Cyber Threat Hunters Handbook

Applying advanced analytics, automation, and
collaborative intelligence for digital defense

David F. Pereira Quiceno

bpb

www.bpbonline.com

First Edition 2025

Copyright © BPB Publications, India

ISBN: 978-93-65898-965

To View Complete
BPB Publications Catalogue
Scan the QR Code:

Dedicated to

My beloved wife Margaret

and

My son David A.

About the Author

David F. Pereira Quiceno is the Founder and CEO of SecPro, a published author, trainer, and digital researcher with over 28 years of experience in cybersecurity and computer forensics. He has led consulting and training initiatives across ethical hacking, malware analysis, penetration testing, and forensic investigations for many international entities. His expertise has impacted sectors such as finance, military, government, and energy. David has been recognized multiple times by EC-Council, receiving awards like Instructor of the Year and Circle of Excellence. He holds over a dozen international certifications, including CCISO, CEH, CHFI, CTIA, and more. As an educator and speaker, he has delivered specialized training for institutions like the FBI, US Marines, Secret Service, Colombia's National Police, and the CERT of multiple countries in Latin America. David is a community-active member and continues to contribute to the global cybersecurity community through teaching, public speaking, and high-impact defense projects.

About the Reviewer

Oleg Bondarchuk is a passionate Azure DevSecOps practitioner with 19+ years of professional experience in Network Security, Cloud Security, Cloud Application Architecture Design, Governance, and Application fitment for cloud. He holds multiple industry certifications in Azure, AWS, Checkpoint, Fortinet, PaloAlto, and ITIL.

He is also a Senior IEEE member, IAHD and IAENG member, Hackathons Judge, peer reviewer for leading journals, and author of many articles in cybersecurity, Blockchain, AI, and STEM fields.

Oleg specializes in developing innovative cloud solutions for security-focused industries and Azure DevOps. He loves working with customers to help them secure and maximize their cloud investment.

He is currently working at Stealthmail and is part of the DevSecOps team.

Acknowledgement

To my beloved wife Margaret, thank you for always being there, for understanding me, and for giving me your infinite love so that I had the freedom to research and write this book in which I have put so much time and effort.

To you, my son David A., who supported me unconditionally with your talent to turn a complex idea into a clear, precise, and didactic visual concept; Without your help, the book would be missing a large component of its essence.

To the entire BPB team with whom I had the honor of working side by side so that this initial idea became this book of which I am proud; thank you very much for your patience, unconditional support, for giving me the freedom to capture without limit such a large amount of concepts and information, without neglecting your attention to detail; You take excellence to a new level.

In my life I have had the great fortune of finding wonderful people on my path who, even without knowing it, become reasons and motives to move forward and trust that if we set out to achieve a result, with effort and dedication, unattainable goals will somehow become palpable achievements; to all my SecPro team who with their work, loyalty, dedication and effort allowed me to have the peace of mind and space to write this book.

To all those who, with their kindness and affection, encourage me to continue spreading knowledge, thank you very much!

Preface

In this wonderful world in which we live and specifically in this evolutionary moment, we find that the information and data ecosystem is one of the most benefited, but at the same time most attacked thanks to the unstoppable advance in the creation of new techniques and malicious tools used by cybercriminals to attack each of their targets in a more effective and undetectable way.

The art of threat hunting becomes a beacon of light and an indispensable tool to be able to detect and countermeasure the increasingly advanced actions of potential adversaries who, day by day, dedicate their time and skills to finding new victims.

When this book was proposed to write, my main objective, which was fully supported by the BPB publishing house, was to capture all the important aspects that allow us to delimit a clear path for a person to become an effective threat hunter, from a practical and proactive point of view, regardless of the capabilities, techniques or tools of his adversary, because the book was first aimed at providing a mindset of the threat hunter and then giving the concepts and tools of the real world to be able to carry out his work in the best possible way, trying to avoid overlooking details that would make all the difference between being able to find an attacker within the environment within a reasonable period of time or allowing him to pass undetected within the infrastructure with the well-known consequences that in most cases are almost impossible to determine.

The composition of the book is as follows:

Chapter 1: Introduction to Threat Hunting- Start your journey with a clear and practical understanding of what threat hunting really is. This chapter walks you through the basics—from the purpose and importance of hunting threats early to the common terminology and techniques used by professionals in the field. It is your foundation for everything that follows.

Chapter 2: Fundamentals of Cyber Threats- Here, we break down today's most pressing cyber threats in a simple and straightforward way. You will learn the main types of threats, how attackers operate, what tactics they use, and who the bad actors are. We also look at where things are headed, so you are not only prepared for now but also for what is next.

Chapter 3: Cyber Threat Intelligence and IoC- Threat intelligence is not just about gathering data; it is about making sense of it. In this chapter, you will learn how to collect, analyze, and use cyber threat intelligence effectively, including how to identify **Indicators of Compromise (IoCs)** that can help you spot threats faster and act smarter.

Chapter 4: Tools and Techniques for Threat Hunting- Knowing what tools to use and how to use them can make all the difference. We will cover essential tools, key frameworks, and powerful techniques for gathering and analyzing data. You will also learn how to streamline your workflow with automation and finish strong with effective documentation.

Chapter 5: Network Traffic Analysis- This chapter teaches you how to analyze network traffic to spot unusual patterns and malicious activity. You will gain practical knowledge of protocols, packet inspection, detection tools, and how to uncover threats hiding in plain sight.

Chapter 6: Operating Systems Analysis- Most attackers go after the systems we rely on every day: Windows and Linux. Here, you will explore how these operating systems work, where their weak points lie, and how to spot malicious activity before it is too late. We also cover the tools used for monitoring and responding to endpoint threats.

Chapter 7: Computer Forensics- When things go wrong, digital evidence tells the story. This chapter explains how computer forensics helps uncover what happened, how it happened, and who did it, without compromising the evidence. You will learn how to preserve, analyze, and extract valuable insights from digital artifacts.

Chapter 8: Malware Analysis and Reverse Engineering- Malware is constantly evolving, and so must we. Here you will learn how to take apart malware, understand how it works, and figure out what it is trying to do. We will explore both static and dynamic analysis, and introduce the tools and skills needed for effective reverse engineering.

Chapter 9: Advanced Persistent Threats and Nation-State Actors- This chapter lifts the veil on the most advanced and dangerous cyber adversaries, APT groups and nation-state hackers. You will learn how they operate, the tools they use, and how to identify and respond to their highly targeted and stealthy attacks.

Chapter 10: Incident Response and Handling- Knowing how to react when a threat becomes an incident is critical. This chapter guides you through every step, from detecting and containing an incident to analyzing what happened and preparing for the next one. You will see how real organizations handle real crises.

Chapter 11: Threat Hunting Best Practices- Now that you have the knowledge and tools, it is time to sharpen your strategy. This chapter outlines the best practices used by top threat hunters; how to plan your hunts, measure success, and continuously improve, even in cloud, IoT, and industrial environments.

Chapter 12: Threat Intelligence Sharing and Collaboration- Cybersecurity is not a solo mission. In this final chapter, we explore how organizations share intelligence to stay one step ahead of attackers. You will understand the platforms, communities, and rules that make collaboration effective and responsible.

Code Bundle and Coloured Images

Please follow the link to download the
Code Bundle and the *Coloured Images* of the book:

https://rebrand.ly/ileljey

The code bundle for the book is also hosted on GitHub at
https://github.com/bpbpublications/Cyber-Threat-Hunters-Handbook.
In case there's an update to the code, it will be updated on the existing GitHub repository.

We have code bundles from our rich catalogue of books and videos available at
https://github.com/bpbpublications. Check them out!

Errata

We take immense pride in our work at BPB Publications and follow best practices to ensure the accuracy of our content to provide with an indulging reading experience to our subscribers. Our readers are our mirrors, and we use their inputs to reflect and improve upon human errors, if any, that may have occurred during the publishing processes involved. To let us maintain the quality and help us reach out to any readers who might be having difficulties due to any unforeseen errors, please write to us at :

errata@bpbonline.com

Your support, suggestions and feedbacks are highly appreciated by the BPB Publications' Family.

Did you know that BPB offers eBook versions of every book published, with PDF and ePub files available? You can upgrade to the eBook version at www.bpbonline. com and as a print book customer, you are entitled to a discount on the eBook copy. Get in touch with us at :

business@bpbonline.com for more details.

At www.bpbonline.com, you can also read a collection of free technical articles, sign up for a range of free newsletters, and receive exclusive discounts and offers on BPB books and eBooks.

Piracy

If you come across any illegal copies of our works in any form on the internet, we would be grateful if you would provide us with the location address or website name. Please contact us at business@bpbonline.com with a link to the material.

If you are interested in becoming an author

If there is a topic that you have expertise in, and you are interested in either writing or contributing to a book, please visit www.bpbonline.com. We have worked with thousands of developers and tech professionals, just like you, to help them share their insights with the global tech community. You can make a general application, apply for a specific hot topic that we are recruiting an author for, or submit your own idea.

Reviews

Please leave a review. Once you have read and used this book, why not leave a review on the site that you purchased it from? Potential readers can then see and use your unbiased opinion to make purchase decisions. We at BPB can understand what you think about our products, and our authors can see your feedback on their book. Thank you!

For more information about BPB, please visit www.bpbonline.com.

Join our Discord space

Join our Discord workspace for latest updates, offers, tech happenings around the world, new releases, and sessions with the authors:

https://discord.bpbonline.com

Table of Contents

CHAPTER 1
Introduction to Threat Hunting

Introduction

In the amazing and dynamic field of cybersecurity, threat hunting is one of the most exciting and interesting areas; you are going to immerse yourself in an exciting hunt for hidden adversaries lurking in the digital wilderness (Your web presence, cloud, network, servers, endpoints, SCADA, IoT, IIoT, etc.). Threat hunting requires analytical skills akin to those of an investigator navigating complex digital terrain.

We need to keep in mind that, unfortunately, most people think that threat hunting is a postmortem activity; you look for clues that show that your infrastructure is already compromised in some way. With that in mind, we are trying to change the paradigm to a more proactive approach.

Threat hunting is not a static nor passive activity; it requires a proactive and curious approach to be effective; in addition, you need to understand the attacker's mindset, including their **Tactics, Techniques, and Procedures (TTP)**; do not worry, we are going to dive deeply into that concept later.

To be an effective threat hunter, you must start thinking out of the box; not all clues can be easily detected. You will analyze abnormal patterns and connect the dots to uncover hidden threats; malicious actors in your infrastructure do not want to be detected, and they use all the tricks in the book. Sometimes, very advanced and undocumented tricks (zero-day) are very difficult to detect, so think about this field as a competition between the bad guys trying to harm, damage, or steal your information and you, the heroic analyst who never stops learning about evolving threats to uncover cybercriminals' actions.

Structure

In this chapter, we will discuss the following topics:

- Threat hunting approach
- Importance of threat hunting
- Key concepts and terminology
- Threat hunting methodologies
- Challenges and limitations of threat hunting

Objectives

After reading this chapter, you should be able to have an informed approach to the world of threat hunting, know the key concepts and definitions you need to understand, be familiar with the threat hunting methodology, and be aware of the challenges that we face every day in front of cybercriminals using sophisticated tools and techniques to countermeasure our defensive architectures and technologies.

Threat hunting approach

The art of combining knowledge and analytical capabilities with a permanent desire to detect and prevent the actions from malicious actors and adversaries; a threat hunter is like a detective who meticulously investigates and analyzes multiple sources of information like network traffic, logs, alerts, malware reports, computer forensic reports, files and system configurations, RAM and more, searching for traces left behind by attackers. The threat hunter proactively seeks out potential threats that may have evaded traditional security measures, aiming to detect and neutralize advanced adversaries before major harm occurs.

Threat hunting is a proactive cybersecurity approach that involves actively searching for and finding potential threats, **Indicators of Attack (IoAs)**, and **Indicators of Compromises (IoCs)** that may have evaded traditional security measures using deceptive methods. It requires a combination of manual and automated techniques to detect and mitigate sophisticated attacks.

Importance of threat hunting

Our ecosystem has more adversaries looking for victims. They are looking for easy money, and there are no more borders or limits. Any person in the world with internet access can become an attacker. The Internet is a very well-suited information repository. It is full of tools, documents, tutorials, malware, and malicious content that can be used against your company. The risk is very real, so let us do this very simple test: open your browser and look for the word hacked in the latest news; as you can see, it is a disturbing landscape that generates uncertainty about your information security and promotes the eternal question: Is the company breached yet?

In front of advanced adversaries or even simple mistakes from a coworker that lead to company information being compromised, we need to be prepared to understand what is going on, what is failing, how the attack was executed, what kind of tools were used, and what can we do to avoid similar results in the future? If the company is going to be attacked in the same way, we need to countermeasure that behavior. In other words, learn the hard lesson to be better prepared the next time, and do not doubt it. There will be a next time.

We have already established that the risk is real, and you need to be proactively in front of the risks. Now, we need to know how to proceed to detect the unwanted actors or behaviors in your infrastructure. That is the purpose of this book: providing a proactive approach to the threat-hunting field, giving you advanced knowledge, techniques, and tools to detect and defend your valuable information from malicious actors.

Key concepts and terminology

In the technological field and even more so in cybersecurity, we find hundreds of different abbreviations and keywords that define either technologies, protocols, mechanisms or even architectures; To achieve a clearer and more direct path to understanding threat hunting, it is important to be familiar with the most relevant terms.

Let us start with your basic guide to threat hunting: The concepts and definitions you need to know.

Indicators of Compromise

IoCs are pieces of digital evidence that suggest the presence of a security breach or compromise. These could include IP addresses, domain names, file hashes, usernames, activity patterns, registry values, or other suspicious indicators that can help identify ongoing or past security incidents.

Some examples of IoCs are as follows:

- Presence of suspicious files in a shared folder

- New users created in an active directory that the system administrators did not authorize

- A defacement in a website (Unauthorized Site Modification)

- Suspicious connections persistent or not, originated from an internal machine against domains found in countries that are not common for the company

Indicators of Attack

These indicators tell us that somebody is executing an attack against our infrastructure. However, that does not mean they succeeded. They are alert about an ongoing adversarial action, especially useful for training the different security and alert technologies that learn from detected behaviors. It is almost a rule that the adversaries execute some tasks against their potential targets before the real and definitive attack; those actions are known as precursors. Some examples are **port scanning**, **banner grabbing**, and **DNS record queries**.

Some examples of IOAs are as follows:

- Huge and unexpected amounts of traffic in a specific server, that is, a web server.
- Continuous attempts to access a user account showed a wrong password on each try.
- Receive an email alerting you to an attempted password change for a specific mail account.
- The antimalware solution in an email detects a malicious document.

Threat intelligence

Threat intelligence refers to information about potential or actual cyber threats gathered from various sources, including Open-Source Intelligence, commercial feeds, and internal security data like logs or alerts. It supplies valuable insights into threat actors' TTPs, enabling organizations to enhance their detection and response capabilities.

Tactics, Techniques, and Procedures

TTPs are the methods and strategies employed by threat actors during the various stages of a cyberattack. Understanding the TTPs used by adversaries can help threat hunters find patterns, predict their actions, and effectively detect and mitigate potential threats.

Pyramid of pain

This is a remarkably interesting concept created by *David Bianco*. It refers to the distinct behaviors and tools that a malicious actor can use in a compromise, and the detection of each one by the security mechanisms or threat hunters.

At each level, the difficulty in detecting adversarial action increases proportionately to the damage to the malicious operation results if the victim detects it.

Refer to the following figure:

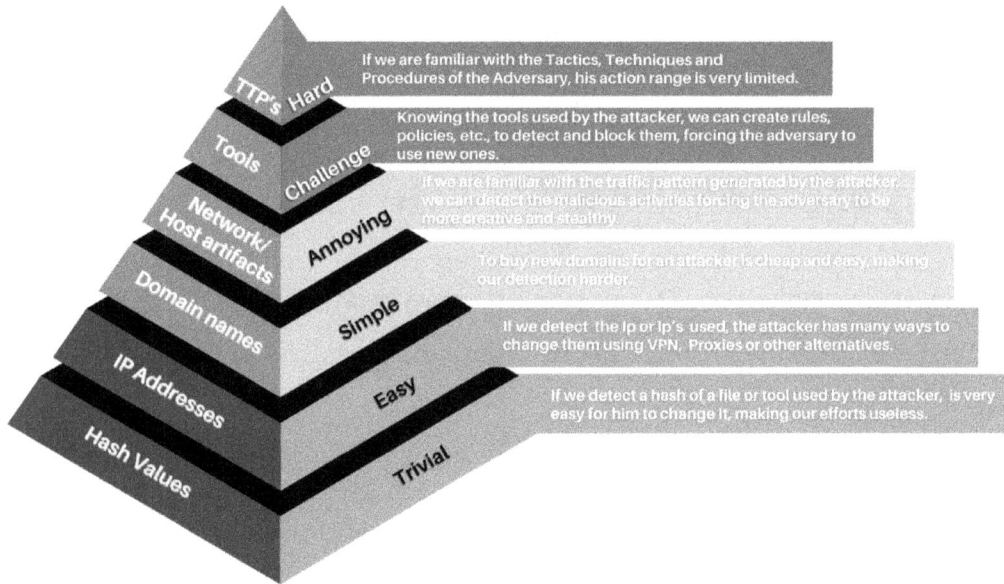

Figure 1.1: Pyramid of pain by David Bianco

Cyber kill chain

Lockheed Martin created this framework to identify and provide a step-by-step orientation about the activities of an adversary; it is formed of seven stages in the life of an attack:

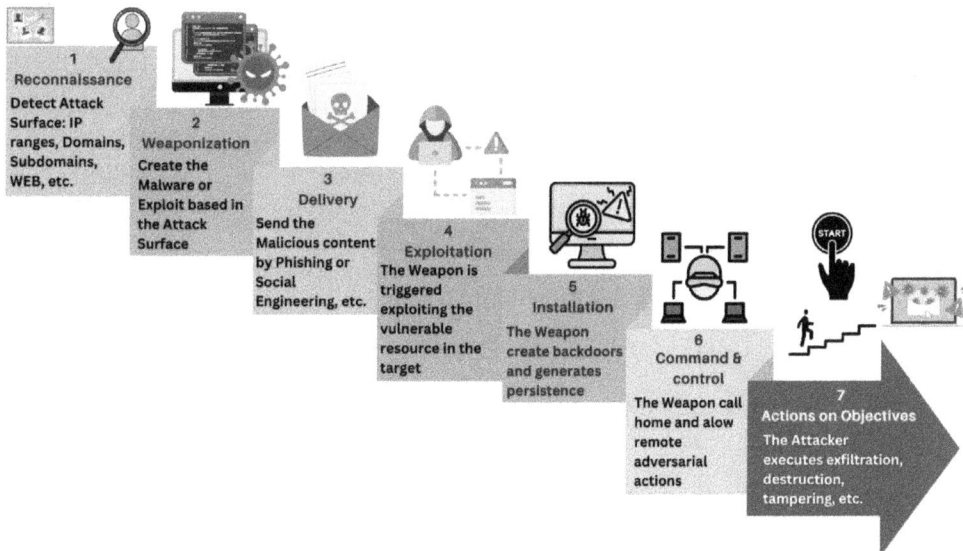

Figure 1.2: Cyber kill chain

Red Team

This group of **offensive experts,** composed of ethical hackers, oversees simulating adversarial actions against infrastructure in a controlled and authorized way. They use the same TTPs that the malicious actors use to evaluate the real security posture of a company. Some of the questions they can answer are:

1. How effective are the detection mechanisms?

2. How effective are the alert technologies?

3. Are there implemented response mechanisms in place?

4. How aware is the personnel in case to are attempted victims of a social engineering attack?

In any case, they try to answer this question: *How mature is our cybersecurity model, and how prepared are we to face a potential cyberattack?*

Some of the actions executed by the Red Team are as follows:

- Controlled phishing campaigns

- Controlled malware campaigns

- Controlled deny-of-service attacks

- Controlled exploitation of vulnerabilities

Blue Team

This team of **defensive experts** oversees detecting and counteracting the actions of a potential adversary. Normally, threat hunters are part of this interdisciplinary group. A company can have different areas to detect and respond to an attack, like a **Security Operations Center** (**SOC**) or the **Cyber Security Operations Center** (**CSOC**). These areas are the Blue Team of the company, which day by day tries to solve vulnerabilities detected by the Red Team, harden the infrastructure, configure security technologies, and detect abnormal or malicious activities in the entire ecosystem.

Some of the actions executed by the Blue Team are as follows:

- Patch management.

- Vulnerability remediation

- Hardening

- Forensic computing

- Malware analysis

Purple Team

In some cases, we have a mix of offensive and defensive teams, so this group of experts has the knowledge and capabilities to execute controlled attacks on the infrastructure and to solve and remediate detected vulnerabilities. Normally, this team comprises seasoned experts with experience in different fields, including architecture, infrastructure, and ethical hacking.

Hackers classification

Based on their actions, mindset, and objectives, different classifications of **hackers** were created. Let us discuss them.

Cracker or black hat hacker

Here, we have the cybercriminals who use their knowledge to steal, damage, or tamper with a company's information using advanced (or not) hacking techniques.

Gray hat hacker

Depending on the case, these people can work offensively or defensively; they travel by a more blurred road and can have a more **flexible** group of ethical principles.

White hat hacker or ethical hacker

This group of experts is included in the Red Team; they use their knowledge and capabilities to test security in many different technologies and scenarios, since a cloud infrastructure passes through a Web application, ending with an active directory. It is important to note that the main difference between a cracker and an ethical hacker is that the ethical hacker is authorized to execute the different attacks used in an adversarial scenario.

Red hat hackers

In this classification, we find hackers who fight battles against black hat hackers, destroy their infrastructure, report them to the authorities, etc.

Blue hat hackers

This type of consultant tests software before it is launched on the market to detect flaws that could later be exploited by a cybercriminal.

Green hat hackers

This category is used to define people who are starting out in the world of hacking and who have a huge desire to learn. The negative part is that while they learn, by mistake, they can cause great damage to an infrastructure. They are sometimes called **noobs**.

Script Kiddie

There are more classifications, such as **Script Kiddies**, also called **lamers**, who try to hack with little or no technical knowledge and generally do not know how to create their own tools, so they will always be subordinate to the tools of others.

Hacktivist or Hacktivism

In some cases, a hacker or group of hackers have a specific ideology for or against something, and they dedicate their hacking actions to fighting or attacking what they believe is the enemy; We can cite the case of the Anonymous group that has carried out **operations** (as their targeted activities are called) against pedophilia but has also attacked government entities and authorities in several countries.

Vulnerability

A vulnerability is a design, implementation, or configuration weakness in a specific hardware, software, or tool that can lead to an undesired and harmful event for a victim. The main task of the Red Team is to detect vulnerabilities before the attacker does.

Exploit

If a vulnerability exists, the attacker uses an exploit to take advantage of it. It consists of a piece of code (script or program) that executes malicious instructions in the vulnerable device to achieve an unintended or unanticipated behavior, like generating a buffer overflow, injecting a fake user in a service, executing unauthorized queries in a database, etc.

Payload

To explain this concept, let us use an analogy: let us say you have an apartment on the second floor of a building (Infrastructure). You left the front window open by mistake (Vulnerability). The thief needs a ladder (Exploit) to reach the open window, and once inside, the thief decides what to steal: the stereo, the TV, Jewelry, etc. (Payload).

A payload can be used with an exploit and is the action or a group of actions the attacker wants to execute once the exploit succeeds. A payload can:

- Receive a shell from the victim machine.
- Execute a specific command on the victim.
- Extract a specific file from the victim's computer.

Malicious software

Malware (Malicious software) is a piece of software created with the sole purpose of causing harm. The harm can be, among others:

- Alter the information in a system

- Delete or damage information in a system
- Encrypt the information and ask for a ransom to provide the decryption key
- Make a system unusable

There are many different malware types and classifications; in *Chapter 8, Malware Analysis and Reverse Engineering,* we will explain the diverse types of malware and how to analyze their behavior.

Advanced Persistent Threat

Advanced Persistent Threat (APT) refers to a malicious actor (in some cases, states or state-sponsored groups) that compromises infrastructures with different goals. In most cases, they want to spy on the activities of the target side. They use advanced tools and knowledge to try to remain undetected in the affected infrastructure, providing them more **Dwell Time**; that means being undetected for the most time possible to exfiltrate information and generate the biggest persistence mechanisms. Their motivations can be economic or political.

Zero Trust

Zero trust is an approach to a way of acting within the world of cybersecurity; their motto is: Never trust, always verify; It does not refer to a specific technology, but to the way of creating policies, configuring and defensively defining technological architectures to make them more robust against potential attackers.

Common vulnerabilities and exposures

An informational catalog about common vulnerabilities can be found here:

https://www.cve.org/

This catalog helps identify, define, and provide detailed information and resources related to discovered vulnerabilities. For each new publicly disclosed vulnerability, a new record with a respective identifier is created, and the notation is like this:

CVE-YEAR- (Consecutive Number); that is, CVE-2025-441.

Common weakness enumeration

An informational list of common weaknesses can be found here:

https://cwe.mitre.org/index.html

This list is supported by a big community composed of technology industry members; it contains a curated list of common software and hardware known security-related weaknesses. Each element inside the list receives a CWE ID.

Common vulnerabilities scoring system

The vulnerability scoring system site can be found here:

https://www.first.org/cvss/specification-document

This is a scoring system that allows the calculation of the severity and criticality of a specific vulnerability based on specific metrics such as (Version 4):

- Exploitability
- Vulnerable system impact
- Subsequent system impact
- Supplemental metrics
- Environmental
- Threat

Each metric comprises different risk parameters, like attack vector, attack complexity, attack requirements, etc. Impact metrics are related to confidentiality, integrity, and availability. In the end, based on the separated calculations, the vulnerability receives a particular severity score level that can be classified as:

- Low (0.1 to 3.9)
- Medium (4.0 to 6.9)
- High (7.0 to 8.9)
- Critical (9.0 to 10.0)

Refer to the following figure:

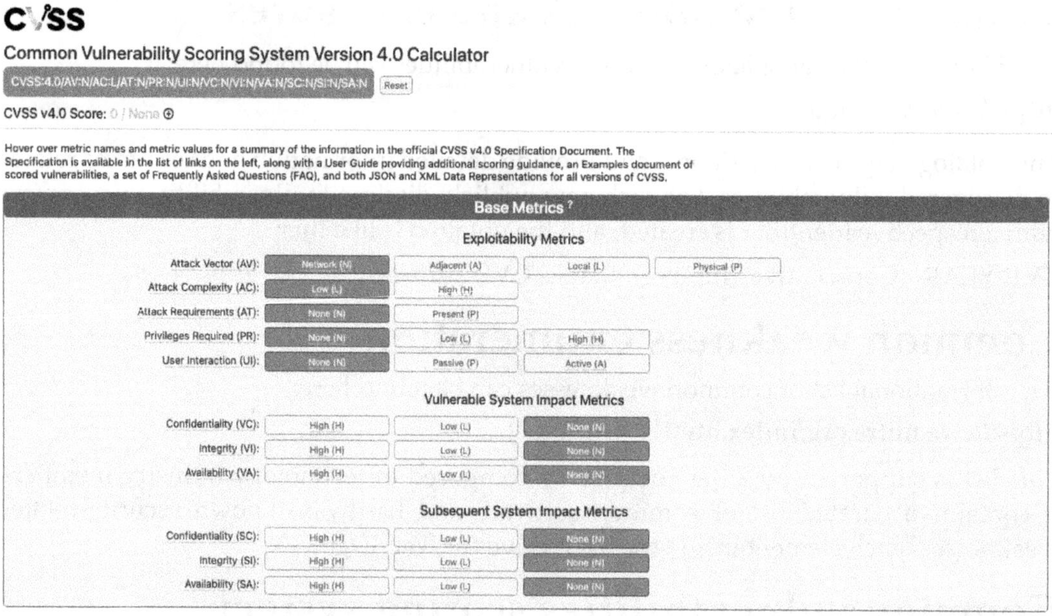

Figure 1.3: CVSS calculator

Data collection and analysis

Data collection and analysis involve gathering and examining security-related data from various sources, such as network logs, system logs, endpoint telemetry, and threat intelligence feeds. Threat hunters use specialized tools and techniques to analyze this data for anomalies, IoCs, IoAs, or patterns that may indicate the presence of threats.

Baseline

You need to understand and identify the difference between a health-hardened, uncompromised system and a compromised one. The healthy system, in other words, normal, is named baseline and is your measurement unit to detect anomalies or differences in a test system or a system under evaluation using comparison mechanisms and tools.

Hunting techniques

Hunting techniques encompass a range of methodologies and approaches used by threat hunters to search for clues and identify potential threats or abnormal records. These techniques may include:

- Log analysis
- Network traffic analysis
- Memory analysis
- Behavioral analysis
- Malware analysis
- Other proactive investigative methods

Forensic computing

This is a discipline that helps the investigators to collect and analyze evidence in a forensically sound manner to try to discover the steps followed by an adversary or criminal in a specific crime related to computers; this process involves the proper capture of the **digital evidence**, chain of custody, and the analysis of this evidence in some cases the Forensic Investigator must appear in court as an **expert witness**.

Adversary behavior analysis

Adversary behavior analysis involves studying threat actors' TTPs to understand their motivations, goals, and capabilities. By understanding how adversaries operate, threat hunters can anticipate their actions, identify patterns, and effectively detect and respond to potential threats.

Incident response and remediation

Incident response and remediation refer to detecting, containing, and mitigating the impact of security incidents. Threat hunters play a crucial role in incident response by providing timely and accurate information about ongoing threats, helping investigate and contain incidents, and helping organizations recover from security breaches.

Types of threat hunting

There are two main ways to hunt for threats in an infrastructure. You can have as basement for your hunting exercises the MITRE ATT&CK framework containing a knowledge database related to the **tactics and techniques** that we know about the adversaries, the attack stages, the tools they use their targets inside an organization, etc. or you can use as starting point an indicator and the information you have about what is going on in the infrastructure. In the following section, we provide the details about the types of hunting.

Structured hunting

The analysis is performed based on an IoA and the TTPs used by attackers. In this hunting type, we use the MITRE **Adversary Tactics Techniques and Common Knowledge** (**ATT&CK**) framework (**https://attack.mitre.org/**) to understand and identify the different stages and attacks from the adversary. Refer to the following figure:

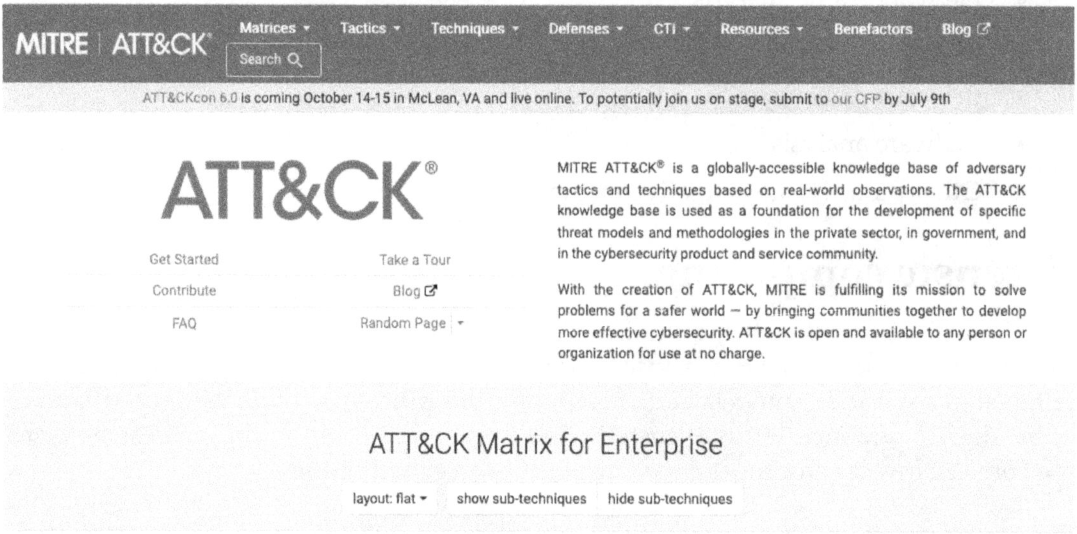

Figure 1.4: ATT&CK matrix

Unstructured hunting

This type of analysis is based on a trigger, normally an IoC. Threat hunters use unstructured hunting to search for patterns, abnormal activities, timelines, and anomalies throughout the system or the infrastructure.

You create a hypothesis, considering the situation and the variables, such as previous attacks received, breaches, information disclosures, attack surface detected from vulnerability assessments, etc. All this information is particular to the organization. You can add security feeds from different sources to compare the current situation with the existing threat landscape and formulate your hypothesis.

Threat hunting methodologies

In threat hunting, you can use different approaches to execute the analysis of the evidence you have, the artifacts, information, IoC, IoA, etc. You can use frameworks or playbooks as a guide, and summarize all your information sources; here the artificial intelligence, in specific Machine Learning helps to detect patterns or abnormal activities in a more efficient way generate your hypothesis, and provide insights about the situation;. Let us discuss the most common approaches.

Hypothesis-based hunting

The investigator uses these resources:

- An attack or threat updated library with the IoA details
- A curated list of TTPs aligned with the MITRE ATT&CK framework.

Using this information, the investigator formulates a hypothesis related to the activities based on the analysis, comparison, and known facts.

Intel-based hunting

This model takes as source the information and indicators generated by the different security mechanisms like IPS, **Security Information and Event Management (SIEM)**, EDR, antimalware, etc., and additional information like hash values, IP addresses, domains, and, in general, any information valuable for the investigation; threat intelligence feeds from crowdsources origins can be used as an element as well. With all the information, the threat hunter looks for patterns to detect and isolate the threat.

Custom or situational hunting

Here, the keywords are **situational awareness**, the investigator looks for clues and evidence in the SIEM, EDR, SASE, or similar technologies; based on the company requirements and political situation (if applicable), the investigator can use an intel-based or a hypothesis-based approach to open the case. This method is customized for the organization.

Threat hunting tools

To be successful in threat hunting, you need information, logs, indicators, etc. There are different technologies and mechanisms that help us to receive the critical information we need to be clear and precise to identify malicious activities in the infrastructure. In the next part, we are going to cover some of the most important sources of information and alerts in your IT ecosystem.

Security Information and Event Management

This technology (SIEM) receives information, logs, alerts, etc., from different devices and mechanisms in the infrastructure, like the Firewall, antimalware console, active directory, authentication servers, etc. This tool is capable of correlating in real-time each feed to detect if something abnormal or unusual is happening, like a threat or attack, allowing us to respond in a faster and smarter way in front of a potential incident.

Endpoint Detection and Response

This tool (EDR) watches the end-user devices to gain visibility about the machine's activities, behaviors, or indicators that can be classified as malicious or abnormal, giving context and early alerts in many cases. Nowadays, most attackers try to compromise the end users with social engineering attacks, so the EDR is one of the most important pieces in our preventive controls and a first line of technical defense.

Extended Detection and Response

The difference between EDR and XDR is the focus of the detection; XDR uses a holistic approach, including not only endpoints but also network, cloud, mail, and applications, providing a wider detection spectrum for threat hunting.

Managed Detection and Response

MDR is a service that provides visibility monitoring and management of the entire IT infrastructure of a company. Normally, it is outsourced and uses EDR as part of the solution.

User behavior analytics

UBA technology can analyze the user's behavior that can be **normal** or **harmless** but uncommon, like visiting new domains, downloading a huge amount of data from a new source, starting sessions on the machine after hours or on holidays, etc. This behavior needs to be reviewed to detect if an attacker generates it or if it is part of the normal operation for the legitimate user.

User and entity behavior analytics

We already talked about user behavior analytics, which is related to the user; well, the **UEBA** can detect abnormal behavior not only from users, but hosts, applications, or devices in the infrastructure. Ultimately, this technology provides our spectrum with another layer of visibility and monitoring. Many UEBA solutions use **artificial intelligence**

(**AI**) to elaborate the **learning map** to differentiate normal usage from potentially harmful activities.

Challenges and limitations of threat hunting

According to my experience, the biggest challenge in the threat-hunting field is detecting an indicator inside a huge amount of data. The best analogy here is to **find a needle in a haystack**. You have clues about what you seek inside an ocean of similar information.

A motivated adversary must detect and exploit one vulnerability to compromise the entire organization. On the other hand, you need to analyze a universe of information to detect the abnormality that guides you to discover the malicious actor. It is not easy, but there are a lot of tools, techniques, and methods that facilitate our task, and we will cover most of them.

The limitations in our field are more related to the expertise of the attackers and the tools they use to compromise our infrastructure. For example, in many cases, you will discover abnormal connections to websites, but they will be encrypted with the TLS protocol, so you cannot inspect the traffic in clear text, of course. Most attackers will try to evade, obfuscate, encrypt, and cover their tracks. It depends on your expertise, creativity, and ingenuity to uncover the veil over their actions.

Conclusion

In this chapter, we learned that threat hunting is a challenging field in which knowledge of malicious tactics and modus operandi of the adversary is decisive to be effective in our work. However, we will face capable, well-trained, and motivated enemies. Remember, we have knowledge, techniques, and methodologies to help us do our best work. We review the different types of threat hunting and the different methodologies we can use to generate analysis and hypotheses with precision, and we define some of the most important tools that help us in our mission.

You have already started an amazing journey in the threat-hunting field. This book is your loyal companion who will help you discover the most astonishing and effective ways to detect and understand the advanced threats we face today.

In the next chapter, we are going to discover the most important and dangerous cyber threats we are facing right now, and we are going to cover the attack vectors used by the cybercriminals to compromise the company's information and infrastructure.

Points to remember

- Threat hunting is an exciting discipline that requires the analyst to have a solid technical basis and the capability to think out of the box.

- The adversaries use nontraditional and not easy to detect methods to accomplish their goals, so in accordance, you need to be aware of evasion techniques, obfuscation, anti-forensics methods, and many more techniques the cybercriminals use to hide their activities.

- With practice, you achieve mastery in this field, and each new case helps you to learn about criminals' behavior and tricks, making you a better analyst.

Multiple choice questions

1. **What is the Blue Team?**
   a. A group of malicious hackers
   b. A security team in charge of defending a computer system
   c. Professional sports team.
   d. A group of software developers

2. **What is an IoC?**
   a. Internet of Connectivity
   b. International Olympic Committee
   c. Inversion of Control in software engineering
   d. Indicator of Compromise in cybersecurity

3. **What is an IoA?**
   a. Indicator of Attack in cybersecurity
   b. Internet of Applications
   c. International Athletics
   d. Inversion of Architecture in software engineering

4. **What is an exploit?**
   a. A type of malware
   b. A piece of software, a chunk of data, or a sequence of commands that takes advantage of a bug or vulnerability to cause unintended or unanticipated behavior
   c. A type of phishing attack
   d. A type of computer hardware

5. **What is malware?**
    a. A type of legitimate software
    b. A type of phishing attack
    c. Malicious software designed to cause damage to a computer system.
    d. A type of computer hardware

Answers

1. b
2. d
3. a
4. b
5. c

References

1. **MITRE: https://www.mitre.org/**
2. **CISA: https://www.cisa.gov/**
3. **NIST: https://www.nist.gov/**

Join our Discord space

Join our Discord workspace for latest updates, offers, tech happenings around the world, new releases, and sessions with the authors:

https://discord.bpbonline.com

CHAPTER 2
Fundamentals of Cyber Threats

Introduction

In this chapter, we provide a clear picture of the most important threats we are currently facing, including the different threat types, vector techniques, and actors that we need to be aware of; in addition, we try to generate some perspective about future cyber threats.

Structure

In this chapter, we will discuss the following topics:

- Understanding the cyber threat landscape
- Types of cyber threats and attack vectors
- Common cyber threat actors
- Impact of cyberattacks
- Future cyber threats

Objectives

As a threat hunter, you need to understand the landscape where malicious actors interact, their capabilities, and tools; in addition, you need to understand the ways that a malicious actor has to deliver an attack (Vectors) and how different attacks can impact the IT ecosystem; having this knowledge, you can extrapolate that information to the different fingerprints and indicators provided by the different security mechanisms to detect and identify potential abnormal activities in the infrastructure.

Understanding the cyber threat landscape

Nowadays, we are facing an extremely dangerous and dynamic landscape for any type of organization; below, you will find a few elements to look for:

- Large numbers and types of malicious actors

- Easy access to attack tools, tutorials, and exploits

- Artificial intelligence at the service of the adversaries

With these ingredients in the risks recipe, we can expect: a substantial number of attacks, many of them using traditional and well known tactics, techniques and procedures, but in addition, a group of advanced attacks (that are increasing day by day) using nontraditional and more difficult to detect **Tactics Techniques and Procedures** (**TTPs**); this generates a big challenge for threat hunters, but at the same time provides us with the opportunity to learn about the mindset of cybercriminals and understand their modus operandi; it is important to mention here that not all cybercriminals are as creative, ingenious and intelligent, most of the time criminals copy the actions from other groups, and repeat their procedures step by step in a kind of copycat attacks but not all of them have the same deep and advanced technical knowledge and capabilities to launch sophisticated and stealth attacks; no matter what the case may be, we need to be prepared for the worst case scenario and never underestimate the capabilities, patience and motivation of the adversary.

Artificial intelligence (**AI**) is a factor that we need to keep an eye out for because it is fertile soil to generate more credible phishing, more complex attacks, well-crafted malware, and easy automation; we need to keep in mind that many actors are creating their AI models oriented to offensive cybersecurity or in some cases cybercrime; some of those are available in clear web and some others in dark web, for example:

- FraudGPT

- DarkGPT

- PoisonGPT

- WormGPT

- WolfGPT

- EvilGPT

The malicious actors can create **On Premise** AI **Large Language Models** (**LLM**) with tools like *GPT4All* (**https://gpt4all.io/index.html**) that allow you to feed the model with the information and documents you want, so you can create an LLM with any kind of content.

Types of cyber threats and attack vectors

In this part, we will cover many cyber threats and attack vectors. Here, it is important to clarify that most communities accept cyber threats and attack vectors to define similar concepts. You will face them in your daily activities as a threat hunter. We will explain some of the most relevant and commonly used cyber threats and attack vectors. As you can imagine, covering all the different cyber threats is impossible, but we will try to include most of them. We are now getting into an interesting part of your knowledge as a threat hunter. This is a critical aspect of your activities because you can classify and separate the distinct kinds of attacks you can receive, and you will be clear about the characteristics and the differences between them.

As we mentioned before, there is a huge list of attack vectors. In the next part of the chapter, we will explore some of the most common attack vectors.

Social engineering attacks

We decided to begin with this group because it is one of the most used by cybercriminals. In most cases, it is easier to deceive a person than force technology or a security mechanism to behave unexpectedly.

This attack relies on deceptive techniques and tools to convince a person to act in a manipulated way or to respond by providing personal or valuable information that the adversary can use in a future attack.

Valuable information that can be extracted by social engineering:

- Usernames
- Passwords
- Banking information (account numbers, credit card number, CVV, expiration date)
- Birthdate
- Passport number
- Other **Personal Identifiable Information (PII)**

Actions that the criminals want to be executed by the victim:

- Open a malicious link
- Visit a malicious website
- Download a file and execute it
- Execute commands in the victim system
- Provide validation codes or tokens
- Connect a malicious USB device to the victim's system

- Connect to a fake Wi-Fi network
- Provide services credentials

In social engineering attacks, we can find many different techniques, as listed in the following table:

Technique	Definition	Mechanisms to deliver
Phishing	Pretend to be a legitimate or trusted entity to reveal sensitive information; criminals pretend to be banks, authorities, service providers, coworkers, etc.	• Email linked with a fake website • Email containing malware • Email containing malicious instructions
Vishing	Voice phishing: Fraudsters use phone calls or voicemail to trick people into executing a specific task or giving them personal or financial information.	• Phone call • Voice mail
Pretexting	In addition to the vishing that allows the criminal to create a more credible scenario, it normally uses pre-recorded sounds like a baby crying or a crowded office.	• Phone call • Voice mail
Smishing	In SMS phishing, fraudsters use text messages to trick people into providing personal or financial information. Often, the text messages appear to come from banks, government agencies, or other trusted organizations and may contain a link to a fraudulent website or a phone number.	SMS
Fake QR codes (QRIshing)	Scammers create fake QR codes that can direct a victim to a phishing website, automatically download malware, or capture personal information.	QR codes
Tailgating/ Piggybacking	Use a pretext to enter a facility without the proper authorization	Physical intrusion

Technique	Definition	Mechanisms to deliver
Baiting	An adversary leaves a device, such as a USB flash drive, where a potential victim can find it. The device is typically labeled with a provocative title to attract the victim's curiosity, leading them to insert the device into a computer. Once inserted, the device can automatically install malware, providing the attacker access to the victim's computer and potentially the entire network.	• USB devices • Phone charger cables • Other devices

Table 2.1: Social engineering attacks

In the following figure, we can see how an attacker performs a phishing attack step by step:

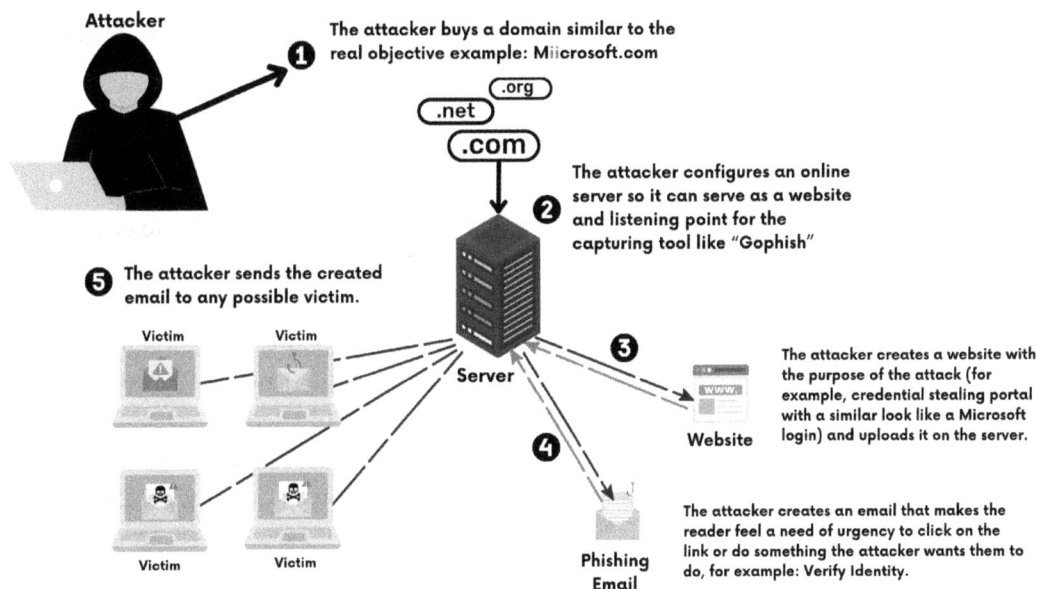

Figure 2.1. Phishing steps

Malicious software

Malicious software or malware is one of the main threats we face. In 1982 the first software created with a malicious intention was discovered (MAC OS Malware), and in 1986, the first PC-oriented malware was discovered. It was named *Brain*. At that moment, we identify them with the classification *Computer Virus*; the word *Malware* comes later to identify all the groups of software created to harm a computing system in some way.

Inside the *Malware* classification, we can group different types of malware. Sometimes, we separate malware based on the infection mechanism, how it behaves, the moment or cause of activation, etc. We will cover these classifications in depth in *Chapter 8, Malware Analysis and Reverse Engineering.*

Here, we are going to include the most common classification list of malware:

Malware type	Effect or activity
Virus	It is a self-replicating malware that infects files and requires the execution of the infected file to generate its malicious activity.
Worm	It is a self-replicating malware that uses the network to spread itself to other hosts.
Trojan	It is malware in disguise. This kind of malware appears in front of the victim as a regular application, but it is malware in the interior; one of the most well-known cases is the **Remote Access Trojan (RAT)**.
Spyware	Malware is created to spy on the activities of the victim.
Ransomware	This type of malware encrypts the victim's information and asks for a ransom to provide the decryption key.
Scareware	Malware is created to spread fear in the victim. The victim can be overwhelmed by disruptive messages based on the unexpected behavior and messages generated by this malware.
Rootkit	Difficult to detect malware that infects critical system files to be protected against antimalware actions and detection.
Adware	Malware that serves unwanted and annoying advertisements.
Bots	Malware that converts the victim into a bot or zombie under the orders of a command-and-control server, controlled by the cybercriminal to execute different tasks like crypto mining or DDoS attacks.
Fileless malware	Malware that uses tools already implemented in the original operating system to execute the malicious instructions; normally, all their actions only reside in RAM, so when the system restarts, the evidence may disappear
Info stealer	Malware is designed to steal information from the victim.
Wiper malware	Malware that encrypts or damages the files of a system just to create chaos and destruction.

Table 2.2: Classification of malware

Here, we illustrate a Trojan infection process:

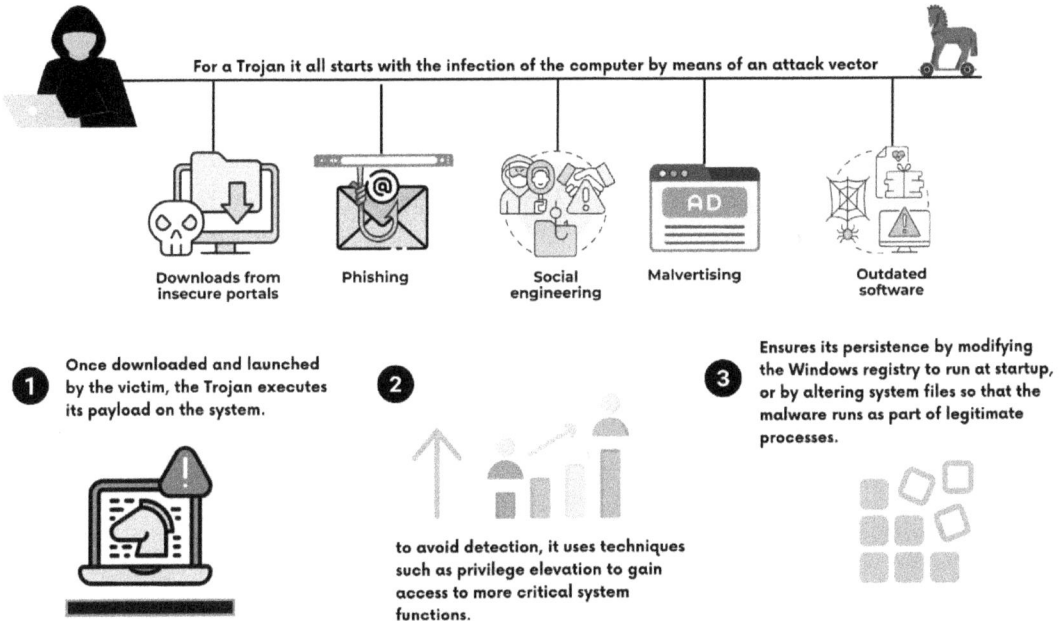

For a Trojan it all starts with the infection of the computer by means of an attack vector

Downloads from insecure portals | Phishing | Social engineering | Malvertising | Outdated software

1 Once downloaded and launched by the victim, the Trojan executes its payload on the system.

2 to avoid detection, it uses techniques such as privilege elevation to gain access to more critical system functions.

3 Ensures its persistence by modifying the Windows registry to run at startup, or by altering system files so that the malware runs as part of legitimate processes.

Figure 2.2: Trojan infection process

A Worm infection process is shown in the following figure:

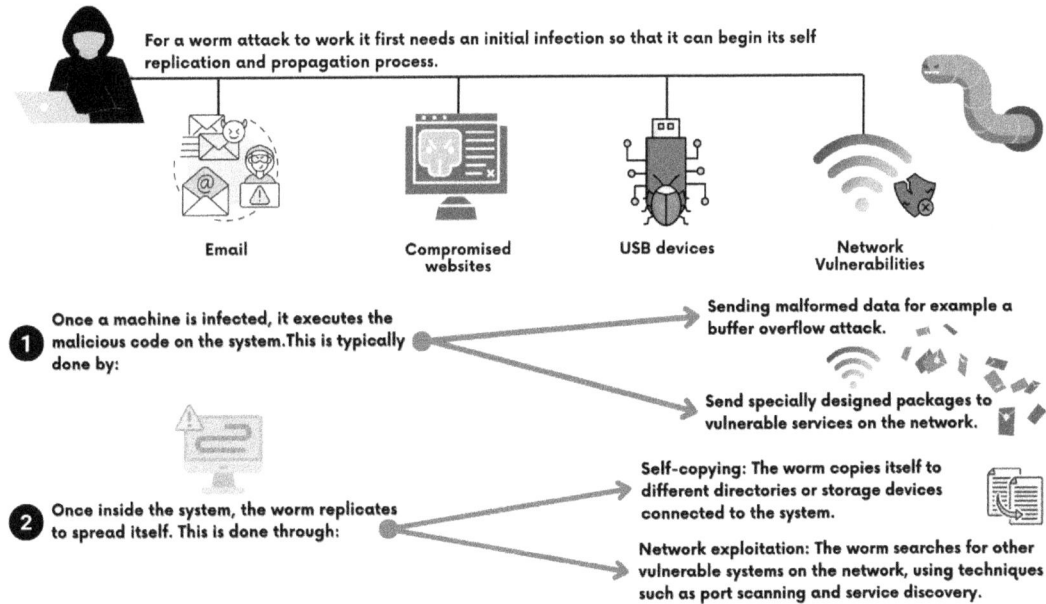

For a worm attack to work it first needs an initial infection so that it can begin its self replication and propagation process.

Email | Compromised websites | USB devices | Network Vulnerabilities

1 Once a machine is infected, it executes the malicious code on the system. This is typically done by:

Sending malformed data for example a buffer overflow attack.

Send specially designed packages to vulnerable services on the network.

2 Once inside the system, the worm replicates to spread itself. This is done through:

Self-copying: The worm copies itself to different directories or storage devices connected to the system.

Network exploitation: The worm searches for other vulnerable systems on the network, using techniques such as port scanning and service discovery.

Figure 2.3: Worm infection process

Ransomware

Let us clarify that *ransomware* is a kind of malware. We decided to put it in an individual category due to its importance and how it has become one of the most critical threats we currently face. This attack can hinder a company from accessing its data or tools. These types of attacks will not go away or change, as these are profitable for cybercriminals.

The main characteristic of ransomware is that after the infection, this malicious software executes different routines, which we will cover in detail in *Chapter 8, Malware Analysis and Reverse Engineering*, but running encryption routines on the files in the victim's computer is most critical. It is important to remember that some ransomware can encrypt not only your internal files but also files contained in external storage devices and your cloud-connected storage. After encryption, the ransomware displays a message to the victim asking for a *ransom* to provide the decryption key to the victim. Normally, this ransom should be paid in some cryptocurrency to make it more difficult for the authorities to trace and locate the cybercriminal.

Here, we illustrate a ransomware infection process:

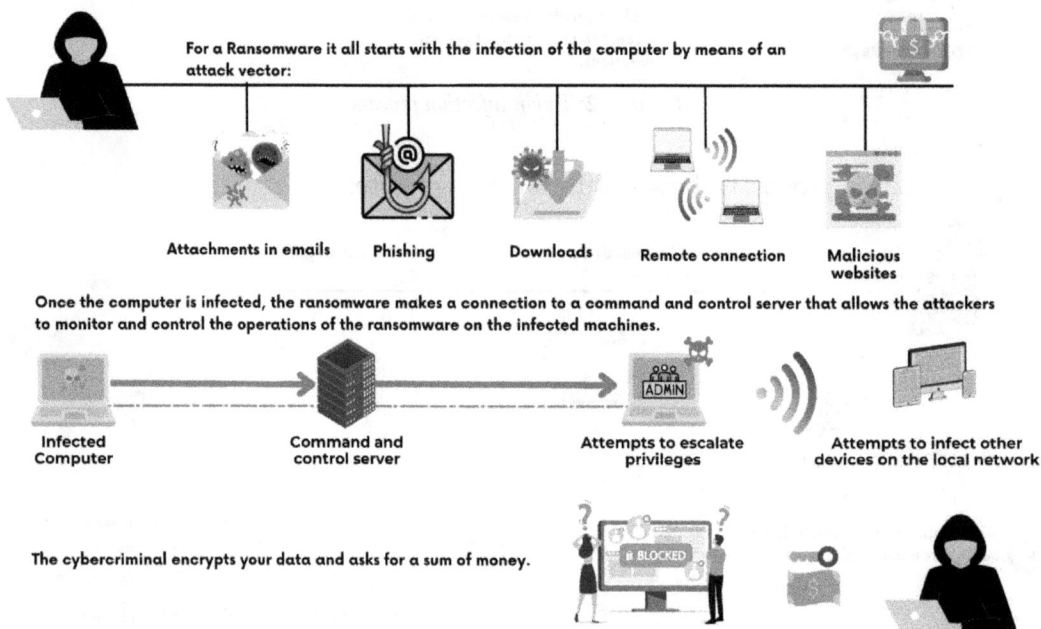

For a Ransomware it all starts with the infection of the computer by means of an attack vector:

Attachments in emails Phishing Downloads Remote connection Malicious websites

Once the computer is infected, the ransomware makes a connection to a command and control server that allows the attackers to monitor and control the operations of the ransomware on the infected machines.

Infected Computer Command and control server Attempts to escalate privileges Attempts to infect other devices on the local network

The cybercriminal encrypts your data and asks for a sum of money.

Figure 2.4: Ransomware infection process

DoS and DDoS attacks

This attack involves deactivating or taking down a service, making it unavailable using different techniques. The attackers can generate excessive amounts of traffic, targeting a specific service. The difference between **Deny of Service (DoS)** and **Distributed Deny of Service (DDoS)** is the number of attack sources, one for DoS and many for DDoS.

The adversaries can use different mechanisms or tools to generate this type of attack:

- Botnets (Zombie networks using PCs, mobile devices, or IoT devices)
- DNS amplification attacks
- Hacktivist collaboration (Hacktivist groups like anonymous often coordinate large-scale DDOS attacks as protest actions)

Let us discuss a few techniques used by our adversaries.

Bandwidth or Volumetric attacks

The attacker or attackers send enormous amounts of traffic with requests to the server, trying to saturate or flood the bandwidth capabilities of the victim's infrastructure. This kind of attack includes:

- ICMP flood
- UDP flood
- Spoofed packets flood

Based on the amount of traffic, this attack can be measured in **bits per second** (**bps**) or **Gigabits per second** (**Gbps**).

Refer to the following figure:

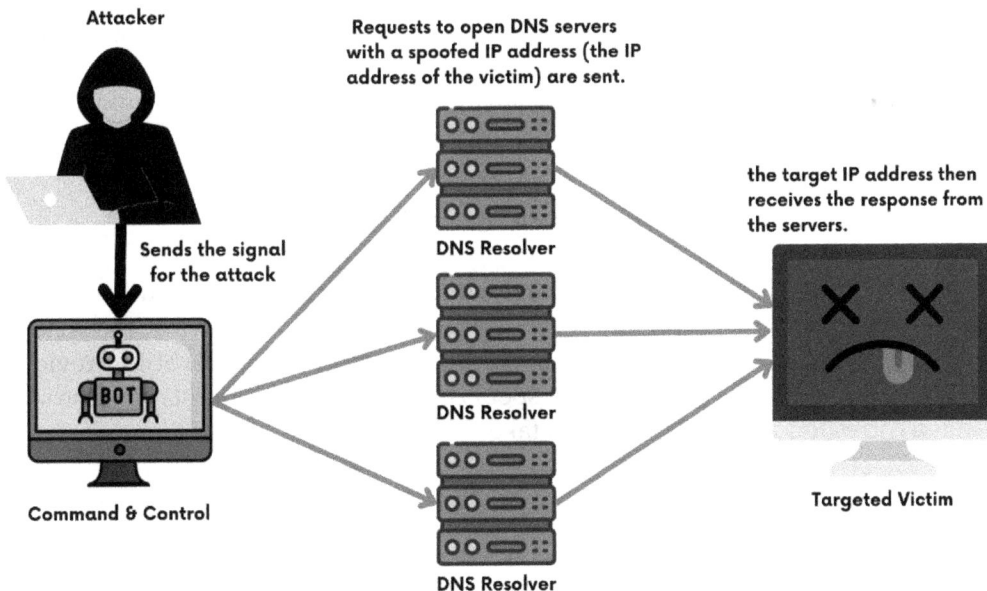

Figure 2.5: Volumetric attack representation

Protocol attacks

This attack takes advantage of the TCP/IP protocol communication parameters, exploiting the regular intended behavior, but in a way that allows the exhaustion of IT Infrastructure resources: Server CPU, Server RAM, network devices, load balancers, routers, etc. This kind of attack is measured in **Packets per second (Pps)**.

The protocol attacks normally target layers three and four of the OSI model (network and transport).

Refer to the following figure:

Network Communication Models Layers Comparison

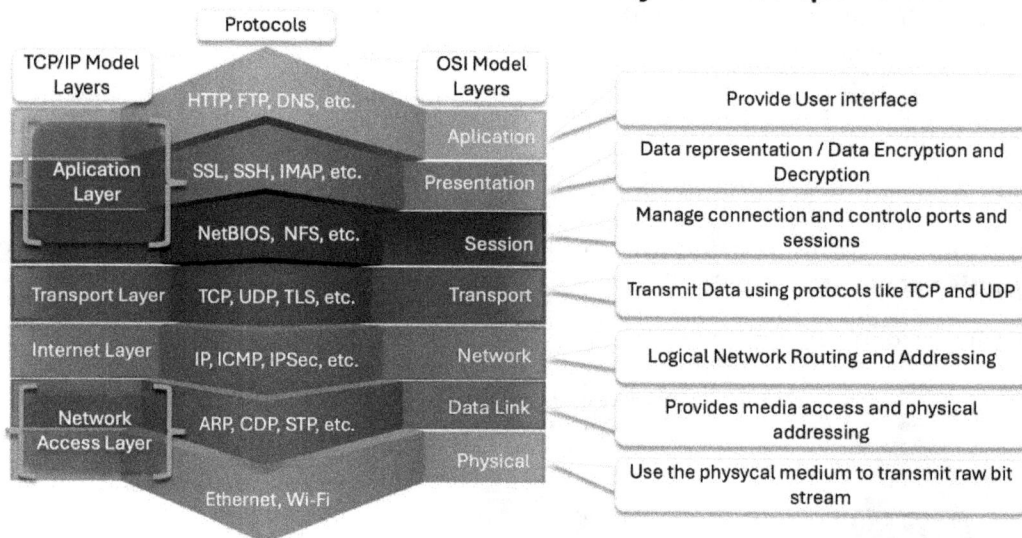

Protocols

TCP/IP Model Layers		OSI Model Layers	
	HTTP, FTP, DNS, etc.	Aplication	Provide User interface
Aplication Layer	SSL, SSH, IMAP, etc.	Presentation	Data representation / Data Encryption and Decryption
	NetBIOS, NFS, etc.	Session	Manage connection and controlo ports and sessions
Transport Layer	TCP, UDP, TLS, etc.	Transport	Transmit Data using protocols like TCP and UDP
Internet Layer	IP, ICMP, IPSec, etc.	Network	Logical Network Routing and Addressing
Network Access Layer	ARP, CDP, STP, etc.	Data Link	Provides media access and physical addressing
	Ethernet, Wi-Fi	Physical	Use the physical medium to transmit raw bit stream

Figure 2.6: Network communication models layers comparison

This is a classic example of using the protocol function against the target differently. For example, suppose the server receives a TCP SYN packet on an open port, for each package received by the server. In that case, the server is forced by the protocol to provide an answer (TCP SYN-ACK), so the adversary spoofs many TCP SYN requests, and the server generates a corresponding answer to each fake package.

A list of protocol attacks:

- TCP SYN floods
- TCP SYN-ACK floods
- IP fragmentation
- UDP floods

- DNS amplification

- SSDP amplification

Refer to the following figure:

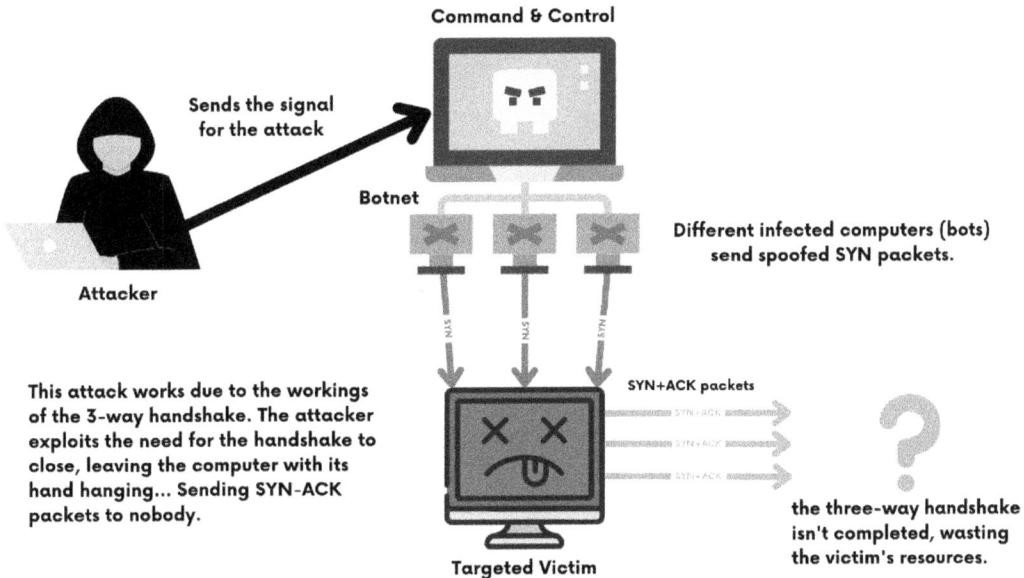

Figure 2.7: Protocol attack representation

Application layer attacks

This type of attack is directed against web server applications. The idea is to send legitimate requests with some specific parameterization to try to generate delays or overload in the web servers or the connection from the web server to the database server, tending to slow down the speed of the server's responses.

This attack is directed against layer seven of the OSI model and is measured in **requests per second** (**Rps**). They are more difficult to detect because they normally do not use huge permanent amounts of traffic, but you can detect small bursts in the communication channel.

Refer to the following figure:

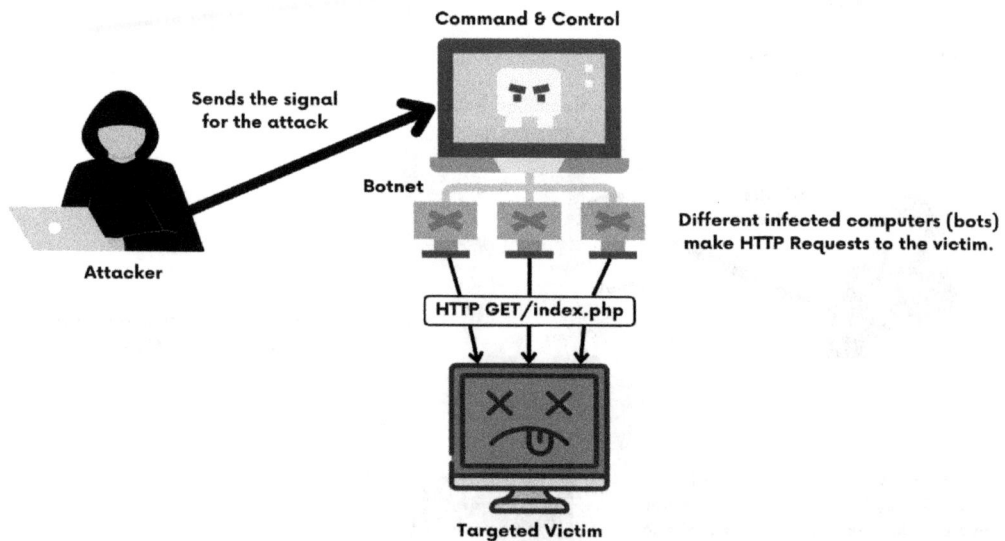

Figure 2.8: *Application layer attack representation*

Compromised credentials

This attack vector is very common. The adversaries can use different attacks to recover a victim's password. This can be achieved using techniques such as:

Password attack type	Description
Brute force attack	Attempts to guess the password by trying every possible combination of characters until the correct one is found. It is the most basic method and the most resource-intensive.
Dictionary attacks	This attack uses a predefined list of words (dictionary) to guess passwords. It is effective against weak passwords that are common words or phrases.
Hybrid attacks	These combine dictionary attack techniques with common character substitutions and additions, such as numbers or symbols at the end of dictionary words, to improve the chances of guessing the correct password.
Pass the Hash (PtH)	Instead of decrypting a password, this attack uses the captured password hash (an encrypted representation of the password) to authenticate as the user without knowing the plaintext password.
Password spraying	Unlike brute force attacks that try many passwords for a single user, password spraying targets many users with a few commonly used passwords, reducing the risk of detection.

Password attack type	Description
Rainbow tables	Uses precomputed tables of password hashes to reverse the hashes back to their original passwords. It is effective against systems that use password hashing without **salt** (random data added to the hash to make it unique).

Table 2.3: Password attack type descriptions

Refer to the following figure:

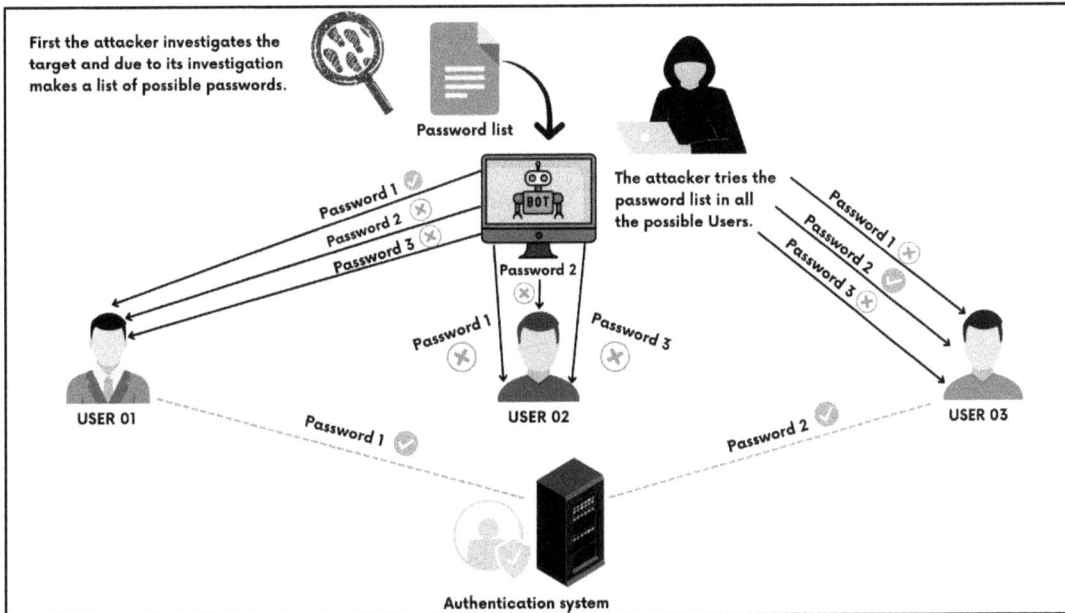

Figure 2.9: Dictionary attack representation

Vulnerability exploitation

Organizations around the world use vast amounts of computing resources. Sometimes, their servers are located on-premises in their own data centers, third-party data centers, or cloud services. In any of these cases, the company is required to keep the operating systems patched and keep up to date all the applications running in the servers; frequently, investigators or even malicious actors detect new vulnerabilities that nobody knew before; these vulnerabilities receive the name of *Zero Day*, the problem is that in many cases there is no protection or workaround to solve the problem and at that moment the infrastructure becomes vulnerable until the moment that the vendors create a patch or an update to eliminate or control the *Zero Day*.

Commonly, companies do not patch immediately because they need to test the new patch or update in their *testing* environment before it can be applied in the *production* infrastructure to avoid malfunctions or new problems generated by the updates.

When a server's operating system or an application running on a server is out of date, or the proper patches are not applied, this device becomes vulnerable, and an adversary can use an exploit to compromise that infrastructure. There are many resources that the adversaries can use to find the exploit code for specific vulnerabilities, such as:

- Exploit-DB (**https://www.exploit-db.com/**)
- CX Security (**https://cxsecurity.com/exploit/**)
- Vulnerability Lab (**https://www.vulnerability-lab.com/**)
- 0day Today (**https://0day.today/**)
- Packet Storm (**https://packetstormsecurity.com/files/tags/exploit/**)
- Rapid 7 (**https://www.rapid7.com/db/**)

Refer to the following figure:

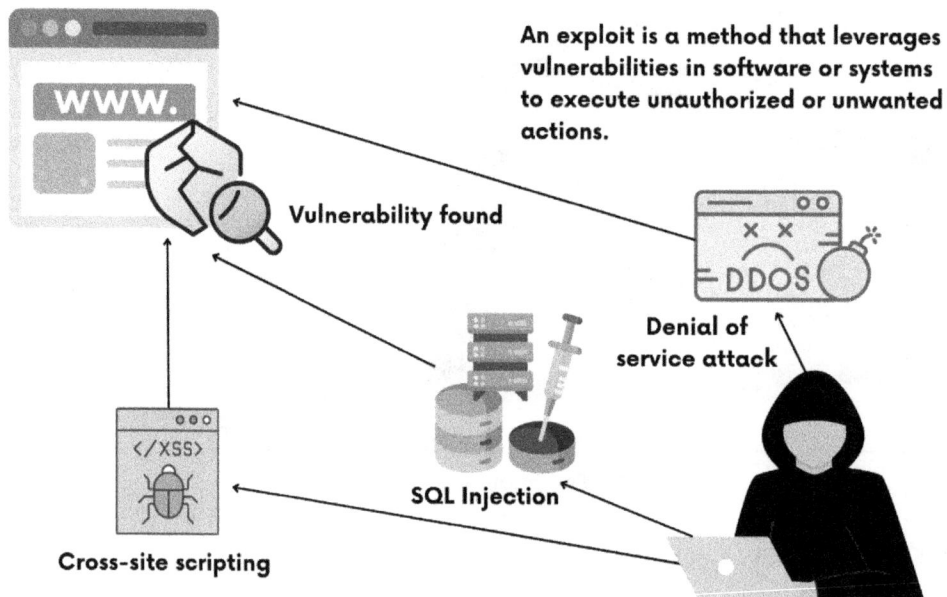

Figure 2.10: Exploit representation

Configuration mistakes

A different threat is generated when the person or persons in charge of deploying or managing a specific device make mistakes, inadvertently forget to remove dangerous or vulnerable configuration files, select a weak password, or keep a default credential in service; these kinds of mistakes can lead to a compromise of the company infrastructure, and the cybercriminals find a low hanging fruit with this behavior. This kind of mistake can be encountered in any infrastructure: Servers, network devices, Firewalls, endpoints, mobile devices, cloud, IoT, etc.

Man-in-the-middle attack

The man-in-the-middle attack implies that the attacker intercepts the traffic directed to a device and, in this way, captures and analyzes it later. The appropriate security mechanisms, such as IDS, IPS, HIDS, HIPS, etc, can easily detect it.

This attack requires several factors on the attacker's part, such as being in the same network as the victim or the network where it is connected, and being trusted by the victim. The next step is to generate fake packets within the network. Usually, the malicious traffic is composed of ARP packets that generate fake updates of the victim's routing table. The modification in the routes directs the traffic to the machine of the attacker's choice and thus allows sniffing and capturing credentials and sensitive information. In some cases, the attacker alters the information and replays it to the destination in a tampered form. Due to the man-in-the-middle attack, it is highly recommended to encrypt the traffic within the network whenever possible.

The protocols that send the information in clear text are the most vulnerable to this attack.

A variant of this attack can generate a denial of service on a specific machine, a group, or an entire network:

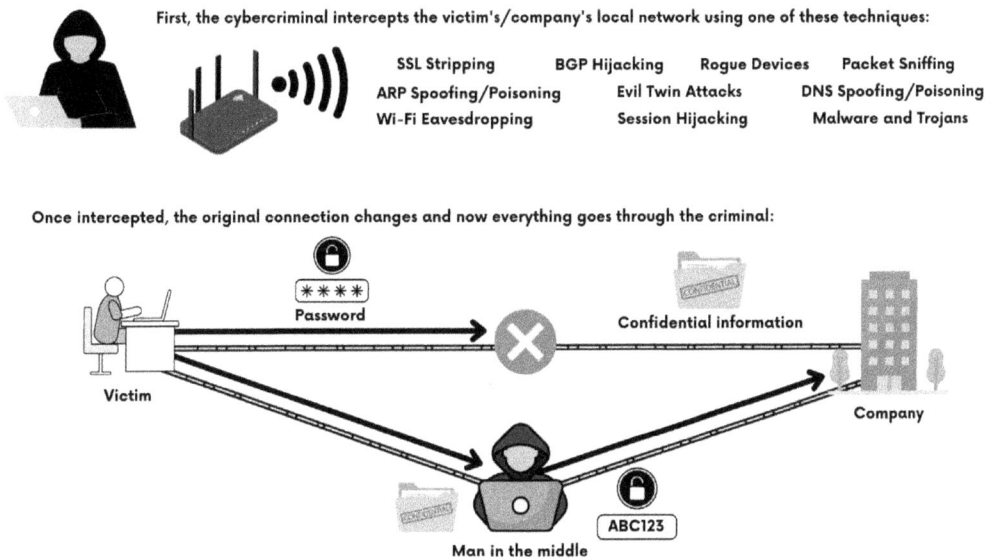

Figure 2.11: Man-in-the-middle representation

Insider threats

Insiders are within an organization as employees, contractors, partners, etc. They are in a position of annoyance or dissatisfaction with the entity to such a degree that they can damage the company. These types of attacks are very difficult to detect since the insider knows the most relevant factors of the organization at the cybersecurity level, such as:

- Cybersecurity policies
- Password policies
- Technical staff
- Security mechanisms
- Anti-malware mechanisms, etc.

It should be clarified that an insider may voluntarily execute malicious actions against the company or may do so unintentionally, simply by being tricked or by a lack of cybersecurity awareness:

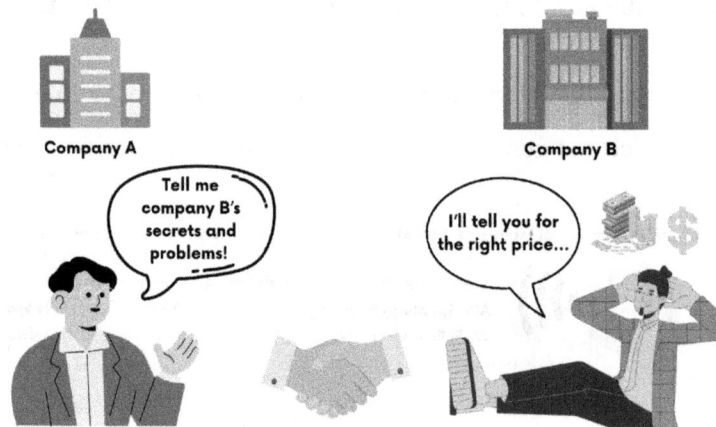

Figure 2.12: Insider threat representation

Common cyber threat actors

Nowadays, organizations face different actors that can generate attacks against them, motivated by different reasons, like financial gain, reputational damage, service disruption, terrorism, hacktivism, etc. No matter what, we can try to summarize the list of potential adversaries.

Malicious hackers

In the previous chapter, we defined the different types of hackers. In this case, we are talking about the crackers or malicious adversaries who possess great knowledge and use these capabilities for nefarious purposes. In some cases, these malicious actors do not target your company from the beginning. They execute automated scans for vulnerabilities in servers and devices connected to the Internet. Unfortunately, they find a vulnerable server in your infrastructure and compromise that resource with an exploit or a specific attack. They can execute different adversarial actions in your infrastructure, like deploying ransomware to encrypt your information and ask for a later ransom, exfiltrate data and sell it on black markets, etc.

One common new practice is to steal the company's information, capture evidence, and blackmail the company if they do not report the incident or compromise with the proper authorities. For example, suppose you are a public company in the United States and suffer an effective cyberattack. In that case, you must disclose and report the incident to the Securities and Exchange Commission (**https://sec.gov**). Here, you can find the *Cybersecurity Disclosure Statement* from December 14, 2023:

https://www.sec.gov/news/statement/gerding-cybersecurity-disclosure-20231214

So, the criminals threaten you if you avoid reporting the incident to the proper authorities and force you to pay blackmail to keep the criminals quiet. As you can see, the message here is: *If, unfortunately, you are a victim of a cybercriminal, report the incident to the proper authorities and follow all the regulations.*

The motivation of the Cyber Criminals: Financial Gains (Profit)

Advanced Persistent Threat groups

We already explained **Advanced Persistent Threats** (**APTs**) in the previous chapter.

They are groups of smart and capable people, creating a model for criminal entrepreneurship. They count on very proficient technical, tactical, and strategy experts to execute their advanced attacks against different industries or market segments, like defense, finance, energy, oil & gas, etc.

In many cases, they are associated with state-sponsored groups due to the sophistication of their techniques, tools, and the budget they must have to achieve their goals.

You can find a curated list of APT groups in this link from MITRE:

https://attack.mitre.org/groups/

Refer to the following figure:

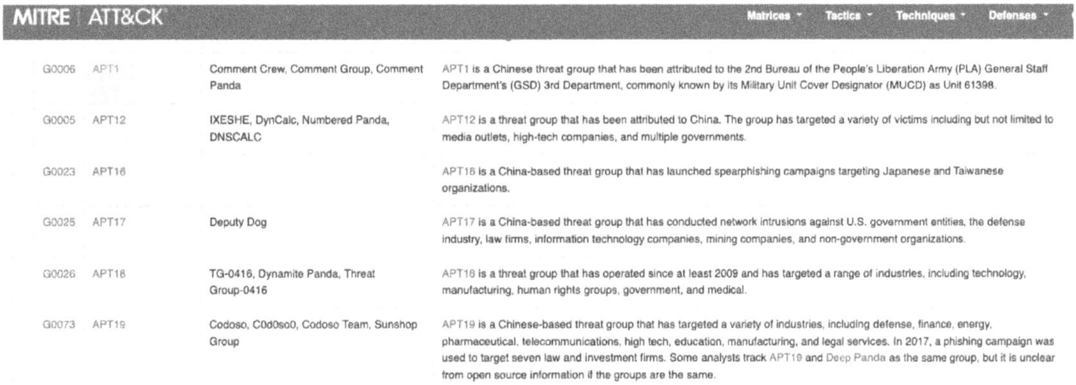
MITRE | ATT&CK — Matrices · Tactics · Techniques · Defenses

G0006	APT1	Comment Crew, Comment Group, Comment Panda	APT1 is a Chinese threat group that has been attributed to the 2nd Bureau of the People's Liberation Army (PLA) General Staff Department's (GSD) 3rd Department, commonly known by its Military Unit Cover Designator (MUCD) as Unit 61398.
G0005	APT12	IXESHE, DynCalc, Numbered Panda, DNSCALC	APT12 is a threat group that has been attributed to China. The group has targeted a variety of victims including but not limited to media outlets, high-tech companies, and multiple governments.
G0023	APT16		APT16 is a China-based threat group that has launched spearphishing campaigns targeting Japanese and Taiwanese organizations.
G0025	APT17	Deputy Dog	APT17 is a China-based threat group that has conducted network intrusions against U.S. government entities, the defense industry, law firms, information technology companies, mining companies, and non-government organizations.
G0026	APT18	TG-0416, Dynamite Panda, Threat Group-0416	APT18 is a threat group that has operated since at least 2009 and has targeted a range of industries, including technology, manufacturing, human rights groups, government, and medical.
G0073	APT19	Codoso, C0d0so0, Codoso Team, Sunshop Group	APT19 is a Chinese-based threat group that has targeted a variety of industries, including defense, finance, energy, pharmaceutical, telecommunications, high tech, education, manufacturing, and legal services. In 2017, a phishing campaign was used to target seven law and investment firms. Some analysts track APT19 and Deep Panda as the same group, but it is unclear from open source information if the groups are the same.

Figure 2.13: *MITRE APT groups*

(Source: https://attack.mitre.org/groups/)

State-sponsored actors

As we mentioned, many APT groups can be related to states that want to generate specific geopolitical results using cyberattacks as a main mechanism or tool in the biggest scenario. In some cases, a state decides to create groups of cyber warriors at its service to carry out cyberattacks directed against its geopolitical enemies, its opposition, or, in some cases, an uncomfortable critic.

Cyberterrorists

Some groups only want to generate fear and chaos and use their technical knowledge and capabilities to achieve that infamous goal. In most cases, they are based on some kind of ideological violence and use cyberattacks in that way.

Hacktivists

Sometimes, a hacker or group of hackers has a specific ideology for or against something, and they dedicate their hacking actions to fighting or attacking what they believe is the enemy. We can cite the case of the anonymous group that has carried out **operations** (as their targeted activities are called) against pedophilia but has also attacked government entities and authorities in several countries.

Insiders

A disgruntled employee or a person who, for some reason, executes actions against the company or the organization they work for is called an insider, because they are **inside** the organization that will be attacked. This is one of the most dangerous actors because they are difficult to detect. They are also familiar with all the policies and technologies in place and have deep knowledge about the people and workflows in the target organization. By all, it affects the organization's trust in these actors. They can generate a huge impact due to the wide range of attacks they can achieve. For example, espionage, sabotage, disclosure, leak, etc.

Thrill-seekers

This category refers to the people who want the *rush* or the adrenaline shot that comes with success in an attack, or just want to be famous, or want the exposure or merits that come with a successful attack against an important target, like a government agency, military, police, or big companies. In some cases, they are looking to demonstrate the limited capabilities of their targets and show their **superiority**.

Impact of cyberattacks

Being a victim of a cyberattack is a hard time for many companies and individuals. There are different consequences and results in the aftermath of an attack, but in any case, most outcomes are negative. The only **positive** result that we can mention is that we can generate lessons learned if we decide to make changes, increase the cybersecurity level in the organization, and improve the cybersecurity maturity model to reduce the risk after a successful attack against us.

In the negative list of impacts that we mentioned before, we can include:

- **Data leaks or loss of privacy:** Some attacks are oriented to leak information from the victim due to espionage reasons or blackmail the owner of the information to prevent their competitors, clients, or partners from receiving that data. Regulations are an additional layer here. The adversaries force the victim to pay to **buy** the criminal's silence in front of the authorities to avoid a fine, etc.

- **Reputational damage:** Unfortunately, the public and the clients and stakeholders of a company, the victim of a cyberattack, do not always understand that a **Safe IT Infrastructure** is an ideal scenario impossible to accomplish no matter how much effort, budget, and technology you have, so it is common to receive the accusation that says: *You did not take all the steps needed to protect our information* (in some cases it is true). What remains popular is the belief that you are responsible for the events, and that can completely affect a company's reputation. It is even worse when your business is the information. Remember that it takes years to forge a reputation and seconds to destroy it.

- **Loss of productivity:** Destructive attacks like ransomware and DoS/DDoS not only affect your reputation due to the impossibility of serving and providing your services to the world, but your operational costs never stop. Payroll, infrastructure, lease, etc., continue, and you cannot produce revenue to keep the company going if you are solving a disaster or an incident. That is why elements like a business continuity plan, **Business Impact Analysis (BIA)**, incident response plan, and disaster recovery are critical parts of the survival guide for an organization.

- **Increased costs:** As a result of an attack, it is possible that the company needs to make additional financial efforts to replace technologies, acquire new services, hire outsourced consulting, etc.

- **Fines or legal cases:** Whether you belong to a regulated industry or are a public company, you may have **Service Level Agreements (SLAs)** that are metrics used to measure the quality and availability of your services. If you receive an attack, the most probable outcome is that you cannot accomplish your SLAs, and you can receive fines or be involved in legal cases against you due to noncompliance with agreements. On the other hand, if you fail to report the incident to the proper authorities when you are a public entity, you can receive additional fines.

Future cyber threats

Unfortunately, threats advance at such a dizzying pace that it is almost impossible for us to keep up with the adversaries and cyber criminals who update their TTPs daily to attack us. Let us look at the complete current panorama. We see how AI is gaining ground and advancing with more capabilities day by day, which can be (and are) used by criminals to compromise organizations around the world.

During the research process for the creation of this book, we came across a very interesting report created by the **European Union Agency for Cybersecurity (ENISA)**, which talked about the cyber threats we would face in 2030. Surprisingly, all those threats we expected to combat within six years are already here.

Here you can review the report (Published on November 11, 2022):

https://www.enisa.europa.eu/news/cybersecurity-threats-fast-forward-2030

The infographic is here:

https://www.enisa.europa.eu/news/foresight_2030_infographic.png

The final message is to prepare to face the threats of tomorrow that are here today.

Conclusion

In this chapter, we took a tour of the current panorama of actors and attack techniques, and we included the new capabilities and tools available to criminals, such as AI. We see in the list of cyberattacks, which is by no means exhaustive, and many possibilities for adversaries. We know that it is a completely unequal territory where we, as part of the Blue Team, must be able to detect any anomaly in an immense ocean of technologies and devices, and the criminal only requires one error, one forgetfulness on the part of the victim company to compromise it. Ultimately, we see that our commitment is to learn more every day and acquire more skills and abilities to keep up with an increasing number of motivated malicious actors just waiting for the right moment to attack.

In the next chapter, we will explore threat intelligence and IoCs that allow us to obtain useful intelligence to keep our revision lists up-to-date and make them a fundamental element within the threat-hunting exercise.

Points to remember

- AI LLM tools can be used for good or evil, depending on who uses them. Cybercriminals are using them to create better scams for phishing, for example, where they can create credible message bodies with perfect grammar and spelling, regardless of the language. On the other hand, malicious actors can use AI to create malware that is difficult to detect, create new tools and scripts, and additionally automate tasks within their attacks.

- It is almost impossible to include all the possible cyber threats in a list to which a company is exposed. The creativity and permanent search for new attack vectors by cybercriminals increases daily. As we mentioned in the beginning, more and more actors are trying to profit from their attacks.

- A disgruntled employee who becomes an insider is much more dangerous for a company than a well-trained and motivated cybercriminal.

Multiple choice questions

1. **What is social engineering?**
   a. The process of designing social media algorithms.
   b. The study of societal behavior about infrastructure.
   c. The technique of manipulating people so they give up confidential information.
   d. A branch of civil engineering related to societal structures.

2. **What is a volumetric attack?**
   a. A type of security breach where the attacker steals large volumes of data.
   b. A type of DDoS attack that aims to overwhelm the bandwidth of a targeted system.
   c. A type of attack where the attacker uses a large volume of noise to disrupt communications.
   d. An attack is where the attacker fills a physical space with a large volume of physical materials.

3. **What is a dictionary attack?**
   a. It is an attack where the hacker speaks to the victim in a secret code language.
   b. It is an attack where the hacker throws dictionaries at the victim's house.
   c. It is an attack where the hacker changes the meanings of words in the victim's dictionaries.
   d. It is a type of cyberattack where an attacker tries to gain unauthorized access to a system by systematically trying every word in a dictionary as a password.

4. **What is a man-in-the-middle attack?**
   a. It is a type of attack where a hacker disguises, as an employee.
   b. It is an attack where the attacker intercepts and possibly alters the communication between two parties who believe they are directly communicating with each other.
   c. It is an attack where a hacker infiltrates a network from the inside.
   d. It is a physical attack by an intruder between two communicating parties.

5. **What is an insider attack?**

    a. An attack that originates from inside a computer system

    b. A type of attack where an insider uses their authorized access in a harmful way or to the detriment of the organization.

    c. An attack that occurs inside a building

    d. A physical attack by an employee on their colleagues

Answers

1. c.

2. b.

3. d.

4. b.

5. b.

References

1. MITRE ATT&CK: https://attack.mitre.org/

2. Hack Central YouTube channel: https://www.youtube.com/@secproint/videos

Join our Discord space

Join our Discord workspace for latest updates, offers, tech happenings around the world, new releases, and sessions with the authors:

https://discord.bpbonline.com

CHAPTER 3
Cyber Threat Intelligence and IoC

Introduction

Cyber threat intelligence is a discipline that provides a methodology and structure to take information from multiple sources about actors, targets, motivation, and malicious behavior; the information goes through a cycle of capture, analysis, cleansing, and delivery to keep the most relevant data that can help mitigate risks or detect materialized attacks. With the intelligence gathered on actors, tactics, etc., we can then generate a more accurate database of **Indicators of Compromise (IoC)** that we can use in threat hunting to be more proactive in front of the potential risks.

Structure

In this chapter, we will discuss the following topics:

- Introduction to cyber threat intelligence
- Cyber threat intelligence cycle
- Sources of CTI
- Threat intelligence platforms and tools
- Threat intelligence sharing standards
- Indicators of Compromise

Objectives

The adversaries evolve day by day, and from our defensive and detective perspective, we need to have enough up-to-date sources of information to keep our security mechanisms tuned and well-configured to be effective in trying to detect elusive small bits of information that becomes clues that you compare with your IoC lists to detect abnormal behaviors or anomalies that lead you to confirm that your infrastructure is a victim of a compromise.

The objective of this chapter is to introduce you to the cyber threat intelligence cycle, the different elements that you need to consider when creating an effective process, and how to incorporate tools that help to keep and use the IoC effectively.

Introduction to cyber threat intelligence

This proactive discipline helps companies understand their risks. What are the most likely threats that they will face depending on their market, location, activities, clients, etc? Due to the vast possibilities of threats, not all of them apply to all companies. With threat intelligence information, the company can improve its level within the maturity model and be more proactive in the face of risks, and even have certain advantages.

In the threat intelligence process, data is collected from multiple sources, processed, cleaned, and analyzed to have a better understanding of malicious actors, their attribution, **Tactics, Techniques, Procedures (TTP)**, motivations, and targets.

There are many advantages in the use and application of threat intelligence, such as being better prepared for a potential attack, better understanding how the minds of potential adversaries work, mitigating risks more effectively in connection with C- level to achieve better IT governance, i.e. the actions of the company's cybersecurity area are aligned with the business goals.

There are different types of cyber threat intelligence, and this is related to the objective that the intelligence information will cover; we can divide the types into the following three categories:

- **Strategic threat intelligence:** This intelligence is related to the complete or even global panorama of what is happening and the company's position within this space; its nature is conceptual, in a non-technical, summarized language. This type of information is intended to inform C-levels about current events and potential threats that the organization may face.

    The data relates to the company's market type, its geographical location, geopolitics, etc., and with this data, the company can update its risk map, rethink decisions, and change its position at a given time.

- **Operational threat intelligence:** This data has a more preventive objective against potential attacks. They are normally technical and include details of TTP and attack vectors. It is useful to identify potential adversaries for the organization and serve to make proactive decisions.

- **Tactical threat intelligence:** This type of intelligence focuses directly on the IoC and is very useful for SOCs, threat hunters, and cybersecurity teams. It allows them to directly search for anomalous elements within the infrastructure, such as a domain, file headers, hashes, etc. This information serves as input for threat-hunting teams as it allows them to perform more precise searches within the data to find malicious actors and their actions.

Understanding the different types of cases of cyber threat intelligence and their uses is essential for aligning cybersecurity. The following figure summarizes the cyber threat intelligence uses:

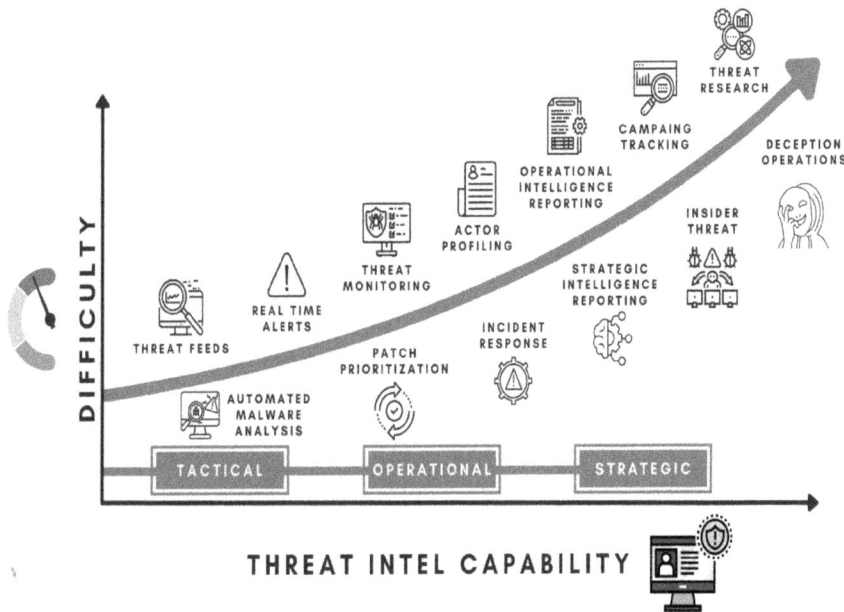

Figure 3.1: Cyber threat intelligence uses

Cyber threat intelligence cycle

Cyber threat intelligence must be carried out permanently in an iterative manner to produce better information.

The cyber threat intelligence lifecycle allows you to transform raw or disorganized data into a useful and, ideally, preventive intelligence product. Each step allows you to improve and purify the data received to ultimately receive information that allows you to make assertive decisions. This cycle is composed of the following six steps, as shown in the figure:

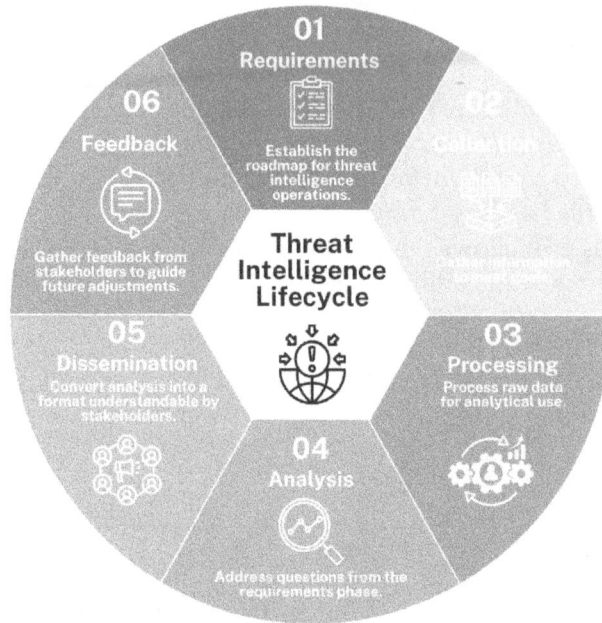

Figure 3.2: Cyber threat intelligence lifecycle

The six steps are explained in detail in the following:

1. **Planning and requirements list:** Good planning is essential for the success of the entire cycle. In this crucial phase, critical decisions are made that should normally involve the C-level and, if not everyone, at least the CISO, who oversees the organization's general cybersecurity guidelines. In this phase, the main factors are defined, such as:

    a. Objectives of the cyber threat intelligence process

    b. Methodology

    c. Attack surface to protect

    d. Actions to execute

2. **Threat data collection:** There are many data sources and multiple ways to collect information on potential threats based on the first stage, where the requirements and goals are defined. Among the potential data sources, we can include free community feeds and private or commercial feeds; in some cases, they provide raw data (*threat data feeds*) or already curated and parsed information. The sources are mentioned in the following:

    a. **Internal sources:**

        i.   Security mechanisms logs

        ii.   Operating systems logs

      iii.   Network device logs

  b. **External intelligence sources (threat intelligence feeds):**

      i.   **Open-Source Intelligence (OSINT)**

      ii.   CISA automated indicator sharing: AIS (**https://www.cisa.gov/ais)**

      iii.   Alien Vault OTX **(https://otx.alienvault.com/browse/global/pulses?include_inactive=0&sort=-modified&page=1&limit=10)**

      iv.   Spamhaus (**https://www.spamhaus.org/sbl/)**

      v.   Honey Database (**https://honeydb.io/threats)**

      vi.   Malware Information Sharing Platform (**https://www.misp-project.org/)**

      vii.   Advanced Persistent Threat Intelligence

3. **Processing:** From the universe of information collected, we must take what is useful to us, that is, we must filter the data. For this purpose, we carry out different steps, such as aggregating, standardizing, correlating the different data, eliminating false positives, etc. There are automated tools for this task, but we must clarify that they are not perfect and that the human factor is always recommended at this stage. Once the information is refined, in many cases, it can be correlated with threat intelligence frameworks such as MITRE ATT&CK.

4. **Analysis:** Now that the information is already refined and organized, we can proceed to the analysis, which is a crucial stage in the process. Here we are going to seek the answer to the questions that were asked in stage one of the cycle. In this phase, we make the data actionable through verification, look for patterns, and connect the dots, which allows us to have a better understanding and accurate information that allows us to make decisions.

5. **Dissemination:** In this phase, we deliver our opinions and recommendations to the stakeholders, so that they can take appropriate actions; these actions can be very varied, for example:

  a. Changing a rule in the anti-spam filter

  b. Blocking a range of IP addresses

  c. Creating a rule in the anti-malware against a certain type of file

  d. Creating an alert in the EDR

6. **Feedback:** In this stage, analysts and stakeholders evaluate whether the objectives and requirements set out in stage one were met. This way, corrective measures can be taken and applied in the planning and requirements stage.

Sources of CTI

As we explained previously, there are many useful sources of information that we can use in threat intelligence. We know the local origins and have clarity about them, every company's machines and devices can generate useful data to generate intelligence, these categories include all types of data logs and alerts generated by the entity's security mechanisms. Apart from them, we have external sources that help us visualize a broader panorama, whether at a regional or global level.

Internal company information space

Within an organization, various internal information sources play a critical role in identifying, analyzing, and responding to security threats. These sources provide valuable insights into system behavior, user activity, and potential IoC. In the internal company space, we have information sources like:

- Firewall logs
- Active Directory logs
- Operating systems logs
- Application logs
- Network device logs
- Network traffic logs
- Mail server logs
- Antispam logs
- Cloud technologies logs
- **Intrusion Detection System / Intrusion Prevention System (IDS/IPS)** logs
- **Security Orchestration, Automation, and Response (SOAR)** logs
- **Endpoint Detection and Response / Extended Detection and Response (EDR/XDR)** logs
- **User Behavior Analytics / User and Entity Behavior Analytics (UBA / UEBA)** logs and alerts
- **Data Leak Prevention (DLP)** logs and alerts
- Antimalware logs

In order to summarize, each device in the infrastructure can be configured to generate logs that can be received in a **Security Information and Event Manager (SIEM)** or in any kind of correlation engine that assists you in detecting the relation between events that can be related to an adversary action.

The SIEM subject is going to be explicated in depth in *Chapter 4, Tools and Techniques for Threat Hunting*.

External space information

In the external feeds group, we have a huge number of different sources, both open-source, private, and commercial. These feeds can be received in specific technologies that use protocols created for this purpose. In most documents, these protocols are identified as sharing standards. Let us understand some of the best-known open-source feeds.

Open-source feeds

AlienVault OSSIM® Open Threat Exchange®(OTX™) (**https://otx.alienvault.com/dashboard/new**). It is A free, open-source SIEM platform developed by AlienVault, which has services like log management, event correlation, asset discovery, vulnerability assessment, and intrusion detection in a unified platform. They use *pulses* as alerts of malicious or abnormal behavior. The main service and information are free; if you want to integrate them with a third-party application or tools, they have a price. The interface looks something like the following figure:

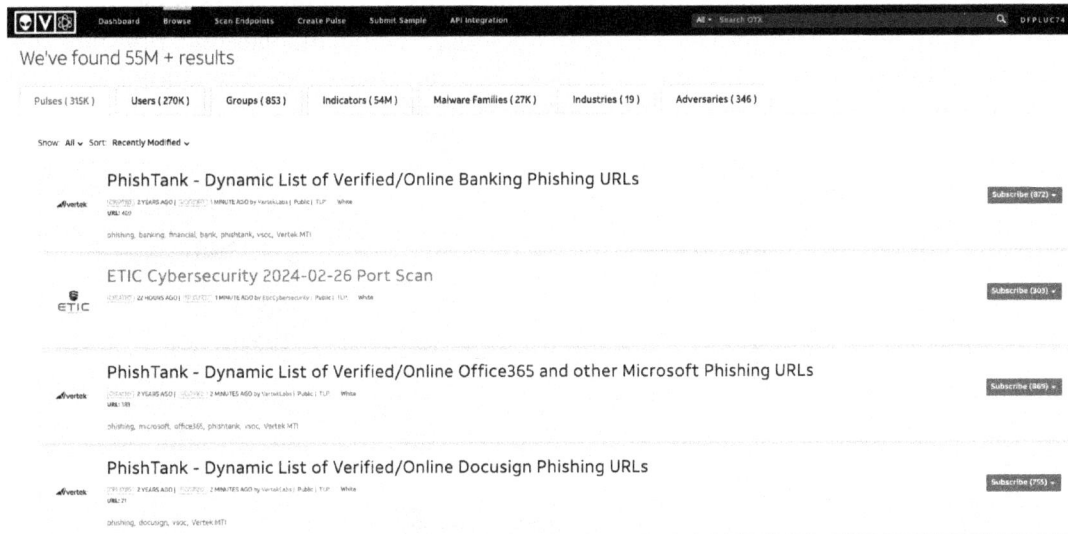

Figure 3.3: AlienVault threat exchange browse page

URLhaus (**https://urlhaus.abuse.ch/**) is a community-driven threat intelligence project designed to collect, track, and share URLs that are being used to distribute malware. The service is completely free. In the following figure, you will be able to see what the homepage looks like:

URLhaus Database

Here you can propose new malware urls or just browse the URLhaus database. If you are looking for a parsable list of the dataset, you might want to check out the URLhaus API.

There are **2'732'581** malicious URLs tracked on URLhaus. The queue size is **9**.

Submit a URL

In order to submit a URL to URLhaus, you need to login with your abuse.ch account

Browse Database

domain, url, md5, sha256, tag:SocGholish, filetype:doc or url_status:online   [Search]

Dateadded (UTC)	Malware URL	Status	Tags	Reporter
2024-02-26 21:35:32	http://59.93.187.174:43598/Mozi.m	Online	elf Mozi	lrz_urlhaus
2024-02-26 21:34:38	http://117.208.91.167:45366/Mozi.a	Online	elf Mozi	lrz_urlhaus
2024-02-26 21:34:29	http://101.67.200.201:44556/Mozi.m	Online	elf Mozi	lrz_urlhaus

Figure 3.4: URLhaus database browse page

Spamhaus (**https://www.spamhaus.org/**) is an organization dedicated to tracking spam, malicious internet activity, and cyber threats such as phishing, malware distribution, and botnet operations. Focused especially on Email Domains Blacklists. The following figure provides a visual representation of the workings of Spamhaus:

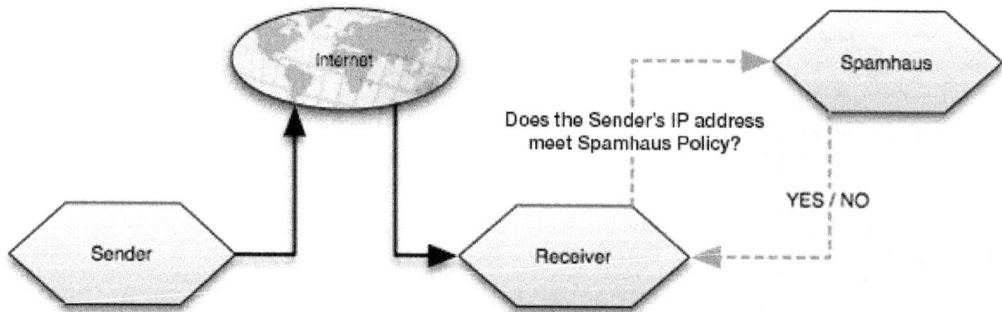

Figure 3.5: Spamhaus workings
(Source: https://www.spamhaus.org/whitepapers/dnsbl_function/)

The following are Combined / PAID / PRIVATE feeds:

- **Mandiant cyber threat intelligence platform:** The Mandiant **threat intelligence platform** (**TIP**) is a cloud-based solution that delivers real-time, actionable threat intelligence gathered from global incident response operations, dark web monitoring, and malware analysis. The following figure depicts the homepage of Mandiant TIP. (**https://www.mandiant.com/advantage/threat-intelligence**):

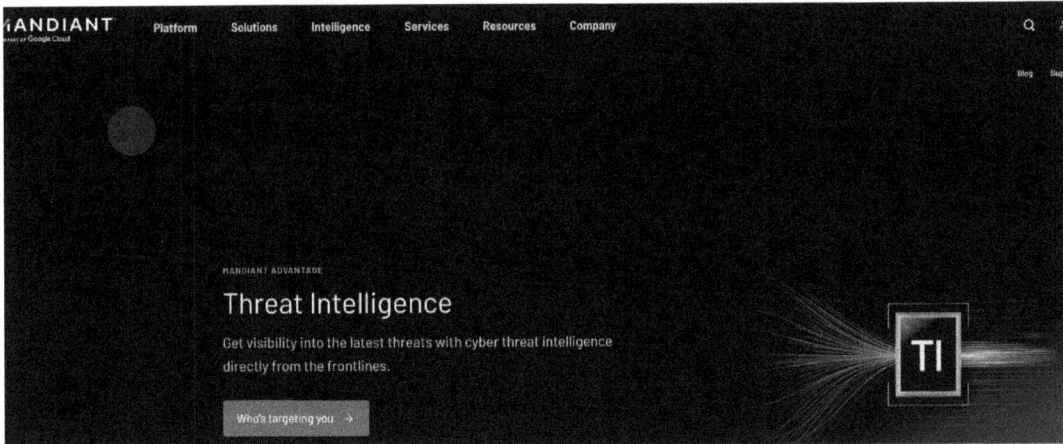

Figure 3.6: Mandiant cyber TIP

- **Cisco Talos Intelligence Center:** Cisco Talos Intelligence Group is the threat intelligence division of Cisco, providing research, analysis, and real-time intelligence on cyber threats, malware, vulnerabilities, and attack campaigns. (**https://www.talosintelligence.com/**)

  For intelligence search, refer to this link **https://www.talosintelligence.com/ reputation_center**

  The following figure will preview the Cisco Talos Intelligence homepage:

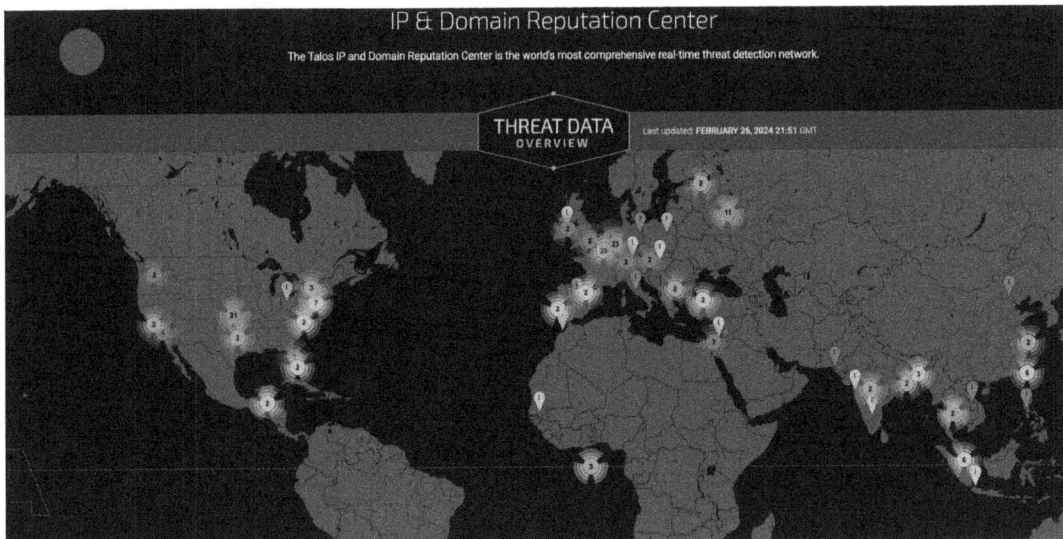

Figure 3.7: Cisco Talos Intelligence Center

- **CrowdSec:** CrowdSec is an open-source, collaborative cybersecurity platform that uses behavior-based threat detection and a crowdsourced threat intelligence network to protect systems and networks from malicious actors. Shown below is an example of how the home interface is presented: (**https://www.crowdsec.net/product/threat-intelligence**)

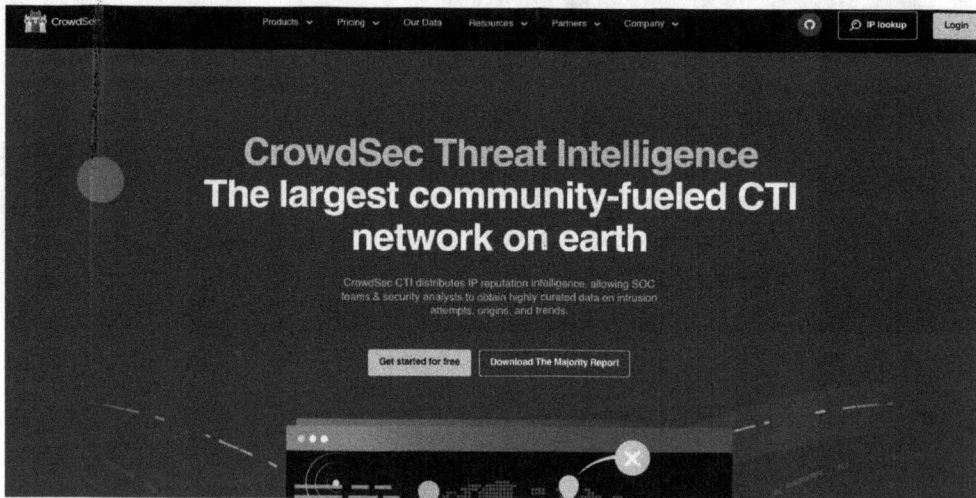

Figure 3.8: *CrowdSec home page*

- **Palo Alto Wildfire:** Palo Alto Networks WildFire is a cloud-based malware analysis and advanced threat detection service that uses sandboxing, machine learning, and static/dynamic analysis to identify zero-day threats, malware, and exploits. The WildFire homepage, as depicted in the following figure, offers users a streamlined view of threat submissions. (**https://www.paloaltonetworks.com/network-security/wildfire**)

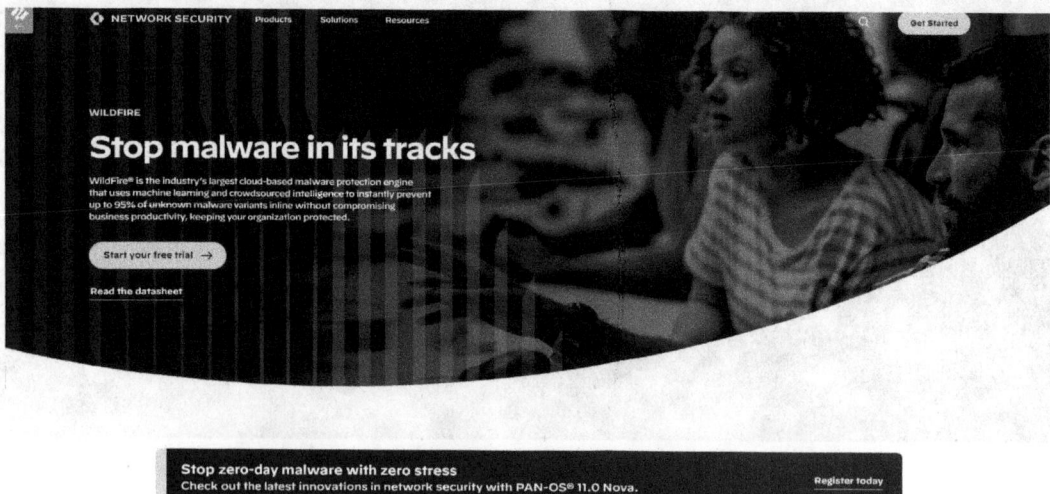

Figure 3.9: *Palo Alto Wildfire home page*

The following are the special mentions to informational sources:

- **Internet Storm Center:** The **Internet Storm Center (ISC)** is a free threat monitoring and analysis platform that provides real-time insights into malicious activity across the internet (**https://isc.sans.edu/index.html**)

Threat intelligence platforms and tools

These platforms are tools that bring the integration of multiple cyber threat intelligence feeds to provide aggregation, depuration, correlation, and generate threat intelligence reports that will allow the Blue Team to take proactive or reactive actions to countermeasure existing threats.

An effective TIP helps to obtain greater precision in the process of identification, investigation, and response to threats, saving time and resources, and allowing analysts to focus on valuable information. They do not have to deal with the enormous amounts of data generated by different feeds. In addition, you can use automation to reduce operational costs and allow the analysis and evaluation that would not be possible in a manual way for the analysts.

Here are some recommendations or best practices related to TIP, so you can obtain the best performance and receive actionable intelligence:

- It should update the information in real-time.

- The TIP should receive and integrate internal and external feeds.

- It should be capable of being integrated with incident handling and event management tools.

- The platform should be capable of being configured to automate tasks and workflows.

We can enumerate many TIPs in the market, including some Open-Source examples. Let us review some of the common:

Name	Type	URL
MISP- Malware Information Sharing Platform	Free	**https://www.misp-project.org/**
Open CTI	Free	**https://github.com/OpenCTI-Platform/opencti**
IBM X-Force Exchange	Paid	**https://exchange.xforce.ibmcloud.com/**
Palo Alto Networks AutoFocus	Paid	**https://docs.paloaltonetworks.com/autofocus**
Anomali Threatstream	Paid	**https://www.anomali.com/products/threatstream**

Table 3.1: Threat intelligence platforms

Threat intelligence sharing standards

The need to standardize how threat intelligence information is shared and disseminated led to the evolution of existing mechanisms until reaching current transmission and structuring standards.

The current standards are:

- **Structured Threat Information eXpression** (STIX)
- **Trusted Automated eXchange of Intelligence** (TAXII)
- **Malware Information Sharing Platform Format** (MISP)

Each one fulfills a different but complementary role. Let us go deep into the definition and characteristics.

STIX

It is a standardized language that allows representing and characterizing objects and information related to cyber threats, their relations, and links in a clear and detailed manner. This provides benefits to analysts, such as the compatibility of this data with different tools and the ease of communication of key information using a JSON structure.

The STIX standard, currently in *version 2.1,* approved on 10 June 2021, is supported and maintained by the **Organization for the Advancement of Structured Information Standards** (**OASIS**). They are a non-profit international group that promotes open, collaborative development of specifications based on public standards.

STIX uses JSON (**http://www.json.org/**) as a schema. The extract example is shown in the following:

```
1    {
2        "type": "bundle",
3        "id": "bundle--02c3ef24-9cd4-48f3-a99f-b74ce24f1d34",
4        "spec_version": "2.1",
5        "objects": [
6            {
7                "type": "x-mitre-collection",
8                "id": "x-mitre-collection--90c00720-636b-4485-b342-8751d232bf09",
9                "spec_version": "2.1",
10               "x_mitre_attack_spec_version": "2.1.0",
11               "name": "ICS ATT&CK",
12               "x_mitre_version": "10.0",
13               "description": "The ATT&CK for Industrial Control Systems (ICS) knowledge base categorizes the unique
14               "created_by_ref": "identity--c78cb6e5-0c4b-4611-8297-d1b8b55e40b5",
15               "created": "2020-10-27T14:49:39.188Z",
16               "modified": "2021-10-21T14:00:00.188Z",
17               "object_marking_refs": [
18                   "marking-definition--fa42a846-8d90-4e51-bc29-71d5b4802168"
19               ],
20               "x_mitre_contents": [
21                   {
22                       "object_ref": "attack-pattern--19a71d1e-6334-4233-8260-b749cae37953",
23                       "object_modified": "2021-10-08T15:14:01.612Z"
24                   },
25                   {
26                       "object_ref": "attack-pattern--2900bbd8-308a-4274-b074-5b8bde8347bc",
27                       "object_modified": "2021-10-08T13:04:01.612Z"
28                   },
```

Figure 3.10: STIX extract example

The STIX *Version 2.1* structure allows presenting any kind of complex data, some are mentioned below:

- Threat actor profiles
- Attack patterns
- Location
- Relations
- Files
- Malware objects
- IP addresses
- Incident response tactics

The standard defines 18 domain objects, as shown in the following figure:

Figure 3.11: *STIX domain objects*

STIX example showing a malicious URL scenario **https://oasis-open.github.io/cti-documentation/examples/indicator-for-malicious-url**

The following figure presents a STIX representation of a malicious URL scenario, showing how structured threat intelligence can capture and communicate detailed relationships and information.

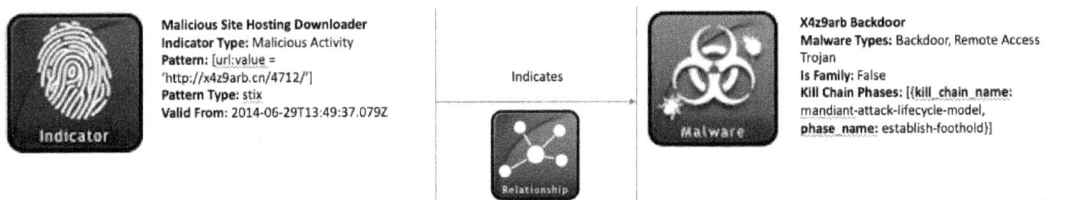

Figure 3.12: *STIX malicious URL scenario*

The STIX JSON schemas can be difficult to interpret directly, so an STIX visualizer is provided to create a graphic representation of the JSON files: **https://oasis-open.github.io/cti-stix-visualization/**.

We can try this example to visualize an indicator of a malicious campaign:

1. Go to: **https://github.com/oasis-open/cti-stix2-json-schemas/blob/master/examples/indicator-to-campaign-relationship.json**.

2. Copy the JSON content or download the file.

3. Paste it into the STIX Visualizer **https://oasis-open.github.io/cti-stix-visualization/**

To better understand how threat intelligence elements relate to each other, the STIX Visualizer provides a graphical way to explore the data, as shown in the following figure:

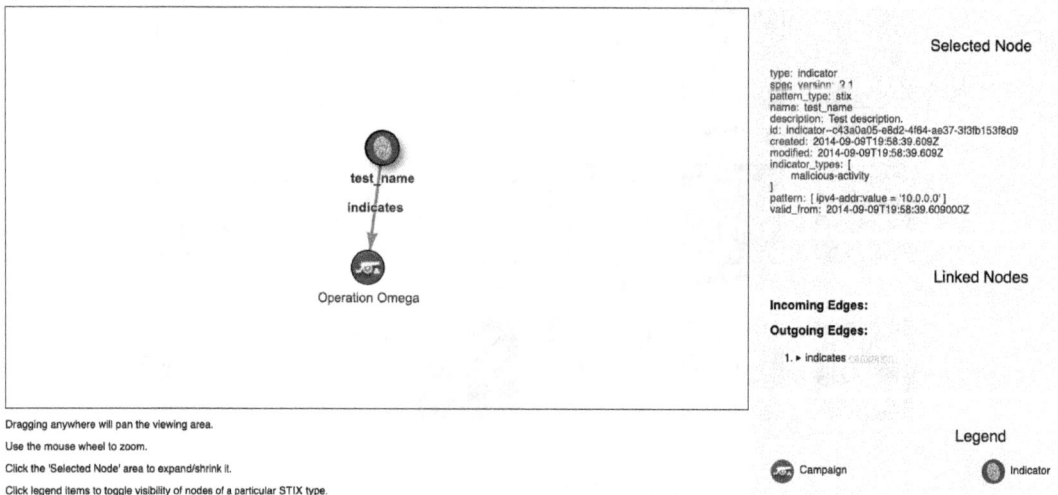

Figure 3.13: STIX Visualizer

For more information about STIX, you can visit: **https://docs.oasis-open.org/cti/stix/v2.1/csprd01/stix-v2.1-csprd01.html**

TAXII

It is a communication protocol that allows the exchange of cyber threat information contained or documented in STIX format. This protocol is aimed at maintaining the security of information along with the automation in the delivery of data. Refer to the following points for a better understanding:

- **TAXII server:** Hosts structured threat data in STIX format, enabling client query and retrieval.

- **TAXII client:** The client can exchange (send and receive) information from a TAXII server, receive updates, and feed the local database.

- **TAXII collections:** They are connections to a database of cyber threat intelligence in a TAXII server that is used to feed the requests from clients.

- **TAXII channels:** TAXII servers maintain the channels and allow the clients to exchange information with other TAXII clients. They can publish messages and subscribe to specific channels to receive information, each server can host multiple channels.

To understand how threat intelligence is exchanged between systems, consider having a look at the TAXII 2.1 protocol, which defines the mechanisms for exchanging STIX data. (Refer to the following link for the official TAXII 2.1 specification and implementation details:

https://docs.oasis-open.org/cti/taxii/v2.1/taxii-v2.1.html).

To illustrate how threat intelligence is shared between systems, the following figure shows the structure of TAXII channels used for exchanging data.

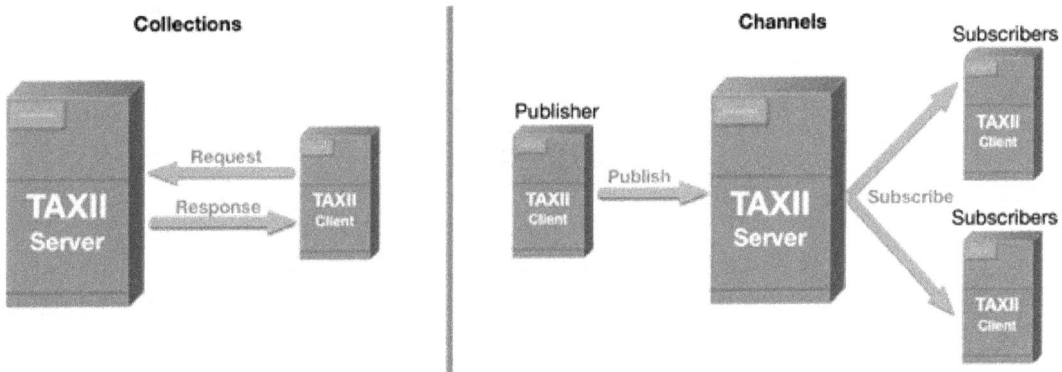

Figure 3.14: TAXII Channels

This protocol supports different information-sharing models using an API:

Sharing Model	Description
Source | Subscriber	Single origin of information for different destinations
Hub and Spoke	Single Information repository
Peer to Peer	Information is shared between Peers and Groups

Table 3.2: Sharing models

To demonstrate how consumers receive threat intelligence, the subscriber model shown in the following figure shows how TAXII enables clients to subscribe to specific data feeds and receive updates automatically:

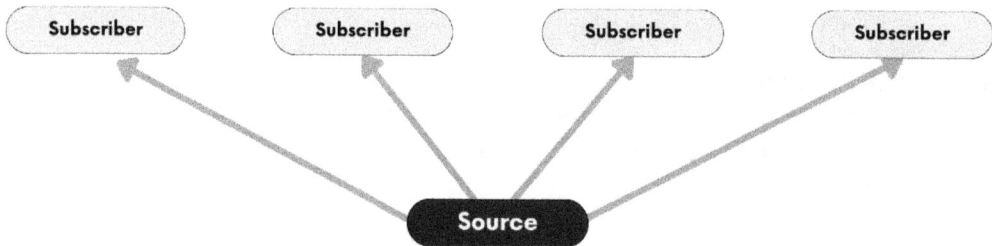

Figure 3.15: Subscriber model

The illustration of the hub and spoke model is shown in the following figure:

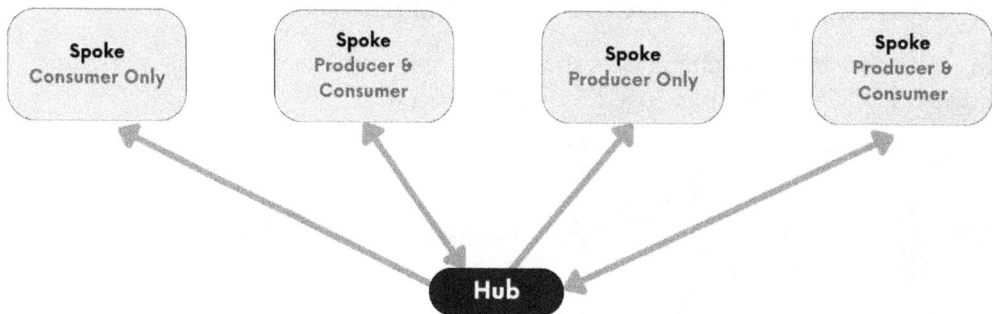

Figure 3.16: Hub–Spoke model

In contrast to the subscriber model, the peer-to-peer model shown in the following figure illustrates how TAXII allows systems to share threat intelligence directly with one another, enabling more decentralized and collaborative information exchange:

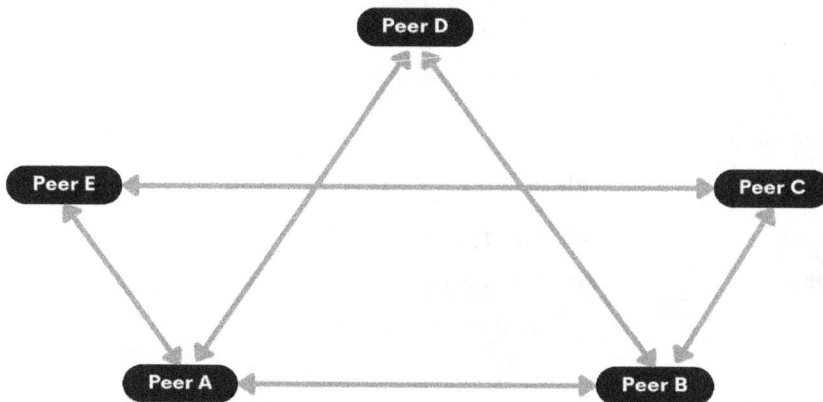

Figure 3.17: Peer–to–peer model

More information about TAXII is mentioned in the following link: **https://docs.oasis-open. org/cti/taxii/v2.0/cs01/taxii-v2.0-cs01.html#_Toc496542700**

Malware Information Sharing Platform

We know that a **Malware Information Sharing Platform** (**MISP**) is a TIP, but it uses a specific format to be able to exchange information and deliver threat intelligence data to different platforms. Let us discuss how it works. MISP can enumerate the attributes within an attack and describe them using a specific behavioral pattern, such as MITRE ATT&CK, and represent the data in JSON format. In addition, it can be used through an API.

MISP uses the following formats:

Refer to the following source for a better understanding: **https://github.com/MISP/MISP-rfc**

MISP format	Description
misp-core-format	Describes the core JSON format of MISP
misp-taxonomy-format	Describes the taxonomy JSON format of MISP
misp-galaxy-format	Describes the galaxy template format used to expand the threat actor modeling of MISP
misp-object-template-format	Describes the object template format to add combined and composite objects to the MISP core format

Table 3.3: *MISP formats*

It is important to keep in mind that MISP is specifically oriented to its platform; the information generated is interpreted on devices that have MISP installed, unlike STIX, which is compatible with almost any TIP.

MISP uses expansion modules to extract data from multiple sources, for example, **Autonomous System Numbers** (**ASN**), **Common Vulnerabilities and Exposure** (**CVE**) to provide detailed vulnerability information, and domain tools to provide Whois (which is the public information related to the domain owner, creation date, expiration date, etc.) data, among many other expansions.

In the same way, you can export data in multiple formats such as **Common Event Format** (**CEF**), PDF, CSV, THREAT STREAM, etc.

MISP can also import information from many data sources, for example, STIX, MALTEGO, OCR, etc.

More information about current expansions, export modules, and import modules is mentioned in the following link: **https://github.com/MISP/misp-modules**

MISP Galaxy

MISP Galaxy allows you to create a detailed graph about the steps, nodes, IPs, artifacts, etc. involved within an attack, like STIX, but STIX can become more detailed to describe the relationships between different objects.

A simple way to present a large object called a **cluster** is that it can be connected to MISP events or attributes. A cluster can be composed of different numbers of objects. Elements are identified as **key values**. There is a default knowledge base with data like:

- Threat actors
- Tools
- Ransomware
- ATT&CK arrays

This knowledge base is available in MISP Galaxy, but it can be overwritten, replaced, updated, forked, and shared as needed:

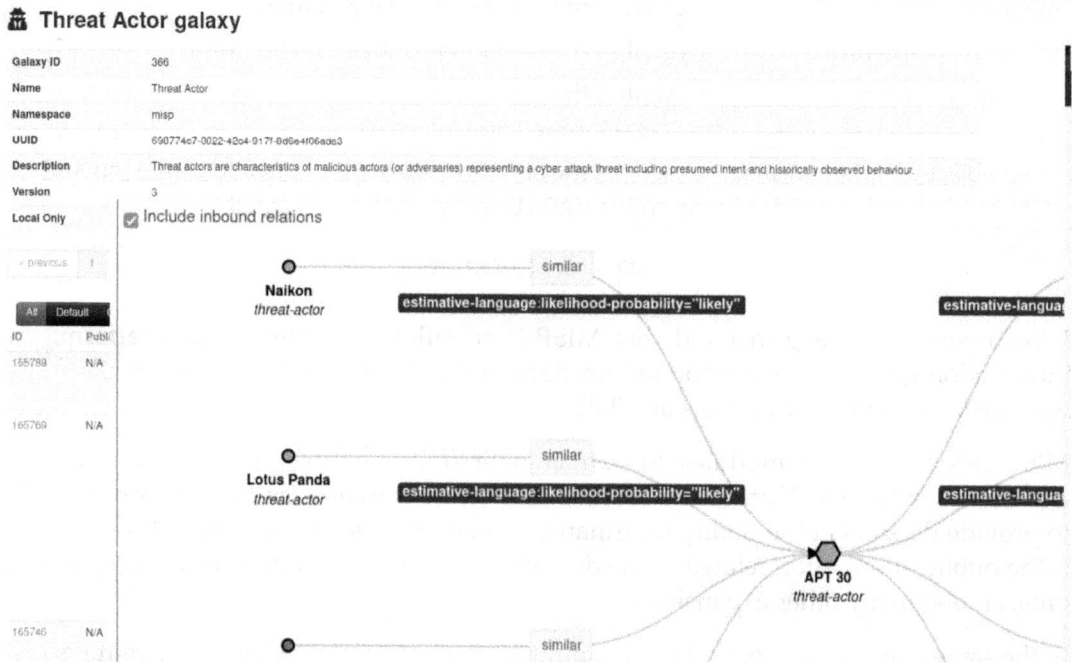

Figure 3.18: MISP Galaxy

(*Source: https://raw.githubusercontent.com/MISP/misp-galaxy/
aa41337fd78946a60aef3783f58f337d2342430a/doc/images/galaxy.png*)

Refer to this link for more information about MISP: **https://www.misp-project.org/tools/**

Indicators of Compromise

We are already familiar with the concept of IoC. We are already familiar with the concept of IoC. These are the traces that an attacker leaves behind during an intrusion, compromise, or attack. IoCs can be shared across the cybersecurity community to raise awareness about specific threats. These threats may include particular attacks, malware variants, threat actors, and more. Sharing this information helps blue teams strengthen their defenses and improve their overall cybersecurity posture.

In this space, we are going to explore the technical point of view of the characterization, types, and analysis of IoCs.

Indicators of Attack versus Indicators of Compromise

The main difference between **Indicators of Attack (IoA)** and IoCs is the moment when they are generated. IoA occurs in real-time (dynamic) and does not mean that your company is already compromised. They indicate that somebody has the intention to compromise the company or is executing a precursor behavior. An IoC (static) tells an organization that the attack was already successful.

Elements revealing an indicator of compromise

IoCs can be very helpful in grabbing information about the adversary, its **Tactics, Techniques, and Procedures** (**TTP**), etc. We can enumerate some of the most important factors:

- TTPs used in an attack
- Attribution (Who is the attacker)
- Capabilities
- Compromise focus
- Severity of the incident
- Mitigation areas

Types of IoC

In your environment, you can detect different objects, parameters, or artifacts that can be created or manipulated by malicious actors to accomplish their attack goals. We use them as IoC, which leads us to know if there is an abnormal behavior or a compromised resource. We can see a short list of them in the following table:

Indicator type	Specific indicators	Possible location	Detection technology
Network-based indicators	• Ip Address / Ip Range • Domain Names • Specific TCP/UDP ports • ARP Tables • Routing Tables • DNS Cache • FQDNS • URL • URI	• Host / Server Operating Systems Configuration Files and Logs • Network Devices Configuration and Log files. • Security mechanisms Log • DNS Servers • Active Directory Information • LDAP Servers	• **Intrusion Detection System (IDS)** • **Intrusion Prevention System (IPS)** • **Extended Detection and Response (XDR)** • **Security Information and Event Management (SIEM)**
File based indicator	• File Headers (Magic Numbers) • File Extensions • File Hash • File Content (Strings)	• Local filesystems • Shared Folders/Directory • NFS (Network filesystem) • Any kind of Storage • MBR	• **Endpoint Detection and Response (EDR)** • Antimalware Console • Sandbox
Host based indicator	• Configuration Files • Windows OS Registry Hives	• Windows OS Registry Values • Registry HKLM Values • Registry HKCU Values • Configuration Directories	• Endpoint Security • EDR • XDR
Behavior based indicator	• Failed Login Attempts • Abnormal Time Activities • Abnormal Connections • Files or Content in a different language	• Logs • Event Managers	• **User Behavior Analytics (UBA)** • **User and Entity Behavior Analytics (UEBA)**

Table 3.4: Types of IoC

True or false, positives and negatives explanation

As a threat hunter, you need to be familiar with different IoCs. Still, at the same time, you also need to be careful because not all abnormal or unusual behavior means imminent malicious activity. In some cases, we are in front of false positives, so you need to fine-tune your IoC and detection technologies to avoid wasting time and resources.

Similarly, your detection technologies may miss some abnormal behavior (False Negative), or some adversary that is already inside your infrastructure but has not been detected yet.

The following figure illustrates the different possibilities related to the detection of an adversary in your environment:

	Incidence of harmful behavior	Absence of harmful actions
Notification created	**TRUE POSITIVE** The monitoring system detected an incident of harmful behavior.	**FALSE POSITIVE** The monitoring system reported the absence of harmful behavior.
No Notification issued	**FALSE NEGATIVE** Harmful behavior occurred but was not detected by the monitoring system.	**TRUE NEGATIVE** No harmful behavior occurred, and none was detected by the monitoring system.

Figure 3.19: Possibilities of detection

IoC lifecycle

Creating or defining an IoC is very important in the world of threat hunting; IoCs have a lifecycle, starting with the capture of abnormal parameters, and discovery, followed by other crucial steps to be able to take advantage of the detection and fine-tune your mechanisms and analysis to be able to detect that anomalous behavior that we are looking for within our infrastructure. The following figure allows us to see each stage in the life of an IoC:

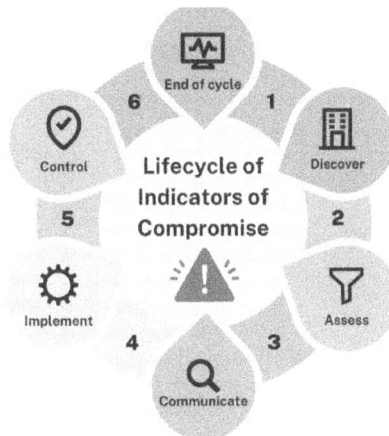

Figure 3.20: IoC lifecycle

The following figure allows us to expand the detail of each stage in the life of an IoC:

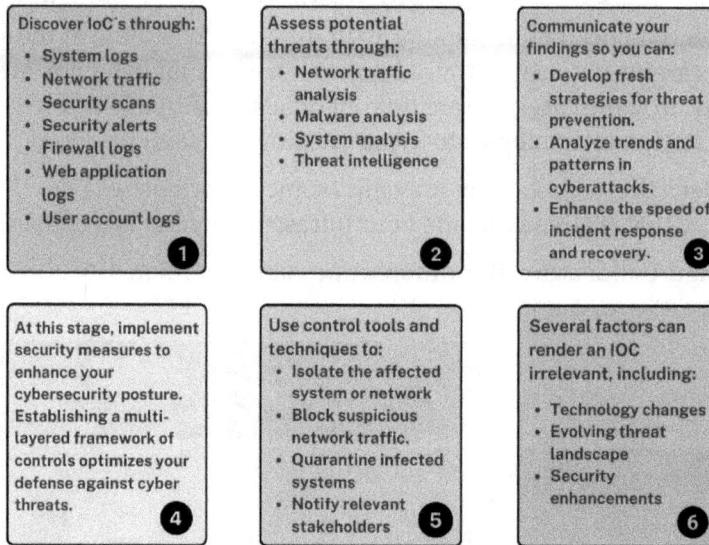

Discover IoC's through:
- System logs
- Network traffic
- Security scans
- Security alerts
- Firewall logs
- Web application logs
- User account logs

1

Assess potential threats through:
- Network traffic analysis
- Malware analysis
- System analysis
- Threat intelligence

2

Communicate your findings so you can:
- Develop fresh strategies for threat prevention.
- Analyze trends and patterns in cyberattacks.
- Enhance the speed of incident response and recovery.

3

At this stage, implement security measures to enhance your cybersecurity posture. Establishing a multi-layered framework of controls optimizes your defense against cyber threats.

4

Use control tools and techniques to:
- Isolate the affected system or network
- Block suspicious network traffic.
- Quarantine infected systems
- Notify relevant stakeholders

5

Several factors can render an IOC irrelevant, including:
- Technology changes
- Evolving threat landscape
- Security enhancements

6

Figure 3.21: IoC lifecycle in detail

Examples of Indicators of Compromise

It is almost impossible to list all the IoCs that an adversary can generate with its actions, but here, we will illustrate some interesting and common examples:

- Anomalies with a specific user account involve an increase in access permissions, using one account to access others that offer additional privileges, or other irregularities related to privileged user accounts.

- Logins to accounts originated from countries or places other than where your business is based, or where your employees are located.

- Numerous unsuccessful attempts to log into a single or multiple accounts.

- An unexpected increase or decrease in network traffic or other unusual activity related to outbound or inbound network traffic.

- Numerous requests are directed toward one specific file.

- Activity in a network port that was previously idle.

- Unauthorized modifications made to your system files or registry.

- Sudden, unexpected DNS requests.

- Abnormal execution of PowerShell, WMIC, or system commands.

- Persistent repetitive actions.

Malicious TTPs and their IoCs

Different types of malicious activities can generate or affect different IoCs. In the next part, we are going to incorporate some different areas in the attack surface, some potential adversarial actions, IoC, what to look for, and attack vectors. It is almost impossible to list all the potential combinations of actions, indicators, and vectors, so we are going to include some of the most relevant and frequently presented:

IoC in user authentication and authorization

Authentication mechanisms are commonly targeted by malicious actors because they serve as the control to access valuable data and systems. By compromising these mechanisms, adversaries can gain unauthorized access to sensitive or critical information, manipulate systems, and disrupt operations. These attacks can involve stealing credentials, exploiting weak authentication methods, or bypassing authentication procedures; the end goal is often to impersonate legitimate users, mask their activities, and evade detection, as shown in the following figure:

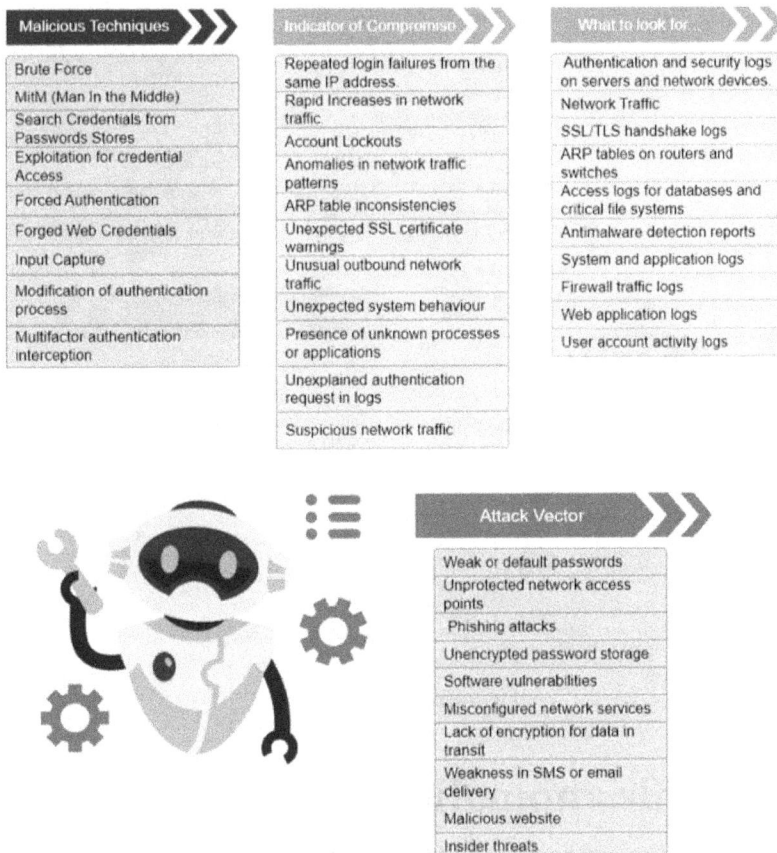

Figure 3.22: IoC in User authentication and authorization

Domain name system

Domain name system (DNS) is a crucial component of the Internet infrastructure, acting as the directory that connects domain names with their corresponding IP addresses. Due to its central role, DNS is a prime target for cyberattackers aiming to disrupt the normal functioning of the internet or redirect users to malicious sites. By compromising DNS servers, attackers can effectively control where traffic is directed, enabling them to intercept, manipulate, or reroute data, leading to data theft, distribution of malware, or denial of service. The following figure will present more information about the subject:

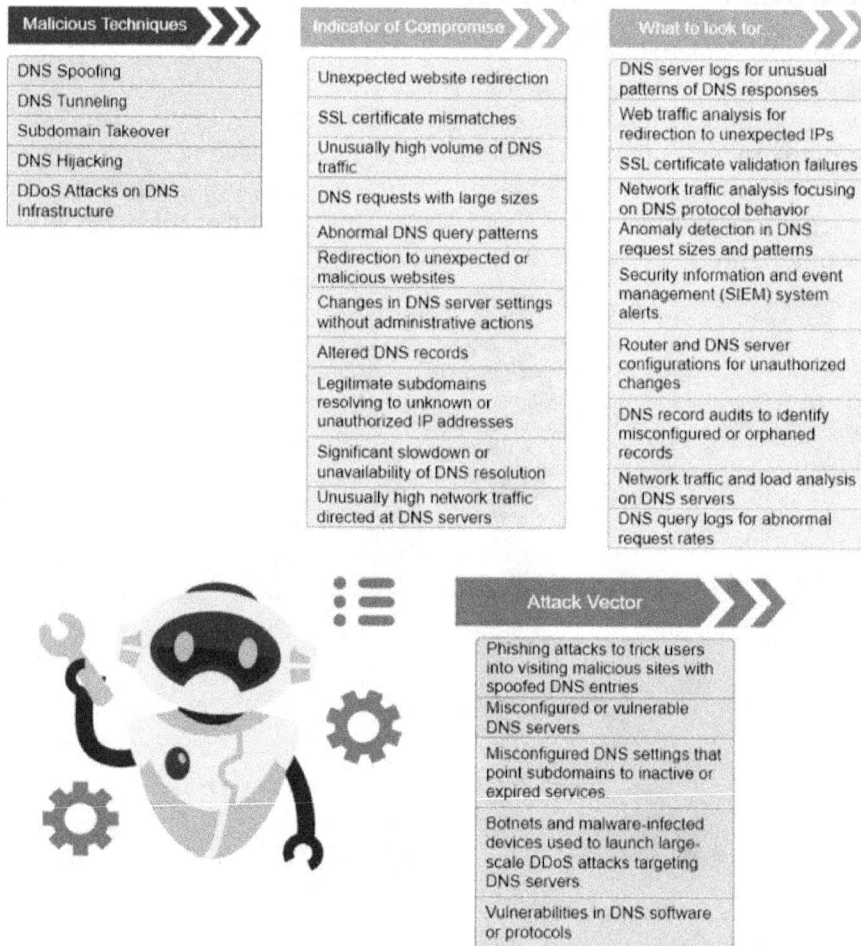

Malicious Techniques	Indicator of Compromise	What to look for
DNS Spoofing	Unexpected website redirection	DNS server logs for unusual patterns of DNS responses
DNS Tunneling	SSL certificate mismatches	Web traffic analysis for redirection to unexpected IPs
Subdomain Takeover	Unusually high volume of DNS traffic	SSL certificate validation failures
DNS Hijacking	DNS requests with large sizes	Network traffic analysis focusing on DNS protocol behavior
DDoS Attacks on DNS Infrastructure	Abnormal DNS query patterns	Anomaly detection in DNS request sizes and patterns
	Redirection to unexpected or malicious websites	Security information and event management (SIEM) system alerts
	Changes in DNS server settings without administrative actions	Router and DNS server configurations for unauthorized changes
	Altered DNS records	DNS record audits to identify misconfigured or orphaned records
	Legitimate subdomains resolving to unknown or unauthorized IP addresses	Network traffic and load analysis on DNS servers
	Significant slowdown or unavailability of DNS resolution	DNS query logs for abnormal request rates
	Unusually high network traffic directed at DNS servers	

Attack Vector
Phishing attacks to trick users into visiting malicious sites with spoofed DNS entries
Misconfigured or vulnerable DNS servers
Misconfigured DNS settings that point subdomains to inactive or expired services
Botnets and malware-infected devices used to launch large-scale DDoS attacks targeting DNS servers
Vulnerabilities in DNS software or protocols

Figure 3.23: IoC in DNS

Network traffic anomalies

Network traffic anomalies are deviations from normal network behavior, which can signal the presence of cyber threats or system issues. These anomalies can result from various causes, including cyberattacks, such as **Distributed Denial of Service (DDoS)** attacks, which flood networks with excessive traffic to disrupt services, or unauthorized access attempts, where attackers probe networks for vulnerabilities. Detecting these anomalies is crucial for maintaining network integrity and security. The following figure will show more information about the traffic anomalies:

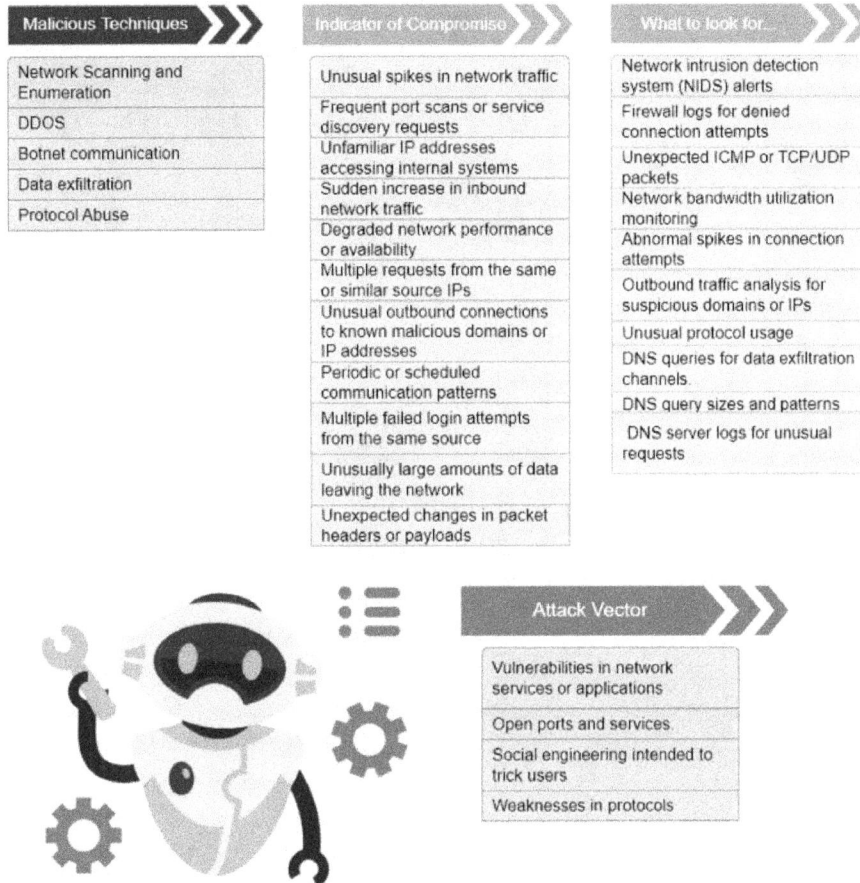

Malicious Techniques ⟩⟩⟩	Indicator of Compromise ⟩⟩⟩	What to look for... ⟩⟩⟩
Network Scanning and Enumeration	Unusual spikes in network traffic	Network intrusion detection system (NIDS) alerts
DDOS	Frequent port scans or service discovery requests	Firewall logs for denied connection attempts
Botnet communication	Unfamiliar IP addresses accessing internal systems	Unexpected ICMP or TCP/UDP packets
Data exfiltration	Sudden increase in inbound network traffic	Network bandwidth utilization monitoring
Protocol Abuse	Degraded network performance or availability	Abnormal spikes in connection attempts
	Multiple requests from the same or similar source IPs	Outbound traffic analysis for suspicious domains or IPs
	Unusual outbound connections to known malicious domains or IP addresses	Unusual protocol usage
	Periodic or scheduled communication patterns	DNS queries for data exfiltration channels.
	Multiple failed login attempts from the same source	DNS query sizes and patterns
	Unusually large amounts of data leaving the network	DNS server logs for unusual requests
	Unexpected changes in packet headers or payloads	

Attack Vector ⟩⟩⟩
Vulnerabilities in network services or applications
Open ports and services.
Social engineering intended to trick users
Weaknesses in protocols

Figure 3.24: IoC in network traffic anomalies

Registry changes

Registry changes refer to modifications in the system registry, a database that stores crucial configuration settings and options on Windows operating systems. Malicious actors often target the registry to embed malware persistently, alter system functionalities, or disable security mechanisms. Timely identification and reversal of malicious registry changes are vital for maintaining system integrity, preventing malware persistence, and ensuring the continued protection of the system against cyberattacks. The following figure will show more details about the registry changes:

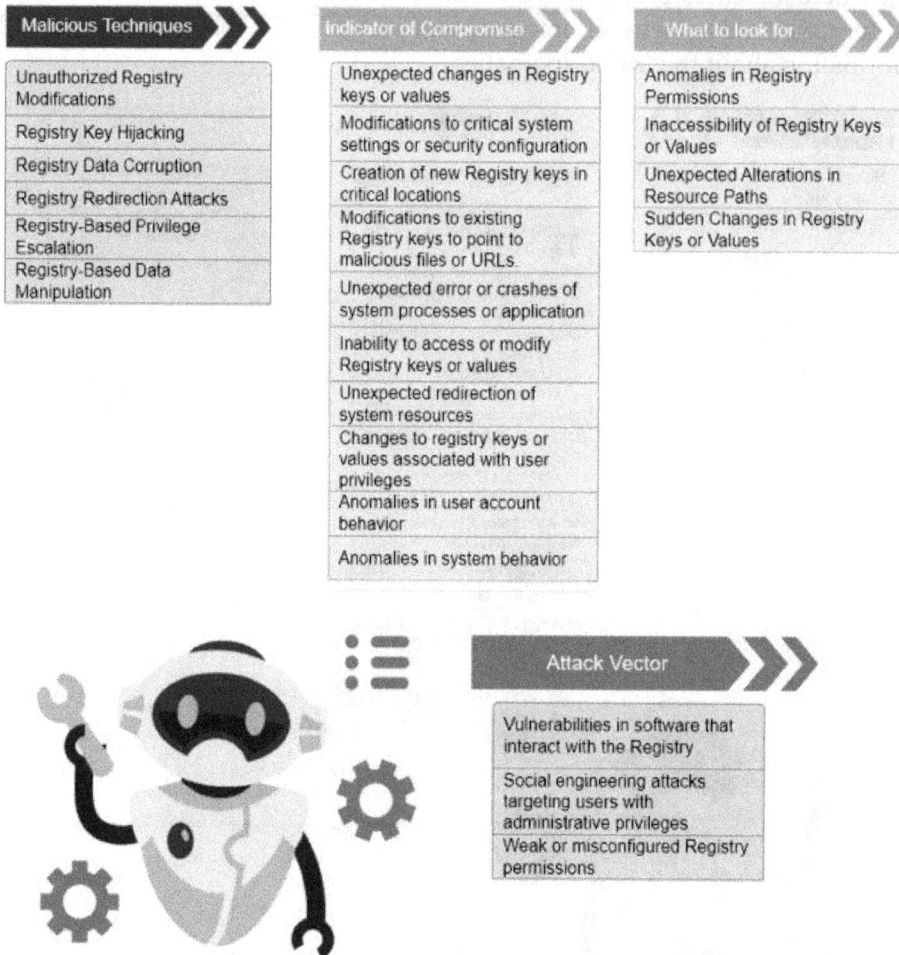

Malicious Techniques
- Unauthorized Registry Modifications
- Registry Key Hijacking
- Registry Data Corruption
- Registry Redirection Attacks
- Registry-Based Privilege Escalation
- Registry-Based Data Manipulation

Indicator of Compromise
- Unexpected changes in Registry keys or values
- Modifications to critical system settings or security configuration
- Creation of new Registry keys in critical locations
- Modifications to existing Registry keys to point to malicious files or URLs.
- Unexpected error or crashes of system processes or application
- Inability to access or modify Registry keys or values
- Unexpected redirection of system resources
- Changes to registry keys or values associated with user privileges
- Anomalies in user account behavior
- Anomalies in system behavior

What to look for
- Anomalies in Registry Permissions
- Inaccessibility of Registry Keys or Values
- Unexpected Alterations in Resource Paths
- Sudden Changes in Registry Keys or Values

Attack Vector
- Vulnerabilities in software that interact with the Registry
- Social engineering attacks targeting users with administrative privileges
- Weak or misconfigured Registry permissions

Figure 3.25: IoC in registry changes

File requests

File requests in a network environment are standard operations where clients ask for specific files from servers. However, when these requests become abnormal or excessive, they can indicate cybersecurity concerns, such as data exfiltration attempts or targeted attacks to exploit server vulnerabilities. Unusually high volumes of file requests, especially for sensitive or critical data, may suggest that an attacker is trying to steal information or that a compromised system is being used to access data illegitimately. The following figure will show more details about the registry changes:

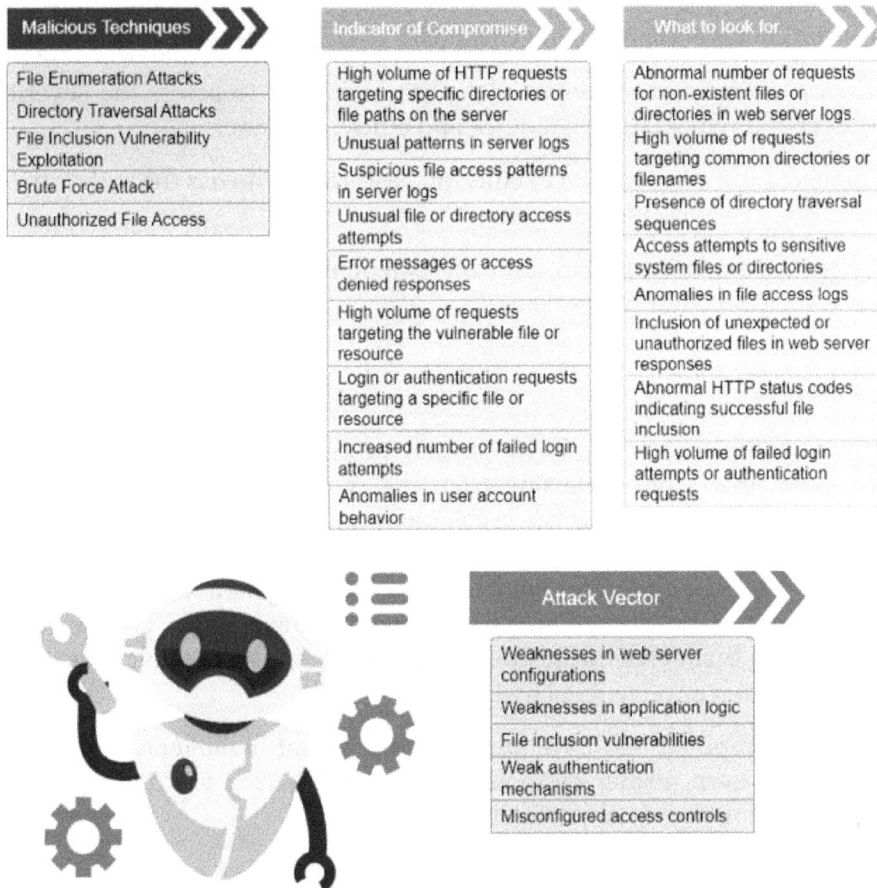

Malicious Techniques ▶▶▶	Indicator of Compromise ▶▶▶	What to look for ▶▶▶
File Enumeration Attacks	High volume of HTTP requests targeting specific directories or file paths on the server	Abnormal number of requests for non-existent files or directories in web server logs
Directory Traversal Attacks	Unusual patterns in server logs	High volume of requests targeting common directories or filenames
File Inclusion Vulnerability Exploitation	Suspicious file access patterns in server logs	Presence of directory traversal sequences
Brute Force Attack	Unusual file or directory access attempts	Access attempts to sensitive system files or directories
Unauthorized File Access	Error messages or access denied responses	Anomalies in file access logs
	High volume of requests targeting the vulnerable file or resource	Inclusion of unexpected or unauthorized files in web server responses
	Login or authentication requests targeting a specific file or resource	Abnormal HTTP status codes indicating successful file inclusion
	Increased number of failed login attempts	High volume of failed login attempts or authentication requests
	Anomalies in user account behavior	

Attack Vector ▶▶▶
Weaknesses in web server configurations
Weaknesses in application logic
File inclusion vulnerabilities
Weak authentication mechanisms
Misconfigured access controls

Figure 3.26: IoC in file request

IoC management best practices

Obtaining sufficient visibility and understanding of what is happening when we are under attack is one of the main advantages of IoCs; sharing information and applying certain rules to our networks can help improve the quality and accuracy of our IoCs. Some recommended best practices are mentioned below:

- Use security tools and technologies like **Managed Detection and Response (MDR)**, **Endpoint Detection and Response (EDR)**, **Extended Detection and Response (XDR)**, and **TIPs to manage IoCs**.

- Share IoCs with industry partners to collectively address cyber threats across your sector.

- Regularly review IoCs and establish a retention policy that aligns with your industry's regulatory requirements and your organization's needs.

- Automate the analysis and correlation of IoCs to prioritize alerts based on their severity, allowing for immediate response to critical threats.

- Develop an incident response plan that uses IoCs to assess the severity of an incident and remediate it in a quick and efficient manner.

- Implement controls for IAM to efficiently ascertain who has the authority to access your data, systems, and networks.

- Segregate your networks to limit the potential damage if a cybercriminal gains access to one of your networks.

Conclusion

In this chapter, we looked at the way we can stay protected and a step ahead of criminals with cyber threat intelligence, starting from the types of threat intelligence that we reviewed, the cyber threat intelligence cycle, tools, and sharing standards, and finishing with the IoC. The topics that we reviewed in this chapter are critically important since the cyber world is becoming more advanced, more evolving, and more dynamic, and it is hard to keep up with everything that is happening and developing. We use cyber threat intelligence with all that encompasses to mitigate and prevent possible attacks that may target our organization or our digital assets.

Now that we are prepared and have studied cyber threat intelligence, we are ready to fortify our defense even further by looking at *Chapter 4, Tools and Techniques for Threat Hunting,* which promises to further enrich our toolkit.

Points to remember

- The cyber threat intelligence cycle is important for foreseeing, detecting, and effectively responding to cyber threats.

- A diverse range of sources and tools enriches understanding and preparedness against cyberattacks.

- TIPs are tools crucial for the efficient gathering, analysis, and sharing of threat information.

- Sharing standards such as *STIX* and *TAXII* facilitate the timely and comprehensible exchange of critical intelligence.

- IoCs are key to swift and accurate detection and response to cyber threats.

- Continuous learning, skill advancement, and collaboration within the security community are essential to confront and overcome cyber threats.

Multiple choice questions

1. **IoCs are important for:**
   a. Slowing down the response to cyber threats
   b. Reducing the need for cybersecurity training
   c. Detecting and responding to cyber threats swiftly and accurately
   d. Eliminating the risk of cyberattacks completely

2. **What is the role of sharing standards like STIX and TAXII?**
   a. To complicate the intelligence-sharing process
   b. To facilitate the exchange of threat intelligence
   c. To limit the sharing of threat information
   d. To increase the cost of cybersecurity defenses

3. **How do TIPs and tools primarily aid organizations?**
   a. By automating all cybersecurity tasks
   b. By enhancing physical security measures
   c. By replacing the need for cybersecurity personnel
   d. By facilitating the efficient gathering, analysis, and sharing of threat information

4. **Which of the following is a key component of the cyber threat intelligence cycle?**
   a. Forecasting
   b. Analysis
   c. Product development
   d. Creation

5. **What are the three types of threat intelligence?**
   a. Strategic, Tactical, and Operational
   b. Economic, Social, and Technological
   c. Internal, External, and Public
   d. Automated, Manual, and Hybrid

Answers

1. c.

2. b.

3. d.

4. b.

5. a.

References

1. **MITRE | ATT&CK Matrix for Enterprise: https://attack.mitre.org**

2. **US-CERT Indicator Bulletins: https://us-cert.cisa.gov/ncas/bulletins**

Join our Discord space

Join our Discord workspace for latest updates, offers, tech happenings around the world, new releases, and sessions with the authors:

https://discord.bpbonline.com

CHAPTER 4
Tools and Techniques for Threat Hunting

In this chapter we will study the recommended tools and techniques that every analyst need to know, and use to be more proficient in threat detection; starting with tool classification, complete framework and data collection to gather enough information to have the elements to detect a threat or disruption, and then we will cover automation tools and mechanisms, subsequently we will finishing with reporting and documentation best practices.

Structure

In this chapter, we will discuss the following topics:

- Essential tools for threat hunting
- Threat hunting frameworks
- Data collection and analysis techniques
- Automation and orchestration in threat hunting
- Threat hunting reporting and documentation
- Setting up your threat hunter environment

Objectives

As a threat hunter you need to understand the landscape where malicious actors interact, their capabilities and tools; in addition, you need to understand the ways that a malicious actor have to deliver an attack (Vectors) and how different attacks can impact the IT ecosystem; having this knowledge you can extrapolate information and obtain different footprints and indicators provided by your security mechanisms to detect and identify potential abnormal activities in the infrastructure. The tools that allow us to detect and understand the malicious actors' behaviors are the main objective of this chapter.

Essential tools for threat hunting

We know that adversaries **Tactics Techniques and Procedures (TTPs)** are different and difficult to detect in most cases when we are facing an individual with advanced techniques, but they are going to leave footprints and evidence of their actions in our systems; here we consider appropriate to remember the Locard's Exchange Principle:

The perpetrator of a crime will bring something into the crime scene and leave with something from it, and that both can be used as forensic evidence.

From the adversary's perspective is almost impossible to remove all clues, but on the other hand they try to make it hard to detect them, that is why we need to cover a wide spectrum of tools and sensors that should be deployed in our infrastructure to try to detect even the smallest bit of uncommon or abnormal behavior, content, or information inside a file.

At this moment, it is possible that you have this question in your mind: where to start? Unfortunately, there is no perfect answer, or an answer that fits all cases, because your strategy is connected with the type of infrastructure and technology you need to analyze; here, different factors need to be considered, such as whether the environment is a Cloud or an on-premises infrastructure.

Well, let us start with the essential tools that we need in our threat hunting tasks.

Common security and network security tools

Here we have the most common tools that are the minimum requirement for cybersecurity in a company such as Firewall, Antimalware or Antivirus, **Intrusion Detection System (IDS)** or **Intrusion Prevention System (IPS)**, because they are sources of information, they give you alerts, well known attacks detection, limited abnormal behavior detection, and provide data and feeds for the threat hunting tools, but the core of those tools is not threat hunting per se, but provide monitoring and security alerts.

Some examples are as follows: Examples of both commercial and open-source firewalls:

Firewalls		
Name	**Type**	**URL**
Check Point Quantum	Paid	**https://www.checkpoint.com/quantum/next-generation-firewall/**
Fortigate	Paid	**https://www.fortinet.com/products/next-generation-firewall**
Paloalto PA-Series	Paid	**https://www.paloaltonetworks.com/network-security/next-generation-firewall-hardware**
OPN Sense	Open Source	**https://opnsense.org/**
PFSense	Open Source	**https://www.pfsense.org/**
IpFire	Open Source	**https://www.ipfire.org/**

Table 4.1: Commercial and open-source firewalls

The following table is an example of antimalware and antivirus solutions:

Antimalware and Antivirus	
Bitdefender	**https://www.bitdefender.com/solutions/total-security.html**
Norton Antivirus	**https://us.norton.com/**
McAfee Antivirus	**https://www.mcafee.com/en-us/antivirus.html**
Malware Bytes	**https://www.malwarebytes.com/**
Sophos	**https://home.sophos.com/en-us/content/best-malware-protection**

Table 4.2: Commercial antimalware and antivirus solutions

The following table is the example of IDS and IPS tools:

Intrusion Detection Systems (IDS) and Intrusion Prevention Systems (IPS)	
AIDE	**https://aide.github.io/**
Hillstone IPS	**https://www.hillstonenet.com/products/network-edge-protection/network-intrusion-prevention-system/**
SNORT	**https://www.snort.org/**
Suricata	**https://suricata.io/**
Solar Winds IDS	**https://www.solarwinds.com/security-event-manager/use-cases/intrusion-detection-software**

Table 4.3: Commercial and open-source IDS/IPS

Endpoint Detection and Response

Users are the most attacked target for cyber criminals, and of course, with a simple mistake or distraction, a user can trash all the security in a company. That is why the EDR mechanisms are useful to monitor and scan the activities performed by the operating system, the applications, and the tools installed in the user's workstations, looking for abnormalities, providing early threat detection, proactive response, and feeds for other threat hunting tools.

Examples of EDR Tools are as follows:

Endpoint Detection and Response (EDR)	
Carbon Black	https://www.vmware.com/products/carbon-black-endpoint.html
Symantec Endpoint Detection and Response	https://www.broadcom.com/products/advanced-threat-protection
CrowdStrike	https://www.crowdstrike.com/platform/endpoint-security/
SentinelOne	https://www.ocntinclone.com/cybersecurlty-101/what-is-end-point-detection-and-response-edr/
TrendMicro XDR	https://www.trendmicro.com/en_us/business/products/detection-response/xdr.html

Table 4.4: Commercial endpoint solutions

Security Information and Event Management

This technology is the foundation stone of the threat hunting for most of the people in the field, the **Security Information and Event Management** (**SIEM**) receives the information, feeds, logs and alerts from the security and telemetry technologies in the company, like Firewalls, Routers, Switches, Antimalware Console, Anti-Spam Technologies, Active Directory, Domain Controller, Endpoint Security, etc. With all these informational sources, the SIEM cleans, normalizes, and standardizes the data to apply correlation and intelligence, trying to detect abnormalities in the network traffic, the endpoints, the Active Directory, etc. One of the most important things here is that the SIEM, having all the logs, can analyze the timeline of the detected activities, so you can follow back the different actions and the kill chain of the adversary step by step. In the following figure, we can observe the functions of the SIEM in an environment:

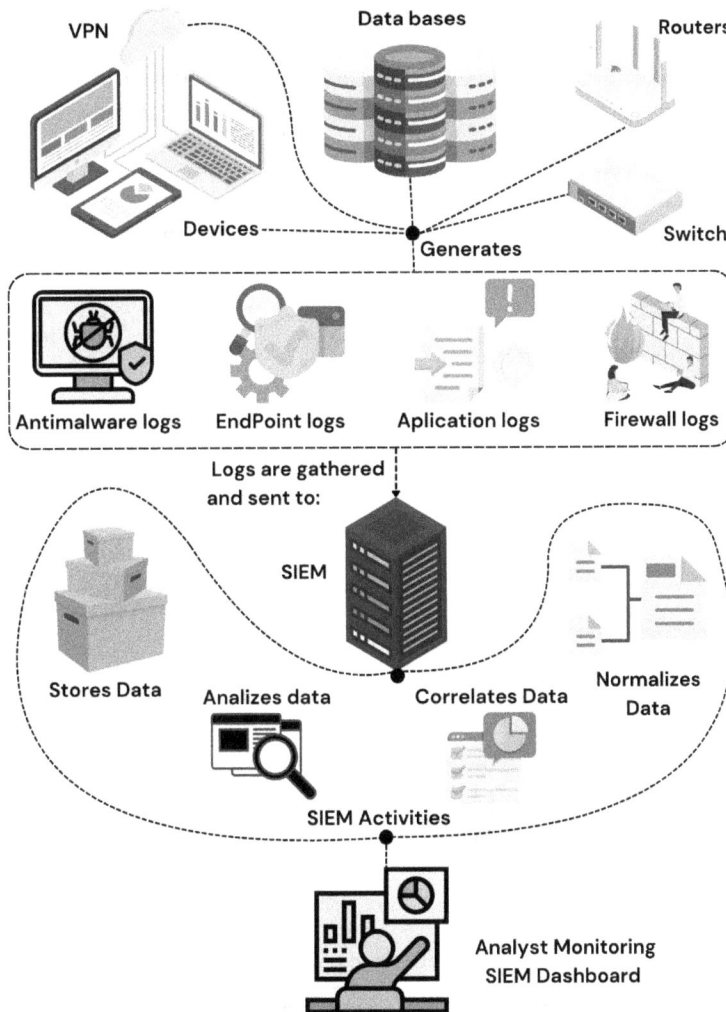

Figure 4.1: SIEM Workflow

The following table shows examples of the SIEM tools:

Security Information and Event Management (SIEM)	
LogRhytm	**https://logrhythm.com/solutions/security/siem/**
IBM QRadar	**https://www.ibm.com/products/qradar-siem**
OSSIM	**https://cybersecurity.att.com/products/ossim**
Elastic SIEM	**https://www.elastic.co/security/siem**
Wazuh	**https://wazuh.com/**

Table 4.5: Commercial and open-source SIEM solutions

Network Detection and Response

These technologies can analyze network traffic, the protocols, and packets, looking for abnormal patterns, or potentially malicious or adversarial activities, and once detected, they are capable to stop threats.

They can detect traffic related to malware, command and control, insider attacks, targeted attacks, exfiltration, and many other network malicious behaviors; in the following figure, we can observe the NDR technology activities:

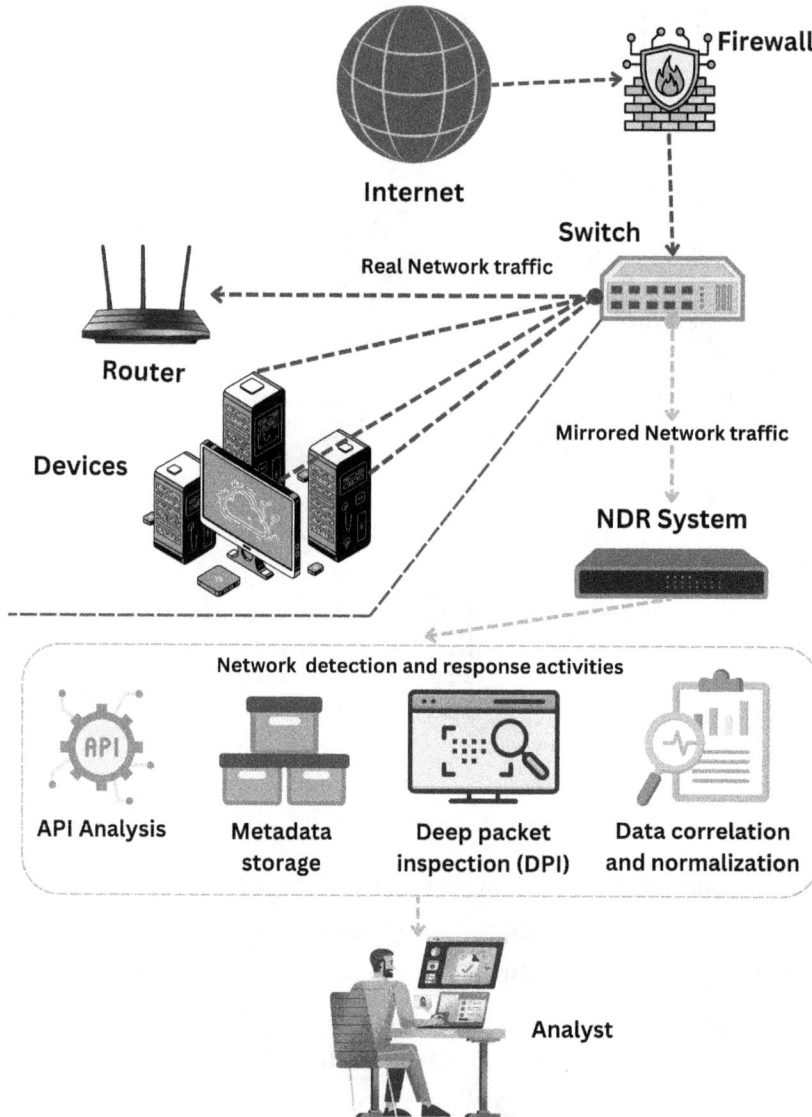

Figure 4.2: NDR workflow

The following table is the examples of NDR tools:

Network Detection and Response (NDR)	
Darktrace	**https://darktrace.com/products/network/detect-respond**
ExtraHop	**https://www.extrahop.com/**
Vectra AI	**https://www.vectra.ai/products/ndr**
Sangfor	**https://www.sangfor.com/**
Cisco NDR	**https://www.cisco.com/c/en/us/products/security/ what-is-network-detection-response.html**

Table 4.6: Commercial NDR solutions

Network sniffers, network monitoring, and packet analyzers

A less advanced technology than **Network Detection and Response** (**NDR**) technologies, these semi-automated or manual tools allow the analyst to capture network traffic and dissect the packets to analyze what is inside the network datagram, source address, destination address, source port, destination port, protocol, flags, etc. These tools can use manual filters to detect specific behaviors or network traffic; they are very useful in threat hunting. In *Chapter 5, Network Traffic Analysis*, we will discuss the usage of these amazing tools to understand and inspect the traffic in the network.

Examples of network sniffers, network monitoring, and packet analyzer tools are as follows:

Network sniffers and packet analyzers	
Wireshark	**https://www.wireshark.org/**
Zeek	**https://zeek.org/**
Xplico	**https://www.xplico.org/**
Ntop NG	**https://www.ntop.org/products/traffic-analysis/ntop/**
OpManager	**https://www.manageengine.com/network-monitoring/?utm_ source=Comparitech&utm_medium=Website-cpc&utm_cam- paign=OPM-NMTools**

Table 4.7: Commercial and open-source network sniffers and packet analyzers

User and entity behaviour analytics

These tools are capable of detecting abnormal user behaviors using machine learning and automation. It is very useful to detect insider attacks, exfiltration command and control, among other malicious activities. Let us clarify the advantages with an example, an employee (Jane) arrives to the office each day at 8:45 AM turns on the computer and logs in her Workstation at 9:00–9:05 AM (Monday to Friday), but one Saturday her workstation is turned on at 3:52 AM, then the user **Jane** is introduced but the password is wrong and the supposed **Jane** person tries four more times with the wrong credentials; here we can see an abnormal behavior and the most probable cause is a remote attacker that has access to the network, knows the username **Jane** but does not know the right password, so executes a dictionary or brute force attack in the workstation; that kind of abnormal behavior is detected by the **User and Entity Behavior Analytics (UEBA)**.

Examples of UEBA tools are as follows:

User and Entity Behavior Analytics (UEBA)	
FortiInsight	**https://fortiinsight.cloud/**
Teramind	**https://www.teramind.co/solutions/user-entity-behavior-analytics**
Forcepoint	**https://www.forcepoint.com/product/ueba-user-entity-behavior-analytics**
Cynet	**https://www.cynet.com/platform/user-behaviour-analytics/**
Securonix	**https://www.securonix.com/**

Table 4.8: Commercial UEBA solutions

Extended Detection and Response

This tool is a traversal approach to cybersecurity in a company; it encompasses monitoring and detection across all surfaces in the entity, like Cloud, Mail, Endpoints, network, etc. In the following figure, you can see the XDR activities:

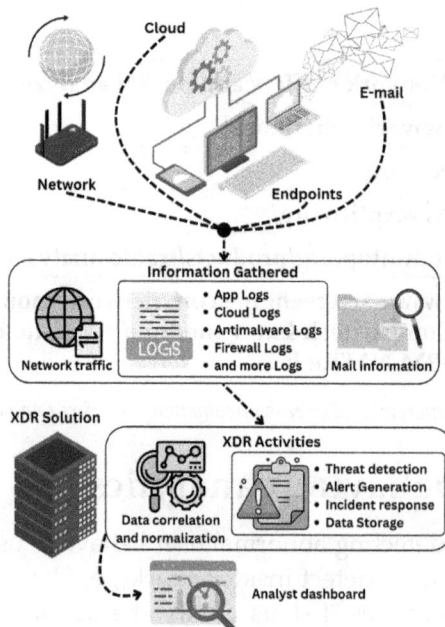

Figure 4.3: XDR Workflow

Examples of **Extended Detection and Response (XDR)** tools are as follows:

Extended Detection and Response (XDR)	
Fidelis	**https://fidelissecurity.com/fidelis-elevate-extended-detection-and-response-xdr-platform/**
Crowdstrike	**https://www.crowdstrike.com/en-us/**
Cybereason	**https://www.cybereason.com/platform/xdr**
Trellix	**https://www.trellix.com/platform/**
Sophos	**https://www.sophos.com/en-us/products/extended-detection-and-response**

Table 4.9: Commercial UEBA solutions

To expand more on XDR, here is a classification table for the tools previously shown:

Tool	Classification	Focus
Fidelis	Network-Centric XDR	Deep network visibility and automated threat response.
Crowd-Strike	Cloud-Native XDR	Cloud-based protection with strong EDR integration and threat intelligence.
Cybereason	Behavior-Based XDR	Behavioral analysis and complex attack detection.
Trellix	Unified Security Platform (XDR)	Integration of McAfee and FireEye technologies into a single XDR platform.
Sophos	Endpoint-Focused XDR	Seamless integration with Sophos ecosystem and simplified threat response.

Table 4.10: Classification of UEBA solutions

Threat hunting frameworks

We are familiar with the different aspects in threat hunting **Indicators of Compromise (IoC), Indicators of Attack (IoA)**, TTPs, etc., now, to put all this information together in a way that allow us to connect this universe of information with the cyber kill chain, providing a better understanding about the attacks, the stages of the attacks and their potential consequences in a logic, structured, repeatable and organized we are going to use threat hunting frameworks.

Let us remember that, depending on the approach we choose for threat hunting, we can start with a hypothesis or a question; the objective is to confirm if we are under attack and how to corroborate it. Here we can take advantage of a methodology that allows us to repeat a process in a coherent and adaptable way.

The framework we choose should provide us with the mechanisms that allow us to confirm whether our hypothesis was accurate, using the most optimal data sources.

Let us discuss the threat hunting frameworks.

Sqrrl threat hunting reference model

Here we should give special recognition to the reference model created by the company Sqrrl, dating back to 2015. This company was later acquired by Amazon (AWS) and its website permanently disappeared in 2019. However, it should be noted that parts of its model are still used in various fields to this day. This reference model primarily focused on the following aspects:

- **Purpose:** Understand the objective for hunting having in mind the context of the threat and the expected goals.

- **Hypothesis:** Formulate educated guesses related to potential threats based on the purpose.

- **Discovery or detection:** Looking for evidence to prove or disprove the hypothesis. This could involve searching for specific IoC or looking for abnormal user behavior, unknown network traffic, or unusual entries in system logs.

- **Investigation:** Verify if the discovered anomalies are indeed threats or false positives.

- **Response:** Execute the appropriate actions to mitigate the threat and prevent future occurrences of the same nature.

Targeted Hunting Integrating Threat Intelligence

TaHiTI framework was created by a consortium of financial institutions known as the *Dutch Payments Association* (**https://www.betaalvereniging.nl/**) and is supported in three phases: **Initiate** (Process Input), **Hunt** (Execution), and **Finalize** (Process Output). One interesting change is that it incorporates threat intelligence inside threat hunting.

In the following figure we can appreciate the model phases and internal tasks:

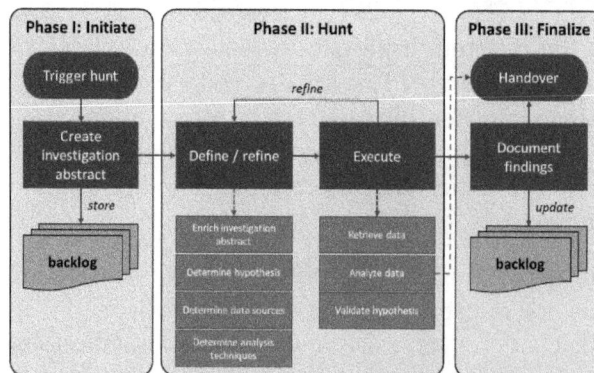

Figure 4.4: TaHiTI phases

(Source: https://www.betaalvereniging.nl/wp-content/uploads/TaHiTI-Threat-Hunting-Methodology-whitepaper.pdf)

Let us analyze each phase:

- **Phase 1 (Initiate):** Within this phase, we receive the input, which is typically triggered by a specific action or artifact. This trigger then becomes an abstract, providing an initial summary of the investigation, and is stored within the hunting backlog. There are various triggers, and the following figure illustrates the different types:

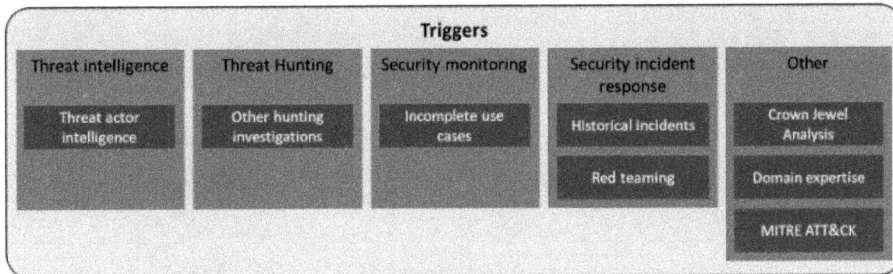

Figure 4.5: TaHiTI triggers

(Source: https://www.betaalvereniging.nl/wp-content/uploads/TaHiTI-Threat-Hunting-Methodology-whitepaper.pdf)

- **Phase 2 (Hunt):** In this phase, the investigation process begins; the first task is called **define or refine**. At this point, the details of the hunt are solidified, and additional information is incorporated if available. This collective information is used to generate the initial hypothesis. Following this, the **execute** step commences, where the formal investigation begins, and data are analyzed. Once the **execute** step concludes, the hypothesis is validated, which can have multiple outcomes:

Hypothesis result	Status
Proven hypothesis	Malicious activity found; incident response started
Disproven hypothesis	No malicious activity found
Inconclusive	Cycle back to the first step (define or refine), change some of the parameters of the hunt, and repeat the execution

Table 4.11: TaHiTI Hunt hypothesis possibilities

- **Phase 3 (Finalize):** Final part of the process to document the results and findings, generate conclusions and recommendations based on the findings, and handover to the other process. Based on the models we can see in the following figure, the process that can receive the results of the investigation as input:

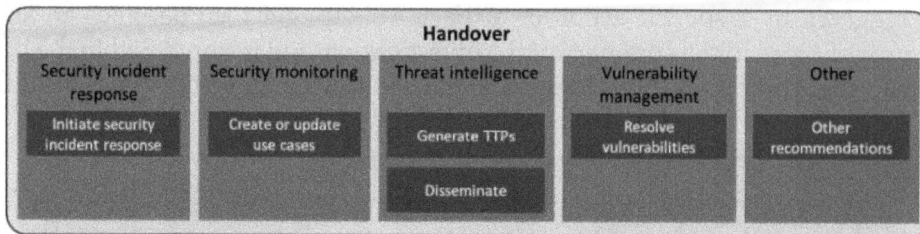

Figure 4.6: TaHiTI Handover possibilities

(Source: https://www.betaalvereniging.nl/wp-content/uploads/TaHiTI-Threat-Hunting-Methodology-whitepaper.pdf)

The TaHiTI methodology utilizes the **Management, Growth, Metrics and Assessment (MaGMa) for threat hunting** tool to facilitate documentations of findings, organize the results of hunting inquiries, and offer guidance for the expansion of the threat hunting procedure; this is an excel file containing instructions and all the fields necessary, ready to receive information; the file can be downloaded in this link: **https://www.betaalvereniging. nl/wp-content/uploads/Magma-for-Threat-Hunting.xlsx**. In the following figure, we can observe the welcome screen of the file:

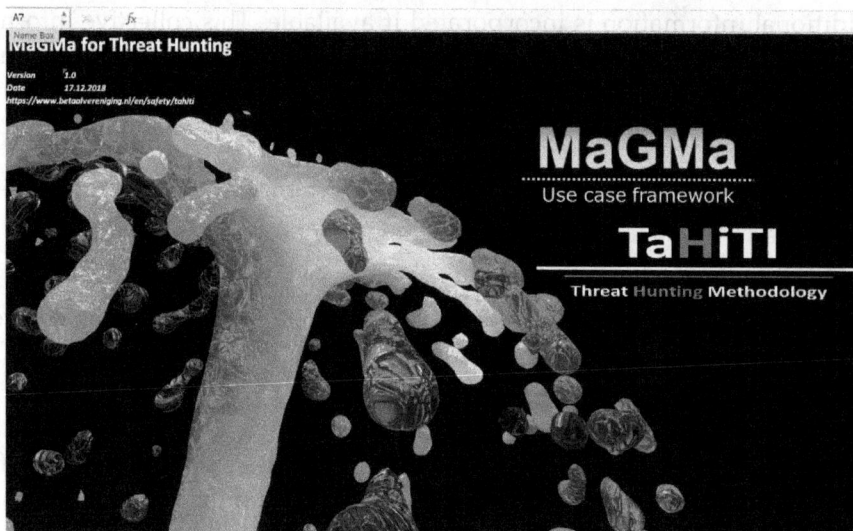

Figure 4.7: Image of the MaGMa tool (Excel File)

Prepare, execute, and act with knowledge

As the name suggests, the methodology consists of three stages: *Prepare, Execute,* and *Act.* In addition, this methodology is somewhat more flexible than previous ones, as it incorporates three different types of hunting:

- **Hypothesis-driven:** Common approach, you start with a supposition related to potential threats that may be affecting the company, and then you use the available data sources to corroborate the hypothesis.

Here we have the graphical representation of the hypothesis-driven hunting process:

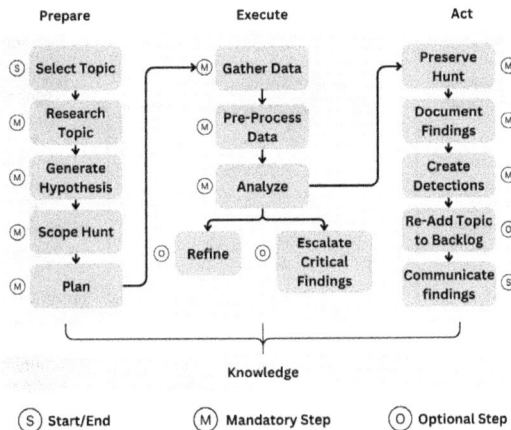

Figure 4.8: PEAK hypothesis-driven hunting process

(**Source:** *https://www.splunk.com/content/dam/splunk-blogs/images/en_us/2023/12/hypothosis-driven-threat-hunting-diagram.jpg*)

- **Baseline hunts:** The threat hunter defines a **baseline** of the normal (Safe) behavior, and looks for abnormalities or unusual activities that can indicate malicious activities.

Here we have the graphical representation of the baseline hunts:

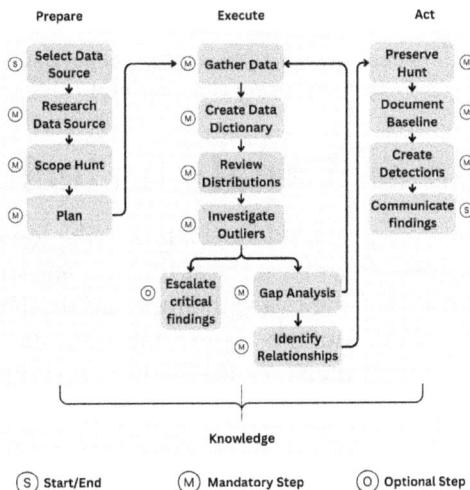

Figure 4.9: PEAK baseline hunts process

(**Source:** *https://www.splunk.com/content/dam/splunk-blogs/images/en_us/2023/12/baseline-threat-hunting-diagram.jpg*)

- **Model-Assisted Threat Hunts (M-ATH):** In this advanced methodology, the hunters use machine learning, taking advantage of the artificial intelligence to create models of **Normal** or safe behavior and **malicious** or abnormal behavior, and then the technologies search for deviations from the models.

Here we have the graphical representation of the M-ATH model:

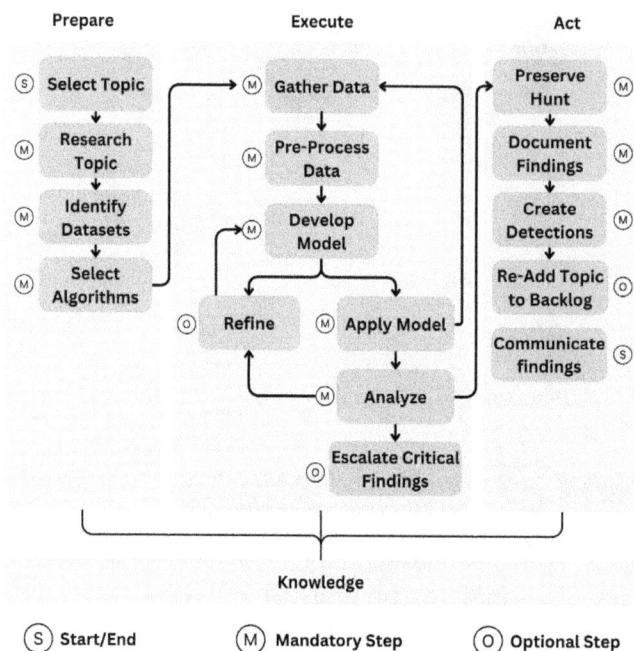

Figure 4.10: PEAK model-assisted threat hunts

(Source: https://www.splunk.com/content/dam/splunk-blogs/images/en_us/2023/12/model-assisted-threat-hunting-diagram.jpg)

Data collection and analysis techniques

Data collection refers to the data provided by the tools, like logs, network traffic, sample files, file system integrity reports, etc., that serve as the fundamental source and foundation for performing effective threat hunting tasks; the more accurate information we have, the better analysis we can execute. Without the appropriate data, our task becomes impossible to carry out. Therefore, it is vital to ensure the highest possible quality of the data we analyze.

Data quality

When we refer to data quality, we mean that it should meet the specific requirements of the threat hunting team, with the aim of ensuring that hunting tasks are executed effectively;

thinking about that, the data should follow some specific parameters or at least be oriented to these goals:

- **Integrity:** The data should be accurate, devoid of any errors or deviations, so it does not impact the conclusions drawn from the analyses.

- **Consistency:** The data must be coherent, which simplifies its analysis and handling regardless of its size.

- **Automation ready:** The data should be normalized and readied for use by automated tools and artificial intelligence, to lessen the burden on the analyst.

We can add here more characteristics about the quality of the data, there is a very interesting document, generated by the United States **Department of Defense (DoD)** named **DoD Data Strategy** that can be applied to the threat hunting data.

Here is the link to the document: **https://media.defense.gov/2020/Oct/08/2002514180/-1/-1/0/DOD-DATA-STRATEGY.PDF**

Data collection

We know that different devices in the infrastructure can provide different data, and it is important to remember that for each hunt you can use and need different data. That is way we need to select the specific kind of data that we are going to use for each analysis The suggestion is to utilize the MITRE ATT&CK Matrix (**https://attack.mitre.org**), which provides an abstract for each kind of attack that we might investigate, along with a list of devices and data sources that can be used to carry out the hunting.

Following is an example of the list of data sources and data components for the drive-by compromise along with a useful explanation of each potential detection:

ID ∨	Name ∨	Domain ▼	Description
DS0026	Active Directory	Enterprise	A database and set of services that allows administrators to manage permissions, access to network resources, and stored data objects (user, group, application, or devices)
DS0015	Application Log	Enterprise ICS	Events collected by third-party services such as mail servers, web applications, or other appliances (not by the native OS or platform)

Figure 4.11: MITRE ATT&CK detection data source example

For ease of use, the ATTACK-Python-Client (attackcti) **https://attackcti.com/intro.html** tool is available. This tool can be easily installed and enables command-line queries about the ATTACK Framework. The commands for installation are as follows:

You can install it via PIP:

```
$ pip install attackcti
```

Or clone the repository:

```
git clone https://github.com/OTRF/ATTACK-Python-Client
cd ATTACK-Python-Client
pip install .
```

This is a Python module as defined in the documentation:

A Python module to access up to date ATT&CK content available in STIX via public TAXII server. This project leverages the Python classes and functions of the cti-python-stix2 and cti-taxii-client libraries developed by MITRE.

Analysis techniques

In the previous section, we explored the various tools and frameworks used for threat hunting. We also discussed the types of data and insights each tool can generate. Now, we will shift our focus to the vast amount of information produced by these interconnected technologies. With a dataset composed of indicators, logs, and alerts, we need to determine the most effective way to analyze it and proceed with our threat hunting efforts.

Once you have the data, you need a way to solve and analyze the information. There is a group of techniques to help you to be efficient and effective in the task. Let us discuss them:

- **Searching:** You query the data, looking for specific artifacts, like a hash, file name, strings inside a file, an IP address, etc. The problem or disadvantage here is that you need to know what to look for, in other word you need specific information to execute the related queries, or the results are going to be enormous, vague or useless and you can miss important information and connections between the data. It is essential to strike the right balance in the level of detail for what we are searching for. This will prevent us from being overwhelmed by too many results or left wanting by too few, both scenarios that will not be beneficial to our work.

- **Stack counting:** This is the most recommended technique when investigating a hypothesis; the number of occurrences relating to events, types of incidents, or indicators within the overall results must be recorded. It is necessary to have the most complete and refined dataset possible for this technique, to be most effective. The best practice for this technique is to apply it to similar or equal artifacts, looking for similarities between them. Some examples of data that can be analyzed with stack counting are: same files executed in different machines, same user logged in different applications on the same day at the same moment, traffic with the same destination from different hosts, etc.

- **Clustering:** In this technique, the aim is to identify artifacts that share resemblances or characteristics within the overall data set. These similar artifacts are then grouped together into what are known as clusters. An example here is to analyze a log containing a considerable amount of data and with technologies like machine learning you can create the clusters of related activities depicted in the log. One of the most useful aspects of clustering is to discover abnormal number of occurrences of an uncommon behavior.

- **Grouping:** In this technique, like clustering, a collection of unique artifacts is grouped together, but subsequently, the circumstances that triggered the multiple occurrences of these artifacts, leading to their initial grouping, are analyzed. In many cases, grouping is considered the logical next step after clustering.

Automation and orchestration in threat hunting

As we have observed, the volume of information that can be gathered within a company through various security, monitoring, and alert systems is immense. It is almost impossible to manually analyze all this data and connect the dots in an effective and useful way or at least is inefficient to do it manually. Furthermore, human reaction speed is comparatively slower than the technological tools available to us. Given this, let us discuss the automation of the mechanisms that can assist in making the process of threat hunting more efficient and comprehensive.

Security orchestration, automation and response

Security Orchestration, Automation, and Response (SOAR), represents an interconnected suite of technologies. As the name implies, the primary function of SOAR is not only to facilitate better integration among various cybersecurity technologies but also to provide a more comprehensive view of security events. This enhanced visibility leads to a significant improvement in the capabilities of incident response. By streamlining and simplifying the traditionally complex processes, SOAR technologies enable organizations to respond to security incidents more swiftly and efficiently, effectively minimizing potential threats and reducing the time spent on manual tasks; in the following figure, we can observe the SOAR activities:

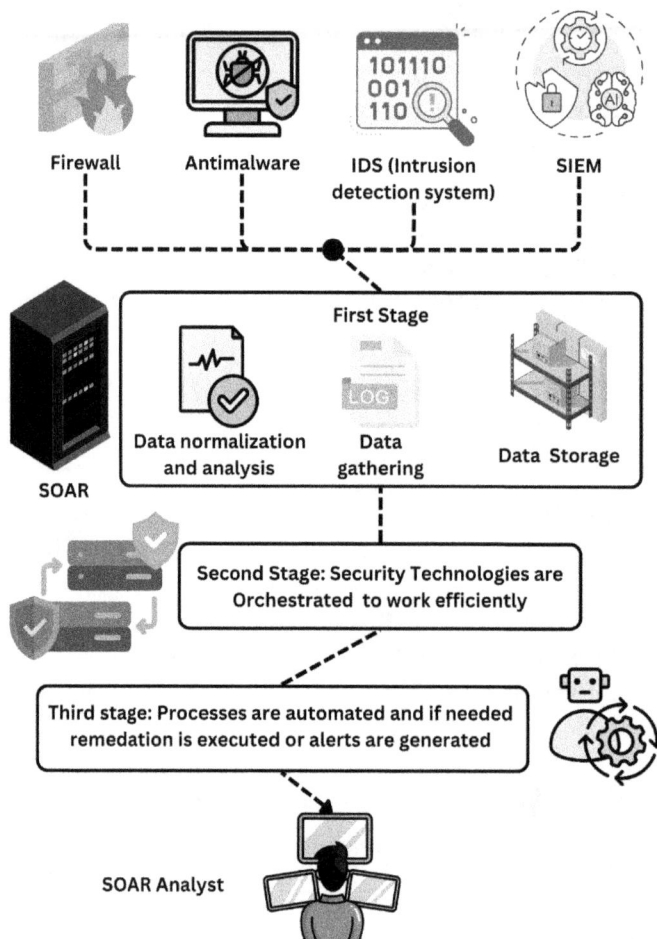

Figure 4.12: SOAR explained

In the following table, we mention some of the most important SOAR tools in the market:

Security Orchestration, Automation and Response (SOAR)	
SWIMLANE	**https://swimlane.com/**
Splunk	**https://www.splunk.com/en_us/products/splunk-security-orchestra-tion-and-automation.html**
Cortex XSOAR	**https://www.paloaltonetworks.com/cortex/cortex-xsoar**
FortiSOAR	**https://www.fortinet.com/products/fortisoar**
Smart SOAR	**https://d3security.com/**

Table 4.12: SOAR solutions

Threat hunting reporting and documentation

The creation of a well-structured threat hunting report is as crucial as the threat hunting process itself. An excellent hunting exercise is futile if the outcomes are not shared in a coherent and useful manner with other involved departments. We must always bear in mind that there are numerous stakeholders who should be able to derive benefit from a threat hunting report, including but not limited to: Executives, IT Directors, IT Managers, CISO, Blue Team members, Incident Responders, and so on. Therefore, we will allocate space to this topic of utmost importance, where, unfortunately, many hunters often fall short.

There are some characteristics that a good report should accomplish (not only a Threat hunting report):

- **Clarity:** The report should be easily comprehensible even for individuals without an extensive technical understanding; overly technical language should be avoided, particularly within the executive summary of the report.

- **Enhance the report:** Do not skimp on resources that can improve the quality of the report, such as graphs, summary tables, or images that allow a clearer understanding of the information presented in the document.

- **Keep a common thread:** The report should include detailed descriptions of the stages and steps followed during the exercise. This allows for a clearer understanding of the actions taken and provides the option to replicate the steps. More importantly, it aids in justifying the conclusions drawn.

- **Deliver solutions:** It is crucial to highlight what is not working correctly, but it is equally, if not more, important to propose solutions or remediation alternatives to the identified issues.

- **Keep up to date:** Regularly update the reports; we understand that threats and risks dynamically change, and as a result, reports should be consistently refreshed.

Following are the recommended components of a treat hunting report:

- **Executive summary:** This summary should be placed in the first section of the report and is targeted towards the company's executives who want to stay informed about the results of the threat hunting exercise. It should offer a high-level overview of the executed exercise and the objectives sought. The recommended components of this summary include:

    o   Main findings from the exercise

    o   Impact analysis on the company

    o   Recommendations

    o   Immediate actions to be taken.

- **Methodology and hypothesis:** In this section of the report, we outline the analytical methodology that we will follow, our hypothesis if applicable, data sources, and the extent of the investigation.

- **Analysis and findings:** In this section, we will detail the identified anomalies, IoA, IoC, and alerted abnormal activities, along with the technologies used and, most importantly, the results and findings achieved that should provide actionable intelligence to make decisions in the company.

  For detailed information about the evidence, logs, and other artifacts, appendices can be attached at the end of the report, containing the evidence that supports the report's findings and conclusions.

- **Correlation analysis (If Applicable):** In the correlation analysis, we assess the existing relationships between the results of our analysis and data we have from other sources such as threat intelligence, MITRE's attack matrix, known adversaries' modus operandi, etc.

- **Impact analysis and risk assessment:** Based on the obtained results and actionable intelligence, is recommended to conduct a risk assessment and impact analysis to understand how the organization could be adversely affected by the attack or by the actions uncovered through our analysis.

- **Mitigation recommendations:** Based on the precise understanding gained from our analysis, we can generate a series of recommendations for implementation within the organization. These recommendations aim to either mitigate the impact of the identified threat or prevent its manifestation in the future.

Setting up your threat hunter environment

Creating your threat hunting environment begins with establishing a solid foundation of virtualization that allows you to safely analyze potential threats while maintaining isolation from your primary systems. From there, we'll explore the essential tools needed for effective threat hunting, including network analysis, endpoint monitoring, log management, and threat intelligence platforms; the list of suggested tools is open-source; the tools depend on several factors, such as budget, architecture, etc. For now, open-source tools are an excellent and powerful alternative.

Virtualization platforms

Virtualization provides the necessary foundation for a threat hunting environment, allowing for isolation, snapshots, and resource management. Let us explore the leading open-source virtualization options in the following section.

Proxmox VE 8.0

Proxmox Virtual Environment has become a favorite among security professionals for its enterprise features available in an open-source package. Its web-based management interface allows you to easily create, manage, and monitor virtual machines and containers from a single dashboard. The cluster management features enable you to scale your environment across multiple physical hosts as your needs grow.

Key benefits for threat hunters include:

- Integrated backup functionality with scheduling
- Live migration of virtual machines between hosts
- Support for both KVM virtual machines and LXC containers
- Advanced networking features including VLANs and Open vSwitch
- Role-based access control for team environments

To install Proxmox VE, follow these steps:

1. Download the latest ISO from the Proxmox website: **https://www.proxmox.com/en/downloads**
2. Create a bootable USB drive with the ISO
3. Install on your physical server, ensuring at least 8GB RAM and a multi-core CPU
4. Configure networking and storage according to your requirements
5. Access the web interface on port 8006 (**https://your-server-ip:8006**)

VirtualBox 7.0

Oracle's VirtualBox remains a popular choice for individual threat hunters or smaller organizations due to its simplicity and cross-platform support.

The latest version introduces significantly improved 3D support, better compatibility with newer operating systems, and enhanced security features. VirtualBox works on Windows, macOS, and Linux, making it an excellent choice for threat hunters who need to work across different host platforms.

Key features relevant to threat hunting include:

- Snapshot functionality for system state preservation
- Host-only networking for isolated environments
- USB device filtering for hardware analysis
- Shared folders for easy data transfer
- Extension packs for additional functionality

VirtualBox works well for smaller-scale operations but may lack the enterprise management features needed for larger teams.

Official website **https://www.virtualbox.org/**

VMware workstation pro or player

While not fully open-source, VMware offers flexible options with VMware Workstation Player and the more fully-featured Workstation Pro, both free for non-commercial use.

The latest versions provide excellent performance, robust networking options, and strong isolation between virtual machines and the host system. VMware's snapshot technology is particularly useful for threat hunters, allowing you to capture the state of a virtual machine before executing potentially malicious code.

Official website **https://www.vmware.com/products/workstation-pro.html**

Network analysis core threat hunting tools

Network analysis core threat hunting tools play a crucial role in detecting hidden threats by providing deep visibility into network traffic patterns and behaviors. These tools, such as Zeek and Suricata allow threat hunters to capture, inspect, and analyze packet flows across the environment, helping to identify anomalies, lateral movement, or data exfiltration attempts.

Zeek 6.0

Zeek has evolved into one of the most powerful network security monitoring frameworks available. The latest version offers improved performance and enhanced protocol analyzers.

To install Zeek on Ubuntu 24.04, add Zeek repository to Ubuntu (each text group is an entire command, and the symbol $ means the Linux prompt):

```
$ echo 'deb http://download.opensuse.org/repositories/security:/zeek/
xUbuntu_24.04/ /' | sudo tee /etc/apt/sources.list.d/security:zeek.list
```

```
curl -fsSL https://download.opensuse.org/repositories/security:zeek/
xUbuntu_24.04/Release.key | \ gpg --dearmor | sudo tee /etc/apt/trusted.
gpg.d/security_zeek.gpg > /dev/null
```

```
$sudo apt update
```

```
$sudo apt install zeek
```

After installation, you can add Zeek directory to the path:

```
echo "export PATH=$PATH:/opt/zeek/bin" >> ~/.bashrc
source ~/.bashrc
```

Zeek's strength lies in its ability to generate highly detailed logs about network activity, which can be used to identify unusual behaviors that might indicate an intrusion.

Official website **https://zeek.org/**

Suricata

Suricata is an excellent open-source network intrusion detection and prevention. The latest version includes improvements to its machine learning capabilities and protocol detection.

To install Suricata on Ubuntu (each text group is an entire command, and the symbol **$** means the Linux prompt):

```
$sudo add-apt-repository ppa:oisf/suricata-stable
$sudo apt update
$sudo apt install suricata
```

Configure Suricata to monitor your network interfaces and integrate it with other tools in your threat hunting stack. The latest version's enhanced performance allows it to handle higher traffic volumes without dropping packets.

Official website **https://suricata.io/**

Endpoint analysis core threat hunting tool

Endpoint analysis tools are essential for gaining detailed insights into activities occurring directly on devices within the environment. Tools like Velociraptor collect telemetry from endpoints, allowing hunters to detect signs of compromise such as unusual process execution, file modifications, or registry changes.

Velociraptor 0.73.4

Velociraptor has emerged as one of the most powerful open-source tools for endpoint visibility and digital forensics. The latest version includes a completely redesigned UI, improved performance, and expanded collection capabilities.

To deploy Velociraptor in Ubuntu Server 24.04 (each text group is an entire command, and the symbol **$** means the Linux prompt):

1. Update your system:

    ```
    $sudo apt update && sudo apt upgrade -y
    ```

2. Visit the Velociraptor releases page and download the latest release for Linux. You can use **wget** to download it directly:

    ```
    $wget https://github.com/Velocidex/velociraptor/releases/download/
    v0.73/velociraptor-v0.73.4-linux-amd64
    ```

3. Make the binary executable:

   $chmod +x velociraptor-v0.73.4-linux-amd64

4. Move the Binary to a Directory in Your PATH:

   $sudo mv velociraptor-v0.73.4-linux-amd64 /usr/local/bin/velociraptor

5. Generate a configuration file and configure each parameter, including username and password:

   $sudo velociraptor config generate -i

6. Start the velociraptor server:

   $sudo velociraptor --config server.config.yaml frontend -v

7. Open your web browser and navigate to **https://your_server_ip:8889**. You can log in using the credentials you set during the configuration step.

   You can see an image like the following figure:

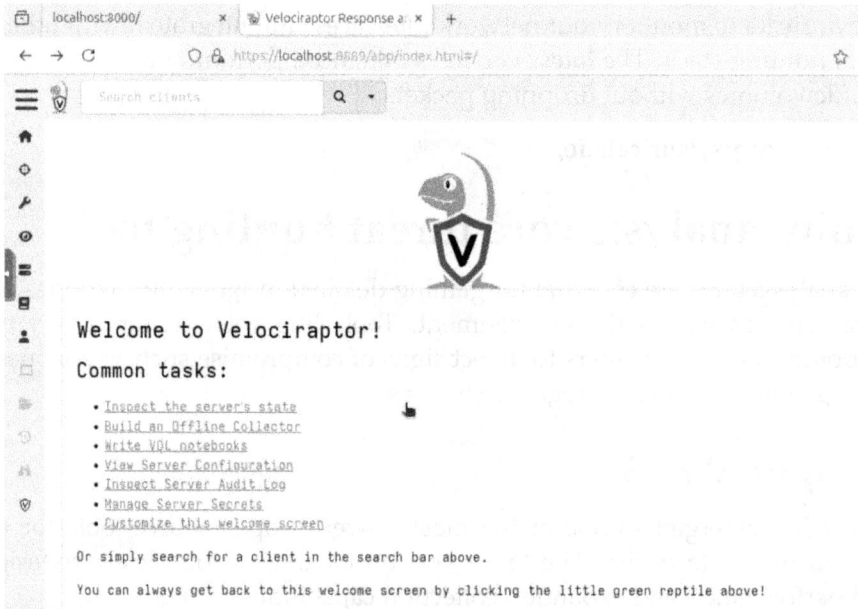

Figure 4.13: Velociraptor tool start page

HIDS core threat hunting tool

Host-based IDSs tools are vital for monitoring and analyzing activities on individual hosts to detect suspicious behavior. Solutions like OSSEC and Wazuh collect log data, monitor file integrity, and track user activities, providing critical visibility into potential threats at the host level.

OSSEC

OSSEC continues to be a reliable host-based IDS. The latest version includes improved rule sets and better integration with other security tools.

OSSEC URL **https://www.ossec.net/ossec-downloads/**

Here are the steps to install OSSEC on Ubuntu 24.04:

1. Update your system:

   ```
   sudo apt update && sudo apt upgrade -y
   ```

2. Install required dependencies:

   ```
   sudo apt install build-essential gcc make unzip sendmail inotify-tools
   expect libevent-dev libpcre2-dev libz-dev libssl-dev libsystemd-dev -y
   ```

3. Download the latest OSSEC version:

   ```
   wget https://github.com/ossec/ossec-hids/archive/refs/tags/3.8.0.tar.gz
   ```

4. Extract the downloaded file:

   ```
   tar -xvzf 3.8.0.tar.gz
   ```

5. Go to the extracted directory:

   ```
   cd ossec-hids-3.8.0
   ```

6. Run the Installation Script:

   ```
   sudo ./install.sh
   ```

   Follow the installation prompts:

   o Select your preferred language.

   o Choose the installation type (for example, local, agent, server).

   o Configure the installation options as prompted.

7. Start the OSSEC service:

   ```
   sudo systemctl start ossec
   ```

8. Enable the OSSEC service:

   ```
   sudo systemctl enable ossec
   ```

9. Verify the installation:

   ```
   sudo /var/ossec/bin/ossec-control status
   ```

Log analysis core threat hunting tool

Log analysis tools enable the systematic examination of log data from diverse sources such as servers, applications, firewalls, and authentication systems. Tools like OpenSearch help threat hunters aggregate, search, and correlate events to uncover suspicious activities.

OpenSearch

OpenSearch is a distributed, open-source search and analytics suite. It was created as a fork of Elasticsearch and Kibana after Elastic NV changed its licensing strategy. OpenSearch is licensed under the Apache 2.0 license, ensuring it remains open-source and free to use, modify, and distribute.

The following are the key features of OpenSearch:

- o **Search and analytics:** Supports full-text search, structured search, and analytics.
- o **Scalability:** Designed to handle large volumes of data across multiple nodes.
- o **Visualization:** Includes OpenSearch Dashboards for data visualization and exploration.
- o **Extensibility:** Supports plugins and extensions for additional functionality.
- o **Security:** Provides features like role-based access control, encryption, and audit logging.

The following are the steps to install OpenSearch on Ubuntu 24.04:

(For latest installation instructions visit: **https://opensearch.org/docs/latest/install-and-configure/install-opensearch/index/**)

1. Update your system and install Docker and Docker compose:

   ```
   $sudo apt update
   $sudo apt install docker.io docker-compose -y
   $sudo systemctl start docker
   $sudo systemctl enable docker
   ```

2. Pull the latest Docker image:

   ```
   $sudo docker pull opensearchproject/opensearch:2
   ```

3. Pull the latest OpenSearch dashboards:

   ```
   $sudo docker pull opensearchproject/opensearch-dashboards:2
   ```

4. Run the Docker image with default parameters, you need to assign an initial admin password in the command as follows:

   ```
   $sudo docker run -d -p 9200:9200 -p 9600:9600 -e "discovery.type=single-node" -e "OPENSEARCH_INITIAL_ADMIN_PASSWORD=<custom-admin-password>" opensearchproject/opensearch:latest
   ```

5. Test the implementation:

   ```
   curl https://localhost:9200 -ku admin:<custom-admin-password>
   ```

Threat intelligence core threat hunting tool

Threat intelligence tools provide crucial contextual information about known adversaries, attack techniques, and IoCs to enhance hunting efforts. Platforms like MISP deliver actionable intelligence that threat hunters can use to proactively search for signs of specific threats within their environment.

MALWARE Information Sharing Platform

The **MALWARE Information Sharing Platform (MISP)** has become the standard for threat intelligence sharing within the security community. The latest version includes improvements to its API and enhanced integration capabilities. Follow these steps:

1. Deploy MISP using Docker:

   ```
   git clone https://github.com/MISP/misp-docker
   ```

2. Go to the new directory:

   ```
   cd misp-docker
   ```

3. Copy the Sample **template.env** file content to .env file:

   ```
   cp template.env .env
   ```

   # Edit .env file with your additional configuration needs (optional).

4. If you have issues, the content of the file can be in this URL:

   https://github.com/MISP/misp-docker/blob/master/template.env

5. Run the Docker image:

   ```
   $sudo docker-compose up -d
   ```

6. Login to **https://localhost**

   - **User**: admin@admin.test
   - **Password**: admin

   This following figure illustrates the MISP welcome screen:

Figure 4.14: MISP threat login platform

7. After login, you receive (refer to the following figure):

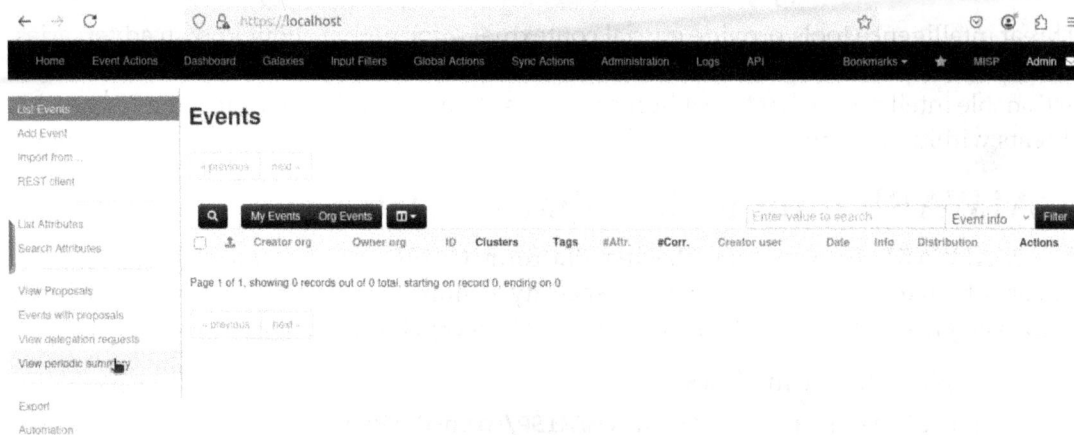

Figure 4.15: MISP tool platform

We can create our laboratory with the level of complexity we want; Of course, having a greater number of tools allows us to compare results, but in the same way, we must properly manage those tools, keep them updated, etc. In the following table, you can find the tools we include in this chapter and some suggestions for additional tools we can add to the lab:

Category	Tool	Description	Official URL
Virtualization	Proxmox VE	Enterprise-level open-source virtualization platform with web-based management interface	**https://www.proxmox.com/en/downloads**
Virtualization	VirtualBox	Cross-platform virtualization software with snapshot functionality	**https://www.virtualbox.org/**
Virtualization	VMware Workstation Pro/Player	Commercial virtualization platform with robust isolation capabilities	**https://www.vmware.com/products/workstation-pro.html**

Table 4.13: Additional virtualization tools

Expanding network visibility and detection capabilities often involves incorporating additional network analysis tools that provide deeper insights into traffic patterns, anomalies, and potential threats; the following table illustrates some of these tools:

Category	Tool	Description	Official URL
Network Analysis	Zeek 6.0 (formerly Bro)	Powerful network security monitoring framework with detailed protocol analysis	**https://zeek.org/**

Category	Tool	Description	Official URL
Network Analysis	Suricata	Network intrusion detection and prevention system with machine learning capabilities	**https://suricata.io/**
Network Analysis	Malcolm	Network traffic analysis platform for security monitoring and forensics	**https://github.com/ cisagov/Malcolm**
Network Analysis	Moloch/ Arkime	Full packet capture and indexing system	**https://arkime. com/**
Network Analysis	Wireshark	Network protocol analyzer	**https://www.wire-shark.org/**
Network Analysis	tcpdump	Command-line packet analyzer	**https://www.tcp-dump.org/**
Network Analysis	NetworkMiner	Network forensic analysis tool	**https://www.ne-tresec.com/?page=-NetworkMiner**
Network Analysis	Brim	Open-source desktop application for analyzing network traffic and logs	**https://www.brim-data.io/**

Table 4.14: Additional network analysis tools

To strengthen endpoint visibility and detection, additional tools can be integrated to provide deeper behavioral analysis, threat detection, and forensic capabilities; the following table illustrates some of these tools:

Category	Tool	Description	Official URL
Endpoint Analysis	Velociraptor 0.7	Advanced endpoint visibility and digital forensics platform with VQL query language	**https://docs.veloci-raptor.app/**
Endpoint Analysis	OSSEC 3.7	Host-based IDS with file integrity monitoring	**https://www.ossec. net/**
Endpoint Analysis	Wazuh 4.7	Comprehensive security platform combining SIEM XDR and compliance monitoring	**https://wazuh.com/**
Endpoint Analysis	osquery	Operating system instrumentation framework for querying and monitoring	**https://osquery.io/**

Table 4.15: Additional endpoint analysis tools

Effective threat hunting relies heavily on comprehensive log management, and incorporating additional tools can enhance log collection, normalization, and analysis; the following table highlights some of these tools:

Category	Tool	Description	Official URL
Log Management	Graylog 5.2	Scalable log management platform with search capabilities and visualization	**https://www.graylog.org/**
Log Management	Open-Search 2.10	Search analytics and visualization platform forked from Elasticsearch	**https://opensearch.org/**
Log Management	Logstash	Data processing pipeline for ingesting data from multiple sources	**https://www.elastic.co/logstash/**
Log Management	Vector	High-performance observability data pipeline	**https://vector.dev/**

Table 4.16: Additional log management tools

Enhancing threat hunting operations often requires the use of additional threat intelligence tools that provide enriched context, indicators, and deeper insights into adversary behaviors; the following table highlights several of these tools:

Category	Tool	Description	Official URL
Threat Intelligence	MISP 2.4.172	Malware Information Sharing Platform for threat intelligence sharing	**https://www.misp-project.org/**
Threat Intelligence	TheHive 5.2	Security incident response platform with case management	**https://thehive-project.org/**
Threat Intelligence	OpenCTI	Open cyber threat intelligence platform	**https://www.opencti.io/**
Threat Intelligence	CRITs	Collaborative Research Into Threats	**https://crits.github.io/**

Table 4.17: Additional threat intelligence tools

To streamline and enhance threat hunting activities, additional integrated platforms can be leveraged to unify data sources, automate workflows, and improve overall threat visibility; the following table presents several of these platforms:

Category	Tool	Description	Official URL
Integrated Platforms	HELK Stack	Hunting ELK stack combining multiple security tools	**https://github.com/Cyb3rWard0g/ HELK**

Category	Tool	Description	Official URL
Integrated Platforms	Security Onion	Network security monitoring distribution	**https://securityonionsolutions. com/**
Integrated Platforms	AlienVault OSSIM	Open Source Security Information and Event Management	**https://cybersecurity.att.com/ products/ossim**
Integrated Platforms	ROCKS Cluster	Security-focused big data analytics platform	**https://rocknsm.io/**

Table 4.18: Additional integrated platforms

Advanced threat hunting often depends on powerful data analysis tools that can process large volumes of information, uncover hidden patterns, and identify subtle anomalies; the following table highlights several tools that support these capabilities:

Category	Tool	Description	Official URL
Data Analysis	Kibana	Data visualization dashboard for Elasticsearch	**https://www.elastic.co/kibana/**
Data Analysis	Grafana	Observability and data visualization platform	**https://grafana.com/**
Data Analysis	Stream-lit	Framework for creating data applications	**https://streamlit.io/**

Table 4.19: Additional data analysis tools

Conclusion

In this chapter, we have discussed the tools that can be used in threat hunting, as well as the different frameworks that assist us in providing a logical and repeatable structure to our exercises. Subsequently, we discussed recommendations for collecting and analyzing information from various available sources. Following the logic of making our work more viable, we continued with the different ways we can automate the threat hunting process, where possible. We concluded with recommendations and best practices for managing our documentation and generating reports. These reports will be used by various departments within the company to apply remediations, change policies, or improve any necessary aspect of security.

In the next chapter, we explore the exciting world of network traffic analysis; given that an attacker is going to use the network in any of the phases of their attack, this is a front that we must know in detail and that we must monitor in depth.

Points to remember

- We have referred to numerous tools throughout this chapter; however, it is crucial to remember that the number of tools we have only affects the dataset that we can assess. What truly makes a difference is the quality of the analysis performed, based on that dataset.

- The various frameworks that are available assist us in creating a logical guide to streamline the execution and repeatability of our threat hunting activities.

- Different information analysis techniques can be integrated to better understand and connect the data universe we have, thereby enabling us to find groups, similarities, and anomalies.

- An analysis can be quite insightful and yield significant findings, however, if these are not presented in a clear, comprehensible, and useful manner, they will not achieve the appropriate relevance or the desired outcome.

Multiple choice questions

1. **Which of the following is considered the foundation stone of threat hunting for many experts in the field?**

   a. Endpoint Detection and Response (EDR)

   b. Security Information and Event Management (SIEM)

   c. User and Entity Behavior Analytics (UEBA)

   d. Network Detection and Response (NDR)

2. **What is the primary role of Endpoint Detection and Response (EDR) mechanisms?**

   a. To monitor and scan activities performed by the Operating System, Installed Applications, and local Antimalware, looking for abnormalities

   b. To cleanse, normalize and standardize data from various sources

   c. To analyze network traffic, protocols, and packets

   d. To detect abnormal user behaviors using machine learning and automation

3. **Which tool uses machine learning and automation to detect abnormal behaviors in users and entities?**

   a. Network Sniffers, Network Monitoring and Packet Analyzers tools

   b. Extended Detection and Response (XDR) too

   c. Security Information and Event Management (SIEM) tools

   d. User and Entity Behavior Analytics (UEBA) tools

4. **Which technology is a traversal approach to cybersecurity in a company and monitors and detects across all surfaces in the entity, like Cloud, Mail, Endpoints, network, etc.?**

    a.   Extended Detection and Response (XDR)

    b.   User and Entity Behavior Analytics (UEBA)

    c.   Network Detection and Response (NDR)

    d.   Security Information and Event Management (SIEM)

5. **What kind of tools allow the analyst to capture the network traffic and dissect the packets to analyze what is inside the Network Datagram?**

    a.   Endpoint Detection and Response (EDR) tools

    b.   User and Entity Behavior Analytics (UEBA) tools

    c.   Network Sniffers, Network Monitoring, and Packet Analyzers tools

    d.   Extended Detection and Response (XDR) tools

Answers

1. b.
2. a.
3. d.
4. a.
5. c.

References

1. **ATTACK-Python-Client:**

   https://github.com/OTRF/ATTACK-Python-Client/tree/master

2. **TaHiTI: a threat hunting methodology:**

   https://www.betaalvereniging.nl/wp-content/uploads/TaHiTI-Threat-Hunting-Methodology-whitepaper.pdf

3. **Introducing the PEAK Threat Hunting Framework:**

   https://www.splunk.com/en_us/blog/security/peak-threat-hunting-framework.html

4. **Gartner XDR Reviews:**

   https://www.gartner.com/reviews/market/extended-detection-and-response

5. **Data, analytics, and artificial intelligence adoption strategy:**

   https://media.defense.gov/2023/Nov/02/2003333300/-1/-1/1/DOD_DATA_ANALYTICS_AI_ADOPTION_STRATEGY.PDF

Join our Discord space

Join our Discord workspace for latest updates, offers, tech happenings around the world, new releases, and sessions with the authors:

https://discord.bpbonline.com

CHAPTER 5
Network Traffic Analysis

Introduction

Networks are one of the preferred targets for malicious actors and are almost impossible for the adversaries to completely hide the malicious or adversarial activity in the network, if you know where to look; the attackers execute many activities in the network like: *Host Scanning, Resources Enumeration, Lateral movement, Password Spraying*, etc.

This kind of attacks can be detected with the proper technologies and knowledge to do it. This chapter covers everything you need to detect and discover abnormal behaviors in your traffic and connections.

Structure

In this chapter, we will discuss the following topics:

- Introduction to network traffic analysis
- Network protocols and packet analysis
- IoC and IoA communication and implementation

Objectives

In any attack, whether remote or local, network communication plays a major role in the success of the cybercriminal's malicious activities, and it is almost impossible for the adversary to eliminate all traces (IoA) generated by the communication he has established; in this chapter we will explore in depth the analysis of the network traffic, the models, the protocols, and we will go deep into the traffic packets to extend our search for anomalies; for this we will use the most advanced and effective tools so far.

We would feel that this chapter is incomplete if we do not start with a review of the connectivity models we use, how they work, the functions of their layers, a visualization of the network protocols and then delve into the detail of the analysis of network traffic, because logically you will not be able to properly analyze what you do not fully understand.

Introduction to network traffic analysis

The analysis of network traffic is one of the most important tasks that a threat hunter must execute, and to achieve the highest proficiency he must have a deep technical knowledge about how data networks and their corresponding protocols work; In the following sections we will be discussing many technical details that are exciting and that allow us to easily detect anomalies if we understand the mechanic of communications.

To be able to analyze the traffic of a network, we will usually use various tools, such as sniffers, packet analyzers, monitoring tools, but at the end it is the skill and knowledge of the analyst that make the difference between finding the attacker's fingerprints or not. In this chapter we are going to focus on delivering as much practical and effective knowledge as possible to make the task of threat hunting more efficient.

The networks we use today have a fundamental basis or models, which determine how they work and the performance of various **layers** that ultimately make up the whole foundation of the networks. There are two models we currently use, but in reality, one model is derived from the other, and currently, it is the TCP/IP model that we commonly use. This explanation, which may sound complicated, will be understood very easily with a graph in which we will be able to understand how the models are complementary to each other.

To be able to communicate between computer devices from different manufacturers and different services, a standardized communication model is necessary.

Let us start by explaining the first model in the following section.

Open systems interconnection model ISO/IEC 7498-1

You can find the technical documentation about the model in this link: **https://www.iso. org/obp/ui/#iso:std:iso-iec:7498:-1:ed-1:v2:en**

In 1973, an experimental packet-switching system in the United Kingdom identified the requirement for defining higher-level protocols. In the late 1970s, the International

Standards Organization - ISO undertook a program to develop general standards and networking methods. In 1983, the **Open System Interconnection (OSI)** model was initially intended to be a detailed specification of real interfaces and in 1984, the OSI architecture was formally adopted by ISO as an international standard.

OSI is a conceptual model, which allows various communication systems to be connected using standard protocols, so OSI provides a standard for different equipment systems to communicate with each other.

The OSI model can be seen as a universal language for connecting computer networks. It is based on the concept of dividing a communication system into seven abstract layers, each stacked on top of the previous one, each layer accomplishes specific functions and allows the interaction between each layer (refer to *Figure 5.1*):

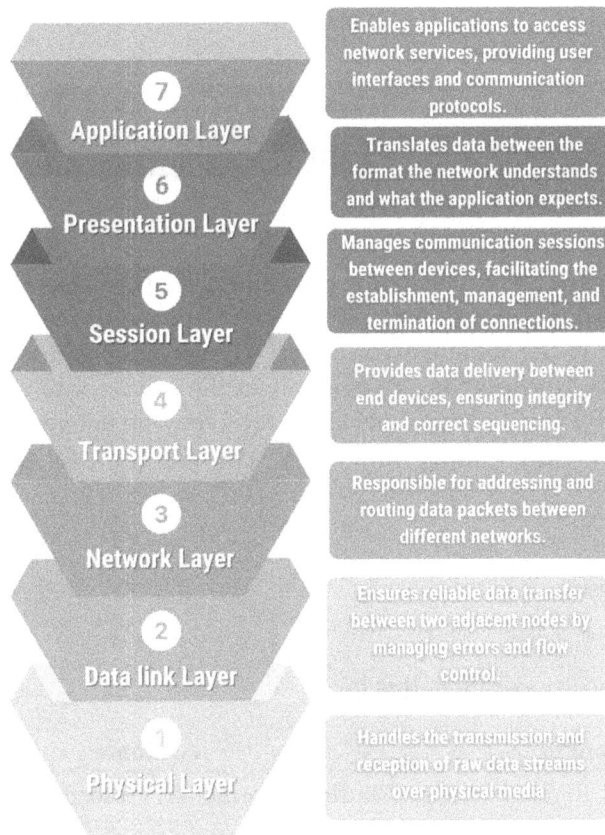

Figure 5.1: Layers of the OSI model

Let us look at the different layers:

- **Layer 1, Physical layer:** This layer includes the physical devices (Hardware) involved in data transfer, such as cables, network cards, routers, and network switches. In this layer, the data is converted into a sequence of bits.

For example:

o Cable

o Network Cards

- **Layer 2, Data link layer:** This layer oversees the transmission of information between two linked devices on the same network. The data link layer is responsible for dividing packets coming from the network layer into smaller segments, known as frames. In addition, this layer carries out the management of the data flow and the error control in the communications that take place within the network.

For example:

o MAC Addresses like: 00:11:22: 33:44:55

o Switches

Example of *Layer 2* traffic:

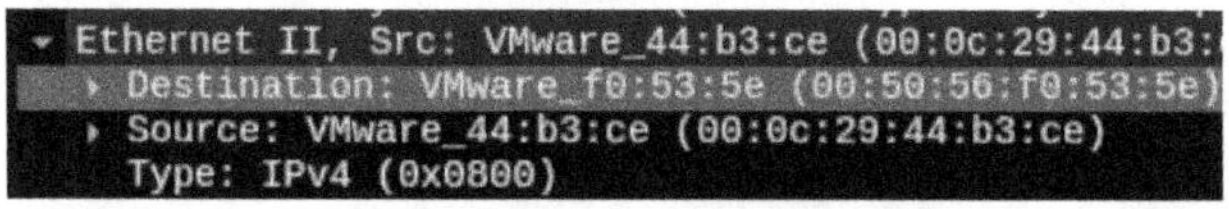

Figure 5.2: Data link layer traffic

- **Layer 3, Network layer:** Unlike the data link layer, the network layer takes care of the transfer of data between two different networks. If the communicating devices are connected to the same network, then the network layer is not necessary. This layer splits the transport layer segments at the sender into smaller units, called **packets**, and rejoins these packets at the receiver. The network layer also executes routing; that means looking for the best physical path for the data to reach its destination.

For example:

o IP Address

o Routers

Various protocols operate at this layer:

Acronym	Name
RIP	Routing Information Protocol
OSPF	Open Shortest Path First
IPv4 / IPv6	Internet Protocol v. 4 and v. 6
IPsec	Internet Protocol Security
ICMP	Internet Control Message Protocol
IGMP	Internet Group Management Protocol

EGP	Exterior Gateway Protocol
EIGRP	Enhanced Interior Gateway Routing Protocol
DDP	Datagram Delivery Protocol
CLNS	Connectionless-mode Network Service
LLARP	Low Latency Anonymous Routing Protocol
IPX	Internetwork Packet Exchange
PIM	Protocol Independent Multicast

Table 5.1: Network Layer Protocols

Example of *Layer 3* actual traffic capture:

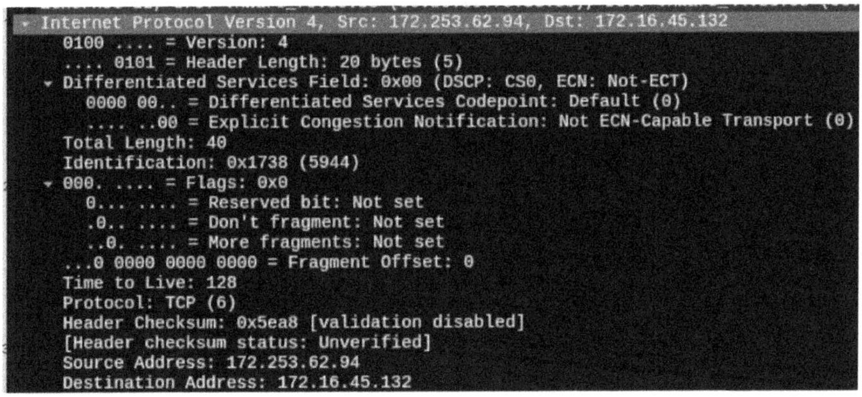

```
▼ Internet Protocol Version 4, Src: 172.253.62.94, Dst: 172.16.45.132
     0100 .... = Version: 4
     .... 0101 = Header Length: 20 bytes (5)
  ▼ Differentiated Services Field: 0x00 (DSCP: CS0, ECN: Not-ECT)
     0000 00.. = Differentiated Services Codepoint: Default (0)
     .... ..00 = Explicit Congestion Notification: Not ECN-Capable Transport (0)
     Total Length: 40
     Identification: 0x1738 (5944)
  ▼ 000. .... = Flags: 0x0
     0... .... = Reserved bit: Not set
     .0.. .... = Don't fragment: Not set
     ..0. .... = More fragments: Not set
     ...0 0000 0000 0000 = Fragment Offset: 0
     Time to Live: 128
     Protocol: TCP (6)
     Header Checksum: 0x5ea8 [validation disabled]
     [Header checksum status: Unverified]
     Source Address: 172.253.62.94
     Destination Address: 172.16.45.132
```

Figure 5.3: Network layer traffic

- **Layer 4, Transport layer:** This layer is responsible for flow control, packet sequencing and error control by exchanging acknowledgment of data and retransmission of lost packets. This type of communication is called end-to-end or point-to-point communication. In this layer, the data is divided into parts called **segments**. The flow control allows determining the optimum speed to balance the transmission between a fast and slow actor to avoid overflows in the communication.

Protocols operating at this layer:

Acronym	Name
TCP	Transmission control protocol
UDP	User datagram protocol

Table 5.2: Transport layer protocols

Example of actual TCP traffic capture:

```
- Transmission Control Protocol, Src Port: 443, Dst Port: 54968, Seq: 4319, Ack: 582, Len: 0
    Source Port: 443
    Destination Port: 54968
    [Stream index: 70]
  ▸ [Conversation completeness: Incomplete, DATA (15)]
    [TCP Segment Len: 0]
    Sequence Number: 4319      (relative sequence number)
    Sequence Number (raw): 980256437
    [Next Sequence Number: 4319     (relative sequence number)]
    Acknowledgment Number: 582    (relative ack number)
    Acknowledgment number (raw): 3080391533
    0101 .... = Header Length: 20 bytes (5)
  ▸ Flags: 0x010 (ACK)
    Window: 64240
    [Calculated window size: 64240]
    [Window size scaling factor: -2 (no window scaling used)]
    Checksum: 0x9354 [unverified]
    [Checksum Status: Unverified]
    Urgent Pointer: 0
  ▸ [Timestamps]
  ▸ [SEQ/ACK analysis]
```

Figure 5.4: Transport layer traffic

- **Layer 5, Session layer:** This layer oversees creating the sessions between devices, that is, opening and closing the communication between them; when communication opens, a session is established between the two devices. This layer allows the session to remain open while data is transferred from one node to another; Once the data exchange is finished, the session is terminated.

  To reduce the loss of time and resources when communications fail, this layer establishes checkpoints every certain amount of data transferred to synchronize the data, so that if the connection is interrupted, the data exchange can be resumed from the last checkpoint.

- **Layer 6, Presentation layer:** This layer prepares the data to be presented to the next layer, the **application layer**, by executing tasks such as translation of the various encoding, encryption or decryption, and data compression; at the end of the day, this layer makes the data *readable*.

- **Layer 7, Application layer:** This is one of the most interesting layers, because it is the one that allows the user interaction with the data using specific protocols such as **Hyper Text Transfer Protocol (HTTP)**, WEB Real-Time Communication, **Internet Mail Access Protocol (IMAP)**, **Post Office Protocol (POP)**, **Simple Mail Transfer Protocol (SMTP)**, etc. Those protocols are interpreted by tools such as internet browsers, video conferencing clients, email clients, etc.

At this point, it is essential that we address how the encapsulation and de-encapsulation of information works in the data flow in the network; remember that the flow is bidirectional, that is, from node A, data flows to node B and vice versa. To achieve this flow, the data undergoes certain changes and additions in the process, such as adding a header, dividing the data into smaller parts, etc. The following figure will allow us to understand more easily how the process works:

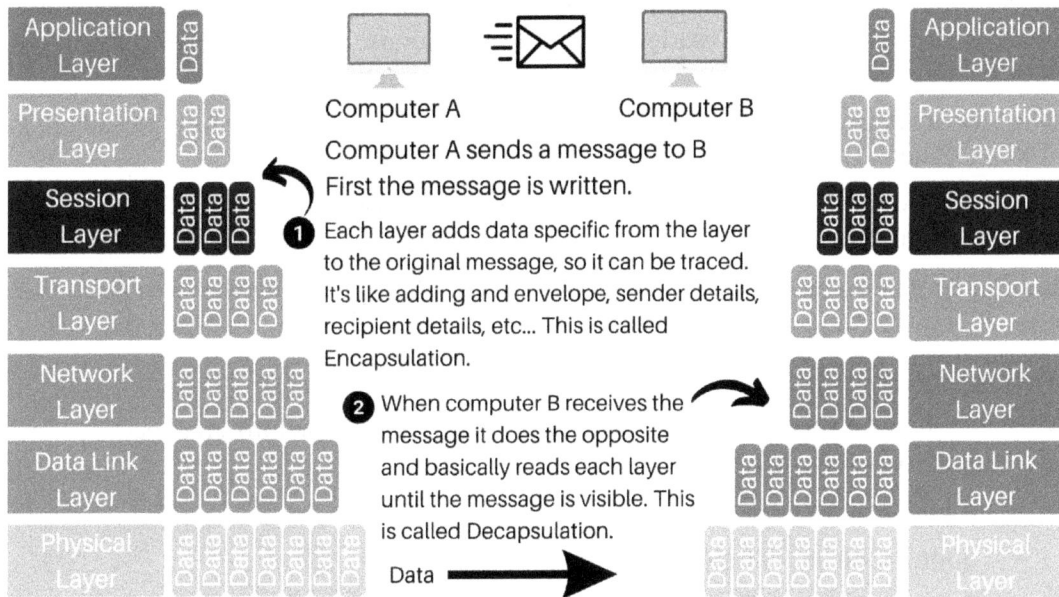

Figure 5.5: *Encapsulation and decapsulation process*

TCP/IP model

In 1974, *Vint Cerf* and *Bob Kahn* published a paper *A Protocol for Packet Network Intercommunication* describing the TCP/IP model - **https://web.eecs.umich.edu/~prabal/ teaching/eecs582-w13/readings/CK74.pdf;** By 1978, testing and development of this language led to a new set of protocols called TCP/IP. In 1982, it was decided that TCP/ IP should replace NCP as the standard language of ARPAnet. On January 1, 1983, ARPAnet switched to TCP/IP. ARPAnet ended its existence in 1990. TCP/IP is the model currently used worldwide for the interconnection of systems; the abbreviation stands for Transmission Control Protocol and **internet protocol (IP)**, they are different protocols but work together.

Internet protocol

The IP is the fundamental communication protocol that forms the backbone of the internet. Think of it as the digital postal service of the internet. It defines how data is packaged, addressed, transmitted, and received across networks, allowing devices worldwide to communicate with each other.

Key characteristics of IP

IP operates at the network layer (Layer 3) of the OSI model and serves two primary functions:

Addressing: IP assigns unique numerical addresses (IP addresses) to devices on networks, similar to how postal addresses identify physical locations. These addresses come in two main versions:

- **IPv4**: Uses 32-bit addresses written as four numbers separated by periods (e.g., 192.168.1.1)

- **IPv6**: Uses 128-bit addresses to accommodate more devices (e.g., 2001:0db8:85a3: 0000:0000:8a2e:0370:7334)

Routing: IP determines the path data packets should take across networks to reach their destination, navigating through various routers and network segments along the way.

Working of IP

When you send data across the internet, IP breaks the information into small packets. Each packet contains:

- A header with source and destination IP addresses

- Information about how packets relate to each other

- The actual data payload

These packets may travel different routes through the network, potentially arriving out of order. Higher-level protocols (like TCP) then reassemble them correctly at their destination.

IP is connectionless and operates on a *best effort* delivery model, meaning it doesn't guarantee packet delivery or proper sequencing. Those responsibilities are handled by transport layer protocols like TCP, which build reliability on top of IP's foundation.

The elegance of IP lies in its simplicity and flexibility, allowing diverse networks and technologies to interconnect and exchange information regardless of their underlying hardware or software implementations.

Transfer control protocol

This is a client-server connection-oriented protocol in charge of controlling errors in transmission and uses a handshake that allows you to establish the session between the devices prior to the start of sending data.

In TCP/IP, each service that can be used, for example, HTTP, DNS, or POP, has a port assigned within a list of a total of 65535 ports = 2^{16}. There are many ports that do not have assigned services, but are used in the establishment of sessions, for example if there is a session between a client and a WEB server, the client uses a source port to the destination port of the specific service and then the server responds to the source port on the client. In the following figure we can easily see it:

TRAFFIC BETWEEN HOSTS

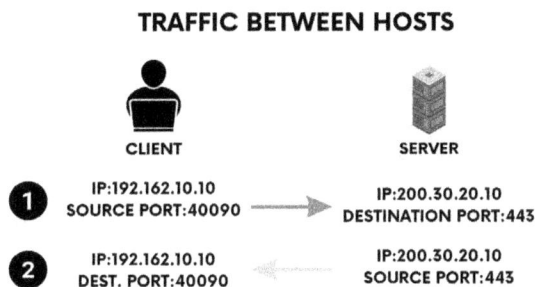

Figure 5.6: Traffic between the host in TCP/IP

TCP ports examples:

Protocol	Stands For	Assigned port/ports
HTTP	Hyper Text Transfer Protocol	80, 81, 8080
DNS	Domain Name System	53
POP	Post Office Protocol	110
SMTP	Simple Mail Transfer Protocol	25
HTTPS	Secure HTTP	443

Table 5.3: TCP port examples

List of assigned port numbers:

https://www.iana.org/assignments/service-names-port-numbers/service-names-port-numbers.xhtml

To establish a session, the server must be listening; that means that the port assigned to the service to be used is open. For example, if you want to access an HTTP website, port 80 should be open on the server. The protocol can determine that a port is open or listening by means of the 3-way handshake, which consists of a greeting between client and server where packets are exchanged with certain flags that allow the status of the port to be determined; the flags that can be used are:

Flag	Stands For	Definition	Flags bit	Decimal value
SYN	Synchronization	Initiate the TCP Connection – like the initial greeting between machines	2	2
FIN	Finalization	Gracefully finish a TCP Connection	1	1
ACK	Acknowledge	Acknowledge the bytes received from a peer	5	16

Flag	Stands For	Definition	Flags bit	Decimal value
RST	Reset	Used to abort a connection (Like a closed port attempted connection)	3	4
URG	Urgent	Used to prioritize data	6	32
PUSH	Push	Used to instruct the Operating System to clear the sending or receiving buffer	4	8
ECE	Explicit Congestion Notification (ECN)-Echo	Indicates that the source node is ECN (Explicit Congestion Notification) capable. Used by routers or intermediary devices; when the sources detect this flag, it reduces the transmission rate to avoid congestion.	7	64
CWR	Congestion Window Reduced	Used to acknowledge that the congestion-indication echoing was received.	8	128

Table 5.4: Flags in TCP

Representation of the TCP flags in a real traffic capture:

Figure 5.7: TCP flags in traffic capture

The 3-way handshake looks like this:

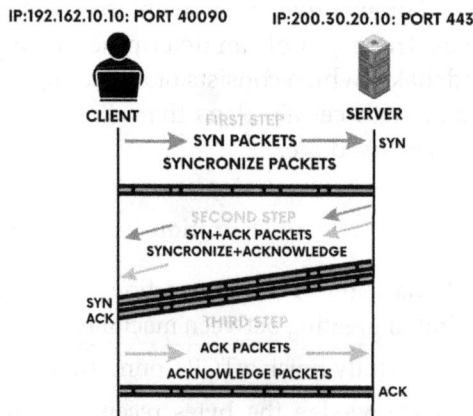

Figure 5.8: 3-way handshake

User datagram protocol

As we have seen, TCP allows an error and flow control that guarantees the quality of the transmitted data, very useful for applications that require that level of certainty in the transmission. Still, some applications do not require that reliability in the data stream. They can use UDP, a datagram, NOT oriented to the connection, that gives greater priority to speed over reliability, which is very effective for protocols such as **Domain Name Resolution** (**DNS**) or video streaming applications.

To provide a better understanding, we present the following figure that allows us to compare the two models, demonstrates the functions of each layer and mentions some of the protocols that transit in each layer:

Network Communication Models Layers Comparison

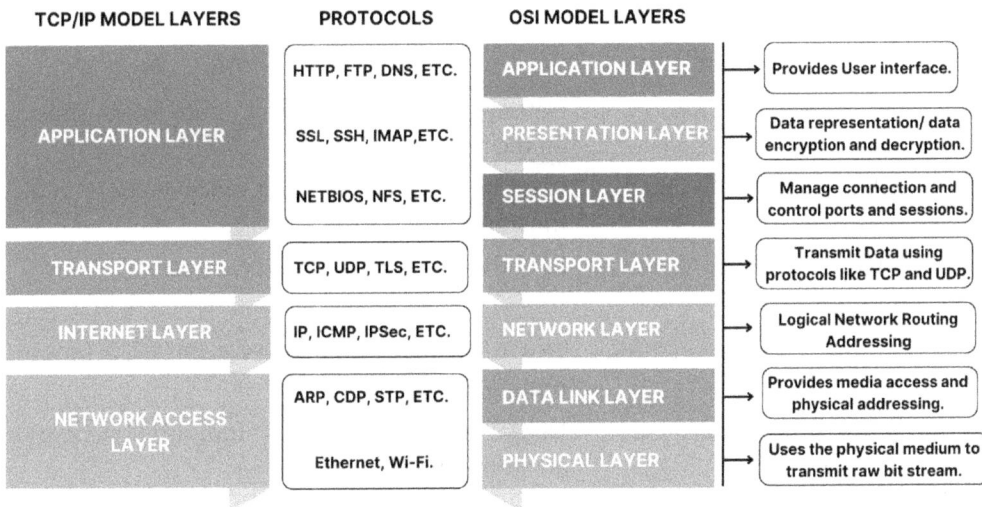

Figure 5.9: OSI and TCP model layers comparison

Network protocols and packet analysis

Network protocols are essentially the languages and rule sets that allow digital devices to communicate with each other. Think of them as the grammar, vocabulary, and etiquette of digital conversation. Without protocols, our devices would be speaking incomprehensible languages to one another.

We recommend the reader to have a small laboratory environment where they can carry out workshops and follow the common thread of the different concepts explained here.

You can use any computer at your disposal and install the Wireshark tool on it, or if possible, (Recommended) implement a virtual machine for this purpose; the virtual isolated machine is recommended because the network traffic you are analyzing can contain malicious artifacts that can compromise the investigative station.

Wireshark can be downloaded from:
https://www.wireshark.org/download.html

Protocols

A protocol is an agreement of rules of engagement by means of which the different interconnected computers will communicate, regardless of the differences in their operating systems or hardware.

As we saw earlier in the definitions and explanations of the models, each network layer uses different protocols according to the type of traffic to be sent. In our world of threat hunting, we need to be able to analyze network traffic and understand the different protocols used by devices on the network, not all devices use the same protocols. For example, routers use protocols such as:

Protocol	Stands For	Definition
BGP	Border Gateway Protocol	Determine the best network route to transmit data on the internet
OSPF	Open Shortest Path First	Used to calculate the most efficient route to direct the traffic
EIGRP	Enhanced Interior Gateway Routing Protocol	Find the best path between routers
RIP	Routing Information Protocol	This is a Distance-Vector Protocol used to update routing tables
IGP	Interior Gateway Protocol	Used to route traffic within individual networks of an autonomous system

Table 5.5: Network routing protocols

From our experience, in the analysis we are going to execute in threat hunting, the common situation is to face protocols that are used both on the Internet and in local networks, for example:

Protocol	Stands For	Definition
HTTP	Hyper Text Transfer Protocol	Used to load WEB content
HTTPS	Hyper Text Transfer Protocol Secure	Extension of the HTTP protocol uses TLS or SSL to encrypt the communication
SSL	Secure Socket Layer	Encrypts the traffic protecting the privacy; it evolves to TLS
TLS	Transport layer Security	Encrypts the traffic protecting the privacy; it replaces in many cases the SSL

Protocol	Stands For	Definition
DNS	Domain Name System	Resolve Names to IP addresses
ICMP	Internet Control Message Protocol	Used to diagnose network communication problems
QUIC	Is not an Acronym	Improves the performance in WEB Applications compared with the TCP Protocol
IPsec	Internet Protocol Security	Secure Protocol was created to protect the communications used in VPN

Table 5.6: Internet and local network protocols

When we are suffering a remote attack, traffic related to that attack will ultimately be generated; in some cases, these attacks present very characteristic behaviors that we can quickly identify, such as, for example, a flood of packets with the SYN flag (Synchronization), almost always associated with a denial of service (SYN Flooding) at the TCP protocol level, and a large amount of traffic with HTTP requests can be associated with a denial of service attempt towards a WEB application.

We have discussed the protocols that we might find in our traffic, and it is impossible to mention them all, but we have already covered the most common ones that we are sure to find. Next, we are going to discuss about the traffic analysis where we are going to learn how to understand traffic, identify legitimate traffic, and detect anomalies that could be malicious traffic.

Packet analysis

Packet analysis is one of the most interesting and exciting activities we do within threat hunting, as we have seen, network traffic is made up of multiple protocols and we must be able to understand those protocols and detect anomalies in that traffic. This is a combination of tools and the analyst's knowledge and expertise. A factor that we must consider, unfortunately, is that there is not always a baseline of the normal traffic of the company or entity, and in this way, we start from scratch in our analysis, since we do not have any point of support or comparison.

To run packet analysis, we need to capture the traffic we are going to analyze, there are several techniques for it. It is very important to understand that in a switched network traffic is only directed to the MAC address of the specific device to which it is directed. If we want to capture that traffic, just connecting a sniffer or capture tool to the network is not enough. We need to connect our sensor in a mirror port or span or tap of a Switch within the network, which is responsible for replicating the entire traffic of the network, in a single port that is the one that is going to deliver the traffic to our sniffer. The following figure gives us a clearer idea of this architecture:

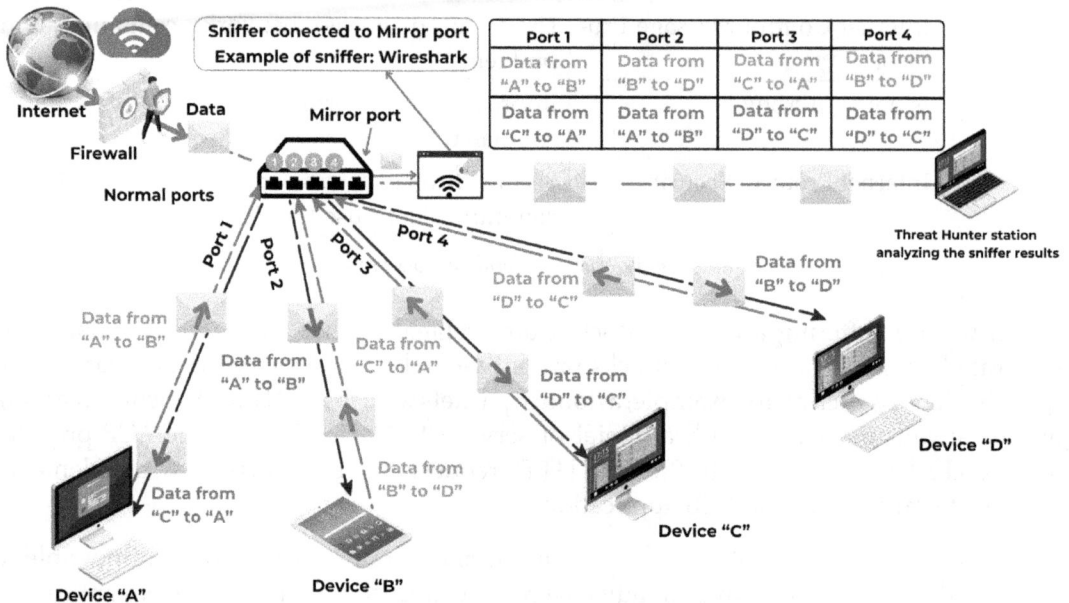

Figure 5.10: Switch architecture

A tap copies network traffic and sends it to a specific device for analysis. It is one of the most used devices to be able to receive the complete traffic of the network, then that device can be connected to Wireshark or some other traffic analysis tool, SIEM, or similar.

There are many tools that will support the traffic analysis, in this chapter, we are going to use Wireshark as main tool. We will see the advantages and we will learn how to use it to be able to detect anomalies in the analyzed traffic.

Wireshark

This open-source tool is a classic of traffic analysis, technically it is a sniffer, which can capture packets layer by layer and by means of filters allow you to see the deepest detail of the traffic, is one of the most widely used applications in threat hunting.

Wireshark can be installed on Windows, MacOS, or Linux and can capture packets in any kind of interface, from Ethernet to Wi-Fi to Bluetooth. It can also open captured traffic files created by other tools.

https://www.wireshark.org/

Here we have the GUI welcome screen of the application.

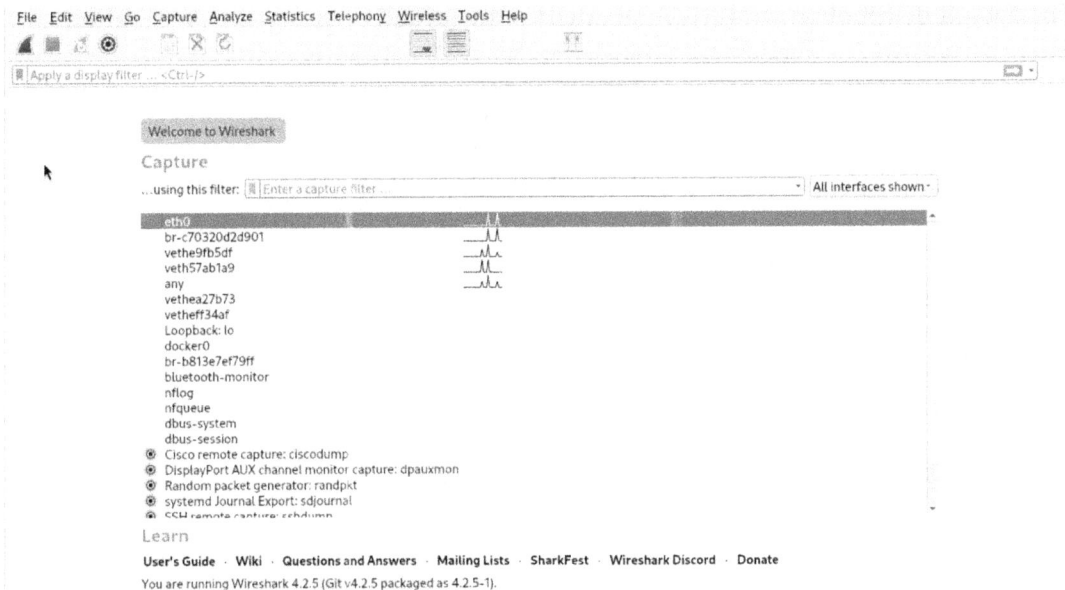

Figure 5.11: Wireshark GUI welcome screen

Let us explain the areas in the capture screen; you have the possibility to configure the layout in the way you need; in the menu: **Edit** | **Preferences** | **Appearance** | **Layout** you can choose the distribution of the three main panels:

- Packet list
- Packet details
- Packet bytes

In the following figure you can see the different configuration options for the three panels:

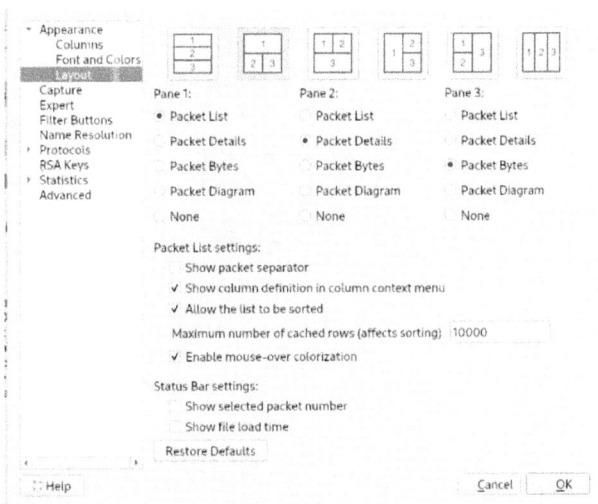

Figure 5.12: Wireshark preferences screen

The default distribution (and recommended) is the second option in the distribution:

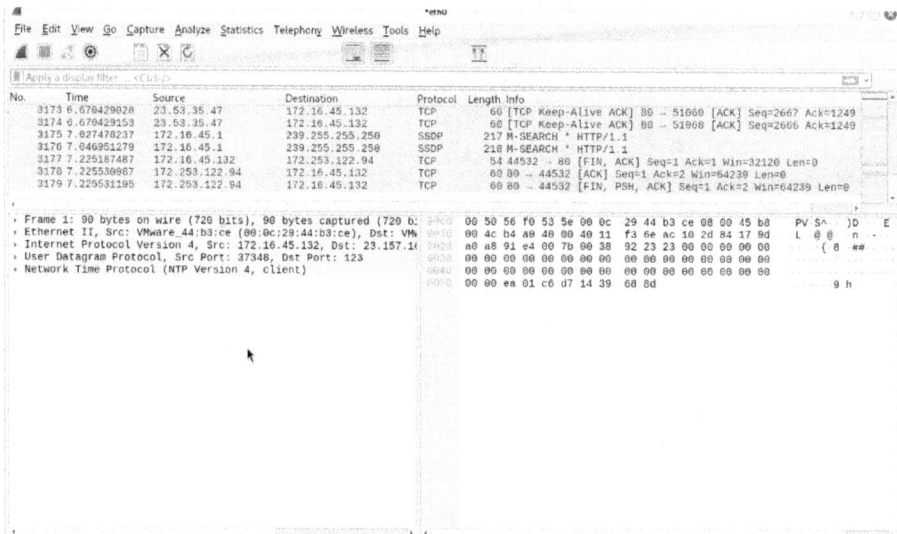

Figure 5.13: Wireshark packet list screen with details

As you can see in the **Packet List** panel, you have the detail of each package: **Timestamp**, **Source**, **Destination**, **Protocol**, **Length**, **Information**. You can add more fields as columns if you need more details, such as **Source port**, **Destination port**, **Destination Address**, etc. The list is huge, and you can arrange or filter for each field in a very easy way; in the following figure we can see the options:

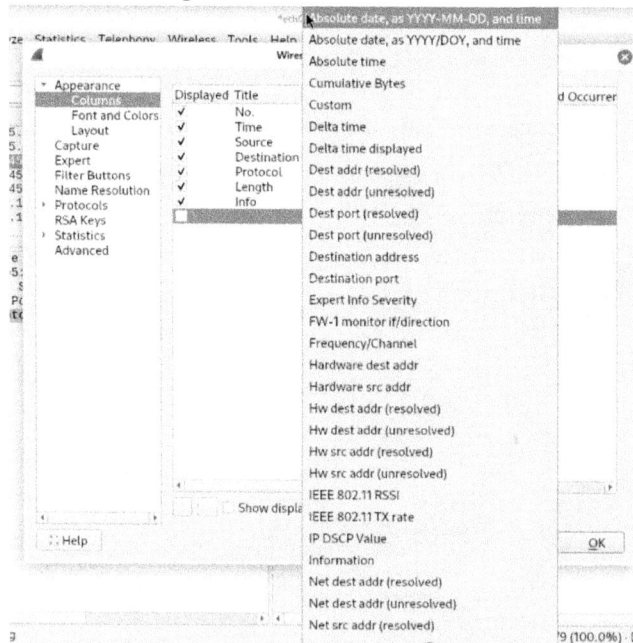

Figure 5.14: Wireshark appearance selection screen

In the following figure, you can see the additional columns such as source port and destination port:

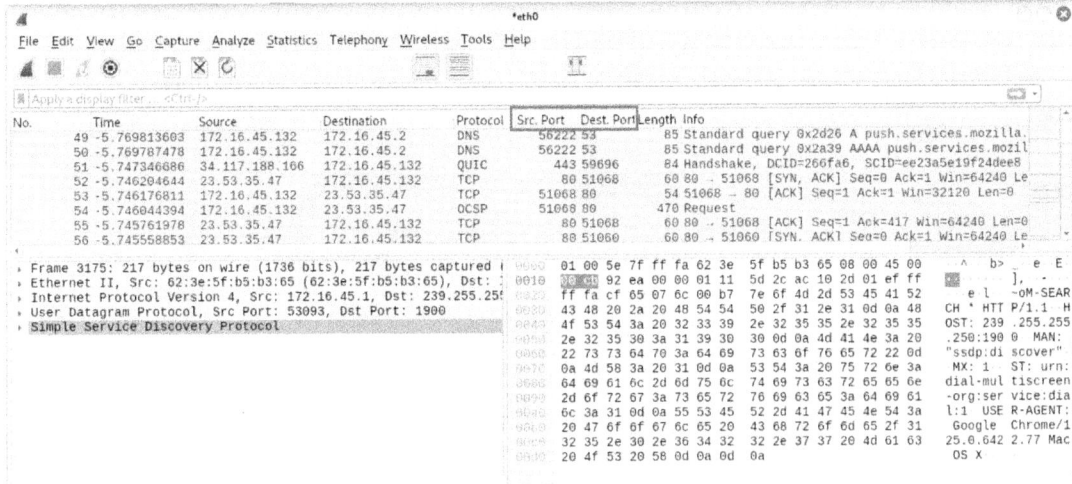

Figure 5.15: Wireshark source and destination port columns

In Wireshark, if you select a packet, you can see in the packet details, all the information in the different layers. Here we select a packet with **Source IP** as **23.53.35.47** and **Destination IP** as **172.16.45.132, TCP Protocol**, **Source Port 80** and **Destination Port** as **51068,** and in the packet details pane we can see the expanded layer one information in the following figure:

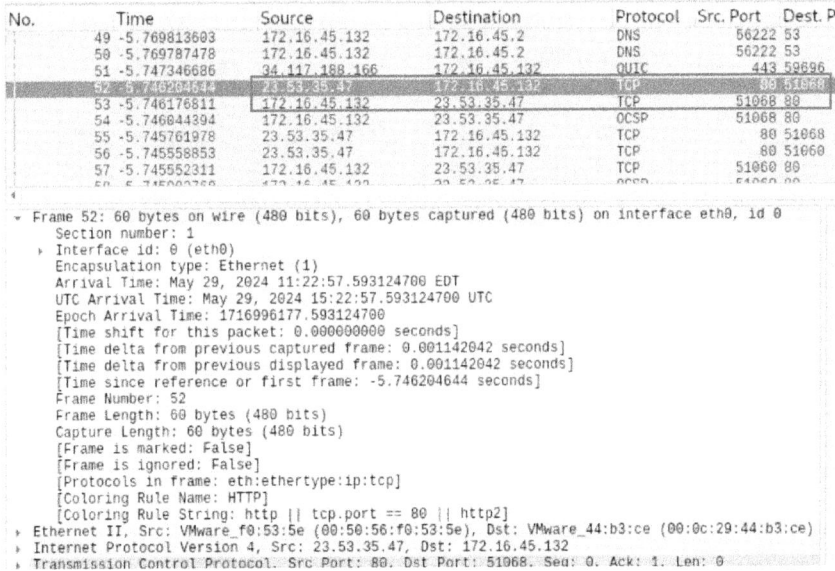

Figure 5.16: Wireshark packet details screen

Layer 2 Ethernet II Information is shown in the following figure:

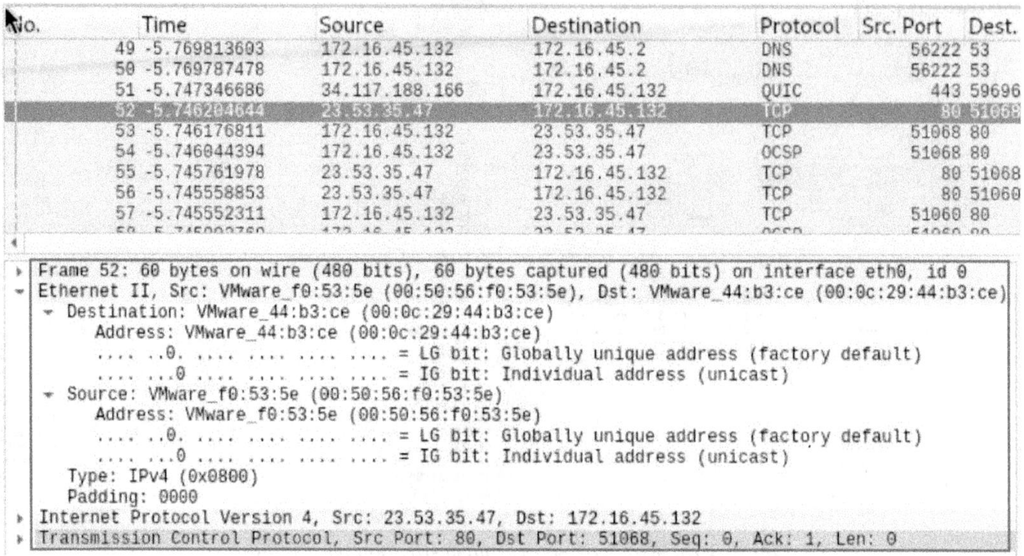

No.	Time	Source	Destination	Protocol	Src. Port	Dest.
49	-5.769813603	172.16.45.132	172.16.45.2	DNS	56222	53
50	-5.769787478	172.16.45.132	172.16.45.2	DNS	56222	53
51	-5.747346686	34.117.188.166	172.16.45.132	QUIC	443	59696
52	-5.746204644	23.53.35.47	172.16.45.132	TCP	80	51068
53	-5.746176811	172.16.45.132	23.53.35.47	TCP	51068	80
54	-5.746044394	172.16.45.132	23.53.35.47	OCSP	51068	80
55	-5.745761978	23.53.35.47	172.16.45.132	TCP	80	51068
56	-5.745558853	23.53.35.47	172.16.45.132	TCP	80	51060
57	-5.745552311	172.16.45.132	23.53.35.47	TCP	51060	80
58	-5.745002760	172.16.45.132	23.53.35.47	OCSP	51060	80

```
▶ Frame 52: 60 bytes on wire (480 bits), 60 bytes captured (480 bits) on interface eth0, id 0
▼ Ethernet II, Src: VMware_f0:53:5e (00:50:56:f0:53:5e), Dst: VMware_44:b3:ce (00:0c:29:44:b3:ce)
   ▼ Destination: VMware_44:b3:ce (00:0c:29:44:b3:ce)
      Address: VMware_44:b3:ce (00:0c:29:44:b3:ce)
      .... ..0. .... .... .... .... = LG bit: Globally unique address (factory default)
      .... ...0 .... .... .... .... = IG bit: Individual address (unicast)
   ▼ Source: VMware_f0:53:5e (00:50:56:f0:53:5e)
      Address: VMware_f0:53:5e (00:50:56:f0:53:5e)
      .... ..0. .... .... .... .... = LG bit: Globally unique address (factory default)
      .... ...0 .... .... .... .... = IG bit: Individual address (unicast)
   Type: IPv4 (0x0800)
   Padding: 0000
▶ Internet Protocol Version 4, Src: 23.53.35.47, Dst: 172.16.45.132
▶ Transmission Control Protocol, Src Port: 80, Dst Port: 51068, Seq: 0, Ack: 1, Len: 0
```

Figure 5.17: Wireshark Ethernet II information screen

The following figure shows the IP:

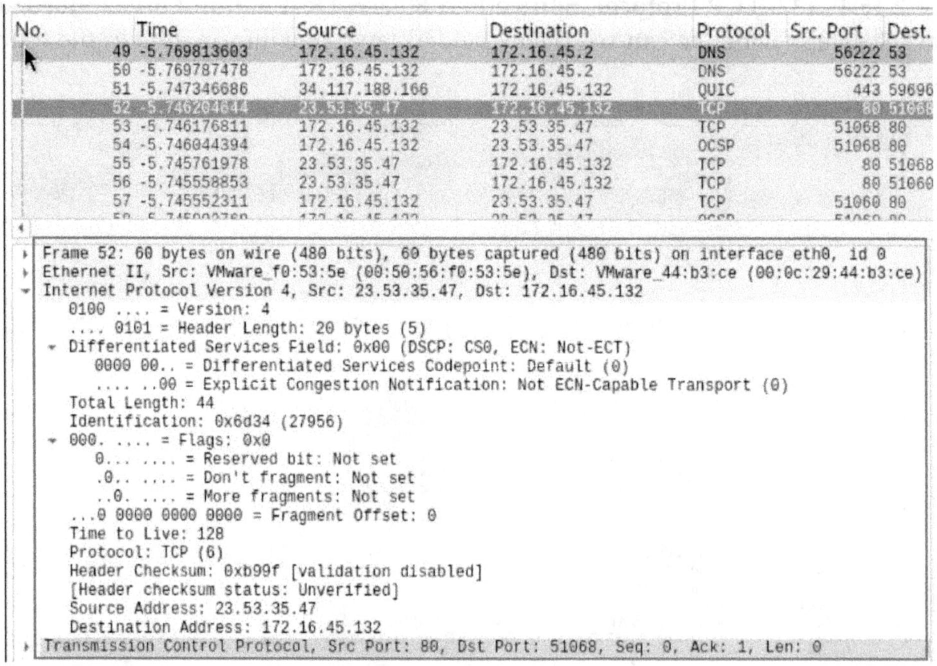

No.	Time	Source	Destination	Protocol	Src. Port	Dest.
49	-5.769813603	172.16.45.132	172.16.45.2	DNS	56222	53
50	-5.769787478	172.16.45.132	172.16.45.2	DNS	56222	53
51	-5.747346686	34.117.188.166	172.16.45.132	QUIC	443	59696
52	-5.746204644	23.53.35.47	172.16.45.132	TCP	80	51068
53	-5.746176811	172.16.45.132	23.53.35.47	TCP	51068	80
54	-5.746044394	172.16.45.132	23.53.35.47	OCSP	51068	80
55	-5.745761978	23.53.35.47	172.16.45.132	TCP	80	51068
56	-5.745558853	23.53.35.47	172.16.45.132	TCP	80	51060
57	-5.745552311	172.16.45.132	23.53.35.47	TCP	51060	80
58	-5.745002760	172.16.45.132	23.53.35.47	OCSP	51060	80

```
▶ Frame 52: 60 bytes on wire (480 bits), 60 bytes captured (480 bits) on interface eth0, id 0
▶ Ethernet II, Src: VMware_f0:53:5e (00:50:56:f0:53:5e), Dst: VMware_44:b3:ce (00:0c:29:44:b3:ce)
▼ Internet Protocol Version 4, Src: 23.53.35.47, Dst: 172.16.45.132
   0100 .... = Version: 4
   .... 0101 = Header Length: 20 bytes (5)
   ▼ Differentiated Services Field: 0x00 (DSCP: CS0, ECN: Not-ECT)
      0000 00.. = Differentiated Services Codepoint: Default (0)
      .... ..00 = Explicit Congestion Notification: Not ECN-Capable Transport (0)
   Total Length: 44
   Identification: 0x6d34 (27956)
   ▼ 000. .... = Flags: 0x0
      0... .... = Reserved bit: Not set
      .0.. .... = Don't fragment: Not set
      ..0. .... = More fragments: Not set
   ...0 0000 0000 0000 = Fragment Offset: 0
   Time to Live: 128
   Protocol: TCP (6)
   Header Checksum: 0xb99f [validation disabled]
   [Header checksum status: Unverified]
   Source Address: 23.53.35.47
   Destination Address: 172.16.45.132
▶ Transmission Control Protocol, Src Port: 80, Dst Port: 51068, Seq: 0, Ack: 1, Len: 0
```

Figure 5.18: Wireshark IP information screen

Following figure shows **Transmission Control Protocol Layer**:

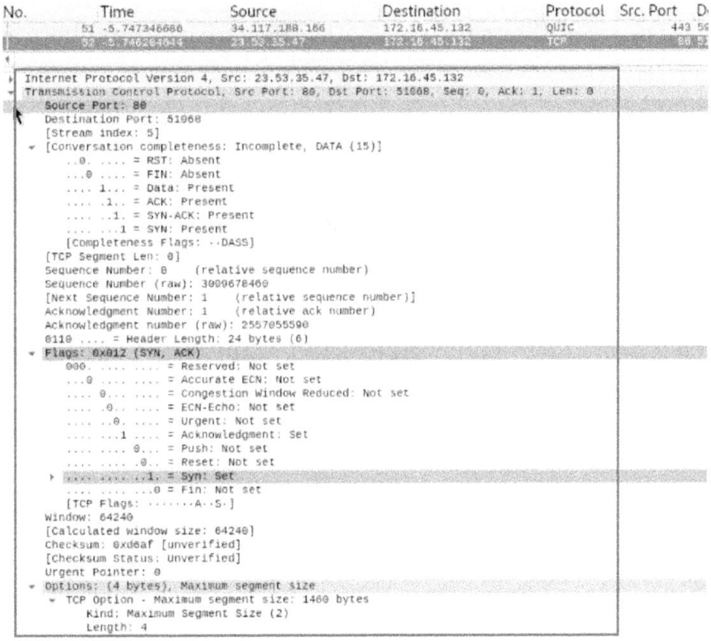

Figure 5.19: *Wireshark Transmission Control Protocol information screen*

If the traffic involves application protocols, you can see additional information. In this case, HTTP and **Online Certificate Status Protocol (OCSP)**, meaning that this connection is validating the revocation status of a X.509 certificate. Refer to the following figure:

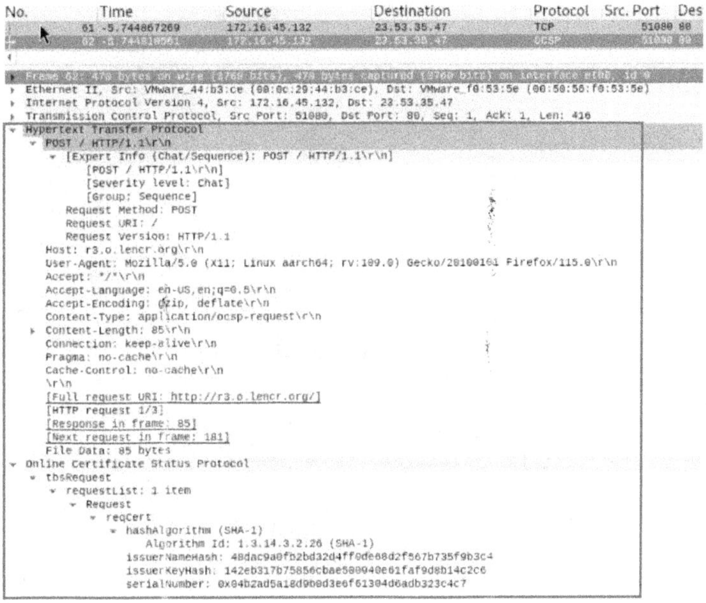

Figure 5.20: *Wireshark Hypertext transfer Protocol information screen*

Filters

There are two main types of filters in Wireshark. They are capture filters and screen filters:

- **Capture filters:** These filters are very useful when we are going to capture live traffic, because they allow us to select beforehand only the traffic of a certain type of protocol (**transfer control protocol (TCP)**, **user datagram protocol (UDP)**, etc.) or if we would, eliminate the DNS traffic, or ignore the traffic of a punctual port, etc. This facilitates the analysis and reduces the amount of information captured, making it more efficient.

To select a capture filter, you need to select: **Capture** | **Capture Filters** menu.

Refer to the following figure:

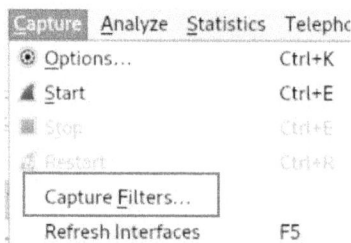

Figure 5.21: Wireshark capture filters option

We are going to receive this screen to select the filter or to create a customized one:

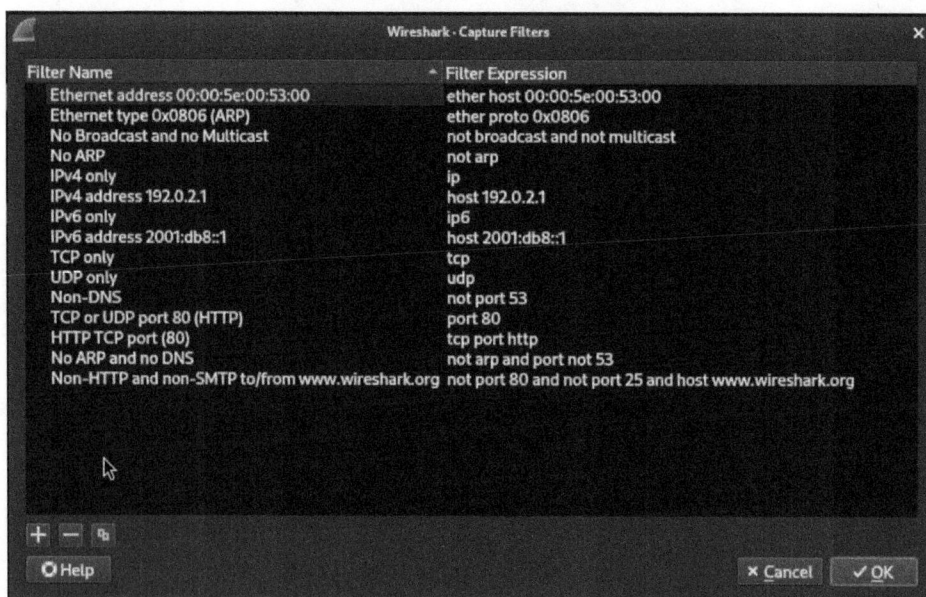

Figure 5.22: Wireshark filters selection screen

- **Display filters:** Once you open a previously captured traffic file such as ***.pcap** or similar or if you make a live capture of traffic, you can apply filters to that traffic to select only the packets of your interest, for example:

  o   Traffic originating from a specific IP

  o   Traffic destined for a specific IP

  o   Traffic generated by a specific protocol

  o   Traffic with a specific flag

  o   And a long, and so on

Building display filter expressions

Here we strongly recommend consulting this URLs : **https://wiki.wireshark.org/ DisplayFilters** and:

https://www.wireshark.org/docs/wsug_html_chunked/ChWorkBuildDisplayFilterSection. html where it is explained in detail how to create display filters in Wireshark. Henceforth we will assume that the reader has visited that link and has tested screen filters in their environment.

For additional information, you can query the **Wireshark Display Filter Reference** containing more than 300.000 possible filters, in this URL: **https://www.wireshark.org/ docs/dfref/**.

The Wireshark tool has many more options and capabilities, and we could dedicate an entire book to them, but to continue with our main topic, we will assume that the reader has a minimum knowledge of the tool.

In the next section we introduce our own methodology of traffic analysis, which consists of a series of steps that allow us to know more in details of the traffic and gives us clues and elements that we can use quickly.

The following illustrates step by step the traffic analysis methodology:

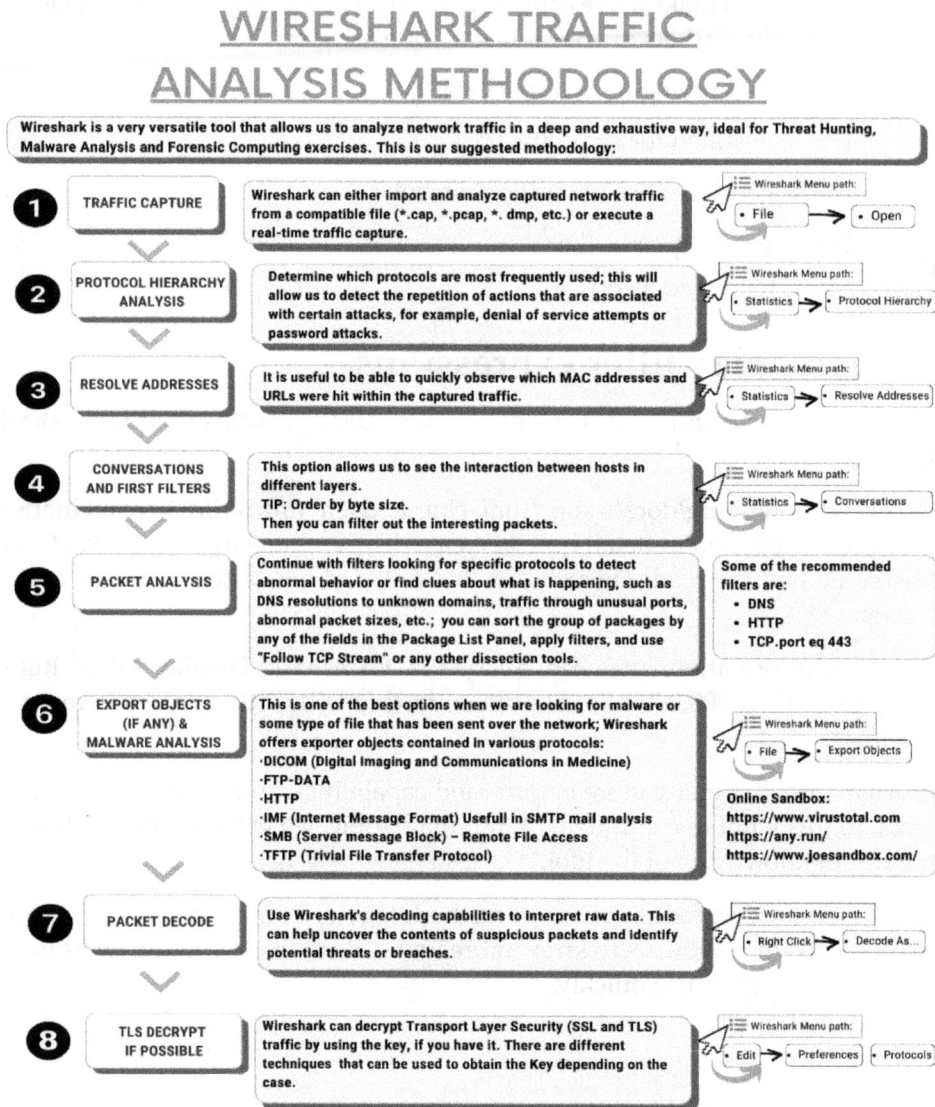

WIRESHARK TRAFFIC ANALYSIS METHODOLOGY

Wireshark is a very versatile tool that allows us to analyze network traffic in a deep and exhaustive way, ideal for Threat Hunting, Malware Analysis and Forensic Computing exercises. This is our suggested methodology:

1 TRAFFIC CAPTURE
Wireshark can either import and analyze captured network traffic from a compatible file (*.cap, *.pcap, *. dmp, etc.) or execute a real-time traffic capture.

Wireshark Menu path:
• File ➔ • Open

2 PROTOCOL HIERARCHY ANALYSIS
Determine which protocols are most frequently used; this will allow us to detect the repetition of actions that are associated with certain attacks, for example, denial of service attempts or password attacks.

Wireshark Menu path:
• Statistics ➔ • Protocol Hierarchy

3 RESOLVE ADDRESSES
It is useful to be able to quickly observe which MAC addresses and URLs were hit within the captured traffic.

Wireshark Menu path:
• Statistics ➔ • Resolve Addresses

4 CONVERSATIONS AND FIRST FILTERS
This option allows us to see the interaction between hosts in different layers.
TIP: Order by byte size.
Then you can filter out the interesting packets.

Wireshark Menu path:
• Statistics ➔ • Conversations

5 PACKET ANALYSIS
Continue with filters looking for specific protocols to detect abnormal behavior or find clues about what is happening, such as DNS resolutions to unknown domains, traffic through unusual ports, abnormal packet sizes, etc.; you can sort the group of packages by any of the fields in the Package List Panel, apply filters, and use "Follow TCP Stream" or any other dissection tools.

Some of the recommended filters are:
• DNS
• HTTP
• TCP.port eq 443

6 EXPORT OBJECTS (IF ANY) & MALWARE ANALYSIS
This is one of the best options when we are looking for malware or some type of file that has been sent over the network; Wireshark offers exporter objects contained in various protocols:
·DICOM (Digital Imaging and Communications in Medicine)
·FTP-DATA
·HTTP
·IMF (Internet Message Format) Usefull in SMTP mail analysis
·SMB (Server message Block) – Remote File Access
·TFTP (Trivial File Transfer Protocol)

Wireshark Menu path:
• File ➔ • Export Objects

Online Sandbox:
https://www.virustotal.com
https://any.run/
https://www.joesandbox.com/

7 PACKET DECODE
Use Wireshark's decoding capabilities to interpret raw data. This can help uncover the contents of suspicious packets and identify potential threats or breaches.

Wireshark Menu path:
• Right Click ➔ • Decode As...

8 TLS DECRYPT IF POSSIBLE
Wireshark can decrypt Transport Layer Security (SSL and TLS) traffic by using the key, if you have it. There are different techniques that can be used to obtain the Key depending on the case.

Wireshark Menu path:
• Edit ➔ • Preferences ➔ • Protocols

Figure 5.23: *Wireshark traffic analysis methodology*

Let us start with a practical example of traffic analysis, using our methodology.

Case 1

Suspected Infection, the malware Latrodectus

> Note: **This is an active malicious sample and can infect your computer if not handled carefully.**

WARNING: **Do not open this file on a non-isolated machine. Use a Linux VM with NAT-only network mode. Malware is live.**

The traffic file for analysis along with other artifacts can be downloaded from: **https://www.malware-traffic-analysis.net/2024/03/07/index.html**

In the following we have explained each step that the analysis methodology follows:

1. **Traffic capture or import compatible traffic captured file:** Wireshark is capable of capturing network traffic in real-time or can import a previously captured traffic file; if you decide to take a real-time capture, remember that the Wireshark must be connected to a SPAN or mirror port of the Switch to receive all the packets on the network.

2. **Protocol hierarchy analysis:** Determine which protocols are most frequently used; this will allow us to detect the repetition of actions that are associated with certain attacks, for example, denial of service attempts or password attacks.

   We will use the option: **Statistics** | **Protocol Hierarchy**. Refer to the following figure:

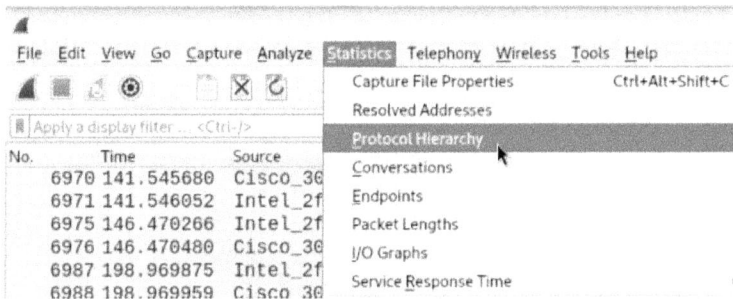

Figure 5.24: Wireshark Protocol Hierarchy option

If you click on **Protocol Hierarchy** option, we receive this detailed information:

Figure 5.25: Wireshark Protocol Hierarchy statistics screen

We can see that most of this traffic is related to TLS (Encrypted Traffic) and is followed by **Simple Service Discovery Protocol (SSDP)** traffic. These two indicators do not tell us much since TLS traffic may be completely normal on the network or could be connected to malicious activity, we do not know yet, so we continue with the next step.

3. **Resolve addresses:** It is useful to be able to quickly observe which MAC addresses and URLs were hit within the captured traffic. We can make filters to look for specific URLs or MACS, but for the filter we would need to know what we are looking for, which does not always happen, so we must go from the general to the particular.

We will use the option: **Statistics | Resolved Addresses**. Refer to the following figure:

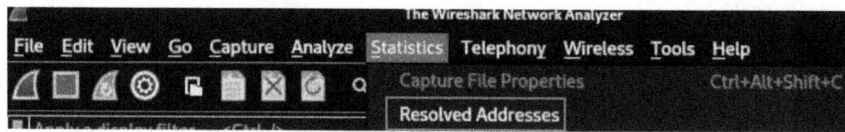

Figure 5.26: *Wireshark Resolved Addresses option*

Figure 5.26 shows the **Resolved Addresses** option available in Wireshark, which allows users to view all the resolved network addresses encountered during packet capture. When this option is selected, Wireshark presents a list of all resolved addresses, as shown in the next figure:

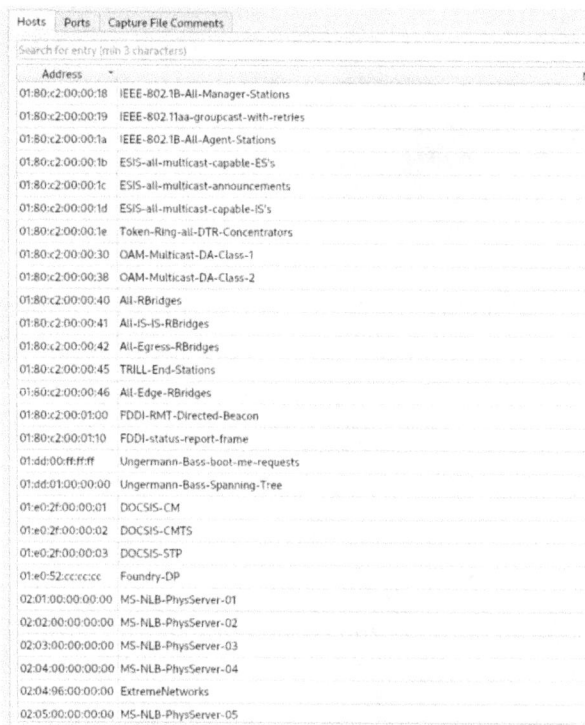

Figure 5.27: *Wireshark Resolved addresses screen*

4. **Conversation analysis:** This is a very useful report that allows us to see very quickly the interaction between hosts in different layers, for example in layer two we can see interactions and broadcasts, and additionally we can see the interactions of IPv4, IPv6, TCP and UDP and then order them by any parameter; my favorite is by byte size. What we are looking for are the interactions with the largest size because they indicate potential file exchange (we can look for malware inside the files), data exfiltration or potential denial of service attempts; we can apply additional filters to these packages.

We will use the option: **Statistics | Conversations**. Refer to the following figure:

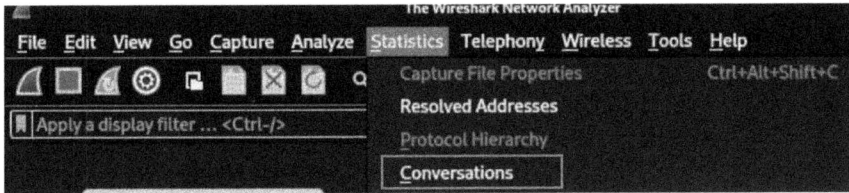

Figure 5.28: Wireshark Conversations option

In the following figure we can see the 6 MB size conversation between the IP; 10.4.9.101 and the 142.250.138.95; that seem interesting to me.

Address A	Port A	Address B	Port B	Packets	Bytes	Packets A →	Bytes A → B	Packets B → A	Bytes B → A	Rel Start	Duration	Bits/s A → B	Bits/s B → A
200.121.1.131	10554	172.16.0.122	80	230	162 k	111	155 k	119	7001	0.000000	135.2297	9217	414
90.162.140.182	21497	172.16.0.122	80	2	1010	0	0	2	1010	1.423515	47.9932	0	168
217.119.117.212	3581	172.16.0.122	80	9	1810	5	943	4	867	3.061139	0.6854	11 k	10 k
87.203.161.150	1666	172.16.0.122	80	10	1364	5	507	5	857	12.253327	0.4937	8215	13 k
41.249.54.225	26773	172.16.0.122	80	20	2288	7	992	13	1296	18.674732	61.2531	129	169
83.29.13.169	2035	172.16.0.122	80	10	1589	6	721	4	868	22.575078	32.5293	177	213
80.54.27.171	12333	172.16.0.122	80	16	3178	9	2206	7	972	26.235145	1.6106	10 k	4827
81.36.38.122	25851	172.16.0.122	80	1	54	0	0	1	54	26.415975	0.0000	–	–
77.125.22.149	1063	172.16.0.122	80	423	377 k	262	367 k	161	9296	26.578456	18.7531	156 k	3965
217.119.117.212	3603	172.16.0.122	80	9	1990	5	1123	4	867	31.647747	0.5684	15 k	12 k
41.232.66.192	60523	172.16.0.122	80	17	1967	9	952	8	1015	33.780133	1.5249	4994	5324
86.158.82.212	4962	172.16.0.122	80	9	1527	5	641	4	886	36.592159	15.3524	334	461
85.18.14.19	14399	172.16.0.122	80	26	11 k	10	6953	16	4129	43.211651	93.4882	594	353
217.119.117.212	3609	172.16.0.122	80	11	3046	6	2125	5	921	44.536196	0.6076	27 k	12 k
80.91.112.106	52995	172.16.0.122	80	10	2595	6	2315	4	280	45.468204	3.3352	5552	671
83.190.80.105	2300	172.16.0.122	80	9	1491	5	623	4	868	52.126180	15.4955	321	448
89.85.51.194	1099	172.16.0.122	80	12	2658	6	1737	6	921	54.758281	0.4205	33 k	17 k
80.90.81.206	2134	172.16.0.122	80	22	9989	11	8762	11	1227	57.683232	12.8947	5436	761
217.119.117.212	3629	172.16.0.122	80	11	2869	6	1936	5	933	58.483801	3.6900	4197	2022
41.250.23.6	45825	172.16.0.122	80	12	3162	7	2195	5	967	72.448185	12.1828	1441	634
217.119.117.212	3641	172.16.0.122	80	9	1926	5	1059	4	867	73.904674	0.6696	12 k	10 k
200.121.1.131	10594	172.16.0.122	80	515	385 k	261	371 k	254	14 k	93.841385	28.8779	102 k	3960
200.72.43.226	62317	172.16.0.122	80	546	429 k	273	409 k	273	20 k	99.866905	29.3974	111 k	5473

Figure 5.29: Wireshark Conversations screen

From this we can filter out this conversation to know more about what is happening:

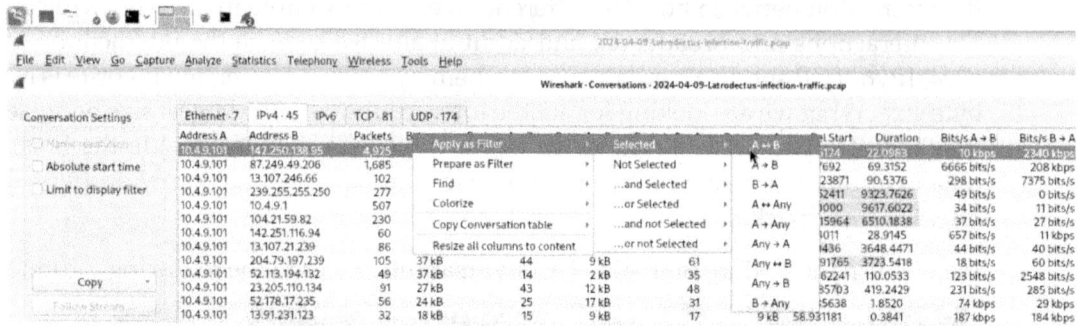

Figure 5.30: Wireshark Conversations screen with filter options

This way we automatically receive in the main panel the filter containing the packages corresponding to the applied selection. As you can see in the filter pane, the automated applied filter was:

ip.addr==10.4.9.101 && ip.addr==142.250.138.95

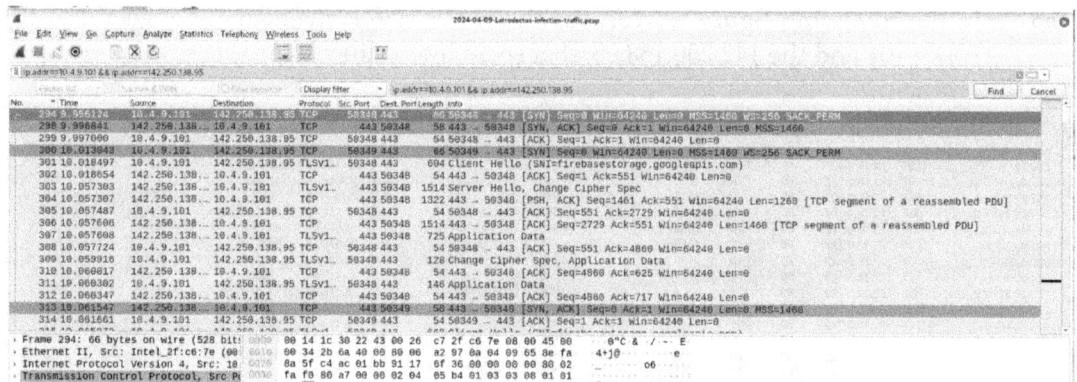

Figure 5.31: Wireshark Conversations screen with filters applied

The actions we see here in order of occurrence are:

a. **Packets 294-299**: We first see the 3-way handshake greeting between the hosts, using port 50348 from the source host 10.4.9.101 (located on a local network) to port 443 of the host 142.250.138.95;

b. **Packet 301 and consecutive**: We see a connection to a Firebase database using TLSv1.3, meaning the connections are encrypted. We can validate the content of the entire transmission with right click over any of the packets, (in this case the 303) and select: **Follow TCP Stream**; this option is great to review the traffic content and we can detect files or specific plain text if the protocols are clear text protocols like HTTP or DNS:

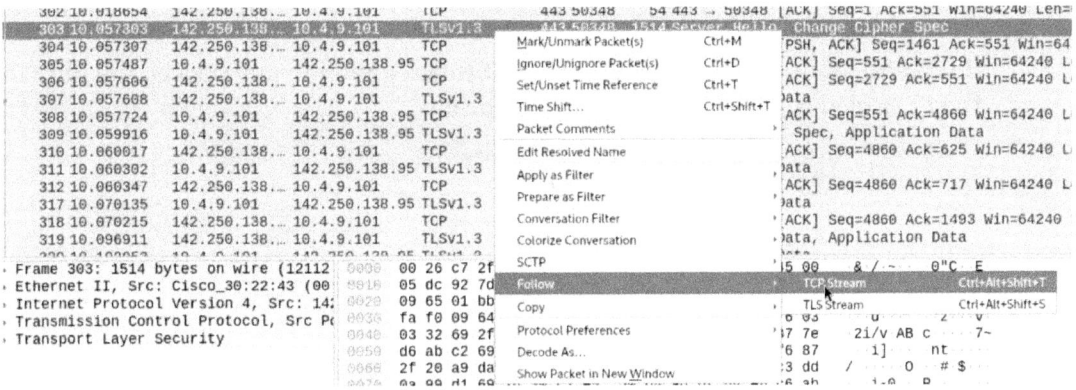

Figure 5.32: Wireshark TCP Stream option

Then we can see the entire content of the stream:

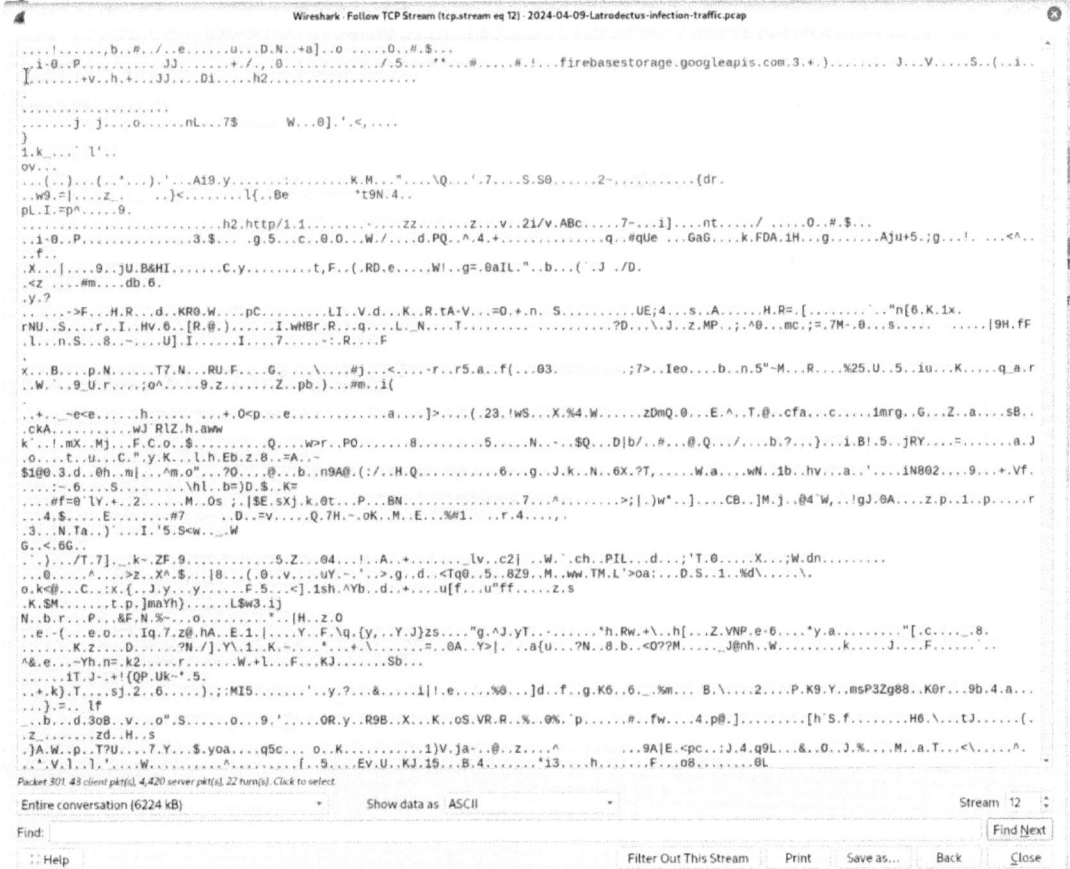

Figure 5.33: Wireshark TCP stream contents

As we can notice this traffic is encrypted.

Be careful; if you apply the **Follow TCP Stream** option to any packet, the filter in the filter filed is going to change automatically.

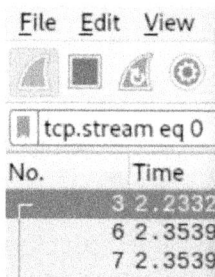

Figure 5.34: Wireshark TCP stream contents to another packet

5. **Packet analysis:** You can continue with the filter pane looking for specific protocols to detect abnormal behavior or find clues about what is happening, such as DNS resolutions to unknown domains, traffic through unusual ports, abnormal packet sizes, etc. For this you can also sort the group of packages by any of the fields in the Package List Panel.

Some of the recommended filters are:

a. DNS

b. HTTP

c. TCP.port eq 443

If you apply the DNS filter, you can see the resolution to different domains in the following figure:

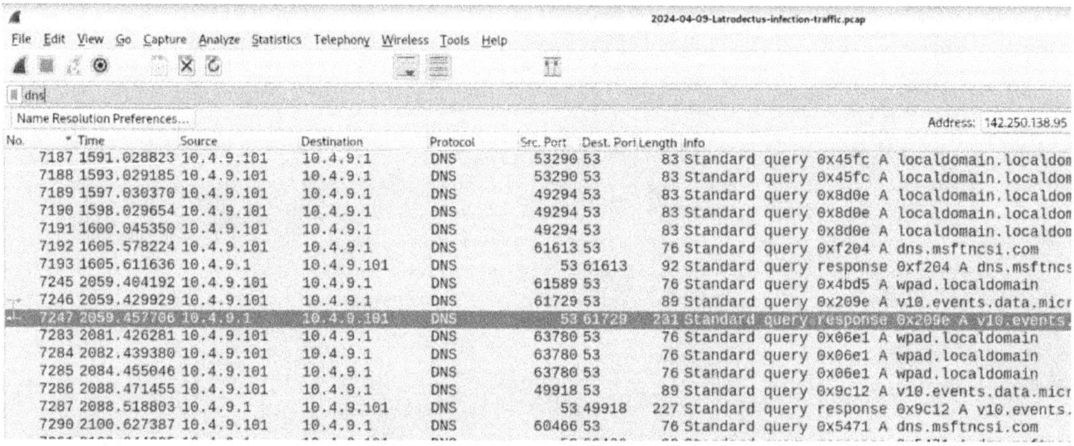

Figure 5.35: Wireshark packet list with DNS filter applied

It is possible that you want to filter out some packets; this is very useful to reduce noise in the data and can be done in this way. Suppose we want to remove from the display all internal resolutions directed to **wpad.localdomain**.

To do this, we will select a package containing this resolution (package 180), right-click and select **Apply as Filter | Not Selected**. Refer to the following figure:

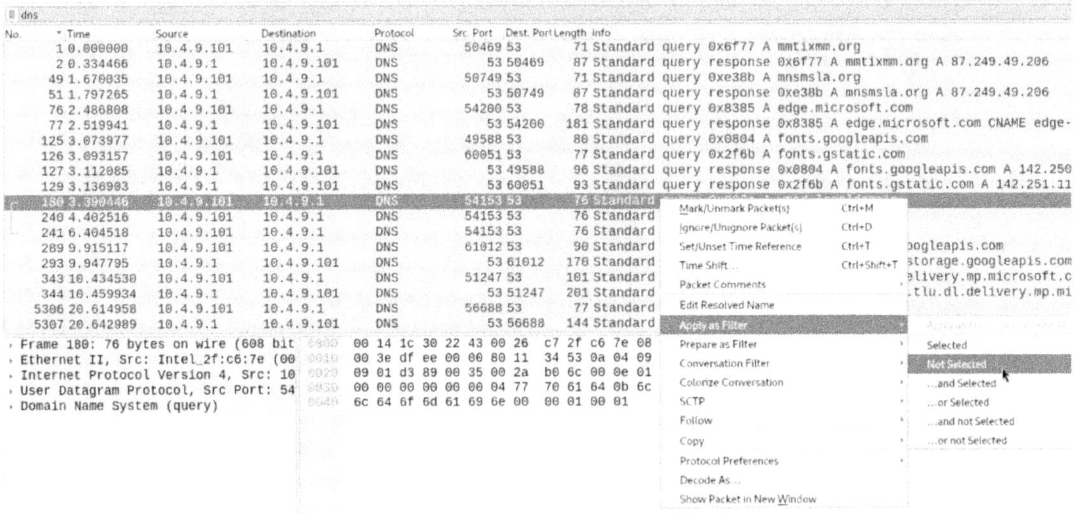

Figure 5.36: Wireshark applies as a filter option

The result will be a list of packets, but without the **wpad.localdomain** packets.

6. **Export objects (artifacts) from the traffic:** This is one of the best options when we are looking for malware or some type of file that has been sent over the network. Wireshark offers exporter objects contained in various protocols:

   a. **Digital Imaging and Communications in Medicine (DICOM)**

   b. FTP-DATA

   c. HTTP

   d. **Internet Message Format (IMF)** useful in SMTP mail analysis

   e. **Server message Block (SMB)** – Remote File Access

   f. **Trivial File Transfer Protocol (TFTP)**

In the traffic we are analyzing right now, we can export HTTP objects:

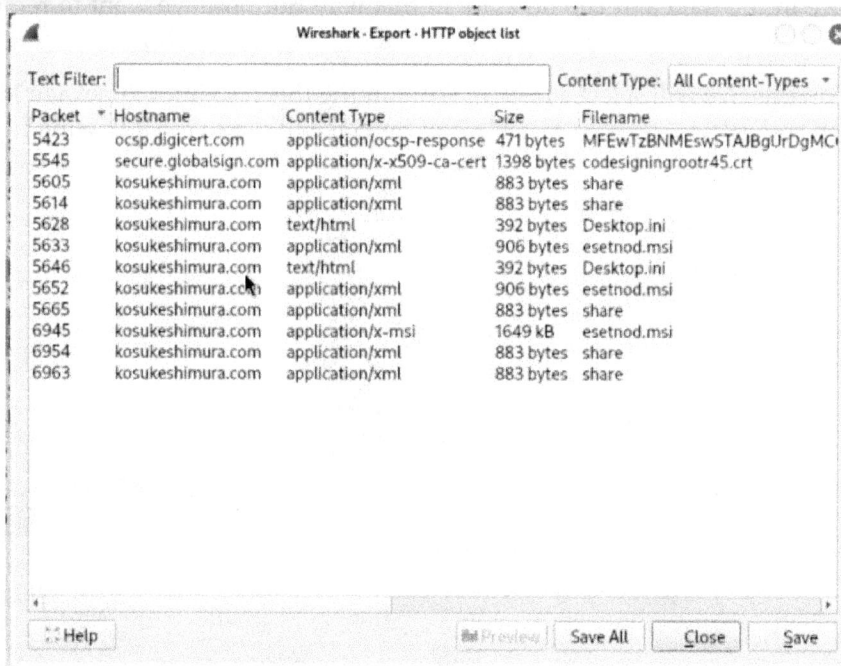

Figure 5.37: Wireshark HTTP object list

We can see that most of the objects come from the *kosukeshimura.com* domain. Several of these objects are very interesting since they are applications, for example, esetnod.msi. The **msi** extension is used by installers on the Windows operating system. The recommendation will be to download all the objects and examine them in detail in sandbox; for this we select the **Save All** option.

Now we have the different files from the traffic sample, refer to the following figure:

Figure 5.38: Files from the traffic sample

We can use an online sandbox to be able to quickly analyze artifacts; in *Chapter 8, Malware Analysis and Reverse Engineering* we will go into the detail of malware analysis, but for now, let us use VirusTotal, (**https://www.virustotal.com/**) one of the most well-known online sandboxes to analyze artifacts. We will find that the file:

esetnod(2).msi contains the **icedid** trojan malware.

The hash SHA256 of the file is:

08075e8a6dcc6a5fca089348edbd5fc07b2b0b26a26a46e0dd401121fdaa88d3

a5fca089348edbd5fc07b2b0b26a26a46e0dd401121fdaa88d3

Figure 5.39: VirusTotal hash SHA256 file report

In VirusTotal we can review the details pane to obtain more information about the artifact:

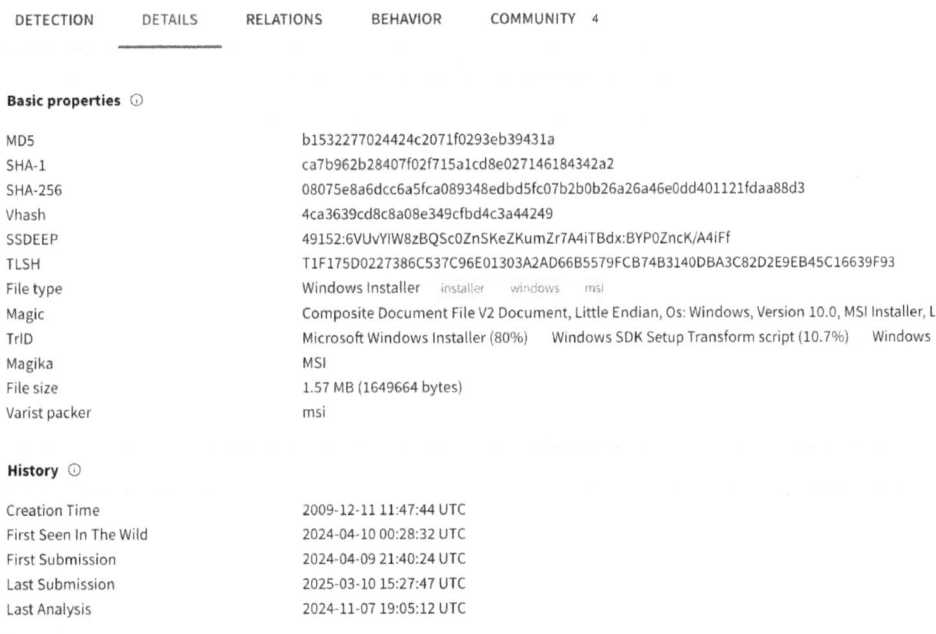

Figure 5.40: VirusTotal hash SHA256 artifact detail pane

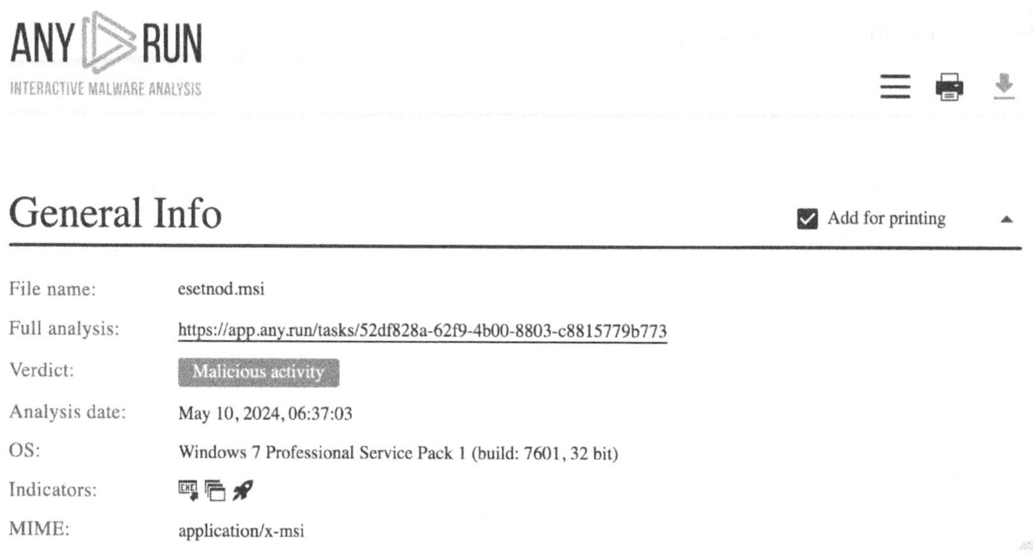

Figure 5.41: *AnyRun report*

Curiously, it is the only result related to this hash:

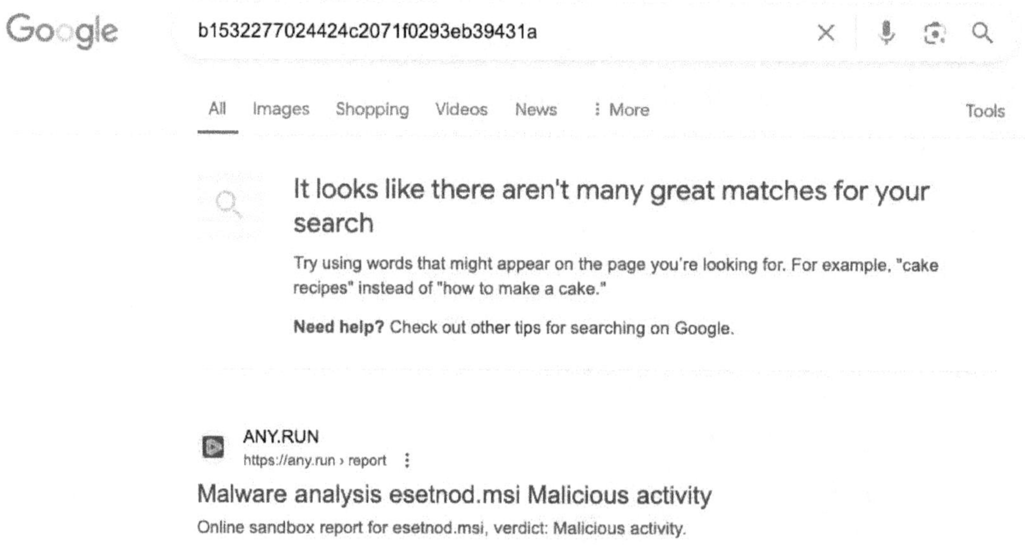

Figure 5.42: *Malicious Hash Google search result*

This forms the perspective of the book that it is very useful because we are doing this exercise with a little-known sample, which allows us to carry out the workshop in a completely realistic way, just like the cases that you are going to face in your day to day.

The next pane in VirusTotal relations, is even more useful for the topic of this chapter because it confirms data that we already had and provides us with context, such as some of the malicious IPs that are contacted by this malware; with these IPs we can begin the next step of our methodology: contrasting data and looking for relationships.

In the figure of the Wireshark traffic analysis methodology, (*Figure 5.23*) we can see that the last steps are:

1. Packet Decode

2. TLS Decryption if possible

These last steps do not always have to be applied and are executed depending on the type of traffic and the needs of the investigation.

We can then continue with the next phase of **traffic analysis** to perform threat hunting, which would be contrasting data and looking for relationships.

In the relations pane from VirusTotal, we have new information:

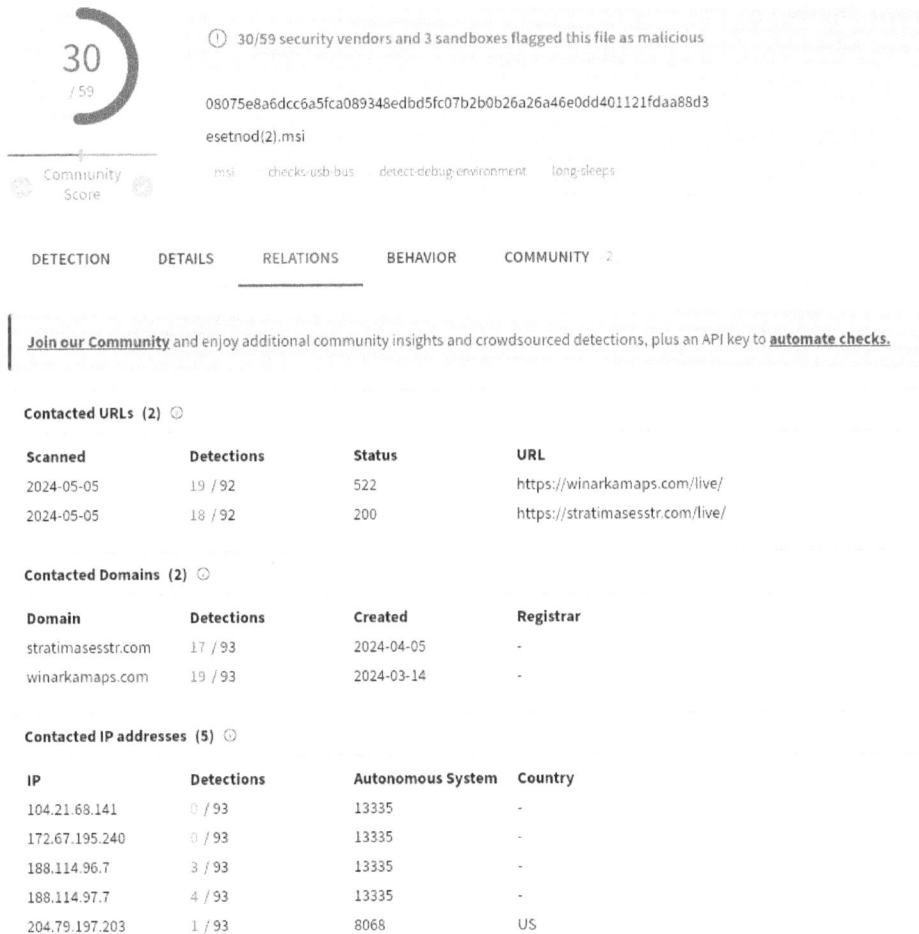

30 / 59

ⓘ 30/59 security vendors and 3 sandboxes flagged this file as malicious

08075e8a6dcc6a5fca089348edbd5fc07b2b0b26a26a46e0dd401121fdaa88d3

esetnod(2).msi

Community Score

msi   checks-usb-bus   detect-debug-environment   long-sleeps

DETECTION   DETAILS   RELATIONS   BEHAVIOR   COMMUNITY 2

Join our Community and enjoy additional community insights and crowdsourced detections, plus an API key to automate checks.

Contacted URLs (2) ◌

Scanned	Detections	Status	URL
2024-05-05	19 / 92	522	https://winarkamaps.com/live/
2024-05-05	18 / 92	200	https://stratimasesstr.com/live/

Contacted Domains (2) ◌

Domain	Detections	Created	Registrar
stratimasesstr.com	17 / 93	2024-04-05	-
winarkamaps.com	19 / 93	2024-03-14	-

Contacted IP addresses (5) ◌

IP	Detections	Autonomous System	Country
104.21.68.141	0 / 93	13335	-
172.67.195.240	0 / 93	13335	-
188.114.96.7	3 / 93	13335	-
188.114.97.7	4 / 93	13335	-
204.79.197.203	1 / 93	8068	US

Figure 5.43: VirusTotal information pane

You can look for the IP addresses that the malware tries to contact within the traffic we are analyzing on Wireshark; for this, we can apply simple filters such as **ip.addr==104.21.68.141**.

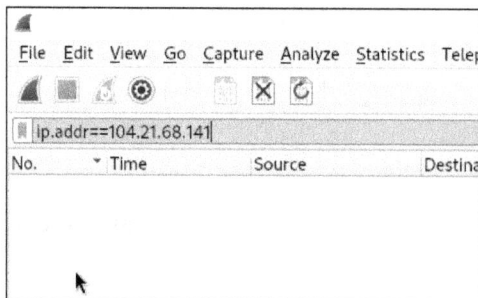

Figure 5.44: Malware contact filter

Unfortunately, none of the IPs appear in the traffic, but we know that the malicious artifact was inside, so we can contrast the malware's contact IP list with the list of IPs existing in our traffic. We can do this very easily with one of Wireshark's tools: Endpoints, which even allows us to export the IP list in CSV, YAML or JSON format.

This menu can be accessed at **Statistics | Endpoints**. Refer to the following figure:

Figure 5.45: Wireshark Endpoints screen

The list of IPs is relatively short, and we can manually check, for example, the first IP that the malware tries to contact: 104.21.68.141, and if we check the list, we find a couple of IPs in a close range:

87.249.49.206	1,685	2 MB	1,409	2 MB	276	58 kB
104.18.21.226	12	3 kB	6	2 kB	6	487 bytes
104.21.37.64	74	16 kB	37	10 kB	37	5 kB
104.21.59.82	230	53 kB	111	22 kB	119	31 kB
104.91.175.23	14	2 kB	7	916 bytes	7	924 bytes

Figure 5.46: Malware´s contacted IP´s

We can then review the packets related to those IPs, to try to understand what protocol is being used and the context of the connection; to do this we right-click on the IP, select **Apply as Filter** | **Selected**. Refer to the following figure:

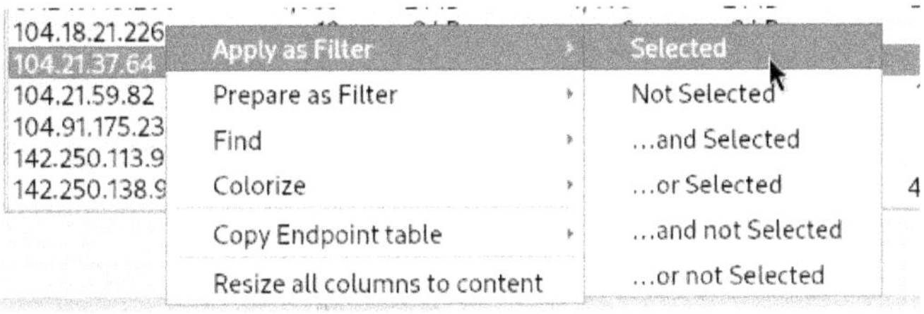

Figure 5.47: *Malware´s contacted IP´s apply as filter option*

In the packet list panel, we will find a 3-way handshake using port 443 against that IP address:

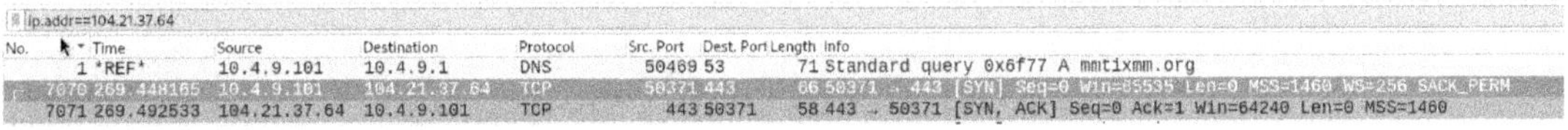

Figure 5.48: *3-way handshake using port 443*

By doing the traceability of the packet with right click and Follow TCP Stream, we get a domain that VirusTotal had mentioned to us, **winarkmaps.com** as we can observe in the following figure:

Figure 5.49: *Malicious Domain found in VirusTotal*

If we look up that domain on Google, we will find that this domain is detected as malicious in multiple services as shown in the following figure:

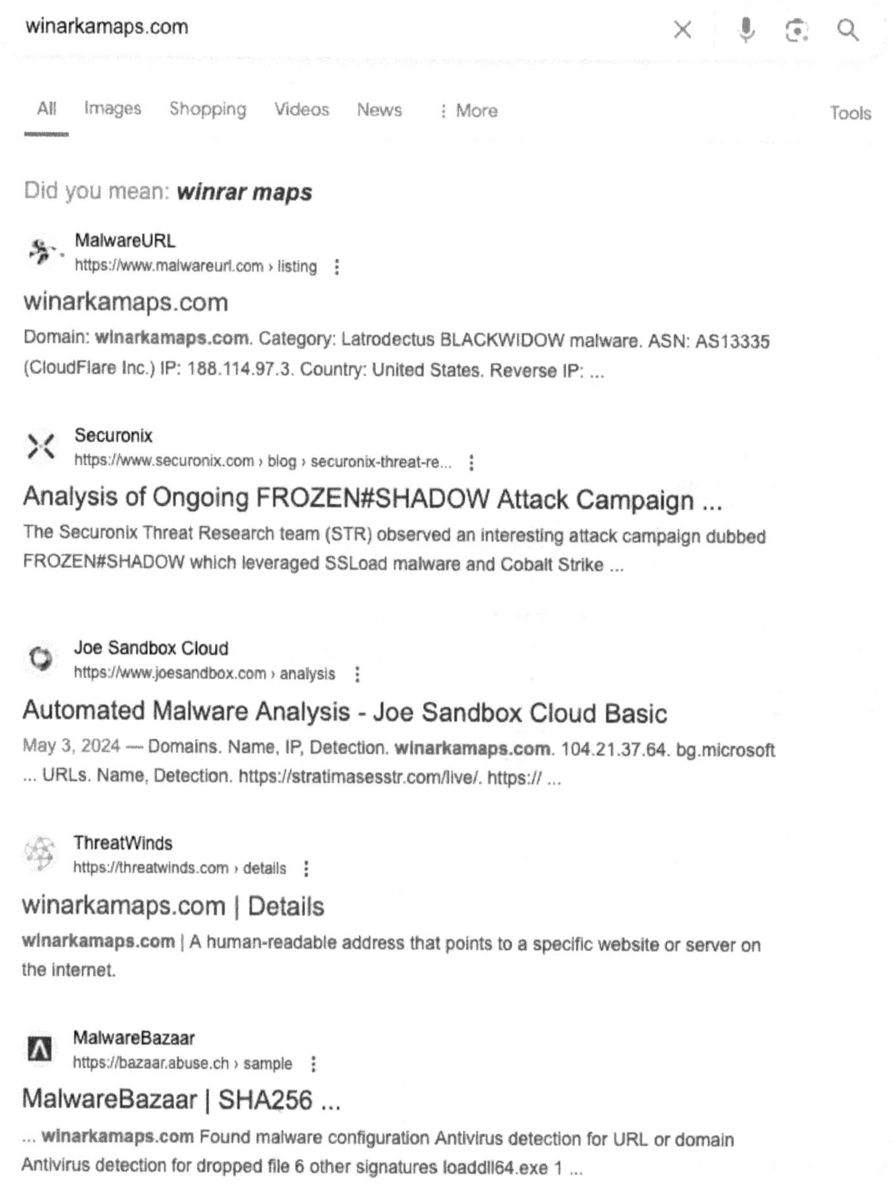

winarkamaps.com

　　×　🎤　📷　🔍

All　Images　Shopping　Videos　News　⋮ More　　　　Tools

Did you mean: **winrar maps**

MalwareURL
https://www.malwareurl.com › listing　⋮

winarkamaps.com

Domain: **winarkamaps.com**. Category: Latrodectus BLACKWIDOW malware. ASN: AS13335 (CloudFlare Inc.) IP: 188.114.97.3. Country: United States. Reverse IP: ...

Securonix
https://www.securonix.com › blog › securonix-threat-re...　⋮

Analysis of Ongoing FROZEN#SHADOW Attack Campaign ...

The Securonix Threat Research team (STR) observed an interesting attack campaign dubbed FROZEN#SHADOW which leveraged SSLoad malware and Cobalt Strike ...

Joe Sandbox Cloud
https://www.joesandbox.com › analysis　⋮

Automated Malware Analysis - Joe Sandbox Cloud Basic

May 3, 2024 — Domains. Name, IP, Detection. **winarkamaps.com**. 104.21.37.64. bg.microsoft ... URLs. Name, Detection. https://stratimasesstr.com/live/. https:// ...

ThreatWinds
https://threatwinds.com › details　⋮

winarkamaps.com | Details

winarkamaps.com | A human-readable address that points to a specific website or server on the internet.

MalwareBazaar
https://bazaar.abuse.ch › sample　⋮

MalwareBazaar | SHA256 ...

... **winarkamaps.com** Found malware configuration Antivirus detection for URL or domain Antivirus detection for dropped file 6 other signatures loaddll64.exe 1 ...

Figure 5.50: Malicious Domain Google Search

For example, we can review the **https://www.malwareurl.com** report, confirming that it is a URL related to the Latrodectus BLACKWIDOW malware, which is a variant of icedid as shown in the figure:

Entry matching **winarkamaps.com** was found in our database.

15512 other active domains were found on 77086 IP(s) for AS13335 (CLOUDFLARENET)

Show the report for AS13335 (CLOUDFLARENET)

MalwareURL Domain Reputation Report

Domain: winarkamaps.com

Category: Latrodectus BLACKWIDOW malware

ASN: AS13335 (CloudFlare Inc.)
IP: 188.114.97.3
Country: United States
Reverse IP:

Figure 5.51: Malwareurl report

If we apply a similar process of analysis to the traffic related to the next IP in the list of our traffic near the IP as 104.21.68.141, we find that we have in the traffic the IP as **104.21.59.82**.

87.249.49.206	1,685
104.18.21.226	12
104.21.37.64	74
104.21.59.82	230
104.91.175.23	14
142.250.113.95	33

Figure 5.52: Traffic IP analysis

Following the same steps as above, we find the domain **grizmotras.com** in the stream, which is not mentioned in the VirusTotal analysis, but which we can then consult on Google. In the follow stream option in Wireshark we can observe this domain:

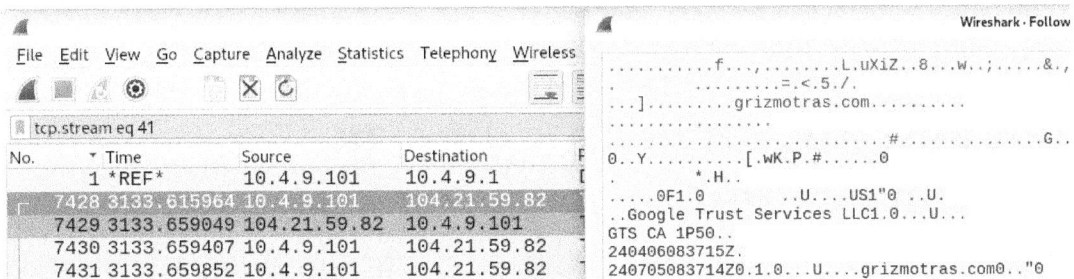

Figure 5.53: grizmotras.com details in Wireshark

Google search results in very good data for our hunt as shown in the figure:

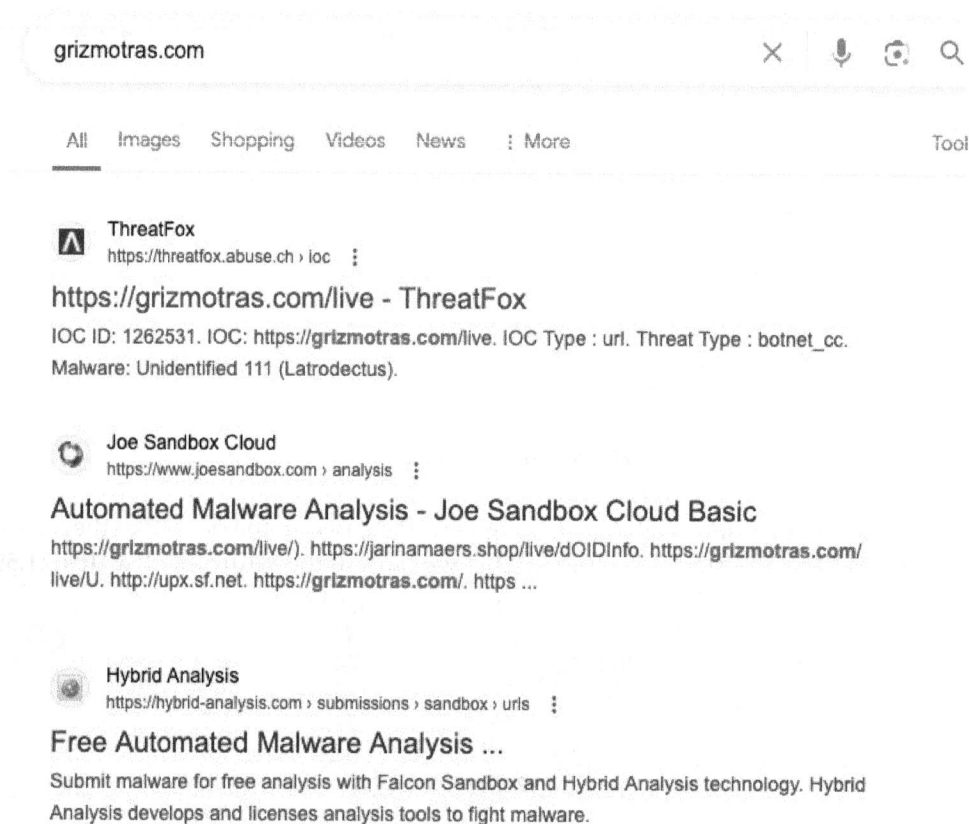

grizmotras.com   ✕   🎤   📷   🔍

All   Images   Shopping   Videos   News   ⋮ More   Tool

ThreatFox
https://threatfox.abuse.ch › ioc ⋮

https://grizmotras.com/live - ThreatFox

IOC ID: 1262531. IOC: https://**grizmotras.com**/live. IOC Type : url. Threat Type : botnet_cc.
Malware: Unidentified 111 (Latrodectus).

Joe Sandbox Cloud
https://www.joesandbox.com › analysis ⋮

Automated Malware Analysis - Joe Sandbox Cloud Basic

https://**grizmotras.com**/live/). https://jarinamaers.shop/live/dOIDInfo. https://**grizmotras.com**/
live/U. http://upx.sf.net. https://**grizmotras.com**/. https ...

Hybrid Analysis
https://hybrid-analysis.com › submissions › sandbox › urls ⋮

Free Automated Malware Analysis ...

Submit malware for free analysis with Falcon Sandbox and Hybrid Analysis technology. Hybrid
Analysis develops and licenses analysis tools to fight malware.

Figure 5.54: grizmotras.com Google Search

If we review the first result of **https://threatfox.abuse.ch**, we can find IoCs that we can apply along with all the previous IoCs found to our security and monitoring tools, and that exactly takes us to the last part of the analysis.

IoC and IoA communication and implementation

Once we have performed the traffic analysis we can compare our results with lists of **Indictors of Compromise (IoC)** or **Indicators of Attack (IoA)** in order to have a clearer idea of what is happening and once confirmed, with all the data collected so far, we can deliver the information to the appropriate areas of the entity so that they can update the IoCs and IoA in the monitoring, detection and security mechanisms so that if any of the indicators are presented, they are quickly detected and neutralized.

Here we have an example related to the case we are evaluating:

https://threatfox.abuse.ch/ioc/1262531/ as we can see in the following figure:

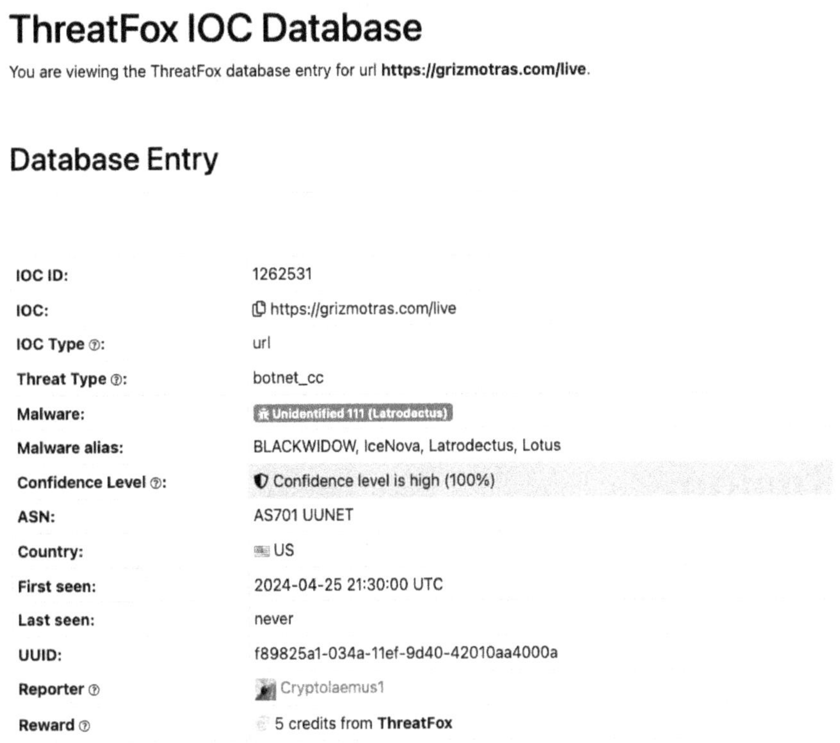

ThreatFox IOC Database

You are viewing the ThreatFox database entry for url **https://grizmotras.com/live**.

Database Entry

IOC ID:	1262531
IOC:	◨ https://grizmotras.com/live
IOC Type ⑦:	url
Threat Type ⑦:	botnet_cc
Malware:	🕷 Unidentified 111 (Latrodectus)
Malware alias:	BLACKWIDOW, IceNova, Latrodectus, Lotus
Confidence Level ⑦:	🛡 Confidence level is high (100%)
ASN:	AS701 UUNET
Country:	🇺🇸 US
First seen:	2024-04-25 21:30:00 UTC
Last seen:	never
UUID:	f89825a1-034a-11ef-9d40-42010aa4000a
Reporter ⑦	🐾 Cryptolaemus1
Reward ⑦	5 credits from **ThreatFox**

Figure 5.55: grizmotras.com threatfox details

Here is a resume of a post-analysis of the IoC:

Indicator type	Value	Source
File Hash (SHA256)	08075e8a6dcc6a5fc...	Virus Total
Domain	winarkmaps.com	Traffic Stream
IP Address	104.21.59.82	Wireshark Export
Filename	esetnod.msi	HTTP Export

Table 5.7: Post-analysis of IoC

In this chapter, we carry out traffic analysis using Wireshark as a primary tool, but there are many other alternatives that have similar functionalities. Following is a list of interesting alternatives:

Tool	Description	URL
Tshark	Command-Line Network Protocol Analyzer version of Wireshark	**https://www.wireshark.org/docs/man-pages/tshark.html**
TCPDump	Command-Line Packet Analyzer	**https://www.tcpdump.org/**
Ngrep	Network Packet Analyzer	**https://github.com/jpr5/ngrep**
Sniffnet	Network Monitoring tool	**https://sniffnet.net/**
NetworkMiner	Network Forensics Tool	**https://www.netresec.com/?page=Network-Miner**

Table 5.8: Wireshark Alternatives

Use Wireshark for protocol learning; use TShark for automation; use NetworkMiner for forensic review.

Conclusion

In this chapter we discussed in detail the operation of data networks, their different models, we understood the operation of different protocols and we discussed traffic analysis where we understood that any type of interaction through a data network will leave evidence that will not allow with the correct analysis to understand what is happening, extract artifacts and be able to evaluate those artifacts to determine if they are related to malicious activity.

We take advantage of a traffic analysis methodology through a specific tool to determine if there is abnormal behavior within a traffic sample. In this methodology, we follow the recommended steps to find evidence connected to IoC or IoA that allows us to establish that there is a threat in the corporate infrastructure.

From this case, we also learned that traffic analysis is a powerful technique not just for detection but also for understanding how threats operate on the network level. The patterns and artifacts we identified could be translated into SIEM rules or alert logic to improve threat detection in real-time. Furthermore, these insights could be used to develop custom detection scripts or signatures in tools like Suricata or Zeek, allowing for automated recognition of similar malicious behavior in future network traffic.

In the next chapter, we explore the operating system analysis, how to hunt threats in Microsoft Windows, in Linux OS, fundamentals of Operating Systems Security and Incident Response.

Points to remember

1. To capture network traffic, there are several mechanisms, but the most used and recommended in the field of threat hunting are: Tap and Port Mirror or Span Port on a Switch.

2. It is essential to understand the operation and mechanics of data transmission in a network to analyze traffic behavior.

3. It is recommended to follow the traffic analysis methodology to optimize threat hunting processes.

Multiple choice questions

1. **What is a common method used by threat hunters to detect harmful network activity?**

    a. Manual inspection of each packet

    b. Random sampling of network traffic

    c. Analyzing network traffic patterns

    d. Ignoring encrypted traffic

2. **Which protocol is most used for secure network communications, and is therefore important in network traffic analysis for threat hunting?**

    a. HTTP

    b. FTP

    c. DNS

    d. TLS

3. **What is a potential indicator of compromise (IoC) in network traffic analysis?**

    a. Regular data transfers during business hours

    b. Outgoing traffic to trusted domains

    c. High volume of data transfers at unusual times

    d. Incoming traffic from local IP addresses

4. **What tool is commonly used for real-time network traffic analysis and threat hunting?**

    a. Wireshark

    b. Microsoft Excel

    c. Notepad++

    d. Google Docs

5. **In the context of network traffic analysis for threat hunting, why is it important to understand the baseline of normal network behavior?**

   a. To make the job more challenging

   b. To identify deviations that could indicate a cyber threat

   c. Because it is a requirement for all IT jobs

   d. To ensure all data transfers are encrypted

Answers

1. c.

2. d.

3. c.

4. a.

5. b.

References

1. **OSI model: https://www.iso.org/obp/ui/#iso:std:iso-iec:7498:-1:ed-1:v2:en**

2. **TCP/IP model: https://web.eecs.umich.edu/~prabal/teaching/eecs582-w13/readings/CK74.pdf**

3. **TCP protocol: https://en.wikipedia.org/wiki/Transmission_Control_Protocol**

4. **Wireshark users guide: https://www.wireshark.org/docs/wsug_html_chunked/**

5. **Traffic samples: https://wiki.wireshark.org/SampleCaptures**

6. **Malicious traffic samples: https://www.malware-traffic-analysis.net/**

7. **IoC database: https://threatfox.abuse.ch/browse/**

Join our Discord space

Join our Discord workspace for latest updates, offers, tech happenings around the world, new releases, and sessions with the authors:

https://discord.bpbonline.com

CHAPTER 6
Operating Systems Analysis

Introduction

Operating systems are the fundamental basis of our interactions with the information systems; Within them we implement websites, databases, VPNs, artificial intelligence systems, etc. Given the above, it is critical to be able to quickly diagnose if there is any type of alteration or modification in the functions of the operating systems that could indicate a materialized attack and therefore a compromise of the machine and the information it contains.

In this chapter we will study the main areas of the Microsoft Windows and Linux operating systems, analyze various aspects used by attackers to compromise these operating systems, and explore the spaces where they are most frequently compromised.

Structure

In this chapter, we will discuss the following topics:

- Laboratory recommendations
- Microsoft Windows Operation
- Microsoft Windows Security fundamentals
- Linux operation
- Linux security fundamentals

- Endpoint Detection and Response tools
- Hunting for endpoint-based threats
- Incident response on endpoints

Objectives

Knowing where to look for potential compromises and alterations in an operating system is one of the most critical knowledge that a threat hunter must have. This chapter aims to familiarize the reader with the key aspects of the sensitive areas of the O.S. and to understand how adversaries act, to compromise their functioning. In this space, we will discuss malicious techniques and tools used by the attackers. In the same way, we will explore mechanisms that we can use to detect compromises.

Laboratory recommendations

This chapter contains references to several tools that the reader can try for themselves; for this we recommend having a small laboratory environment where they can carry out tests and follow the common thread of the different concepts explained here.

You can create your own lab using desktop virtualization tools such as:

- **VMware workstation:**

  https://www.vmware.com/products/desktop-hypervisor/workstation-and-fusion
- **Virtual box:**

  https://www.virtualbox.org/

  You can download Microsoft server or workstation operating systems from these links:
- **Windows 11 virtual machines:**

  https://developer.microsoft.com/en-us/windows/downloads/virtual-machines/
- **Download Windows Server 2022 ISO:**

  https://info.microsoft.com/ww-landing-windows-server-2022.html
- **Linux Server and Workstation Virtual machines repository:**

  https://www.osboxes.org/

Microsoft Windows Operation

The Microsoft Operating System is present in workstations, on-premises servers, and cloud infrastructure. Following are some examples of the different versions available:

Operating System	Function
Windows Server 2025	Server
Windows Server 2022	Server
Windows Server 2019	Server
Windows Server 2016	Server
Windows 11 Pro	Workstation
Windows 10 Pro	Workstation
Azure Windows Virtual Desktop	Cloud

Table 6.1: Microsoft operating systems

The Microsoft Operating System is monolithic in its kernel and uses MS-DOS as a foundation. The operating system structure consists of several main components:

Component	Definition
Kernel	This is the core of Windows and is responsible for managing resources, for example, RAM, Processing, etc. In turn, it controls critical aspects such as security, communications, and the file system.
	Kernel oversees process management, handling the execution of applications and processes, ensuring they run appropriately without interference.
File System	The file system is the architecture through which data is organized and stored so that it can then be accessed. Microsoft Windows uses **New Technology File System** (**NTFS**).
Device Drivers	These are software components created to allow interaction with the machine's hardware, such as USB ports, HDMI ports, hard drives, etc.
User Interface	The graphical user interface, known as GUI, is one of the most representative elements of Microsoft Windows; it is the mechanism by which the user interacts with the computer directly and is composed of icons, toolbars, windows, cursor, etc.

Table 6.2: Microsoft operating system structure

When dealing with Microsoft Windows Server systems, there are components that are an essential part of their operation. Among others, we may include the following:

- **Server manager:** Windows Server includes Server Manager, a tool that helps administrators manage roles and features that are installed on servers. This includes managing multiple roles like DNS, DHCP, file services, and more.

- **Active Directory:** One of the most crucial components in Windows Server environments, **Active Directory** (**AD**) is used for user and resource management across a network. It allows for domain services, managing user data, security settings, and resource allocation.

Hyper-V: This is a hypervisor built into Windows Server, allowing administrators to create and manage virtual machines. This is crucial for consolidating server hardware and for testing environments.

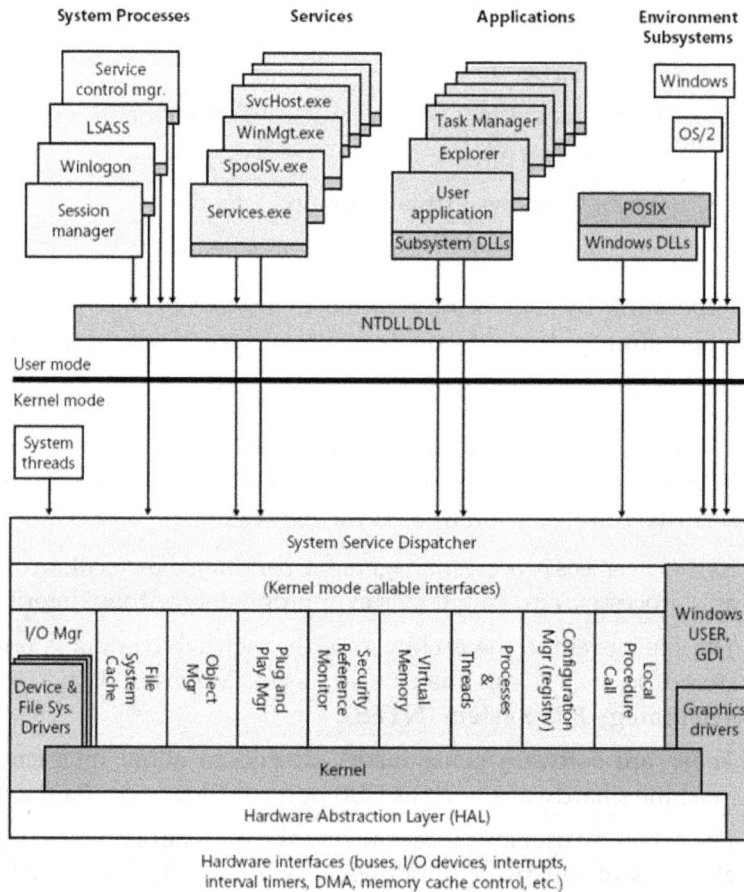

Figure 6.1: *Windows Server hypervisor*
(Source: https://learn.microsoft.com/en-us/windows-hardware/drivers/kernel/overview-of-windows-components)

Microsoft Windows comes with some useful tools to verify and, in some cases, repair problems in the operating system, protected system files, which are commonly targeted by adversaries. One of these tools is the **system file checker (SFC)**, you can visit the following source for a better understanding:

- **System file checker (SFC): https://support.microsoft.com/en-us/topic/use-the-system-file-checker-tool-to-repair-missing-or-corrupted-system-files-79aa86cb-ca52-166a-92a3-966e85d4094e**

You can use the tool sfc with the parameter **/VERIFYONLY** to verify the protected files without executing any repair, so the evidence is going to be untampered in case a protected file has issues. The following figure illustrates the output of the SFC tool when executed with the **/VERIFYONLY** parameter.

```
C:\Windows\System32>sfc /VERIFYONLY

Beginning system scan.  This process will take some time.

Beginning verification phase of system scan.
Verification 100% complete.

Windows Resource Protection did not find any integrity violations.

C:\Windows\System32>
```

Figure 6.2*: SFC with the parameter /VERIFYONLY executed.*

- **File Signature Verification (Sigverif):** This tool allows you to validate digital signatures in critical files, which allows you to easily detect alterations or changes. In the following figure you will see the tool in command line:

```
C:\Windows\System32>sigverif
```

Figure 6.3: *SFC with the parameter Sigverif*

Once a sigverif scan is executed, a window is presented. The next figure shows the verification window:

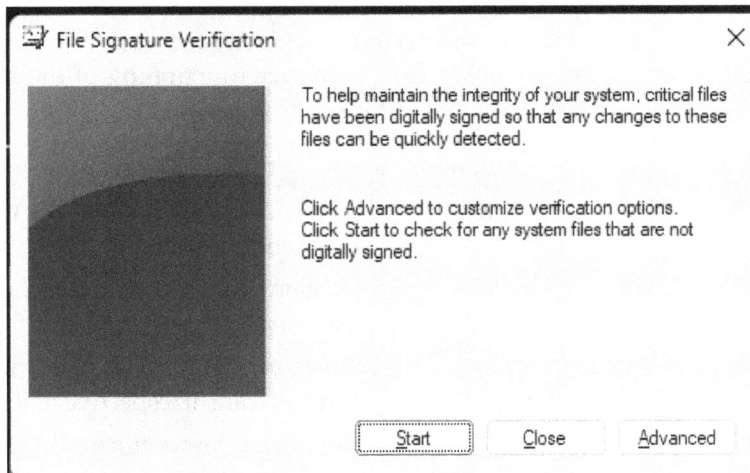

Figure 6.4: *Parameter Sigverif verification*

The following figure shows the results log example:

```
SIGVERIF - Notepad
File  Edit  Format  View  Help
********************************

Microsoft Signature Verification

Log file generated on 6/26/2024 at 8:37 AM
OS Platform:  Windows (x64), Version:  10.0, Build: 17763, CSDVersion:
Scan Results:  Total Files: 104, Signed: 104, Unsigned: 0, Not Scanned: 0

File                    Modified      Version      Status          Catalog                Signed By
----------------        --------      --------     --------        --------               ---------
[c:\windows\system32]
sysfxui.dll             9/15/2018     2:10.0       Signed          Microsoft-Windows-DeMicrosoft Windows
vm3dc003.dll            2/6/2024      9.17.7.2     Signed          vm3d.cat               Microsoft Windows Hardware Compatibility Publisher
vm3ddevapi64.dll        2/6/2024      9.17.7.2     Signed          vm3d.cat               Microsoft Windows Hardware Compatibility Publisher
vm3ddevapi64-debug.d    2/6/2024      9.17.7.2     Signed          vm3d.cat               Microsoft Windows Hardware Compatibility Publisher
vm3ddevapi64-release    2/6/2024      9.17.7.2     Signed          vm3d.cat               Microsoft Windows Hardware Compatibility Publisher
vm3ddevapi64-stats.d    2/6/2024      9.17.7.2     Signed          vm3d.cat               Microsoft Windows Hardware Compatibility Publisher
vm3dgl64.dll            2/6/2024      3.5.3.0      Signed          vm3d.cat               Microsoft Windows Hardware Compatibility Publisher
vm3dglhelper64.dll      2/6/2024      9.17.7.2     Signed          vm3d.cat               Microsoft Windows Hardware Compatibility Publisher
vm3dservice.exe         2/6/2024      9.17.7.2     Signed          vm3d.cat               Microsoft Windows Hardware Compatibility Publisher
vm3dum64.dll            2/6/2024      9.17.7.2     Signed          vm3d.cat               Microsoft Windows Hardware Compatibility Publisher
vm3dum64_10.dll         2/6/2024      9.17.7.2     Signed          vm3d.cat               Microsoft Windows Hardware Compatibility Publisher
```

Figure 6.5: Microsoft signature verification log

Windows Registry

The registry is a hierarchical database that stores configuration data of the operating system and installed applications that require configuring certain parameters that must be stored in the registry database. We can think about it like the backbone of the Windows operating system. The ability to modify registry parameters is one of the objectives pursued by cybercriminals.

The Windows Registry is organized into a tree structure, like a file system, with keys and values instead of folders and files. The structure of the registry and its components are explained in the following:

- **Hives:** These are the main divisions of the registry, and each one contains specific information and data, necessary for the proper functioning of the system. In the following table you will see some of the existing hives:

Hive	Acronym	Description
HKEY_CLASSES_ROOT	HKCR	Stores information about file types and file extension associations.
HKEY_CURRENT_USER	HKCU	Contains configuration information for the user currently logged in.
HKEY_LOCAL_MACHINE	HKLM	Stores configuration data for the computer and software, irrespective of the user.
HKEY_USERS	HKU	Contains user-specific settings for all users on the machine.
HKEY_CURRENT_CONFIG	HKCC	Stores information about the current hardware profile.

Table 6.3: Hive examples

- **Keys and subkeys:** Keys are like directories in the registry, and they can contain subkeys. Each key can store subkeys, creating a hierarchical structure. Keys are used to organize and categorize the registry values.

- **Values:** Values are the actual data entries within the keys. Each value has a name, a type, and data. Common types of registry values include:

  o **String (REG_SZ)**: Plain text.

  o **Binary (REG_BINARY)**: Raw binary data.

  o **DWORD (REG_DWORD)**: 32-bit integer.

  o **QWORD (REG_QWORD):** 64-bit integer.

  o **Multi-String (REG_MULTI_SZ)**: Multiple strings.

  o **Expandable String (REG_EXPAND_SZ)**: String containing variables that are replaced when called.

Many of the corporate attacks are aimed at modifying certain registry keys. There are some hives more likely to try to be altered, such as **HKCU (HKEY_CURRENT_USER)** to execute malicious code with each machine login as shown in the following figure:

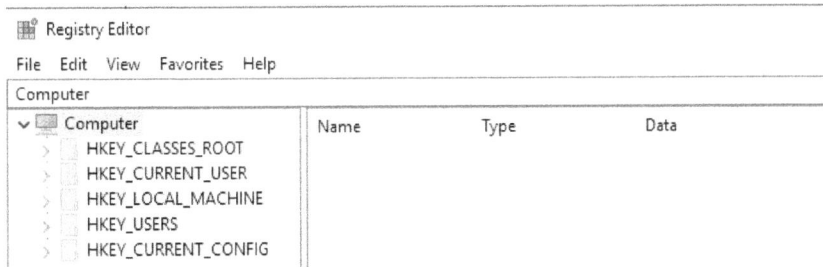

Figure 6.6: *Hives visualized in registry editor*

Microsoft Windows Security fundamentals

The main aspect that we as threat hunters must know about an operating system is related to security. We must understand the mechanisms by which we will be able to detect anomalies and attacks that could affect its functioning.

Microsoft Windows has a series of tools and components aimed at maintaining the security of the operating system, some of the tools are oriented to hardware protection and others are oriented to the OS security. Therefore, many tools used by adversaries are aimed at bypassing these control and detection mechanisms. Let us discuss the mechanisms that Microsoft Windows has:

- **Windows Defender Antivirus:** This is the Microsoft Windows integrated antivirus and anti-malware solution that provides real-time protection against different threats including phishing, malicious web applications, downloaded files containing malware, etc. It is constantly updated and improved, it evaluates the applications running on the machine and the applications that are going to be executed, detecting a wide range of threats and their variants.

- **Windows Firewall:** The Windows Firewall is a critical component that monitors incoming and outgoing network traffic based on predetermined or customized security rules. It acts as a barrier, blocking unauthorized access while allowing legitimate communications to pass through, thus preventing potential attacks or exfiltration from internal or external sources.

- **User Account Control (UAC):** UAC is designed to mitigate the impact of some exploits and malware that tries to elevate privileges. It prompts users for permission or an administrator's credentials before allowing actions that could potentially affect the system's stability or security. This helps prevent unauthorized changes in critical files of the operating system and ensures that only trusted applications and users can perform critical tasks.

- **BitLocker:** BitLocker provides full disk encryption, protecting data on the entire drive from unauthorized access, especially in the event of physical theft. By encrypting the disk, it ensures that even if the hardware is compromised, the data remains inaccessible without proper authentication.

- **Windows Hello:** Windows Hello introduces biometric authentication, using facial recognition, fingerprints, or iris scans to provide a more secure and user-friendly login experience. This reduces reliance on traditional passwords, which are often weak and easily compromised.

- **Secure Boot:** It is part of the **Unified Extensible Firmware Interface (UEFI)** that helps prevent malicious software from loading during the boot process. By ensuring that only trusted software with valid digital signatures can run, it protects the system from rootkits and bootkits that attempt to compromise the boot sequence, that is one of the targets that malicious actors try to compromise.

- **Credential Guard:** It uses virtualization-based security to isolate and protect user credentials. By storing credentials in a secure container, it prevents attackers from accessing them, even if the operating system is compromised.

- **Windows Update:** Regular updates are vital for maintaining security. Windows Update automatically downloads and installs updates, ensuring that the system is always protected against the latest vulnerabilities. This proactive approach helps mitigate risks associated with outdated software. In the server environment, the updates can be controlled by the entire ecosystem, so only the authorized updates are going to be applied.

- **Windows Event Logging:** It provides a centralized way to record log information from both the operating system and applications, software, and hardware. The grouping of this information is called an **Event Log**, and each event has an ID. Microsoft provides different catalogs related to the events so that the threat hunters or the Blue Team can understand the nature of each event in a better way.

Microsoft Windows Server Networking Troubleshooting Events Catalog:

https://learn.microsoft.com/en-us/windows-server/identity/ad-ds/plan/ appendix-l--events-to-monitor

Windows provides the Event Viewer tool so that the administrator or user of the machine can access the operating system log information and thus use this information within the Threat Hunting process, along with any other indicators provided by external tools. The following figure shows the Windows Event Viewer tool:

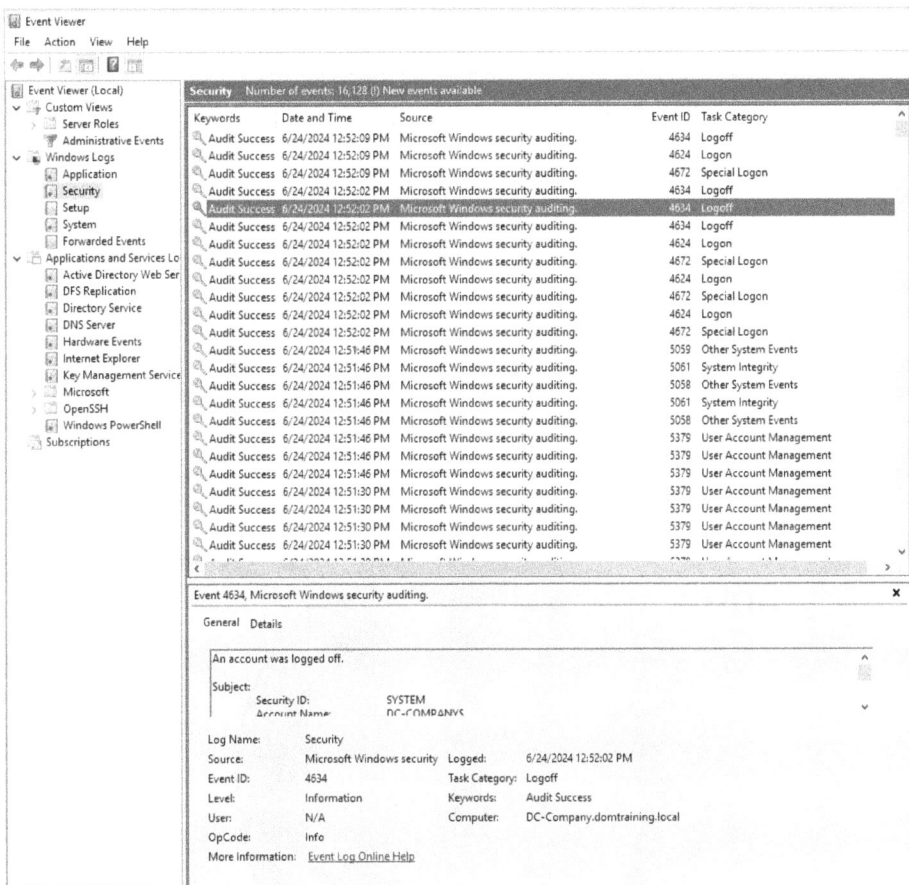

Figure 6.7: *Event Viewer tool*

Microsoft has additional tools such as **Extended Detection and Response (XDR)** or Sentinel, which are proprietary, aimed at facilitating threat detection, but they are paid, so unfortunately, they are not present in all implementations, so in this chapter, we emphasize the tools that are incorporated by default within the operating system.

Linux operation

Linux is an open-source operating system with a huge group of distro flavors developed largely by the community. This operating system is the most used by servers in the world, given its robustness, versatility, capabilities, and tools.

In the following table, we have some examples of Linux distros and flavors:

Linux distribution	Function
Ubuntu Desktop	Workstation
Fedora Workstation	Workstation
Linux Mint	Workstation
Debian	Workstation, Server
CentOS	Server
Red Hat Enterprise Linux (RHEL)	Server
Ubuntu Server	Server
SUSE Linux Enterprise Server	Server

Table 6.4: Linux distribution example

The architecture of the Linux operating system is quite simple to understand. The hardware interfaces with the kernel of the operating system, which is a compressed archive (vmlinuz) at the moment that it is not loaded into RAM memory. Once loaded in RAM, it becomes the kernel that allows the user to interact with the system, and in turn, the applications that are going to be executed. You do it using the system shell. The following figure presents the Linux architecture in a graphical way:

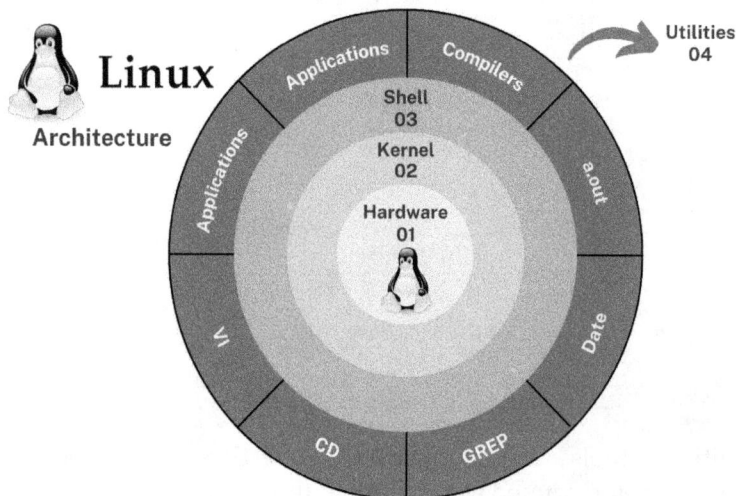

Figure 6.8: Linux architecture

As we saw in the above figure, it presents a graphical view of the Linux architecture, outlining its core layers. To complement this, the following table breaks down the main components of the Linux architecture:

Component	Definition
Hardware Layer	Composed of the peripheral devices (HDD, CPU, RAM, etc.)
Kernel	It is the core of the operating system and oversees control the activity of the hardware elements; additionally, it manages the virtual resources that are assigned for each process that requires them. There are several types of kernels: • Micro Kernel • Monolithic Kernel • Hybrid Kernel • Exo Kernel • Nano Kernel Each of them has different functions and capabilities, but for our interest in Threat Hunting we are not going to delve into them now.
Shell	The shell is responsible for being an interface between the user and the kernel; Users interact with the system via Shell, which spawns a unique session per user. There are several types of shells; among which we can mention: • Bourne Again Shell (Bash) • KornShell (ksh) • Bourne Shell (sh) • Z Shell (zsh) • C Shell (csh)
Utilities	These are the programs that allow the user to take advantage of the operating system.

Table 6.5: Linux architecture components

Linux security fundamentals

Linux has certain characteristics that allow it to become a very robust platform at the security level, with the configuration, tuning, and proper hardening; intrinsically, the system has multiple safety characteristics. The following table is some of the most relevant:

Area	Control	Definition
User and Group Management	Granular permissions	Linux can control the read, write, and execute permissions for individual users and groups

Area	Control	Definition
File System Security	Root User	The root is the superuser, who has complete control over the system. Regular users operate with limited permissions, reducing the risk of accidental or malicious system modifications or activities.
	Access Control Lists (ACLs)	They provide a more granular control of the user/group/other model users' permissions
	Encrypted File Systems	Linux supports various file encryption methods to protect the information even if the attacker has physical access to the storage.
Network Security	Firewall	Linux can use different tools like Iptables, Netfilter, Firewalld to provide firewall functionalities and protect the inbound and outbound connections based on rules and policies.
	Secure Shell (SSH)	Provides encrypted and secure remote access to the system
Software Security	Package Management Systems	Linux can be configured to download applications, updates and security patches only from trusted sources, and you can also use different package managers (APT, YUM, SNAP, etc.) to manage software installations and updates.
	Kernel Security Modules (KSM)	Security-Enhanced Linux (SELinux) and AppArmor provide mandatory access control (MAC) policies, increasing security by enforcing strict access controls to applications.
Process Isolation and Control	Chroot Jail	Chroot is used to isolate processes in a specific directory, preventing them from accessing the broader file system.
	Namespaces and **Control Groups (Cgroups)**	These features provide process isolation and resource limiting, ensuring that processes run in separate spaces and do not interfere with each other or consume excessive system resources.
Logging and Auditing	System logs	Linux can create logs about almost all sections and areas of the operating system; By default, it comes with tools for this purpose, such as syslog, journald, and auditd to collect and store log data. In the area of threat hunting, logs are the main evidence we have, to be able to detect anomalies in the operating system.

Table 6.6: Linux safety characteristics

There are additional security tools in Linux that allow you to strengthen the operating system in a more granular way, for example the Lynis (**https://cisofy.com/lynis/**) tool, which is capable of analyzing a large number of areas of the operating system in order to detect flaws and generate implementation recommendations and adjustments to make the Linux more robust from a security point of view.

Endpoint Detection and Response tools

Endpoints are physical devices that connect to a network system such as mobile devices, desktop computers, virtual machines, embedded devices, and servers. These endpoints are often the primary targets of cyberattacks, making them critical points for monitoring and protection.

Endpoint Detection and Response (EDR) tools are specialized security solutions designed to provide continuous monitoring, detection, and response capabilities at the endpoint level. Unlike traditional antivirus software, EDR tools focus on identifying suspicious behavior and providing visibility into advanced threats that may bypass detection.

Introduction to EDR tools

These tools analyze events related to suspicious behavior and activity on endpoints, including Cloud technologies, **Internet of Things (IoT),** and **Industrial Internet of Things (IIoT).** If an anomalous event exists, an alert is generated by the EDR, which allows the blue team to initiate response protocols depending on the type of alert. The main objective of an EDR is to intercept threats and generate an early warning of any attack to prevent the level of compromise or damage from escalating.

If such events occur, EDR alerts security teams about the issues found by endpoint protection. Thus, you will be able to intercept these threats on time, before the attack has escalated and caused further damage to your systems. EDR tools are doing continuous monitoring for threats and known and unknown attack patterns; in some cases, the EDR is capable to block the threat.

EDR tools have different capabilities and functions and are supported by comprehensive data analytics to pinpoint abnormal or uncommon system behavior and provide detailed information about the event.

The following is a list of EDR tools that are very useful within the threat hunting process:

EDR	URL	Best For
Microsoft Defender XDR	**https://www.microsoft.com/en-us/ security/business/siem-and-xdr/ microsoft-defender-xdr**	Seamless integration with Windows environments; enterprise-grade detection.
Sentinel One	**https://www.sentinelone.com/**	Real-time advanced threat detection.

EDR	URL	Best For
CrowdStrike Falcon Insight	**https://www.crowdstrike.com/ platform/endpoint-security/**	Cloud-native endpoint protection, fast deployment, and threat intelligence-rich
OSSEC	**https://www.ossec.net/**	Small orgs or budget-limited setups
The Hive	**https://thehive-project.org/**	Case management and alert triage
osQuery	**https://www.osquery.io/**	Endpoint visibility via SQL-like queries; investigation and hunting.

Table 6.7: EDR tools

Hunting for endpoint-based threats

Covering all the mechanisms that adversaries can use to compromise an operating system, which we should try to detect in the threat hunting exercise is the subject of this book; However, this topic is very broad and dynamic, so we cannot cover the details of each threat in this book, but we can use as a guide to understand the different activities that we should look for within our analyses the list of data sources of MITRE ATT&CK:

https://attack.mitre.org/datasources/

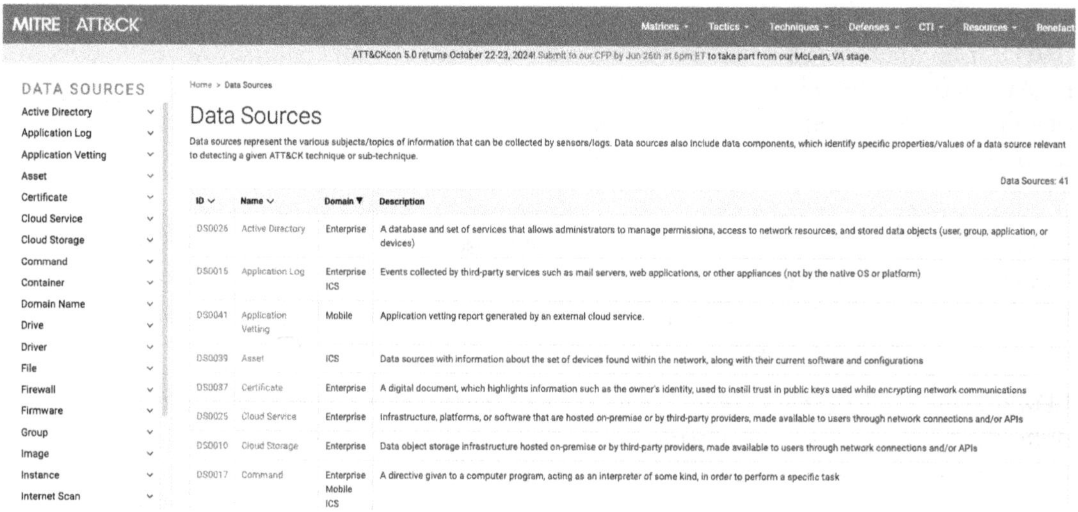

Figure 6.9: List of data sources of MITRE ATT&CK

Although threat hunting methodologies apply equally to any device or operating system, the in-depth detail of what should be monitored or controlled varies in each case. In the following, we are going to give examples of tools and commands that must be monitored in both Microsoft Windows and Linux operating systems. It is almost impossible to provide an absolute and complete guide, since each version of the operating systems can generate changes and even eliminate certain commands or tools, and of course include new ones, so what is explained in the following should serve as a basis and example for the threat hunter of the type of parameters, tools and commands that it could analyze and much more.

Microsoft Windows threat hunting key process

MITRE ATT&CK offers us a very complete matrix exposing the detail of each potential attack that we can receive on Windows (**https://attack.mitre.org/matrices/enterprise/ windows/**) platforms, including the impact that we could suffer. By analyzing this matrix in detail, we will be able to execute our threat hunt in an optimal way, since we not only have information about the attacks, but also **Indicators of Compromise (IoC)** and **Indicators of Attack (IoA)**that we can use to have greater clarity about what is happening. In the following figure we will see the MITRE attack matrix:

Figure 6.10: MITRE ATT&CK Windows attack matrix

In the matrix it is explained that in Microsoft Windows there are many processes and files that can be used maliciously to alter the operation of the system, escalate privileges, exfiltrate information, among many other adversarial activities. In the following we provided an example list of Microsoft Windows processes that should be monitored and evaluated within the operating system, because they are commonly used by adversaries to execute various malicious techniques, such as masking the execution of a malicious process, malware injection, escalating privileges, irretrievably deleting a file, among others. This list is a simple example of the processes and files that can be useful within a threat hunting process, because they are widely used by adversaries to take advantage of them and compromise the system. In no case is this list exhaustive since there is an immense number of this type of services that detection tools monitor, but as threat hunters, we should try to be familiar with the main ones.

Wininit.exe

Wininit.exe is a Windows system file that plays a critical role in system startup and can be relevant when identifying malicious process injection or unauthorized modifications. The following table provides detailed information about the `Wininit.exe` process:

Process	Parent Process	Legitimate Path
Wininit.exe	Created by smss.exe, does not show a Parent Process	`%SystemRoot%\System32\wininit.exe`

Table 6.8: Wininit.exe information

The following points outline the potential threat indicators and recommended tools for analyzing the Windows Initialization Process during threat hunting and system monitoring:

- **Regular use:** Launch the Windows Initialization Process and start the key background process.

- **Threat hunting abnormal indicators:**

  o Only one instance should be running

  o Unusual path or multiple paths

- **Recommended tools for analysis:**

  o **Process explorer: https://learn.microsoft.com/en-us/sysinternals/downloads/process-explorer**

  o **Process hacker: https://processhacker.sourceforge.io/**

  o **Security Information and Event Management (SIEM)**

In the following figure, you will see the properties window of Wininit.exe, which provides useful details such as its file location and digital signature:

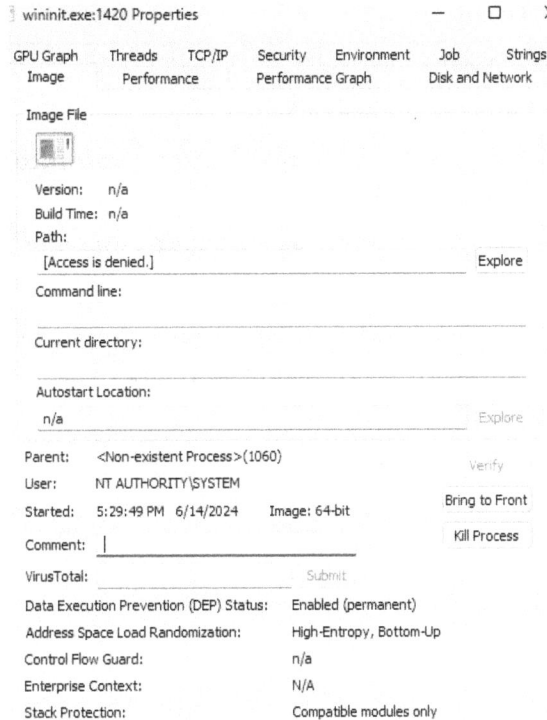

Figure 6.11: Wininit.exe properties

Services.exe

The properties of services.exe offer key information that helps verify its authenticity, such as its file path and important details when assessing potential anomalies. The next table will offer you more information about the process:

Process	Parent Process	Legitimate Path
Services.exe	Wininit.exe	%SystemRoot%\System32\services.exe

Table 6.9: Services.exe information

The following points outline the normal behavior, potential threat indicators, and recommended tools for analyzing services.exe during threat hunting and system monitoring:

- **Regular use:** Start the Service Control Manager, which can start, interact, and end services. Is the parent process of **svchost.exe**, **dllhost.exe**, **spoolsv.exe**, **taskhost.exe**, etc.

- **Threat hunting abnormal indicators:**
  - Only one instance should be running
  - You can monitor this Microsoft Event ID:

- 4697 (security)
- 7045 (system)

- **Recommended tools for analysis:**

  o **Process explorer**: **https://learn.microsoft.com/en-us/sysinternals/downloads/process-explorer**

  o **Process hacker**: **https://processhacker.sourceforge.io/**

  o SIEM

As you will see in the following figure, the properties window of **services.exe** can be reviewed to verify its location, digital signature, and other key details that help confirm it's a legitimate system process:

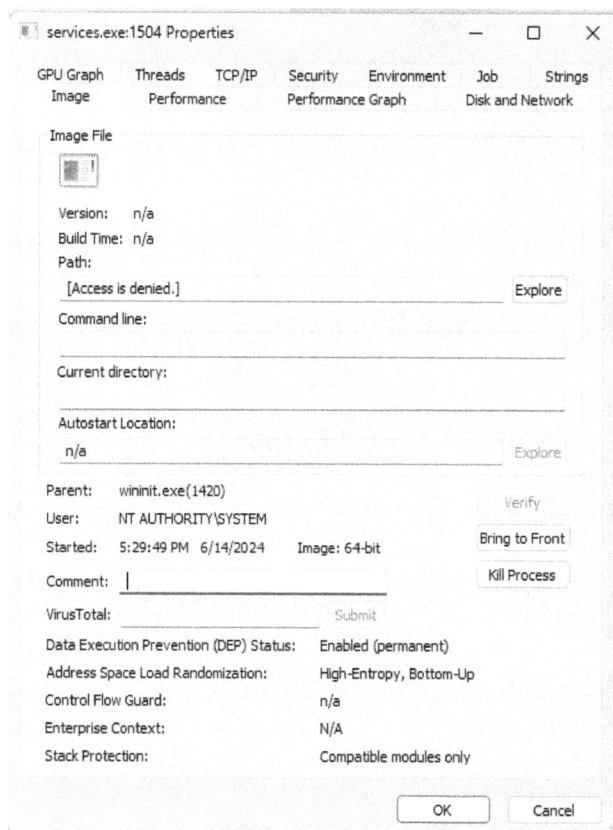

Figure 6.12: Services.exe properties

Svchost.exe

Svchost.exe (Service Host) is a Windows process that groups and runs various system services from DLL files. It helps optimize resource usage by allowing multiple services to share a single process. The following table provides key information about **svchost.exe**:

Process	Parent Process	Legitimate Path
Svchost.exe	Services.exe	%SystemRoot%\System32\svchost.exe

Table 6.10: Svchost.exe information

The following points summarize the typical behavior of svchost.exe, indicators of suspicious activity, and recommended tools for effective analysis during threat hunting:

- **Regular use:** Running Service DLL, Outbound Connections, Starts Services

- **Threat hunting abnormal indicators:**

  o Parent process different than **services.exe**

  o Svchost.exe located in a different path or multiple paths

  o Normally, you can find many **svchost.exe** processes running at the same time, but if you find an excessive amount, it is recommended to review each one in detail

- **Recommended tools for analysis:**

  o **Process explorer**: **https://learn.microsoft.com/en-us/sysinternals/downloads/process-explorer**

  o **Process hacker**: **https://processhacker.sourceforge.io/**

The following figure displays the properties of **svchost.exe**, which can help with important information about the process:

Figure 6.13: Svchost.exe properties

LSASS.exe

LSASS.exe is a critical Windows process responsible for enforcing security policies, handling user authentication, and generating security tokens, it plays a central role in managing logins, password changes, and access control. The following table provides essential information about **LSASS.exe**:

Process	Parent Process	Legitimate Path
LSASS.exe	Wininit.exe	%SystemRoot%\System32\lsass.exe

Table 6.11: LSASS.exe information

The following points outline the normal behavior of **LSASS.exe**, common threat indicators, and recommended tools:

- **Regular use:** Enforce the security policy in the system; once loaded in RAM, have access to the system passwords. It is targeted to obtain passwords, NT Hashes, LM Hashes, and Kerberos Tickets; to achieve privilege escalation, lateral movement, data theft, etc.

- **Threat hunting abnormal indicators:**
  - Abnormal access to the **LSASS.exe** process
  - Tools execution related to **LSASS.exe** (Commonly trying to dump credentials):
    - `procdump -ma lsass.exe lsass_dump`
    - `rundll32.exe C:\Windows\System32\comsvcs.dll MiniDump PID lsass.dmp full`

- **Recommended tools for analysis:**
  - **Process explorer:** **https://learn.microsoft.com/en-us/sysinternals/downloads/process-explorer**
  - **Process hacker: https://processhacker.sourceforge.io/**
  - SIEM

The following figure displays the properties of **LSASS.exe**, which can help with details of this important process:

Figure 6.14: LSASS.exe properties

Winlogon.exe

`Winlogon.exe` is a core Windows process responsible for handling secure user interactions during the logon and logoff procedures. The following table provides key information about `Winlogon.exe`:

Process	Parent process	Legitimate path
Winlogon.exe	Created by `smss.exe` instance, does not show a Parent Process	`%SystemRoot%\System32\win-logon.exe`

Table 6.12: Winlogon.exe information

The following points describe the normal behavior of `Winlogon.exe`, common IoC, and recommended tools for detection and analysis during threat hunting:

- **Regular use:** Controls interactive users' logon and logoff is responsible for the login prompt to receive username and password and pass those credentials to `lsass.exe` to be validated; Once authentication is successful, Winlogon initiates the process by loading the user's **NTUSER.DAT** into the HKEY_CURRENT_USER Registry Hive. Following this, it launches the user's shell, explorer.exe, through **Userinit.exe**.

- **Threat hunting abnormal indicators:**
  - ○ Shell modifications; (Different shell than `explorer.exe`)
  - ○ Some attacks try to bypass the credentials requirement, so the user can log into the machine without credentials just pressing <enter> in the credentials
  - ○ ls prompt; tools like Kon Boot are used by attackers (**https://kon-boot.com/**)
- **Recommended tools for analysis:**
  - ○ **Process explorer:** **https://learn.microsoft.com/en-us/sysinternals/ downloads/process-explorer**
  - ○ **Process hacker**: **https://processhacker.sourceforge.io/**
  - ○ SIEM

The following figure displays general information about `Winlogon.exe`, providing an overview of its properties within the system:

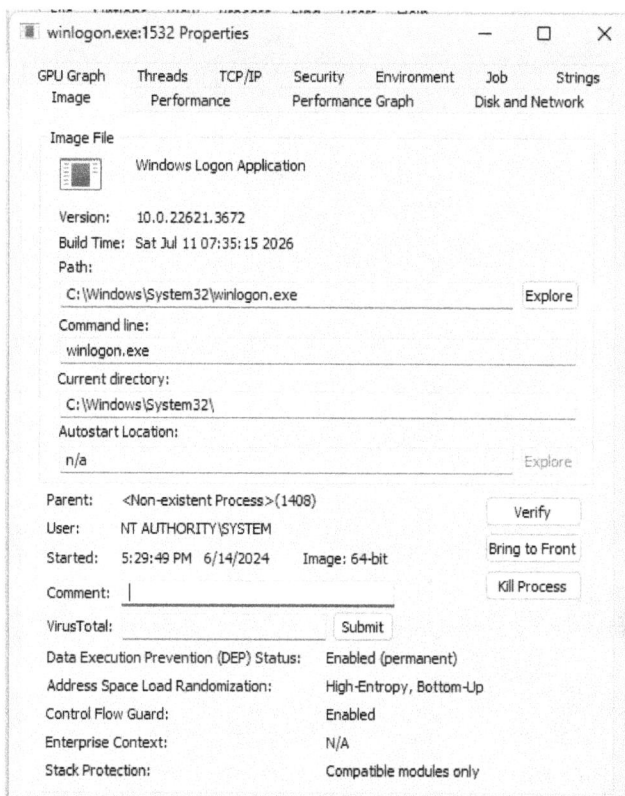

Figure 6.15: Winlogon.exe properties

Within threat hunting activities, the behavior of many variables, commands, processes, registry keys, file integrity verification, etc., must be analyzed. We could dedicate an entire book just to this aspect, given the depth of each operating system. As a closing of this part, we leave some recommendations of processes and parameters to be evaluated in Microsoft Windows operating systems:

o PowerShell commands that can be used by attackers

o Windows Instrumentation Console Commands

o Psexec command

o Certutil command

o Vssadmin

o Schtasks

o Utilman

o MSHTA and hundreds more

Due to the many processes that the Windows operating system presents, here is a summary table of Windows threat hunting:

Element	Monitor it	Indicators to watch (IoA/IoC)
Wininit.exe	Initializes services during boot. Hijacked for persistence or privilege escalation	Unsigned child processes, abnormal startup params
Services.exe	Manages system services. Target for service creation or modification	Suspicious new services, unexpected registry entries
Svchost.exe	Hosts services. Commonly injected with malicious code	Unusual services, network traffic, unsigned DLLs
LSASS.exe	Handles credentials. High-value target for dumping hashes	Access attempts, memory reads, use of procdump/mimikatz
Winlogon.exe	Manages user logins. Used in persistence or credential theft	Unusual registry mods (Shell, Userinit), abnormal DLLs
powershell.exe	Automation tool, heavily abused for payload delivery or execution	Encoded commands, download strings, "-nop", "-w hidden" flags
wmic.exe	Executes WMI commands. Used for lateral movement or evasion	Unusual queries, remote exec, persistence indicators
psexec.exe	Remote command execution	Lateral movement, use from non-admin accounts
certutil.exe	Certificate utility, often abused for downloading payloads	"-urlcache", base64 decoding, writing to temp folders
vssadmin.exe	Volume Shadow Copy tool. Used to delete backups pre-ransomware	"delete shadows", used in non-backup contexts
schtasks.exe	Schedules tasks. Commonly abused for persistence	Unexpected tasks, remote scheduling, running malicious scripts

Element	Monitor it	Indicators to watch (IoA/IoC)
`utilman.exe`	Accessibility tool. Often replaced for login bypass (Sticky Keys backdoor)	File hash change, execution at login screen
`mshta.exe`	Executes HTML applications. Used for executing malicious JavaScript/VBScript	Suspicious URLs, hidden scripts, odd parent process
Bitsadmin (Command)	Used to download files or transfer data; commonly leveraged by attackers for **command-and-control** (**C2**) or payload delivery	Background transfers from suspicious URLs, execution within scripts, use of /transfer, /addfile, or /complete flags

Table 6.13: Summary table of windows threat hunting

Linux threat hunting key aspects and tools

For the Linux operating system, we also have the MITRE ATT&CK reference matrix (**https://attack.mitre.org/matrices/enterprise/linux/**) that gives us the details of the malicious techniques used by cybercriminals, the IoC for each attack or technique, and even the tools. This information gives us everything we need to know to be able to perform our analysis in Threat hunting. In the following figure you will see the Linux matrix from MITRE Att&ck:

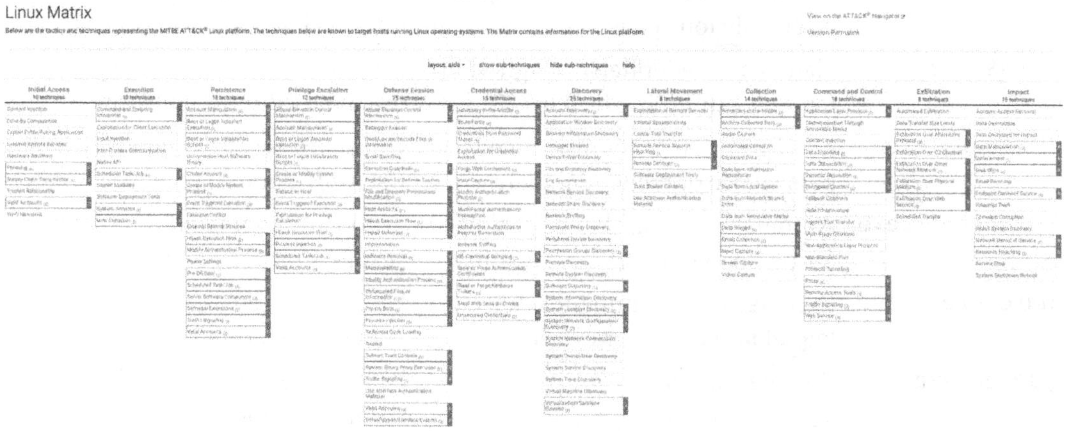

Figure 6.16: MITRE ATT&CK Linux attack matrix

In Linux, most of the attacks can be detected by command execution and process creation events. A great advantage that we have is that the tools necessary to detect these indicators can be easily installed in the operating system. Let us start by talking about the Linux Audit System controlled by the daemon or service **auditd**.

Linux audit system

Auditd is a tool used on Linux systems for monitoring and recording activities. It helps track which user did what and when on the computer. This tool is useful for monitoring and detecting system changes and identifying potential security issues. It provides detailed logs that can be reviewed later to see what actions were taken and by whom.

You can install auditd (**https://linux.die.net/man/8/auditd**) in many flavors of Linux.

In Debian-based Linux distributions, you can install the latest version of auditd and its plugins with this command:

```
sudo apt-get install auditd audispd-plugins
```

In Red Hat Enterprise Linux distributions, the auditd package is installed by default in version 7 and above. If it is not installed by default, the following command will do it:

```
sudo dnf install audit
```

After installation, you can configure a file containing the rules defining what to audit and the conditions; that file is going to be in:

```
$/etc/audit/rules.d/audit.rules
```

An example of this file can be located here: **https://github.com/Neo23x0/auditd/blob/master/audit.rules**

An extract of this file is shown in the following figure:

```
310     ## Suspicious activity
311     -w /usr/bin/wget -p x -k susp_activity
312     -w /usr/bin/curl -p x -k susp_activity
313     -w /usr/bin/base64 -p x -k susp_activity
314     -w /bin/nc -p x -k susp_activity
315     -w /bin/netcat -p x -k susp_activity
316     -w /usr/bin/ncat -p x -k susp_activity
317     -w /usr/bin/ss -p x -k susp_activity
318     -w /usr/bin/netstat -p x -k susp_activity
319     -w /usr/bin/ssh -p x -k susp_activity
320     -w /usr/bin/scp -p x -k susp_activity
```

Figure 6.17: Audit.rules file extract

You can create and configure the rules in the way you need and use auditd as one of the effective tools to create the necessary logs whenever an anomalous activity occurs in the operating system.

Linux key alerts

Linux systems, like Windows, are exposed to a variety of adversarial techniques detailed in the MITRE ATT&CK Matrix for Linux. The table below highlights key alerts and events that should be monitored during threat hunting to identify early signs of compromise.

Aspect /tool/event	Importance in Threat Hunting	Indicators to watch (IoA/IoC)
Auditd (Linux Audit System)	Core for monitoring system calls, file access, user actions, and permission changes.	Unauthorized access to `/etc/shadow`, permission changes, `execve` logs
Command execution (**execve**)	Most Linux attacks rely on command-line tools and scripts.	Use of `bash`, `sh`, `python`, `perl`, suspicious flags or encodings
Unauthorized Privilege Escalation	Attackers may try to gain root through local exploits or sudo misuse.	`sudo` activity from non-admin users, SUID file changes
SUID Binary Creation/ Modification	Often used to maintain privileged access.	New SUID/SGID files, `chmod 4777`, in uncommon paths like `/tmp`
Execution from Temp Paths	`/tmp`, `/dev/shm`, and `/var/tmp` are commonly abused for malware execution.	Script or binary execution from temp directories
Cron Job Modifications	Persistence via scheduled tasks.	New entries in `/etc/cron*`, user-specific cron jobs running unknown scripts
Network Activity Monitoring	Outbound connections to C2 servers, port scanning, reverse shells.	Use of `nc`, `nmap`, `Socat`, `cryptcat` connections to rare IPs or high ports
Use of Living off the Land Binaries (LOLBins)	Attackers abuse native tools for stealth operations.	`curl`, `wget`, `scp`, `rsync`, `base64`, `openssl` usage patterns
Filesystem Changes	Creation or modification of sensitive files indicates compromise or persistence.	Changes to `/etc/passwd`, `/etc/sudoers`, `/root/` directory files
SSH Key Injections	Adversaries may insert their keys for persistent access.	New keys in `~/.ssh/authorized_keys`
Log File Deletion or Tampering	Indicators of anti-forensic behavior.	Truncation or deletion of `/var/log/auth.log`, use of `logrotate`
Kernel Module Loading	Rootkits and stealth malware may load malicious modules.	`insmod`, `modprobe` usage, presence of unsigned or unknown modules

Table 6.14: Linux key alerts

Incident response on endpoints

We know that currently the risks are increasing, and in most cases, the question does not arise: *Are we going to be hacked?* rather, the right question is: *When and how are we going to be hacked?* Given the above, prevention and detection play a preponderant role within threat hunting because, when well executed, they help us to reduce the risk levels of the entity. In the following figure, you will see a graphical interpretation of the previously discussed subject:

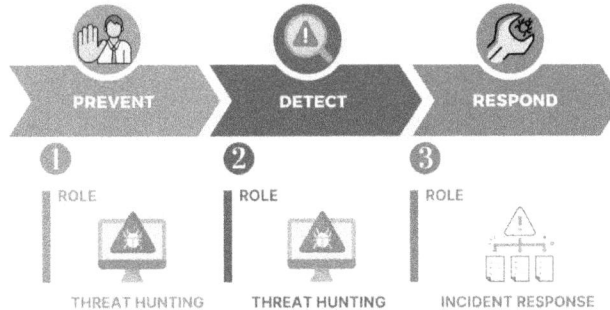

Figure 6.18: Threat hunting risk reduction roles

The order that companies follow in their Cyber defense process is: **Prevent | Detect | Respond**. We have already talked about preventive technologies such as Antimalware, Antispam, etc., and detection technologies such as SIEM, XDR, etc. As we can see, both prevention and detection are broadly related to threat hunting. The response part is not part of threat hunting, but we consider it important to mention it and outline the steps to follow within incident response. If you want to go further in detail, we can involve the **National Institute of Standards and Technology (NIST)** cybersecurity framework in its version 2.0 **https://www.nist.gov/news-events/news/2024/02/nist-releases-version-20-landmark-cybersecurity-framework** that includes IT governance as part of the process, as you will be able to see in the following figure:

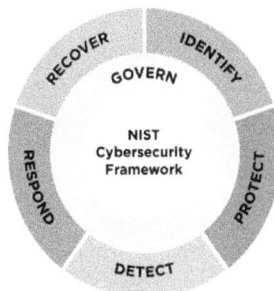

Figure 6.19: NIST CSF 2.0 functions
(Source: https://www.nist.gov/)

Incident response is an organized and strategic process to countermeasure a cyberattack or data breach, including how an organization executes mechanisms of damage control of such an incident. The goal is to effectively and efficiently manage incidents to minimize damage to systems, data, and reputation, and reduce recovery time and cost.

Incident response is made up of a series of steps and stages that we detail in the following:

1. **Incident Response Plan (IRP):** This is the planning phase, here you create a well-documented and structured IRP that defines the procedures for detect, respond, and recover from security incidents.

2. **Incident response team:** Form a dedicated team with clear roles and responsibilities for handling incidents.

3. **Communication plan:** Develop a communication strategy that includes internal notifications and external communications.

4. **Detection and analysis:** Implement tools and processes for early detection of incidents.

5. **Containment strategy:** Have clear procedures for containing the incident to prevent further damage. This may include isolating affected systems or networks.

6. **Eradication and recovery:** Develop methods to remove the cause of the incident and to restore systems to normal operation.

7. **Training and drills:** Regularly train the incident response team and conduct simulated drills to ensure preparedness.

8. **Documentation and reporting:** Document all incidents and responses for future reference, legal requirements, and to aid in continuous improvement of the IRP.

The following figure presents the fundamentals of incident response, outlining the key phases:

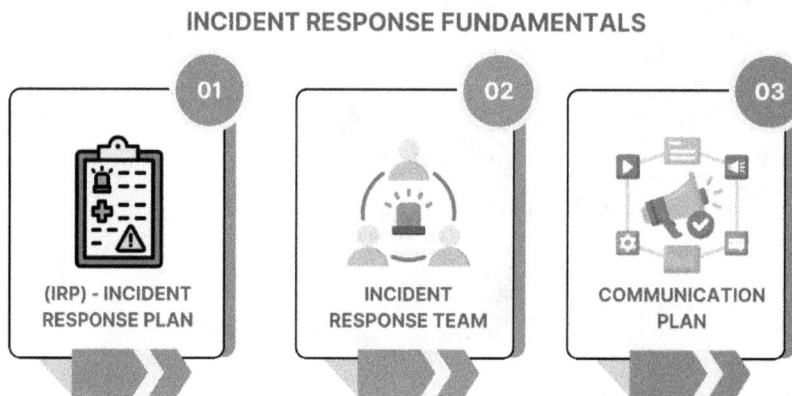

INCIDENT RESPONSE FUNDAMENTALS

01 (IRP) - INCIDENT RESPONSE PLAN

02 INCIDENT RESPONSE TEAM

03 COMMUNICATION PLAN

Figure 6.20: Incident response fundamentals

Conclusion

In this chapter we explore the basic architecture of the Microsoft Windows and Linux operating systems, we mention their most important security features and then we discuss the tools at our disposal at the methodological level to be able to detail the malicious activity within a system leveraged by means of the MITRE ATT&CK matrices for both Microsoft Windows and Linux.

Everything stated in this chapter indicates that the capacity, creativity, lateral thinking, and reasoning of the analyst are the preponderant and decisive factors within the threat hunting exercises to be able to detect anomalies effectively. The tools and methodologies fulfill the function of saving time, understanding the malicious TTPs and improving efficiency, but the axis of success is the human being.

In the next chapter, readers will explore the world of computer forensics within the context of threat hunting. The discussion will cover the fundamentals of digital evidence collection and preservation, techniques for analyzing both volatile and non-volatile data, and how to effectively use forensic tools in investigations.

Points to remember

- Manufacturers and creators of operating systems have invested a lot of time and resources to create add-ons, tools, and configurations that help strengthen their operation; As threat hunters we must know what these add-ons are because of course the attackers will try to deactivate, alter or uninstall them; detecting these actions helps us within the threat hunting process.

- Each operating system has tools and commands that can help within the threat hunting process. It is convenient to deepen the knowledge of each operating system with which we must work and to know the details of these tools.

- The MITRE ATT&CK matrices are our best ally to know the details of the TTPs used by cybercriminals.

Multiple choice questions

1. **What is Active Directory?**
   a. A file management system used in Linux for storing and organizing files.
   b. A database management system for managing SQL databases in Windows.
   c. A component in Windows Server environments for managing user accounts and security settings
   d. A web server software used for hosting websites and web applications.

2. **What is HKEY_USERS?**
   a. A database management system used in Windows to store user profiles.
   b. A registry hive in Windows that contains information about all user profiles on the system.
   c. A component of Windows used for managing network resources.
   d. A security protocol in Windows for encrypting user data.

3. **Which is the third layer of the Linux architecture?**
   a. Kernel
   b. Shell
   c. Hardware
   d. Utilities

4. **What is LSASS.exe?**
   a. A system file in Windows responsible for managing the graphical user interface.
   b. A process in Windows that handles the execution of applications and system commands.
   c. A process in Windows that enforces the security policy, handles user logins, and manages password changes.
   d. A network service in Windows that facilitates internet connections.

5. **What is the Linux Audit system?**

    a. A software for managing network configurations in Linux.

    b. A utility to manage user accounts and permissions.

    c. A program for creating and managing disk partitions in Linux.

    d. A tool to monitor and track system activities for security and compliance purposes.

Answers

1. c.

2. b.

3. b.

4. c.

5. d.

References

1. **Windows security documentation: https://learn.microsoft.com/en-us/windows/security/**

2. **Review events and errors using Event Viewer: https://learn.microsoft.com/en-us/defender-endpoint/event-error-codes**

3. **Sysinternals Suite: https://learn.microsoft.com/en-us/sysinternals/downloads/sysinternals-suite**

4. **OS Credential Dumping: LSASS Memory: https://attack.mitre.org/techniques/T1003/001/**

5. **LSASS Memory: https://redcanary.com/threat-detection-report/techniques/lsass-memory/**

6. **Detecting and preventing LSASS credential dumping attacks: https://www.microsoft.com/en-us/security/blog/2022/10/05/detecting-and-preventing-lsass-credential-dumping-attacks/**

7. **Linux Audit Record Types: https://docs.redhat.com/en/documentation/red_hat_enterprise_linux/6/html/security_guide/sec-audit_record_types**

8. **NIST Cybersecurity Framework 2.0: https://nvlpubs.nist.gov/nistpubs/CSWP/NIST.CSWP.29.pdf**

9. **IoC Portal: https://www.vmray.com/analyses/beb260b05891/report/ioc.html**

Join our Discord space

Join our Discord workspace for latest updates, offers, tech happenings around the world, new releases, and sessions with the authors:

https://discord.bpbonline.com

CHAPTER 7
Computer Forensics

Introduction

Understanding the events that have occurred, starting from a group of digital evidence and creating a timeline that allows you to understand the step-by-step actions of an attacker, is a fundamental part of the objective of forensic computing.

In its history, we find that in the 80s, *Peter Norton* published the first version of a software to recover deleted files called **UnErase**, then in the 90s, the **Federal Bureau of Investigation** (**FBI**) influenced a change in criminology, calling it digital evidence of crimes. *P.A. Collier* and *B. J. Spaul* spoke of the term **computer forensics,** and from the following years, international companies, organizations, and associations were created to train professionals in the area, implement manuals, laws, or discuss new advances at an international level.

Computer forensics refers to a group of methodological procedures and techniques that help identify, preserve, extract, interpret, document, and present facts as evidence from computer equipment to be presented either in administrative proceedings or before a court of law.

Structure

In this chapter, we will discuss the following topics:

- Introduction to computer forensics
- Digital evidence collection and preservation

- Analyzing volatile and non-volatile data

- Tools for threat hunting investigations

- Analyzing system artifacts

- Extracting information from captures

- Analyzing malware artifacts and IoCs

- Case studies showcasing computer forensics

Objectives

In this chapter, we explore the vital role of computer forensics applied to threat hunting. Computer forensics helps to identify, analyze, and understand the traces left behind by an attacker. We discuss the techniques and methodologies used in computer forensics to uncover valuable evidence and insights for threat hunting purposes, having as the main purpose to protect the digital evidence and artifacts against tampering so our work is executed without errors.

Introduction to computer forensics

The concept of computer forensics can be expressed with different statements. Among the most accepted, we find the following:

- A methodical set of techniques and procedures for obtaining evidence, from different computer equipment, various storage devices, and digital computing media, in order to present them in a court of law in a coherent and meaningful format

- Preservation, identification, extraction, interpretation, and documentation of computational evidence, including rules of evidence, legal process, integrity of evidence, and providing expert opinion in a court of law or other legal and/or administrative proceeding as to what was found

- Computer forensics is the science of capturing, processing, and investigating information from computer equipment or the like, using an appropriate methodology, so that any evidence discovered is acceptable in a court of law

The objective of forensic computing is to identify evidence quickly, estimate the potential impact of malicious activity on the victim, and assess the intent and identity of the perpetrator.

Digital evidence collection and preservation

Digital evidence is defined as any information of evidentiary value that is stored or transmitted in digital form. Digital information can be gathered while examining any media containing information, monitoring network traffic, or making copies of data found during research.

Digital evidence is found in places such as:

- Image archives
- Audio or video files
- Browsing history
- Server logs
- Word processing files
- Emails
- System or application logs
- Social media
- Instant messaging services etc.

The role of evidence is to establish a credible link between the attacker, the victim, and the crime scene. According to LOCARD's exchange principle, anyone who arrives at a crime scene takes something from the scene and leaves some of it at the scene. For example, in an investigation, if any information from the victim's computer is stored on the server or in the system itself, the researcher can trace that information by examining the logs, browsing history, etc.

The following are different types of evidence that can be included in an investigative process shown in the table:

User-created files	Protected files	Files created by the computer
• Address books • Database files • Multimedia • Official documents • Internet reviews, favorites, etc.	• Compressed files • Files with modified extensions • Password-protected files • Hidden files • Files with steganography	• Backup files • Log files • Configuration files • Cookies • System files • Temporary files • History

Table 7.1: Types of evidence in an investigative process

Digital evidence must have some characteristics that are indispensable for it to be used in a court of law:

- **Credible:** The evidence must be clear and understandable to judges.
- **Precise:** There should be no doubt about the authenticity and veracity of the evidence.

- **Admissible:** The evidence must be related to the fact being proved.

- **Complete:** The evidence must prove the attacker's actions or innocence.

- **Authentic:** The evidence must be real and must be related to the incident in an appropriate manner.

Forensic investigators face many challenges while preserving digital evidence, as it is a chaotic form of evidence, and it is critical to handle it in the right way.

Following are some of the aspects of digital evidence that pose challenges for investigators and threat hunters:

- During the investigation, evidence may be maliciously or unintentionally altered.

- Digital evidence is circumstantial, making it difficult for the forensic investigator to trace system activity.

- Digital evidence is an abstraction of certain events, the resulting activity creates data that gives a not always complete view of the current fact.

Analyzing volatile and non-volatile data

It is important to keep in mind that storage technologies evolve very quickly. Nowadays, for example, we use **Solid State Drive (SSD)** disks that use different storage technologies, like NVMe, which is a semiconductor technology that does not require a continuous power supply to retain stored data.

Non-volatile data

When we talk about non-volatile data, we refer to technologies that store data permanently. They keep data after the power is turned off.

It does not require an electrical charge to maintain the storage state. It is a memory of reading and writing data.

Following we have a table with examples:

Category	Examples
File system data	Files and directories, metadata (timestamps, permissions), file fragments, slack space, unallocated space, file system logs.
Operating system artifacts	Registry (Windows), system logs, error logs, prefetch files (Windows), system configuration files (for example, /etc/).
Application data	Browser data (history, bookmarks, cookies), email archives, messaging app logs, SQLite databases, application logs.

Category	Examples
Storage media artifacts	Disk images, partition tables, **Master Boot Record (MBR)**/ **GUID Partition Table (GPT)**, BitLocker/LUKS metadata.
Network artifacts	Configuration files (VPN, proxy), captured packets (.pcap files), firewall logs, stored Wi-Fi profiles (SSIDs, keys).
Hardware-specific data	Firmware data (BIOS/UEFI), logs from embedded systems (IoT devices, printers).
Removable media data	USB device logs, optical media (CDs, DVDs), SD card files and partitions.
Backup and recovery data	Restore points, cloud backups, local backup files (for example, .bak), recovery images.
Other persistent data	Virtual machine images (`.vmdk`, `.vdi`), residual deleted data, steganographic data, encrypted containers (for example, VeraCrypt).

Table 7.2: Non-volatile data examples

Volatile data

This is information that is stored or that we can access when the device is turned on; the most classic case of this type is **Random Access Memory (RAM)**, which serves as the working memory of computers and other devices for the operating system. All the instructions executed by the **Central Processing Unit (CPU)** and other computer units are loaded into the RAM, as well as containing the data manipulated by the different programs. In the following figure, you will preview the types of RAM:

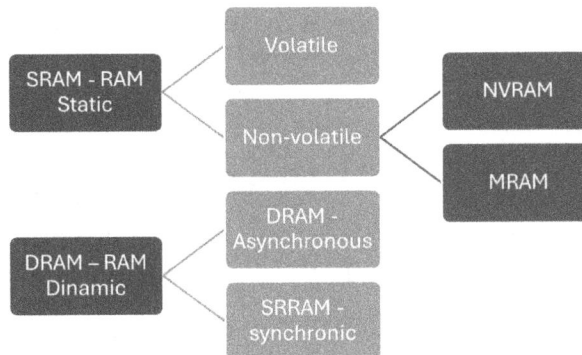

Figure 7.1: Types of RAM

In the following table, we have volatile data with forensic value:

Category	Examples
Memory (RAM)	Running processes, open network connections, loaded libraries or modules, clipboard data, encryption keys, passwords and credentials, command history, chat and messaging sessions.
Network data	Active connections, routing tables, **Address Resolution Protocol (ARP)** cache, **Domain Name System (DNS)** cache, live packet capture.
System state	Open files, logged-in users, system uptime, temporary files.
Operating system and application data	Temporary registry data, cache data, scheduled tasks.
Virtual memory	Pagefile or swap space containing memory pages swapped to disk.
Other volatile information	Logs in memory, environmental variables, kernel structures (for example, system calls, process tables).
Hardware state	CPU registers, hardware-level cache, peripheral device state (for example, USB devices, printers).

Table 7.3: Volatile data examples

Depending on where the data we must analyze is located, we will use different technologies and techniques. The most important thing to consider within the techniques to be used, is that we must protect digital evidence at all costs against any type of alteration or modification, since this can completely ruin an investigative process; however, we must also keep in mind that any forensic tool we use will leave a footprint within the digital evidence.

To discuss the techniques that we can use at the forensic level, we must first understand some critical aspects of the forensic tools that we can use, which we will explore in the following sections.

Tools for threat hunting investigations

Forensic hardware and software tools play a crucial role in threat hunting investigations, allowing to identify, investigate, and understand potential threats in an effective way.

It is almost impossible to detail a complete list of forensic tools that we can use. There is a supremely useful resource called **Computer Forensics Tool Testing (CFTT(** created by the **National Institute of Standards and Technology (NIST)**, which contains a detailed analysis of hundreds of tools and their specifications, performance ratings, etc. It is a valuable resource to be able to choose the right tool for each need and to have this tool recognized by our peers. In the following figure you will preview the home page of the computer forensics program:

Refer to this link for more information about CFTT: **https://www.nist.gov/itl/ssd/ software-quality-group/computer-forensics-tool-testing-program-cftt**

Figure 7.2: NIST tool testing program

This table contains a list of well-known forensic tools, separated by category:

Category	Tool	Purpose	Official website
Memory forensics	Volatility	Analyze memory dumps for malicious artifacts	**Volatility**
	Rekall	Perform memory forensics on live systems or dumps	**Rekall**
Disk and file system forensics	Autopsy	GUI-based platform for analyzing file systems and artifacts	**Autopsy**
	Sleuth Kit	Command-line tools for disk and file system analysis	**Sleuth Kit**
	FTK Imager	Create forensic images and preview data	**FTK Imager**

Category	Tool	Purpose	Official website
Network forensics	Wireshark	Analyze network packets for suspicious activity	**Wireshark**
	Zeek (Bro)	Monitor and log network activity for analysis	**Zeek**
	NetFlow	Examine network flow data for anomalies	**NetFlow**
Endpoint forensics	Velociraptor	Endpoint monitoring and response	**Velociraptor**
	Sysinternals Suite	Tools like Autoruns and Process Monitor for Windows systems	**Sysinternals Suite**
	OSQuery	SQL-powered endpoint investigation	**OSQuery**
Log analysis	Splunk	Log aggregation and analysis	**Splunk**
	ELK Stack	Open-source log analysis and visualization	**ELK Stack**
	Graylog	Centralized log management and analysis	**Graylog**
Malware analysis	IDA Pro	Static binary analysis	**IDA Pro**
	Ghidra	Reverse engineering and malware dissection	**Ghidra**
	Cuckoo Sandbox	Dynamic malware analysis in isolated environments	**Cuckoo Sandbox**
Threat intelligence integration	MISP	Share and analyze threat intelligence	**MISP**
	VirusTotal	Analyze and scan suspicious files and URLs	**VirusTotal**
	Shodan	Identify exposed assets related to investigations	**Shodan**
Automation and orchestration	Cortex XSOAR	Automate repetitive investigation tasks	**Cortex XSOAR**
	Splunk Phantom	Security orchestration, automation, and response	**Splunk Phantom**
	Ansible	Automate data collection and artifact extraction	**Ansible**

Table 7.4: Forensic tools

Analyzing system artifacts

In this space, we are going to briefly discuss the different challenges that we face when we must investigate certain types of information and a series of recommendations and steps to facilitate the task. Let us start by exploring the research on file systems.

To start discussing the investigation in file systems, we must know that there are different organizational structures in which data is stored on media like a hard drive, SSD, etc., and each type of file system has its advantages. Here is a resume of different file structures:

File system	Operating system	Max file size	Max volume size	Journaling
NTFS	Windows	16 EB	256 TB	Yes
FAT32	Windows, Linux	4 GB	32 GB	No
exFAT	Windows, Linux	16 EB	128 PB	No
EXT4	Linux	16 TB	1 EB	Yes
HFS+	MacOS	8 EB	8 EB	Yes
APFS	MacOS	8 EB	8 EB	Yes
XFS	Linux	8 EB	8 EB	Yes
Btrfs	Linux	16 EB	16 EB	Yes
ZFS	Linux, FreeBSD	16 EB	256 ZB	Yes

Table 7.5: File system structures

As you can see in *Table 7.5*, there are many types of file systems that we can use depending on the operating system and the necessities we need to cover. Following is a visual example of the structures:

FILE SYSTEM STRUCTURE

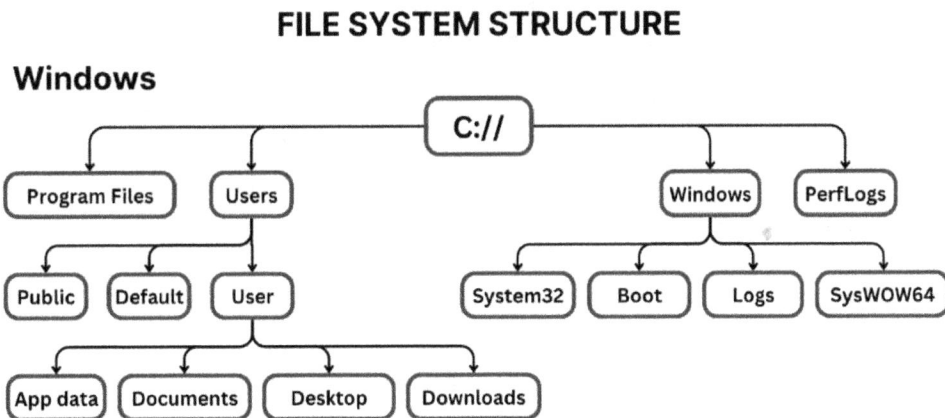

Linux

MacOS

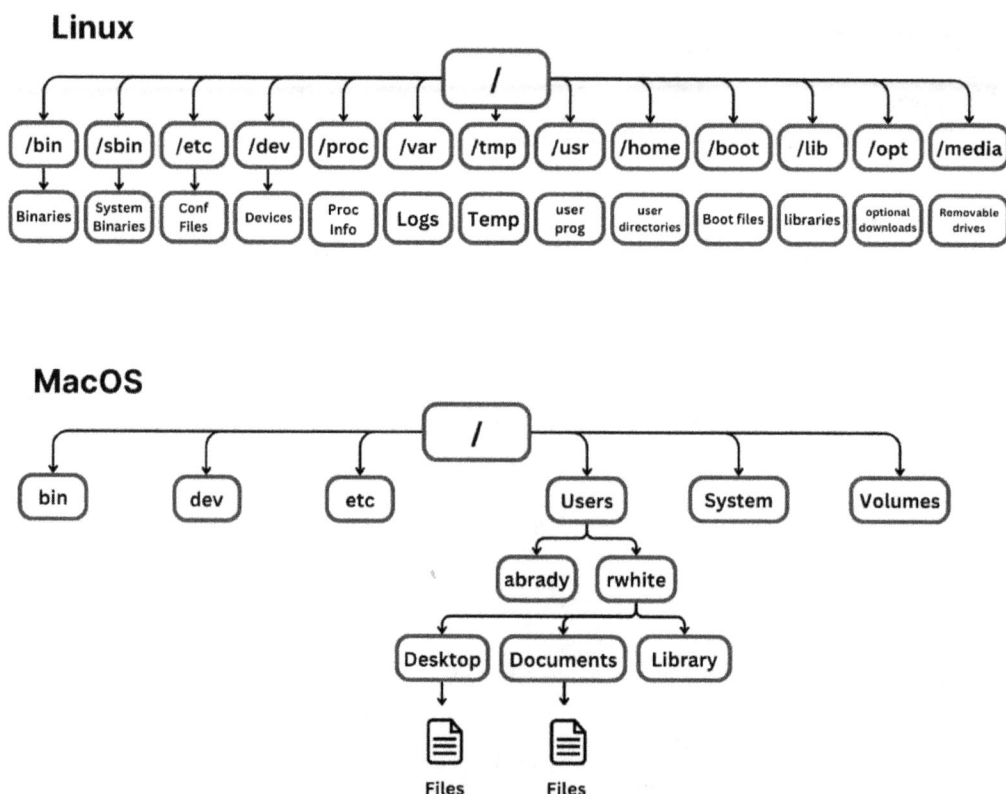

Figure 7.3: Different file system structures

In forensics, there are some key places where we can analyze and gather important or hidden information. For example, in Windows, we have metadata, which is information about a file. This can be descriptive information about the origin of a file, administrative information that defines the treatment given to the item, or structural information that relates to the conformation of the file. From a forensics viewpoint, a lot of information could be crucial to have, so following is a table of places we can search for important data:

Element	Description	Forensic relevance
Master File Table (MFT)	Contains metadata about all files in the NTFS file system	Identifying deleted files, timestamps, and access history
File system journal	Records recent file system changes (NTFS, EXT4)	Recovering deleted or modified files
Shadow copies	Stores previous versions of files (NTFS)	Restoring previous versions of files
Alternate Data Streams (ADS)	Hides additional data within a file (NTFS feature)	Detecting hidden malware or unauthorized data storage

Element	Description	Forensic relevance
Recycle Bin	Stores deleted files before permanent removal	Recovering deleted user data
Prefetch Files	Tracks recently executed applications	Tracking execution of programs, potential malware analysis
Recent Files	Lists recently accessed documents	Revealing user activity and document access
Pagefile and Hibernation File	Stores temporary memory data and hibernation state	Recovering system activity and potential memory artifacts
Superblock (Linux)	Stores metadata about file system structure in Linux	Determining file system structure and history in Linux
Inode table (Linux)	Holds file metadata (ownership, timestamps, permissions) in Linux	Recovering file metadata and detecting unauthorized changes
Symbolic and hard links	References to files that can affect forensic analysis	Investigating redirections or hidden file storage

Table 7.6: Important stored information and the forensic relevance

Registry artifacts

The registry is a big database that contains information about how a system is configured. It has information about the software, hardware, user, files, programs used, devices connected to the device, and much more. It is a big notebook where we can see configurations. In *Chapter 4, Tools and Techniques for Threat Hunting,* we talked about the registry and its keys and the importance of them in a system.

There are many keys where fundamental information is stored and where criminals tend to alter or use their functions. Following is a list where you can see some registry keys and the forensic relevance:

Registry Key	Description	Forensic Relevance
`HKEY_LOCAL_MACHINE\SAM`	Stores local user account information and credentials	Identifying user accounts and password hashes
`HKEY_LOCAL_MACHINE\SOFTWARE\ Microsoft\Windows\CurrentVersion\ Authentication\LogonUI`	Displays last logged-in user	Tracking last logged-in users
`HKEY_CURRENT_USER\Software\ Microsoft\Windows\CurrentVersion\ Run`	Lists programs that run at startup for current user	Detecting persistence mechanisms

Registry Key	Description	Forensic Relevance
`HKEY_LOCAL_MACHINE\SOFTWARE\ Microsoft\Windows\CurrentVersion\ Run`	Lists programs that run at startup for all users	Detecting persistence mechanisms
`HKEY_LOCAL_MACHINE\SYSTEM\ CurrentControlSet\Enum\USBSTOR`	Records USB devices that have been connected	Identifying unauthorized USB device usage
`HKEY_CURRENT_USER\Software\ Microsoft\Windows\CurrentVersion\ Explorer\RecentDocs`	Stores recently accessed files and documents	Recovering evidence of file access
`HKEY_LOCAL_MACHINE\SOFTWARE\ Microsoft\Windows NT\ CurrentVersion\Winlogon`	Can be modified by malware for persistence (Shell key)	Checking for persistence or system modifications
`HKEY_LOCAL_MACHINE\SOFTWARE\ Microsoft\Windows\CurrentVersion\ Uninstall`	Contains installed software information	Finding traces of installed and uninstalled software
`HKEY_LOCAL_MACHINE\SYSTEM\ CurrentControlSet\Services`	Lists services running on the system	Identifying unauthorized service installations
`HKEY_LOCAL_MACHINE\SYSTEM\ CurrentControlSet\Control\Session Manager\Memory Management`	Controls virtual memory settings	Checking for potential memory-related modifications
`HKEY_LOCAL_MACHINE\SYSTEM\ CurrentControlSet\Control\ TimeZoneInformation`	Stores system time zone information	Identifying time zone manipulations (potential anti-forensic activity)

Table 7.7: Common affected registry keys

Event logs

The investigation of event logs allows us to reconstruct a detailed record of the actions on a compromised system, detect malicious activity, and attribute actions to users or attackers. Event correlation, timestamp analysis, and the use of advanced tools allow forensic analysts to generate detailed and conclusive investigation and reports.

On Windows, event logs are stored in **%SystemRoot%\System32\winevt\Logs** and on Linux, event logs are stored in directories located in **/var/log/**. Following is a list of some examples of different logs depending on the operating system:

Log Type	Log Path	Description	Key Events
Security Log (Windows)	`%SystemRoot%\System32\winevt\Logs\Security.evtx`	Records authentication attempts, logins, and security events	4624 (Login Success), 4625 (Login Failure), 4672 (Elevated Privileges)
System Log (Windows)	`%SystemRoot%\System32\winevt\Logs\System.evtx`	Logs system-level events like hardware failures and shutdowns	6005 (System Start), 6006 (System Shutdown), 6008 (Unexpected Shutdown)
Application Log (Windows)	`%SystemRoot%\System32\winevt\Logs\Application.evtx`	Records application-specific events and errors	Application errors and crashes
Audit Log (Windows)	`%SystemRoot%\System32\winevt\Logs\Security.evtx`	Tracks changes to security policies and permissions	4719 (Audit Policy Change), 4902 (Firewall Policy Change)
PowerShell Log (Windows)	`%SystemRoot%\System32\winevt\Logs\Micro-soft-Windows-Pow-erShell%40opera-tional.evtx`	Stores events related to PowerShell commands and scripts	4104 (Script Execution), 4105 (Remote Session Creation)
Authentication Log (Linux)	`/var/log/auth.log` (Debian/Ubuntu), `/var/log/secure` (CentOS/Red Hat)	Stores authentication attempts and SSH logins	Accepted password for user, Failed password for user
Syslog (Linux)	`/var/log/syslog` (Debian/Ubuntu), `/var/log/messages` (CentOS/Red Hat)	General logging framework for system messages	System messages and errors
Web Server Log (Linux)	`/var/log/apache2/access.log`, `/var/log/nginx/access.log`	Records HTTP requests, errors, and web access	HTTP request details, error messages, access records

Table 7.8: Different key event logs

Extracting information from captures

In digital forensics, extracting valuable information from memory captures and network captures is essential for identifying malicious activity, reconstructing events and understanding the scope of a security incident. Both sources provide detailed insight into the system state and data traffic. In this section, we will go into more detail about the memory than the network analysis, as we have previously talked about networks in *Chapter 5, Network Traffic Analysis.*

When we are extracting information from the memory of the device, we analyze the memory dumps of the system, and they contain the current state of RAM, including running processes, active network connections, loaded modules, and temporary data. Analyzing these dumps helps to identify in-memory malware, plaintext credentials, and executed commands.

To analyze the memory dumps of any system, we need tools, and a very common one is volatility. This software is an open-source forensic tool for computer incident response and RAM analysis. It is developed in Python and compatible with Windows, Mac OS X, and Linux systems. Once installed on the device, we can run many commands. The recommended steps are shown in the following table:

Step	Description	Volatility command
Verify integrity	Calculate the image hash to ensure integrity.	`sha256sum memory.dmp`
Identify profile	Determine the correct operating system profile.	`volatility -f memory.dmp imageinfo`
Confirm profile	Verify the profile with another command.	`volatility -f memory.dmp --profile=Win7SP1x64 kdbgscan`
List active processes	Identify active processes in the memory dump.	`volatility -f memory.dmp --profile=Win7SP1x64 pslist`
Detect hidden processes	Find hidden processes using anti-forensic techniques.	`volatility -f memory.dmp --profile=Win7SP1x64 psscan`
Analyze process hierarchy	Show parent-child relationships between processes.	`volatility -f memory.dmp --profile=Win7SP1x64 pstree`
List DLLs in processes	List loaded DLLs in specific processes.	`volatility -f memory.dmp --profile=Win7SP1x64 dlllist -p <PID>`
Detect code injections	Identify processes with injected code (malware).	`volatility -f memory.dmp --profile=Win7SP1x64 malfind`
Analyze network connections	Examine active network connections and open sockets.	`volatility -f memory.dmp --profile=Win7SP1x64 netscan`
List handles	List resources opened by processes (files, registry keys).	`volatility -f memory.dmp --profile=Win7SP1x64 handles`
Explore Windows Registry	List registry hives in memory.	`volatility -f memory.dmp --profile=Win7SP1x64 hivelist`

Step	Description	Volatility command
Extract password hashes	Extract password hashes stored in the **Security Account Manager (SAM)**.	`volatility -f memory.dmp --profile=Win7SP1x64 hashdump`
Search for clear text credentials	Scan memory for clear text credentials.	`volatility -f memory.dmp --profile=Win7SP1x64 credscan`
Analyze browser history	Retrieve browsing history in Chrome or IE.	`volatility -f memory.dmp --profile=Win7SP1x64 chrome-history`
Dump suspicious processes	Dump suspicious processes for malware analysis.	`volatility -f memory.dmp --profile=Win7SP1x64 procdump -p <PID> -D ./dump`

Table 7.9: Step guide for volatility

Analyzing malware artifacts and IoCs

Malware artifacts are traces or footprints left by malware (malicious software) on a compromised system, including malicious files, system changes, suspicious processes, and registry modifications. Due to the traces left by the malware, there are signals or indicators that tell us if the system has been infected or modified without the user's knowledge, and we call this **Indicators of Compromise (IoC)**.

Malware artifacts are the primary source from which IoCs are derived. During malware analysis, specific details such as hashes, IP addresses, domains, modified records, etc. are extracted and then converted into IoCs. For example:

- **Malware Artifact:** `C:\Windows\System32\malicious.dll`.
- **Derived IoCs:**
  - MD5 hash of file: `d41d8cd98f00b204e9800998ecf8427e`
  - File name: `malicious.dll`
  - Path: `C:\Windows\System32\`

Case studies showcasing computer forensics

Computer forensics plays a vital role in uncovering digital evidence, responding to security incidents, and supporting legal investigations. The following section *Case studies* illustrate how forensic techniques are applied in threat hunting scenarios.

Volt Typhoon discovery

Volt Typhoon (APT Group) is a cyber-espionage group using legitimate Windows tools to operate undetected. A company affected by this group became suspicious of a possible intrusion when it noticed unusual activity on its network, such as unexpected remote connections and commands being executed at unusual times. Although the security systems did not detect any threat, the behavior raised suspicions of a possible compromise of the systems. Determined to investigate further, they gathered a threat hunting team.

This criminal group used standard Windows tools like PowerShell and WMI to perform what appeared to be normal administrative tasks but with criminal intention and left no trace. To find out what was happening in the systems, the threat hunting team used the following forensic analysis methods:

- **Evidence collection:** They compiled a list of actions performed on the computers, including the commands issued and the remote sessions established. They paid much attention to PowerShell since it was used in a way that was not typical for the tool, the application was running without generating any output and storing it on the disk. This is the typical practice of experienced hackers to make sure that there is nothing to relate or involve them.

- **Memory analysis:** The RAM memory of the computers was also analyzed to see if there were programs or scripts that were running without being logged in the normal logs. Hence the malicious scripts were discovered to be running in the background, and the PowerShell was used in a stealth mode.

- **Behavioral patterns:** The logs were checked for any unusual behavior, and they found that some devices were:

  o Performing administrative tasks by users when they should not be able to.

  o Forming remote connections to other machines in the same network without a clear reason.

  o Very long and complex commands which looked like they had been written for the purpose of moving from one computer to another without being detected.

- **Event correlation:** All these events were linked together using a tool called **Security Information and Event Management (SIEM)**. This enabled the company to realize how the attackers were able to gain access to the computers using stolen credentials. Also, they identified the unusual traffic to and from the internal network, which appeared to be normal internet traffic, but was communication with the attackers to give them instructions.

Here is a case study mapping table for the Volt Typhoon case:

Category	Details
Threat group	Volt Typhoon (APT)
Target environment	Enterprise Windows network

Category	Details
Initial indicators	Unusual remote connections and commands executed at irregular times without triggering alerts
Initial access	Use of stolen credentials
Execution technique	PowerShell and WMI are used for stealthy command execution
Persistence mechanisms	WMI event subscriptions and scheduled tasks to maintain long-term access
Privilege escalation	Use of native tools and compromised accounts to gain elevated access
Defense evasion	Living off the Land tactics: no custom malware, silent PowerShell execution with no output written to disk
Credential access	Reuse of valid credentials from earlier breaches
Lateral movement	Remote access through legitimate administrative tools and internal RDP sessions
Command and Control (C2)	Outbound traffic disguised as normal internet traffic to receive remote instructions
Volatile Data Evidence	Memory-resident PowerShell scripts and active network sessions
Non-Volatile Evidence	Registry modifications, scheduled task artifacts, Windows Event Logs, and MFT entries
Behavioral Indicators	Administrative actions from unauthorized users; Unexplained remote connections; Obfuscated, unusually long command sequences
Forensic Tools Used	Volatility, Rekall, Sysinternals Suite, Event Viewer, PowerShell logs, SIEM platform (e.g., Splunk or Elastic)
Detection Methods	Memory forensics, log analysis, behavioral pattern detection, and event correlation
SIEM Correlation Outcome	Identified attacker movement across the network, unauthorized access timeline, and covert communications with external infrastructure
Incident Outcome	Confirmed compromise attributed to Volt Typhoon, updated detection use cases, enhanced threat hunting strategies

Table 7.10: case sturdy for Volt Typhoon

Turla group network discovery

In the case of Turla, also an advanced cyber espionage group, forensic analysis was also used in the threat hunting process to help discover how they were operating in an organization's network. It all started with an increase in network traffic to external servers, which seemed to be normal but had some unusual communication patterns. Furthermore, some DNS queries had confusing behavior, which included repeated queries to domains that were not known. Like in the case of Volt Typhoon, the security systems did not raise an alarm on any danger. To investigate further, the security team set up a group that used different forensic analysis techniques to reveal the true reason behind these connections. The following will detail more about the case:

- **Evidence collection**: The team seized network traffic logs, DNS events, and endpoint logs, and the focus was on unusual DNS queries and persistent communication with external servers. The focus was on identifying the communication patterns that were apparently benign but were covering the exfiltrated commands and data to Turla's C2 servers.

- **Network traffic forensics**: They analyzed the connections to external domains that appeared safe but were command and control servers. Normal browsing was hidden behind the HTTP traffic, while the exfiltration was done through DNS queries, which were broken down into small, seemingly unharmful requests. The team was able to determine how Turla was using a technique called DNS Tunneling by recognizing these patterns.

- **Malware Forensics**: Samples of custom malware from the compromised endpoints were also identifies. It was determined through static and dynamic analysis (we will talk about these types of analysis in detail in *Chapter 8, Malware Analysis and Reverse Engineering*) that the malware used encryption and obfuscation to conceal its payload and control messages. Also, the malware was made to use covert channels of communication to enable Turla to work in the network without raising any alarm.

- **Behavioral forensics**: Anomalous user and system behavior was reviewed to include unusual remote connections and commands run at unconventional times. It was discovered that Turla was using stolen credentials to move around the network and that it was using the privileges of legitimate administrative accounts to conceal its malicious activities. These events were, therefore, correlated to identify the chain of events in the attack.

- **Forensic event correlation**: The following pieces of evidence were integrated to link all of them through the SIEM tools, which analyze the endpoint logs, network traffic, and DNS events. This made possible the mapping of the entire attack path and seeing how Turla gained access to the network, moved within it using stolen credentials, and left the network with the valuable data through the back door via DNS and HTTP.

Conclusion

In this chapter, we have discussed the world of computer forensics in relation to threat hunting and talked about the fundamentals and approaches that enable us to gather, preserve and analyze digital evidence.We also discussed the basic ideas of computer forensics, the importance of these kind of processes and the kinds of digital evidence (volatile and non-volatile) that our devices work with.

As pointed out in previous chapters, this chapter continues to develop the role of the threat hunter, and as such, focuses on the need for precision, discipline, and creative problem solving. Digital evidence is growing and becoming more significant with the technology being used in our daily lives and the sophistication of cyber threats on any device.

In practice, a solid live response starts by focusing on what is most likely to disappear first—things like RAM and active network connections. These pieces of volatile data can hold critical clues and need to be captured quickly. Tools like Volatility and Rekall help us dig into memory and uncover signs of malicious activity. From there, analysts turn to the registry, event logs, and the MFT to spot how attackers may have gained persistence or moved through the system. Looking at real-world case studies and using SIEM tools to connect the dots helps us understand the attacker's behavior and timeline. And through it all, it is essential to double-check what the tools are telling us and make sure everything is properly hashed and documented, so the evidence stays intact and trustworthy.

In the next chapter, which is called **malware analysis,** we will discuss the explanation of what malware does, analyzing the activities, how they are related to the IoC, and how we can use IoC to identify a malware artifact in the system.

Points to remember

- Computer forensics involves a systematic approach to identifying, preserving, extracting, interpreting, and presenting digital evidence for legal or administrative proceedings, ensuring the integrity and authenticity of the evidence.

- Digital evidence must be credible, precise, admissible, complete, and authentic to be considered valid in legal contexts. Maintaining its integrity is crucial for successful investigations.

- IoCs are signals indicating malicious activity. Analyzing malware artifacts and deriving IoCs (For example, file hashes and registry modifications) helps identify and respond to cyber threats effectively.

- Remember to check on the previous chapters, for example *Chapter 3, Cyber Threat Intelligence and IoC,* and *Chapter 5, Network Traffic Analysis,* which will be of great help in investigations.

Multiple choice questions

1. **What is the primary objective of computer forensics?**

    a. To develop new cybersecurity tools

    b. To identify, preserve, analyze, and present digital evidence

    c. To encrypt data to protect it from cybercriminals

    d. To delete sensitive information permanently

2. **Which characteristic is NOT essential for digital evidence to be admissible in court?**

    a. Credible

    b. Precise

    c. Incomplete

    d. Authentic

3. **Which of the following is an example of volatile data?**

    a. Memory (RAM) contents

    b. File fragments

    c. System logs

    d. Browser history

4. **Which tool is commonly used for analyzing memory dumps in digital forensics?**

    a. Autopsy

    b. FTK Imager

    c. Wireshark

    d. Volatility

5. **Indicators of Compromise (IoCs) are used to:**

    a. Encrypt sensitive files

    b. Identify signs of malicious activity

    c. Restore deleted files

    d. Backup critical system data

Answers

1. b.

2. c.

3. a.

4. d.

5. b.

References

1. Computer forensics by CISA: https://www.cisa.gov/sites/default/files/publications/forensics.pdf

2. Computer forensics by IBM: https://www.ibm.com/think/topics/computer-forensics

3. Cybersecurity guide of computer forensics: https://cybersecurityguide.org/careers/computer-forensics/

4. Digital forensics by NIST: https://www.nist.gov/itl/ssd/digital-forensics

5. Digital evidence by NIST: https://www.nist.gov/digital-evidence

6. IoC´s By Microsoft: https://www.microsoft.com/en-us/security/business/security-101/what-are-indicators-of-compromise-ioc

7. IoC´s By CrowdStrike: https://www.crowdstrike.com/en-us/cybersecurity-101/threat-intelligence/indicators-of-compromise-ioc/

8. Artifact Analysis by IBM: https://www.ibm.com/docs/en/qsip/7.5?topic=tools-artifact-analysis-suspicious-malicious-content

Join our Discord space

Join our Discord workspace for latest updates, offers, tech happenings around the world, new releases, and sessions with the authors:

https://discord.bpbonline.com

CHAPTER 8

Malware Analysis and Reverse Engineering

Introduction

In our everyday world, technology has become more fundamental for our lives, technology has become more **intelligent** and has become a part of our daily routine, for example, we have wireless coffee makers, intelligent lights, fridges, washing machines, and many more. By having these types of connectivity, cybercriminals have become more creative in the way they try to exploit our vulnerabilities, leaving us traps that are supposedly helpful, but they have a malicious intent behind them, and by this, it means malicious software or malware.

In this chapter we are going to explore the world of malware, discovering the art of malware analysis and reverse engineering, we will see the techniques and methodologies used to dissect malware and how to uncover the inner workings of malicious software, deciphering its hidden functionality and discovering its impact.

Structure

In this chapter, we will discuss the following topics:

- Introduction to malware analysis
- Malware analysis techniques
- Malware analysis tools and sandboxing

- Reverse engineering basics
- Reverse engineering tools

Objectives

Understanding how to dissect malicious software is one of the most essential skills a threat hunter must possess. This chapter is to familiarize the reader with the key techniques and tools used in malware analysis, allowing them to understand the methods employed by attackers to create malware and how they stay hidden. In this section, we will explore various types of malware, the tactics they use to evade detection, and the steps involved in static and dynamic analysis as well as reversing.

Chapter recommendations

This chapter contains references to several tools that the reader can try for themselves. As we have recommended in previous chapters, it is necessary to have a small laboratory environment where they can carry out tests without compromising their precious information and devices, and follow the common thread of the different concepts explained here.

You can create your own lab using desktop virtualization tools such as:

- **VMware Workstation:**

  https://www.vmware.com/products/desktop-hypervisor/workstation-and-fusion
- **Virtual box:**

  https://www.virtualbox.org/

You can download Microsoft server or workstation operating systems from these links:

Windows 11 Virtual machines:

https://developer.microsoft.com/en-us/windows/downloads/virtual-machines/

Introduction to malware analysis

Let us start by defining the word malware, it is short for malicious software, when put together we have malware. Malware is usually created with the intent to harm, a harmful or malicious intent of some kind. In some cases, what the cybercriminal is looking for is to ask for a ransom, for example, to return our information, as in the case of ransomware.

In other cases, they simply want to disable our information or not allow the use of our devices, it depends. So, let us go a little further into the classification of the different types of malware. There are a lot of different types of malware, depending on the book and the author. You are going to find different types because there is a great variety, but they can be summarized in the following figure:

Types of Malicious Code

Rootkits

Code designed to hide its presence from the scanning of an antimalware or EndPoint solution. It often takes the appearance of an operating system file to go undetected, while taking control of detection tools and staying hidden.

Virus

Malicious code that attaches itself to other programs in order to take advantage of the execution of the infected software to execute itself. Its spreading mechanism is usually the sharing of infected files and the promiscuity of external storage devices.

Trojan (RAT)

Malware composed of two parts. The first is a harmless code that will be used as bait for the victim to initiate the infection process, the second part corresponds to the malicious instructions that will be executed together with the seemingly harmless software.

Worm

Malicious code that replicates itself, without requiring attachment to other programs. Its spreading mechanism is usually transmission through data networks.

Launcher

A program with a short structure that invokes other malware of greater structure and potential. It is useful in cybercrime because its code is not usually identified as a threat by detection tools.

Backdoor

Malicious code that allows an attacker to gain remote access to an infected machine or device. Through the use of a backdoor, commands can be executed remotely on the system by the attacker.

APT (Advanced Persistent Threat)

Malware tailored to particular companies or a specific sector is characterized by being difficult to detect and targeted at different industries.

Spammer

This type of code, when infecting a machine, takes it as a launching pad for SPAM mail, which also sometimes has malicious code included to maintain persistence in multiple victims.

Fileless Malware

Fileless malware is a type of threat that operates directly in a system's memory without writing files to disk, using legitimate system tools to avoid detection.

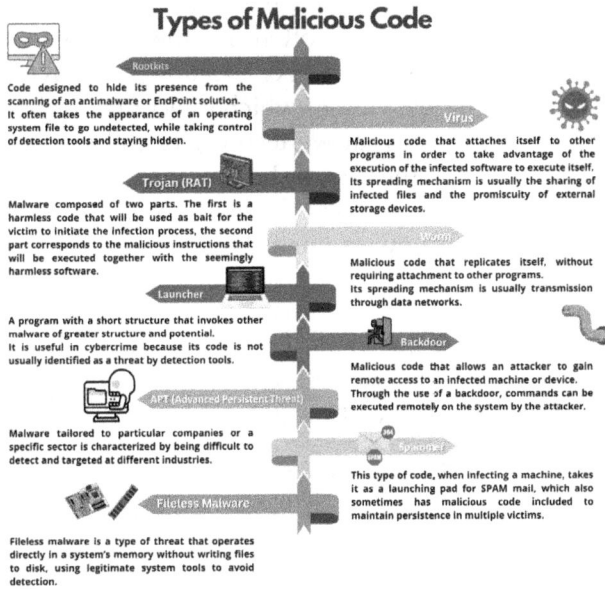

Figure 8.1: Types of malicious malware

Beyond the classic types of malware, today's threats have evolved into far more sophisticated forms that pose serious challenges to security teams. The following figure shows more types of malware and its description:

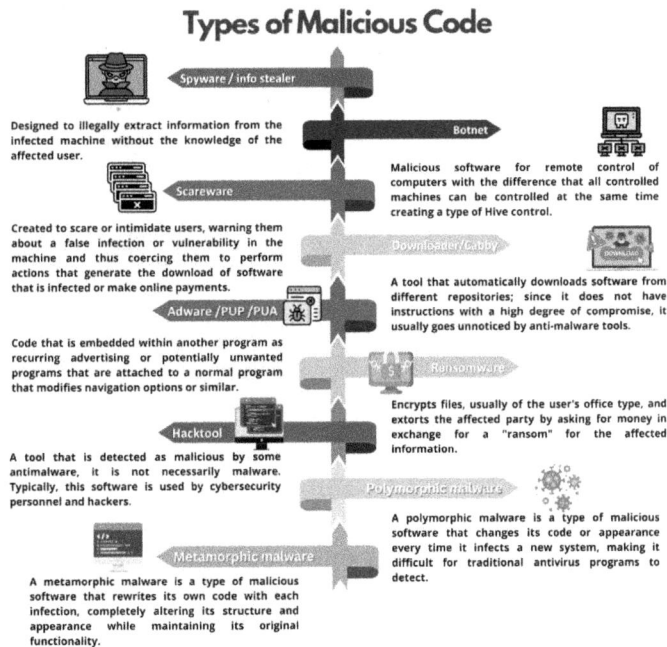

Types of Malicious Code

Spyware / info stealer

Designed to illegally extract information from the infected machine without the knowledge of the affected user.

Botnet

Malicious software for remote control of computers with the difference that all controlled machines can be controlled at the same time creating a type of Hive control.

Scareware

Created to scare or intimidate users, warning them about a false infection or vulnerability in the machine and thus coercing them to perform actions that generate the download of software that is infected or make online payments.

Downloader/Gabby

A tool that automatically downloads software from different repositories; since it does not have instructions with a high degree of compromise, it usually goes unnoticed by anti-malware tools.

Adware /PUP /PUA

Code that is embedded within another program as recurring advertising or potentially unwanted programs that are attached to a normal program that modifies navigation options or similar.

Ransomware

Encrypts files, usually of the user's office type, and extorts the affected party by asking for money in exchange for a "ransom" for the affected information.

Hacktool

A tool that is detected as malicious by some antimalware, it is not necessarily malware. Typically, this software is used by cybersecurity personnel and hackers.

Polymorphic malware

A polymorphic malware is a type of malicious software that changes its code or appearance every time it infects a new system, making it difficult for traditional antivirus programs to detect.

Metamorphic malware

A metamorphic malware is a type of malicious software that rewrites its own code with each infection, completely altering its structure and appearance while maintaining its original functionality.

Figure 8.2: More types of malicious malware

As you can see, there are many types of malware, so you can imagine there are many different classifications of malware. Malware is often classified by the type of file it infects, how it works, or the evasion measures it uses. For example, we have classifications by infected objects, we could talk about file viruses which infect files, or boot viruses, which infect the boot sector of hard disks or what we technically call the **master boot record (MBR)**. So, the MBR or first sector of the disk or boot sector of the disk can be infected with the aim that every time the machine starts, the malware is executed again, avoiding its disinfection. The following figure shows a small classification of malware:

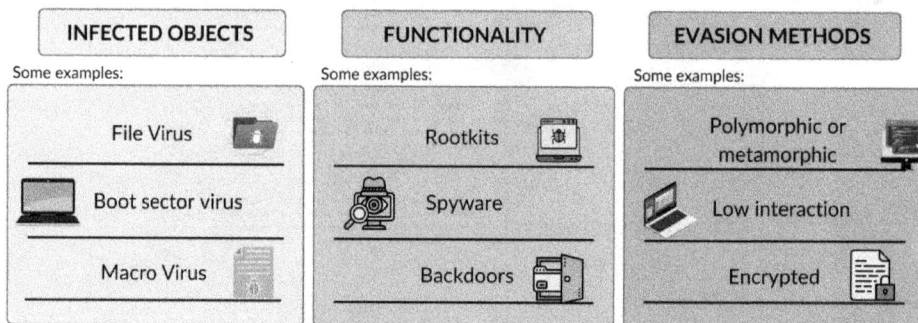

Figure 8.3: Malware classification

Now let us talk about malware analysis, which normally consists of different techniques and tools that we use to be able to perform malware analysis. At the end of the exercise, what we need is to understand how the malware is created, with which tool it was compiled. For example, which areas of our machine or our operating system it affects, how it works, if it has persistence, hiding, and encryption mechanisms it uses, etc. Following figure is an example of the process of malware analysis:

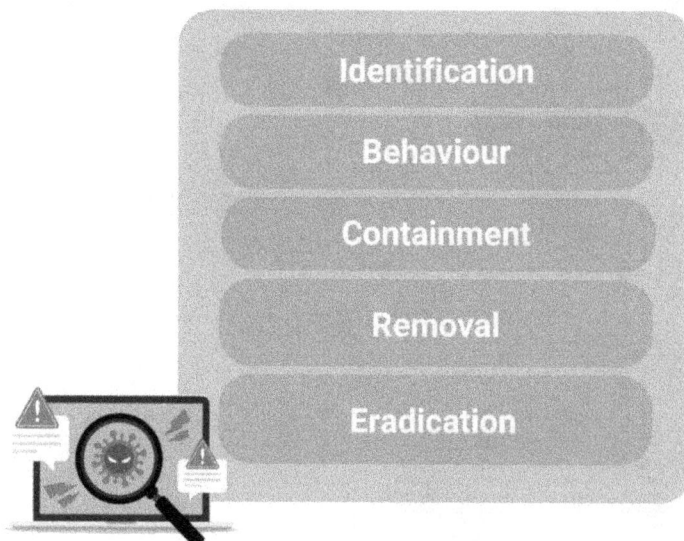

Figure 8.4: Malware analysis process

Activities performed by malware

Typically, a malware might alter an existing process or modify it in some way. Another way is to modify a service running within a system, for example a service like an anti-malware or firewall type service.

They could modify a file system, causing, for example, your **New Technology File System (NTFS)** or **High Throughput File System (HTFS)** to be altered, modifying, for example, the names of the folders you have stored on the machine, and so on. It could modify the registry as well, causing for example an application or software to load every time the Windows operating system boots or they could connect to internal or external networks to send information and exfiltrate data, steal data from our networks, so as you can see there is an infinite number of activities that malware can perform in devices.

Malware can also implement techniques for making itself more difficult to detect and persist for a longer period of time by implementing techniques as shown in the following table:

Techniques	Activity
Code encryption	Use encryption algorithms to protect against malicious code. This decreases the detection surface for automated tools. Since no antimalware solution to date can break encryptions directly. Some of the algorithms used are AES, 3DES, BlowFish, among others.
Code obfuscation	Obfuscation is the technique aimed at making it difficult to understand the execution flow of a program through abrupt changes in the program or the addition of junk or redundant instructions that make it difficult to scan samples. It is often used in conjunction with encryption to hide pieces of malware, exfiltrate information, and give remote instructions.
Code encoding	Rewrites clear text strings, under XOR, Base64, or similar type schemes, or uses unfamiliar or exotic programming languages.
Anti-reversing techniques	They are methods that a developer can implement in their code to prevent it from being easily analyzed by a debugger.
Evasion of signature detection or heuristics	In the antivirus field, heuristics are techniques used to recognize malicious code that is not in its database, based on the recognition of compiled code, disassembly, and de-packaging, among others. To avoid detection, they simply change the signatures recognized by the antivirus (variants) and, for heuristics, they modify the execution times, packers, include obfuscation, coding, and encryption, among others.
Persistence	Persistence consists of a series of techniques that allow the malware to remain on the compromised machine for a long time, even if it is initially detected and removed. There will be another infected file with some kind of additional protection, process, or registry key that will invoke the infection on the machine again.

Table 8.1: Malware techniques

Malware analysis techniques

There are several, and they also depend a lot on the authors; each writer creates their own characterizations. First, we are going to discuss the two types on which we all agree; other types will be listed separately in case a deeper explanation is needed later. The following figure highlights these malware analysis techniques:

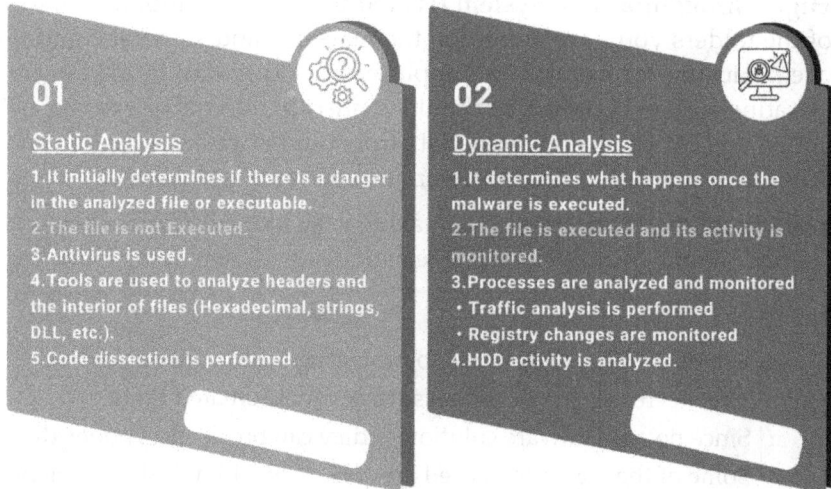

01

Static Analysis

1. It initially determines if there is a danger in the analyzed file or executable.
2. The file is not Executed.
3. Antivirus is used.
4. Tools are used to analyze headers and the interior of files (Hexadecimal, strings, DLL, etc.).
5. Code dissection is performed.

02

Dynamic Analysis

1. It determines what happens once the malware is executed.
2. The file is executed and its activity is monitored.
3. Processes are analyzed and monitored
   - Traffic analysis is performed
   - Registry changes are monitored
4. HDD activity is analyzed.

Figure 8.5: Static and dynamic analysis

These foundational techniques are often complemented by more advanced methods, such as RAM and code analysis, which allow analysts to investigate what happens in system memory and during real-time execution. The following figure illustrates the two approaches:

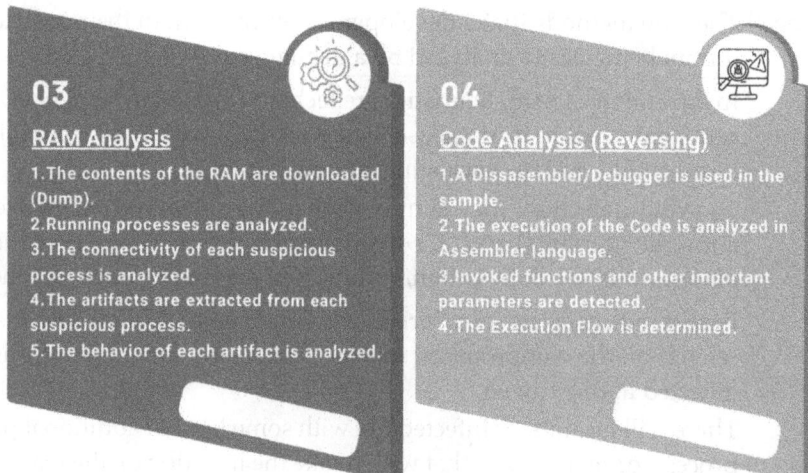

03

RAM Analysis

1. The contents of the RAM are downloaded (Dump).
2. Running processes are analyzed.
3. The connectivity of each suspicious process is analyzed.
4. The artifacts are extracted from each suspicious process.
5. The behavior of each artifact is analyzed.

04

Code Analysis (Reversing)

1. A Dissasembler/Debugger is used in the sample.
2. The execution of the Code is analyzed in Assembler language.
3. Invoked functions and other important parameters are detected.
4. The Execution Flow is determined.

Figure 8.6: RAM and code analysis

Malware analysis techniques

As we have previously mentioned, malware analysis involves examining malicious software to understand its behavior, purpose, and impact. This process is essential for identifying **Indicators of Compromise (IoCs),** detecting hidden threats, and developing effective defenses. In the following sections, various malware analysis techniques will be explained.

Static analysis

We will begin with the static analysis, which consists of analyzing the sample without executing it, in other words, gathering as much information as we can without executing the malware at all. What information could we detect? For example, what the executable or sample is compiled with, what language it was created with, what text strings it has inside, the metadata, when it was created, when it was modified, when it was last accessed, its file header or magic number, and many more information we can find. Normally, in static analysis, we involve or could involve the analysis of the assembler code. However, we will discuss this topic later in the chapter. In the following figure, you will preview the procedure for static analysis:

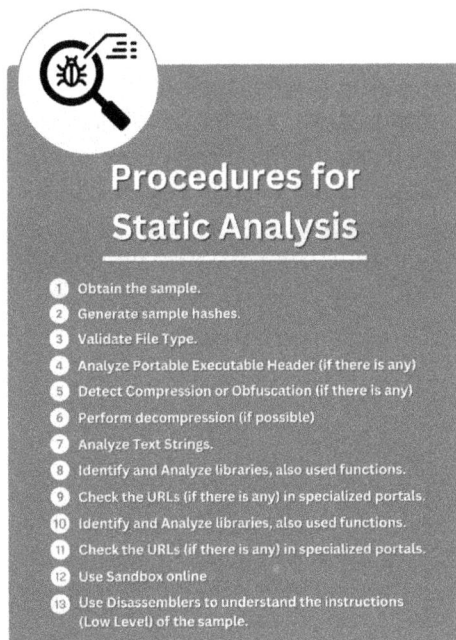

Procedures for Static Analysis

1. Obtain the sample.
2. Generate sample hashes.
3. Validate File Type.
4. Analyze Portable Executable Header (if there is any)
5. Detect Compression or Obfuscation (if there is any)
6. Perform decompression (if possible)
7. Analyze Text Strings.
8. Identify and Analyze libraries, also used functions.
9. Check the URLs (if there is any) in specialized portals.
10. Identify and Analyze libraries, also used functions.
11. Check the URLs (if there is any) in specialized portals.
12. Use Sandbox online
13. Use Disassemblers to understand the instructions (Low Level) of the sample.

Figure 8.7: Static analysis process

Generate sample hashes

The first step we are going to perform to be able to do our static analysis is to generate the hashes of the malware sample. Hashes are algorithms or use one-way encryption algorithms such as MD5, SHA 256, SHA 512, etc. A one-way encryption algorithm is an algorithm that can be received as a result or generates a hash as a result of a checksum or a mathematical function that is used against the contents of a file. In the following figure, you will see an example of an MD5 Hash:

Figure 8.8: MD5 hash example

A hash is usually based on the internal contents of a file, no matter if the file changes its name, the hash will always be the same, this is one of the most important things to keep in mind. To know if a hash is malicious, we can compare it with the previously examined malware in the world. In the section *Malware analysis tools and sandboxing*, you will be able to see some recommended tools.

Validating file type

It is essential that we can understand what type of file we are analyzing or what type of file is the sample we have under study. So, let us talk about the magic numbers. For us to know what type of file each one of the files we are analyzing is, we have the magic numbers or file signature that go inside the file, as you will see in the following figure:

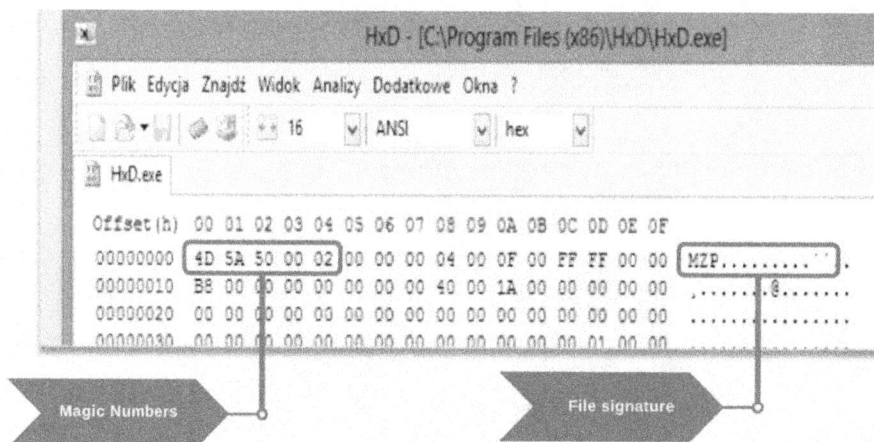

Figure 8.9: Magic numbers and file signature example

Magic numbers have nothing to do with the file extension, the file extension can be modified. In fact, it is a very common technique of cybercriminals to change the extension of a file to divert attention. For example, a JPG or PNG file that is an Excel or Word file.

Normally, the operating system can change the display of the icon with reference to the extension and that makes life a bit more complicated.

Here, we recommend the Gary Kessler website, containing a detailed list of the most important file signatures **https://www.garykessler.net/library/file_sigs.html**

In the following figure you will preview the Gary Kessler website and the file signature:

```
25 50 44 46              %PDF
            FDF, AI   Adobe Portable Document Format, Forms Document Format, and Illustrator graphics files
                      Trailers:
                      0A 25 25 45 4F 46 (.%%EOF)
                      0A 25 25 45 4F 46 0A (.%%EOF.)
                      0D 0A 25 25 45 4F 46 0D 0A (..%%EOF..)
                      0D 25 25 45 4F 46 0D (.%%EOF.)
                      NOTE: There may be multiple end-of-file marks within the
                      file. When carving, be sure to get the last one.
```

Figure 8.10: File signature example

Analysis of the portable executable header

It is very important within the static analysis of the malware to be able to see what sections are within the header and what each of them contains. Let us remember that the structure is what we have in the following figure:

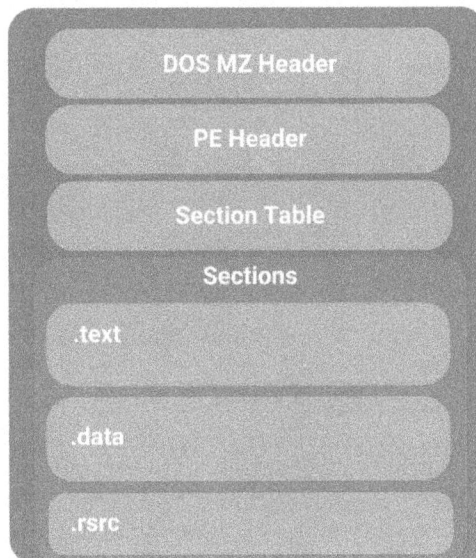

Figure 8.11: Portable header structure

We have the **Mark Zbikowski (MZ)** header, then the **portable executable (PE)** header, and inside the PE header, we have the section table that contains each one of the important sections that can have the rsrc, resources, the edata, data, etc.

The most important sections for us are the .data, which are initialized variables, the **.rsrc** contains all the resources of the file, menus, cursors, etc. We can sometimes have, if it is compressed with upx, an .upx, we have .adata, we also have an .rdata, there are many possible sections within a PE. We check the PE header so we can look through its structure and determine if it is malicious or not, by identifying irregularities in the structure that may indicate that it has bad intent.

Compressors and packers

Malware writers are usually going to try to use a lot of tools that are going to allow them to package the malware to make it much more difficult for us to understand what the malware is doing.

There are a lot of packaging tools. The advantage for us is that we can detect most of them, and in some cases, we can unpack the content of the file. In other cases, when we cannot unpack it, we have to either do a dynamic analysis and execute the malware and extract the information or extract from the RAM memory the malware already unpacked because some of them have keys, decryption procedures, etc. So, it becomes a bit complex. Let us see in the following figure is of the packaging process. Here, we have an **original.exe** where we use a packing algorithm, for example, upx:

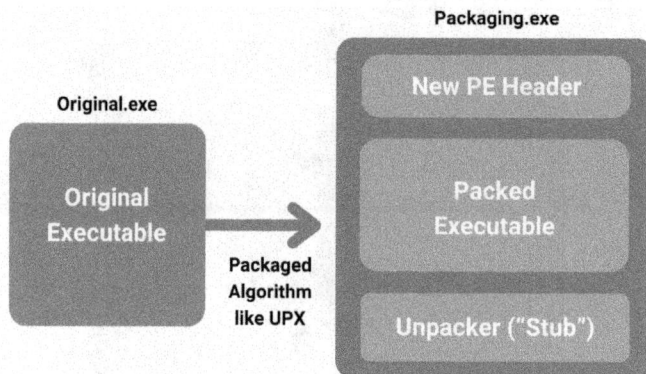

Figure 8.12: Packaging process

Once we pass the original. Exe through the packaging algorithm, we will receive a new file that has a new PE header, the packed executable, and an unpacker called the stub. Inside the stub are the unpacking routines of the packed file. Following figure is an example of the execution of the new file:

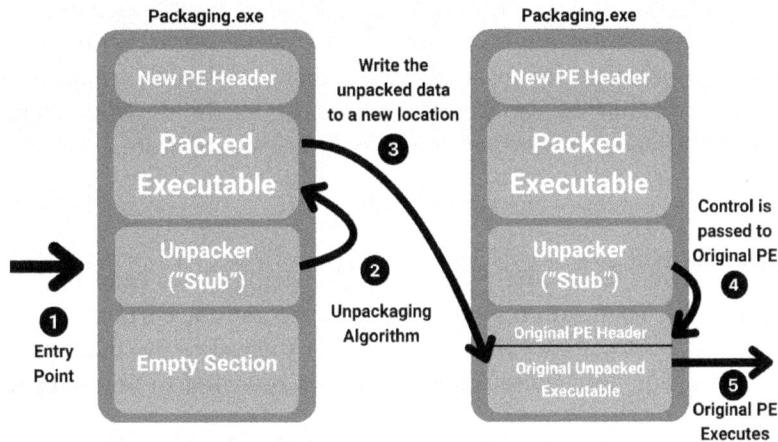

Figure 8.13: *Execution of packaged executable*

First, we have the entry point, which is handled by the stub, which invokes the unpacking algorithm for the packed file. The unpacked data is written to a new location, then control is passed to the original file, and then the original file is executed as it was intended from the beginning. This makes it more difficult for the person analyzing the malware.

Analyzing the text strings

To try to understand and get clues about how malware works, we can extract the character strings that make it up. This is not the same as understanding each instruction, but it can give clues about the activity performed by the program.

Text strings often contain valuable information such as URLs, IP addresses, file paths, API calls, registry keys, or even error messages. These strings can suggest the malware's purpose, such as data exfiltration, communication with a **command-and-control (C2)** server, or modification of system settings.

Extracting strings is typically one of the first steps in static analysis because it is quick, non-intrusive, and can be performed without executing the file. Analysts often use tools to pull out these readable components from binaries or memory dumps. While not all strings are meaningful, and some may be obfuscated, the presence of certain patterns or keywords can guide the direction of deeper analysis.

Detection of DLL libraries

Dynamic Link Library (DLL) libraries are executable files within the operating system that can normally be invoked by malware to be able to access certain functions that are embedded within each of the libraries, functions such as connecting to the internet, reading a file, opening a file, creating it, modifying it, reaching the registry, etc.

It is very important to analyze which libraries a specific malware is invoking because that would allow us to understand a little of how the malware works, with what areas of the operating system it interacts, for example, the registry, network connectivity, files, etc. So, it is very important that we can access the contents of the dependencies, usually the executable files or malware, depending on these libraries to operate.

Check URLS

It is possible that within static analysis, inside the strings, you may find some kind of HTTP address or URL. Then you may need to investigate that URL if it has some kind of malicious content. Therefore, we have some portals that allow us to determine whether a website is malicious or not. These websites will be revealed to you later in the section *Malware analysis tools and sandboxing*.

These URLs can often point to C2 servers, download additional payloads, or serve as destinations for exfiltrated data. Analyzing them can provide important context about how the malware operates and what infrastructure it relies on. It is strongly recommended not to access these URLs directly in a browser or uncontrolled environment, as they may still be active and dangerous.

Instead, analysts use specialized tools and online services that check the URL against threat intelligence databases. These platforms may reveal information such as the domain's reputation, hosting history, associations with known malware, or whether the site has been reported in past incidents.

Online sandbox

Another step-in static analysis is that you should check your results with an online sandbox. There are a lot of online sandboxes that we can use, it is not always going to be the recommended alternative to use online sandboxes, because it is possible that suddenly within the malware we find some kind of confidential content, of a company or personal, we will not want to expose them to the world, but for the cases where we can simply do an analysis and contrast our results with those of a sandbox this step is highly recommended. Later in the section on *Malware analysis tools and sandboxing*, there will be a list of potential sandboxes, all free for the most part, so that you can deliver a sample to these sandboxes and then test or determine what the sandbox says and contrast.

Disassemblers

One of the final phases of static analysis of malware is to disassemble the malware. Disassemblers and debuggers are tools that allow us to see in assembler instructions the samples that we want to analyze, and at a determined moment they allow us to execute them in a spaced way or in a way that allows us to generate breakpoints. This is basically malware reversing and to perform this, it normally requires knowledge of assembler to be able to understand the instructions.

Dynamic analysis

Dynamic analysis basically consists of running tools that allow us to monitor and census the activity inside the computer once we execute the malware to see what changes are generated and, in this way, understand how the malware works. So, within the procedure for dynamic analysis, we have different techniques that we recommend, as you will preview in the following figure:

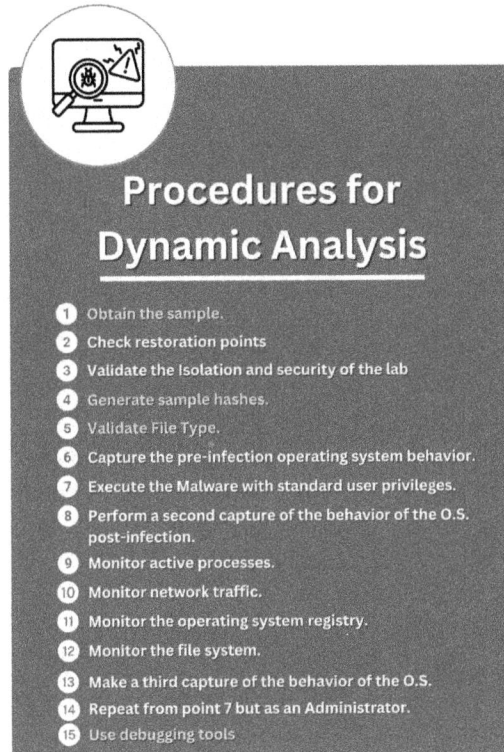

Procedures for Dynamic Analysis

1. Obtain the sample.
2. Check restoration points
3. Validate the Isolation and security of the lab
4. Generate sample hashes.
5. Validate File Type.
6. Capture the pre-infection operating system behavior.
7. Execute the Malware with standard user privileges.
8. Perform a second capture of the behavior of the O.S. post-infection.
9. Monitor active processes.
10. Monitor network traffic.
11. Monitor the operating system registry.
12. Monitor the file system.
13. Make a third capture of the behavior of the O.S.
14. Repeat from point 7 but as an Administrator.
15. Use debugging tools

Figure 8.14: Dynamic analysis process

In the above figure, points *1,4,5,* and *15* were already explained in static analysis, therefore, it is recommended to read those topics again in case you have forgotten them.

Restoration points and validation of isolation

This is a crucial activity, to check the virtualization restore points; in other words, you must capture snapshots, so at a given moment, you can return after having infected the sandbox.

This is essential and the recommendation is that you have a backup copy in an alternate location of the original sandbox, so that if for any reason you were to analyze a malware that has sandbox escaping technologies or that could suddenly exploit a vulnerability of the virtualization tool you are using, you have a backup mechanism of that sandbox. You must validate the isolation and security of the laboratory; only the two virtual machines can be seen against each other, and their network only communicates with each other. It is essential to validate that this isolation between machines is properly maintained.

Capture the operating system behavior

The first point we are going to analyze is capturing the behavior of the operating system, and in this case, we are going to discuss specifically capturing the registry of the Windows operating system.

It is vital to take an initial snapshot of what the registry looks like at a given point in time prior to infection. Take a first snapshot and then infect the machine. The second snapshots must be taken pre-infection and post-infection so we can compare the two moments and understand very quickly what changes were generated.

Once the malware is executed, the recommendation is that we give it about 40 seconds to one minute of execution because it gives time to the malware to perform the malicious activities it is going to perform. Sometimes, you must give it more time because it is possible that the malware stays with stealth technologies or just high latency, stays resident in RAM, and then after 12 hours or 24 hours, executes certain actions. For example, connect to the internet or download another file, etc. If suddenly you do not notice major changes between one execution and the other, it is simply a matter of changing the time parameters to see if it runs in a different way, or if given time, there is a noticeable change that you can notice.

Sample execution

It is very important to keep in mind within the dynamic analysis of the malware that we must run the malware both with normal common user or restricted user privileges and with administrator user privileges, because the malware can behave in a different way. If we do it in only one way, as a normal user for example, we could lose sight of certain behaviors or certain actions of the malware, such as not seeing a network connection because it would not execute, because the malware detects that it does not have sufficient privileges. Other examples can be the modification of a registry key or the creation of a file in a specific folder.

Monitoring of activities

One of the main tasks of the dynamic analysis is to monitor the behavior of the compromised machine during the infection and to list the different changes that occur to it. Points of interest to review are shown in the following figure:

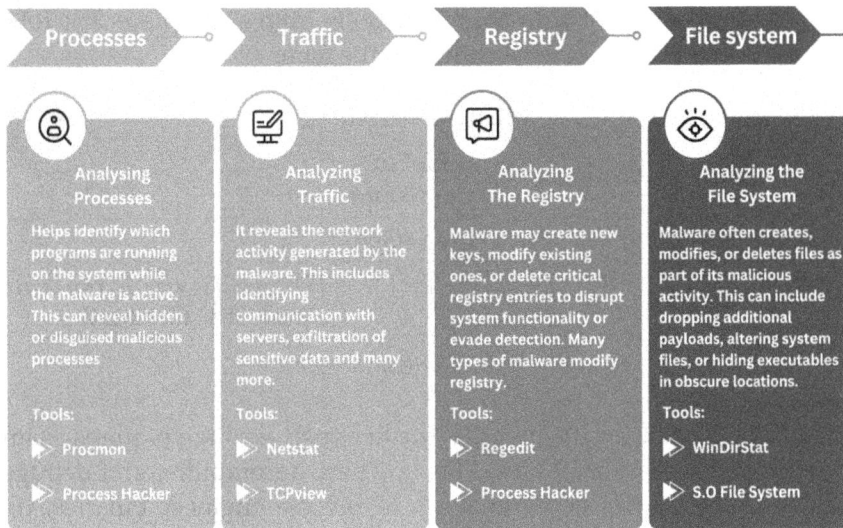

Figure 8.15: Points of interest for monitoring

Traffic monitoring

We are now going to talk about how to capture the traffic that is generated in our machine, you can use in a remnux machine **https://remnux.org/** the command **sudo inetsim** to be able to review the services, then copy the routes that you want to analyze, see that they are being used in the machine and to be able to observe in realtime how the Logs are being modified. In the following, we will see commands and examples of the traffic monitoring:

- **Commands:**
  - **Sudo inetsim**
  - **Cd (Route of the log)**
  -
  - **Tail -f -(name of the log)**
- **Example:**
  - **Sudo inetsim**
  - **Cd /var/log/inetsim/**
  - **ls**
  - **Tail -f -service.log**

Another way to monitor traffic in other types of operating systems is to use tools like Wireshark or TCP view.

Malware analysis tools and sandboxing

For all the tests that we have previously explained, we need tools so we can execute these types of investigations for malware analysis. If you investigate and find better tools, you can use them. However, remember to download them from a safe place. The following are a couple of lists of recommended tools shown in the table:

Generate Hash				
Name	**Linux**	**Windows**	**Tool or Command**	**Link**
Md5sum	X		Command	
Hash my files		X	Tool	**https://www.nirsoft.net/utils/ hash_my_files.html**

Table 8.2: Tools for generating Hash

While hash tools help ensure data integrity, further analysis often requires examining the internal structure and behavior of files. This is where decompiling and debugging tools become valuable. These tools allow analysts to reverse engineer binaries, understand program logic, and identify hidden or malicious functionalities that may not be evident through static inspection alone. The following is a table of debugging tools:

Decompiling and debugging tools				
Name	**Linux**	**Windows**	**Tool or Command**	**Link**
IDA Pro		X	Tool	**https://hex-rays.com/ida-pro/**
WinDbg		X	Tool	**https://learn.microsoft.com/en-us/windows-hardware/drivers/debugger/**
Binary Ninja		X	Tool	**https://binary.ninja/**
Radare	X	X	Tool	**https://www.radare.org/n/**
R2 Ghidra	X	X		**https://github.com/radareorg/r2ghidra**

Table 8.3: Tools for decompiling and debugging

Once a file has been examined at the code level, it is often necessary to confirm its actual type, especially in cases where attackers disguise malicious files by changing their extensions. File type validation tools help determine the true nature of a file based on its internal structure rather than its name or extension, which is crucial in identifying disguised or obfuscated malware. Here is a table of validating file type tools:

Validating File Type				
Name	**Linux**	**Windows**	**Tool or Command**	**Link**
HxD		X	Tool	Comes installed
Gary Kessler File Signatures		X	Tool	**https://www.garykessler.net/library/file_sigs.html**
Cff Explorer		X	Tool	Comes installed
XXD	X		Command	
file	X		Command	

Table 8.4: Tools for validating the file type

After confirming the file type, especially for executable files, a deeper examination of its internal structure is often necessary. Tools that analyze PE headers provide detailed insights into how the file was built, its entry points, linked libraries, and other metadata. This information is essential for identifying suspicious modifications, understanding execution flow, and supporting further reverse engineering. Here is a table of PE Header Analyzer tools:

PE Header Analyzers				
Name	**Linux**	**Windows**	**Tool or Command**	**Link**
PE studio		X	Tool	**https://www.winitor.com/download**
PE Viewer		X	Tool	Comes installed
CFF Explorer		X	Tool	Comes installed
PE Bear	X	X	Tool	**https://github.com/hasherezade/pe-bear**

Table 8.5: Tools for analyzing PE headers

After examining the PE headers, it is also important to determine whether the executable has been compressed or packed. Attackers often use packers to obfuscate malware and hinder analysis by hiding the actual code. Here is a table of compressor and packer tools:

Compressors and Packers				
Name	Linux	Windows	Tool or Command	Link
VMProtect		X	Tool	**https://vmpsoft.com/**
AsPack		X	Tool	**http://www.aspack.com/**
CExe		X	Tool	**https://www.softpedia.com/get/Compression-tools/CExe.shtml**
EXE Stealth		X	Tool	**https://www.webtoolmaster.com/packer.htm**

Table 8.6: Compressors and packers

Once a file has been unpacked or is ready for inspection, analyzing its text strings becomes an effective next step. Tools or commands that extract readable strings from binaries can reveal valuable information such as hardcoded URLs, IP addresses, file paths, commands, or even attacker messages. Here is a table of text string analyzing tools:

Text Strings Analyzing				
Name	Linux	Windows	Tool or Command	Link
Strings		X	Tool	Comes with sysinternals.
WinHex		X	Tool	**https://x-ways.net/winhex/**
BinText		X	Tool	**https://www.majorgeeks.com/files/details/bintext.html**
Grep	X		Command	
Floss	X	X		**https://github.com/mandiant/flare-floss**

Table 8.7: Tools or commands for analyzing text strings

After identifying meaningful strings, the next step often involves examining the libraries the file interacts with. Analyzing imported and linked libraries can uncover the file's dependencies, its intended functionality, and potential misuse of legitimate system functions, all of which are essential for understanding the behavior and risk associated with the file. Here is a table of library detection tools:

Library Detection				
Name	**Linux**	**Windows**	**Tool or Command**	**Link**
PE studio		X	Tool	**https://www.winitor.com/download**
Dependency walker		X	Tool	Comes installed
CFF Explorer		X	Tool	Comes installed
dll files.com	X	X	Website	**https://www.dll-files.com/**
Process Library	X	X	Website	**https://www.processlibrary.com/en/**

Table 8.8: Tools or commands for analyzing libraries

In many cases, malware communicates with external servers or downloads additional components from the internet. For this reason, it is important to verify any URLs found during analysis. URL checkers allow analysts to safely inspect suspicious links, check for known malicious domains, and assess the potential risk of online resources referenced by the file. Here is a table of library detection tools:

URLS Check				
Name	**Linux**	**Windows**	**Tool or Command**	**Link**
URL scan IO	X	X	Tool	**https://urlscan.io/**
AbuseIPDB,	X	X	Tool	**https://www.abuseipdb.com/**
URL Void	X	X	Tool	**https://www.urlvoid.com/**
Virus Total	X	X	Website	**https://www.virustotal.com/gui/home/upload**

Table 8.9: URL checkers

While checking URLs provides insight into external communication, understanding how a suspicious file behaves within the operating system is equally important. Tools that monitor OS-level activity, such as file system changes, process creation, and registry modifications, offer a more complete picture of the malware's behavior and impact on the host system. Here is a table of tools for capturing the operating system behavior:

Capturing the operating system behavior				
Name	Linux	Windows	Tool or Command	Link
RegShot	X	X	Tool	**https://github.com/Seabreg/Regshot**
Regedit		X	Tool	Comes installed
Process Hacker		X	Tool	**https://processhacker.sourceforge.io/**

Table 8.10: Tools for capturing the operating system behavior

In addition to monitoring local behavior, it is also important to analyze network activity. As mentioned before, malware often attempts to connect to remote servers, exfiltrate data, or receive commands. That is why traffic monitoring tools are a must, due to their ability to allow analysts to inspect these connections, detect anomalies, and gather valuable IoCs related to network behavior. Here is a table of tools for monitoring traffic:

Monitoring Traffic				
Name	Linux	Windows	Tool or Command	Link
Wireshark	X	X	Tool	**https://github.com/Seabreg/Regshot**
TCP View		X	Tool	Comes installed

Table 8.11: Tools for monitoring traffic

While monitoring traffic reveals external interactions, analyzing how a file interacts with system components at a lower level is also essential. Tools that monitor drivers and API calls provide insight into how malware communicates with the operating system, accesses hardware resources, or manipulates system behavior, offering a deeper understanding of its capabilities and techniques. Here is a table of tools for monitoring Drivers and API:

Monitoring Drivers and API				
Name	Linux	Windows	Tool or Command	Link
Driver view		X	Tool	**https://www.nirsoft.net/utils/driver-view.html**
API Monitor		X	Tool	

Table 8.12: Tools for monitoring drivers and API

In addition to runtime behavior, it's also important to examine how malware may affect system startup. Some malicious programs are designed to load during boot-up to ensure persistence. Monitoring tools focused on the startup process help detect unauthorized services, scheduled tasks, and registry modifications that enable malware to launch automatically when the system starts. Here is a table of tools for monitoring boot up:

Monitor Boot Up				
Name	**Linux**	**Windows**	**Tool or Command**	**Link**
Auto Runs		X	Tool	**https://learn.microsoft.com/en-us/sys-internals/downloads/autoruns**

Table 8.13: Tools for monitoring boot up

Beyond startup behavior, it is also important to observe how a file affects overall system performance and process activity. Tools that monitor processes and system vitals provide real-time insights into CPU usage, memory consumption, and active threads, helping analysts identify abnormal behavior or resource-intensive operations linked to malicious activity. Here is a table of tools for monitoring process and vitals:

Monitor Process and vitals				
Name	**Linux**	**Windows**	**Tool or Command**	**Link**
Process Explorer		X	Tool	**https://learn.microsoft.com/en-us/sys-internals/downloads/process-explorer**
Sysmon		X	Tool	**https://learn.microsoft.com/en-us/sys-internals/downloads/sysmon**

Table 8.14: Tools for monitoring process and system vitals

Sandbox

Sandboxes are basically used to take a sample of the malware and analyze it under a controlled environment, which is essential for malware analysis.

There are several types of environments. We have virtual labs, which is the most common of all, where you normally use a hypervisor platform such as Hyper V, Vmware, Virtualbox or like create your virtual machines and be able to do the analysis in a safe way.

We have the automated laboratory, which usually requires specialized software, which generates virtualizations and manages these virtualizations. There are several vendors that sell these types of solutions. They can be mounted inside an existing server in the infrastructure, or they are delivered to you as an appliance, as a machine created specifically for that purpose. They have a relatively high cost.

We have the physical labs, on the other hand, a physical lab consists of an actual physical machine that you're going to infect with the sample, with the goal of understanding how the sample works, what the behavior is, what areas of the registry it alters, network connectivity, and so on. It is the best of all basically because many advanced malwares can detect that they are running in a sandbox or in a Sheep Dip machine, which is another name for the sandbox.

In the case of more advanced malware such as **Advanced Persistent Threat (APT)** or similar, in many cases a physical machine is required. In these cases, the physical machines require a restoration mechanism to be able to return them to the previous state.

There are some specific cards for this, you can make a disk image and restore the disk image once the analysis of a sample is finished, among other aspects that could be handled.

Another important thing is that it requires to be completely isolated from the network, it should not have real connectivity to the outside, it should not be connected to a network where there are production machines, it must be a totally isolated environment. Virtualization tools even have an isolation configuration space, this space must be properly configured. In the following table you will find sandboxes where you can handle malware samples:

Sandbox online	Link
Hybrid analysis	**https://www.hybrid-analysis.com/**
Any.Run	**https://any.run/**
Virustotal	**https://www.virustotal.com/gui/home/upload**
Jotty	**https://virusscan.jotti.org/**
Joe sandbox	**https://www.joesandbox.com/#windows**

Table 8.15: Sandbox online

There are a lot of sandboxes online. *Table 8.15* is too short to talk about them all. You can simply do a search on the Internet, just say online sandbox or similar, and you will find a lot of them.

Downloading samples

Something extremely important to be able to do malware analysis is to have samples to analyze. The following table shows a list of potential places where you can download malware or malware samples for analysis:

Malware samples	Link
Hybrid Analysis	**https://www.hybrid-analysis.com/**
Malshare	**https://malshare.com/**
Contagio malware dump	**http://contagiodump.blogspot.com**
Objective-See	**https://objective-see.com/malware.html**
VirusShare	**https://virusshare.com/**
Malware DB = theZoo	**http://thezoo.morirt.com/**

Table 8.16: Online malware samples

Reversing engineering basics

The malware reversing consists of the whole group of techniques that we use to be able to understand in assembler the code of a file that we are analyzing.

Normally, when we try to disassemble the code, we must consider the following. We have a source code where, normally, a pre-processing is done, and it is compiled. When compiling the source code, whether it is in C, Java, etc., we normally make an assembly of the code. That assembly leads us to an object code, and it will normally have some links and some linked DLL, which will be invoked when necessary. At the end, what we receive is an executable code, an .exe or a .scr, depending on what we are creating.

This executable code is already compiled, and if we try to visualize it with a text editor, with a tool such as strings or similar, what we will see are text strings, but we will not be able to really understand what the functions inside this executable code are. That is where code disassembly comes in. When we disassemble code, what we do is take the executable code and take it back to the assembler, to the assembly language, to be able to understand the instructions in the language we call assembler.

So, these are instructions, they are low-level instructions, they are normally the instructions that are loaded into the processor, and we will be able to understand them, but to understand them, we need a certain level of knowledge.

Reverse engineering tools

Reverse engineering is the process of deconstructing software to understand how it works, identify hidden functionality, or detect malicious code. In malware analysis, reverse engineering tools are essential for examining executables. They allow analysts to disassemble code, trace execution flow, identify obfuscation techniques, and analyze embedded resources. Here is a table with a list of decompiling and debugging tools that you can use:

Decompiling and debugging tools				
Name	**Linux**	**Windows**	**Tool or Command**	**Link**
IDA Pro		X	Tool	**https://hex-rays.com/ida-pro/**
OllyDBG		X	Tool	**https://www.ollydbg.de/**
Binary Ninja		X	Tool	**https://binary.ninja/**
Radare	X	X	Tool	**https://www.radare.org/n/**
R2 Ghidra	X	X	Tool	**https://github.com/radareorg/r2ghidra**
Relyze		X	Tool	**https://www.relyze.com/**

Table 8.17: Reverse engineering tools

Conclusion

In this chapter we explored the world of malware and in this case malware analysis, we mention all the malware types that currently exist and how they are classified, we also discussed all the steps for analyzing malware, going into detail in static and dynamic analysis which are the most fundamental analysis that we can perform. We had a look in the tools that we can use, and we entered the basics of malware reversing, an advanced topic due to the knowledge needed to understand the most profound workings of malware.

As stated in previous chapters, this chapter highlights the crucial role of the analyst and how creativity, patience, capacity, and an eye for detail are key for malware analysis. Malware is currently being innovated each day; cybercriminals find a new process that is vulnerable, an innovative and creative way of exploiting a vulnerability in a way that has never been done before, so the analyst will have to overcome new challenges to discover the secrets of malware.

In the next chapter, readers will explore the world of APTs, where topics will include the APT attack lifecycle, common **Tactics, Techniques, and Procedures (TTPs)**, methods for hunting APTs, and approaches to incident response and attribution in high-level threat scenarios.

Points to remember

- It is of deep importance that you check the isolation of the lab you have decided to use, remember that you will be executing real malware, and it can scape, if you are not careful enough, you might get infected, keeping your information and your machine safe is a must.

- Always have a clean snapshot of the machine you are infecting, in any case something goes wrong, it is possible to go back to the start. It is also needed for comparing with future snapshots when it is infected.

- Malware is becoming more advanced, it is crucial that the analyst does too, being up to date with all the techniques and new malware its important.

- Remember to follow the steps when performing the analysis explained in the chapter, they will be of great guide.

Multiple choice questions

1. **What is the primary goal of static malware analysis?**
   a. To execute malware and observe its behavior in a controlled environment.
   b. To analyze the malware without executing it.
   c. To decrypt malware communication.
   d. To reverse engineer the malware's code completely.

2. **What type of malware is designed to replicate itself and spread to other systems?**

   a. Trojan

   b. Rootkit

   c. Worm

   d. Ransomware

3. **What is the purpose of reverse engineering malware?**

   a. To modify the malware's functionality.

   b. To understand the malware's inner workings and design.

   c. To remove the malware from infected systems.

   d. To obfuscate malware code.

4. **In dynamic analysis, what does network analysis typically involve?**

   a. Decompiling the malware's code.

   b. Monitoring malware's impact on system resources.

   c. Tracking malware's communication with suspicious sources.

   d. Running the malware in a disassembler.

5. **Which tool is widely used for disassembling and reverse engineering malware?**

   a. IDA Pro

   b. Process Explorer

   c. Wireshark

   d. Reg Shot

Answers

1. b.

2. c.

3. b.

4. c.

5. a.

References

1. Malware analysis by Fortinet: https://www.fortinet.com/resources/cyberglossary/malware-analysis

2. Malware analysis by crowdstrike: https://www.crowdstrike.com/cybersecurity-101/malware/malware-analysis/

3. Sysinternals Suite: https://learn.microsoft.com/en-us/sysinternals/downloads/sysinternals-suite

4. Static Analysis: https://www.techtarget.com/whatis/definition/static-analysis-static-code-analysis

5. Static and Dynamic analysis: https://www.bitdefender.com/blog/businessinsights/the-differences-between-static-malware-analysis-and-dynamic-malware-analysis/

6. Dynamic Analysis: https://www.techtarget.com/searchsecurity/tip/How-dynamic-malware-analysis-works

7. Reverse engineering: https://www.techtarget.com/searchsoftwarequality/definition/reverse-engineering

8. Malware Reversing: https://www.eccouncil.org/cybersecurity-exchange/ethical-hacking/malware-reverse-engineering/

Join our Discord space

Join our Discord workspace for latest updates, offers, tech happenings around the world, new releases, and sessions with the authors:

https://discord.bpbonline.com

CHAPTER 9

Advanced Persistent Threats and Nation-State Actors

Introduction

Nowadays, the entire cybercrime landscape and ecosystem have undergone a fundamental transformation due to the unprecedented growth of **artificial intelligence** (**AI**). This technological evolution has reshaped attack vectors, defense mechanisms, and the overall security paradigm.

Malicious actors, whether supported or not by states, have achieved unprecedented attacks by taking advantage of several factors that have been enhanced by AI, such as social engineering, NoCode (No-code is a way of building software applications without writing any traditional programming code), and automation through multiple tools; we are going to delve into the world of APTs, their campaigns (Attacks) understand their taxonomy and evaluate countermeasures.

This chapter includes APT case studies that have been discovered in various victims, created by multiple malicious actors. We recommend that the reader explore their analysis and study through the links provided for each case and actor mentioned.

Structure

In this chapter, we will discuss the following topics:

- Understanding APTs and nation-state threats

- APT attack lifecycle
- APT TTPs
- Hunting for APTs and nation-state actors
- APT incident response and attribution

Objectives

This chapter explores the hidden **Tactics, Techniques, and Procedures (TTPs)** employed by nation-state actors and **Advanced Persistent Threats (APT)** groups, shedding light on their motives and capabilities.

Through real-world case studies and expert analysis, readers will gain a comprehensive understanding of the APT attack lifecycle and the methods used by nation-state actors to infiltrate and compromise targeted organizations. We will explore the advanced techniques employed by these adversaries, such as zero-day exploits and advanced social engineering tactics.

In this space, readers will be better prepared to defend against these highly sophisticated adversaries.

Understanding APTs and nation-state threats

In our world of cybersecurity, one of the most feared and complex threats is the APTs. These are not simple and common attacks; they represent strategic, well-funded, and organized operations that aim to infiltrate critical networks and steal valuable information or sabotage key infrastructure, all without being detected. Unlike traditional attacks, APTs do not seek immediate results but rather prolonged and sustained access, which makes them extremely dangerous and difficult to detect. The time they manage to stay within their target undetected is called **Dwell Time**, that is, the time they manage to stay exfiltrating data or generating sabotage to the infrastructure they are attacking without any detection or alert.

Advanced Persistent Threats

An APT is an advanced and persistent threat that is characterized by its sophistication and ability to go unnoticed; they are created either by independent criminal groups or often by groups belonging to or sponsored by Nations. They can behave like very advanced malware and spread like a worm throughout an infrastructure or explore machine by machine looking for a specific target, information or technology to be attacked.

Among the most common objectives of APTs, we have:

- Government espionage
- Corporate espionage

- Exfiltration of sensitive information
- Attacks on critical infrastructure
- Sleeping agents to be activated in certain circumstances

The following figure is from MITRE's website with the most up-to-date list of APT groups:

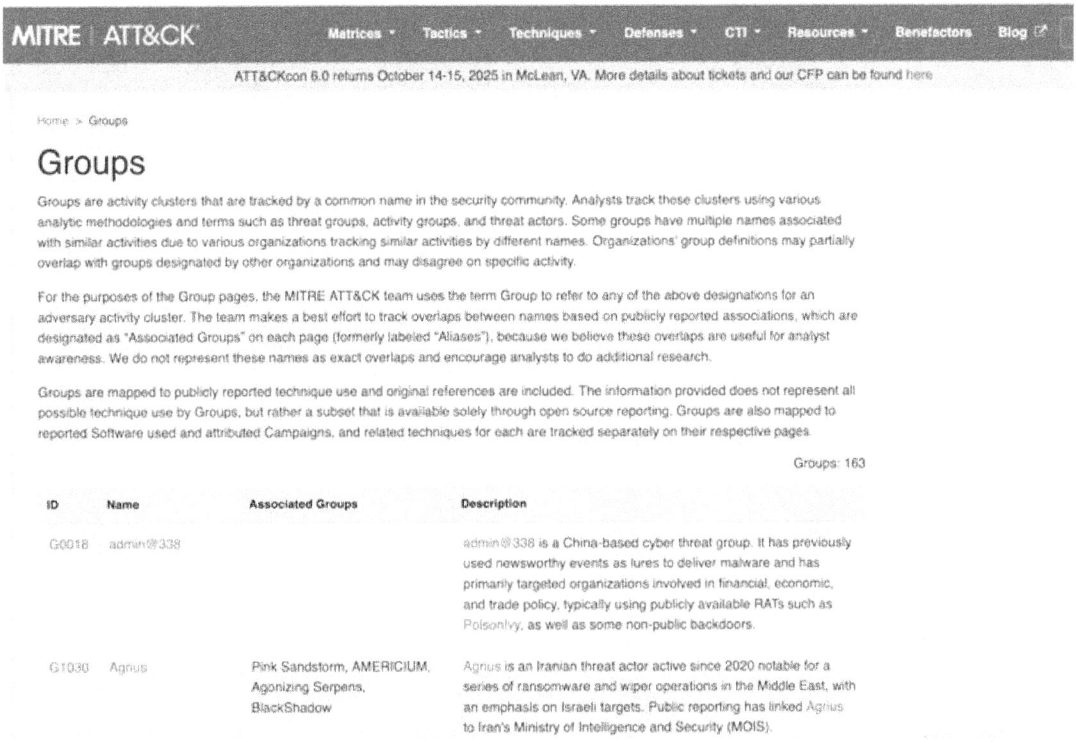

Figure 9.1: MITRE's APT groups
(**Source:** *https://attack.mitre.org/groups/*)

Advanced Persistent Threats attack lifecycle

APTs operate in planned phases to achieve successful infiltration and undetected information extraction. This process is like the *Kill Chain* and usually includes different stages or different focuses. Many cybersecurity companies and authors have differences about the steps or stages of the APT lifecycle. However, we present the most generally accepted:

1. Target definition
2. Target recognition and research
3. Initial infiltration
4. Foothold

5. Privilege escalation

6. Lateral movement

7. Data exfiltration

8. Persistence and evasion

As we can see, we separate the different stages of the life   cycle of the APTs between preparation phases (Target definition, reconnaissance), where the adversary makes a choice of the target and an in-depth study of his potential victim and develops or acquires the necessary tools to be able to attack him in a more profiled way, thanks to the reconnaissance phase. Then comes the intrusion phases (initial infiltration, foothold, and privilege escalation), where the attacker begins the initial attack almost always using social engineering once a foothold is achieved, that is, getting at least one victim to click where they should not or download and execute a file or any other of the possible techniques. We move on to privilege escalation, where the adversary takes more and more capabilities, permissions, and levels within the compromised infrastructure, and finally, we have the phases of active intrusion, where the attacker or adversary owns and exercises control over the victim infrastructure either to execute unwanted actions, spy on it, sabotage it or exfiltrate information. Following figure shows where you will preview the lifecycle of an APT:

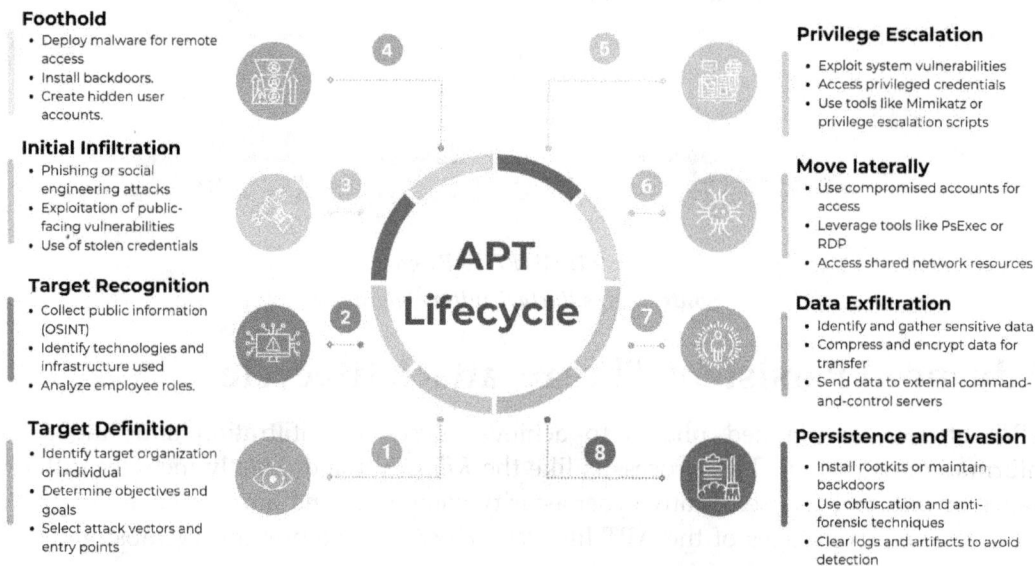

Figure 9.2: APT lifecycle

APT TTPs

The TTPs used by APTs are multiple and varied, and can be combined in many ways, which only adds more complexity to the threat hunting process. However, there is a complete framework that helps us map the activities of the APTs. This is the MITRE ATT&CK shown in the following figure:

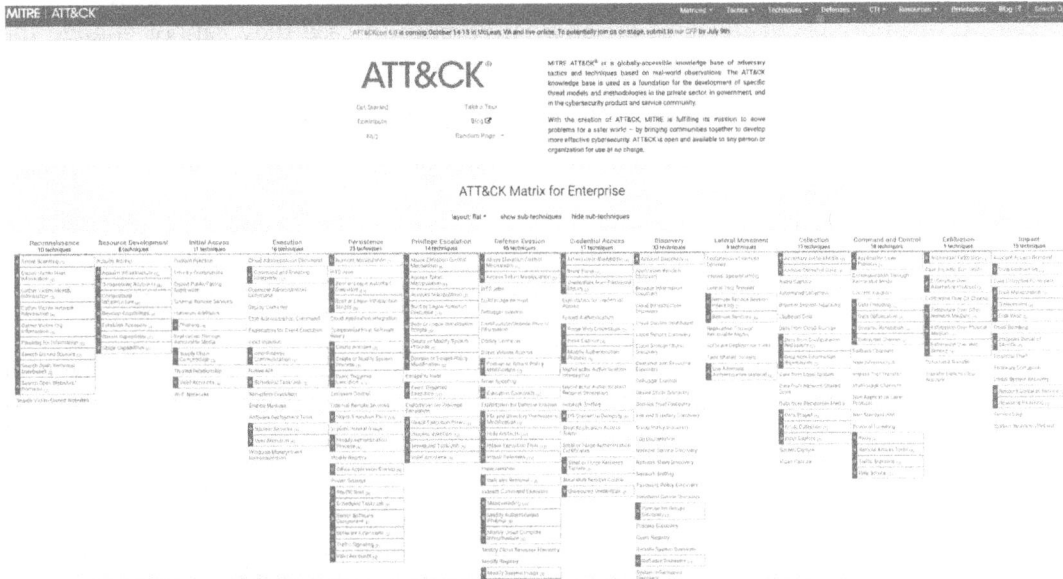

Figure 9.3: *MITRE's TTPs*

This framework contains a matrix with the known attack phases and its different techniques, with complete technical information and many external links that allow us to expand our knowledge and evaluation when analyzing a potential APT campaign. This framework contains examples of known APTs, target platforms, mitigation mechanisms, detection techniques, and reference links.

As threat hunters, we must be familiar with the different phases that make up an APT attack or campaign, and the different TTPs they involve, so in the following, we will analyze each phase, its actions, potential techniques, and some of its TTPs:

1. **Reconnaissance or intelligence gathering:** In this phase, the attacker(s) gather information about their target. They use **Open-Source Intelligence (OSINT)** techniques, collecting data from sources such as:

    a. IT infrastructure (including Cloud, IP ranges, specific versions of each system and application, etc.)

    b. Domains

    c. Subdomains

    d. Social media

    e. Corporate websites

    f. Cloud infrastructure

g. Data leaks

h. Previously stolen information from the target

i. Supply chain (to have an alternative path in case they cannot engage the target directly)

j. Any other public or private information they may find

With this information collected, they usually design an initial infiltration strategy and move on to the next stage.

2. **Infiltration (initial access):** With the data collected in phase one, attackers use advanced methods to infiltrate the target's network. Some of the most common techniques include:

    a. **Phishing, spear phishing, and laser phishing:** Personalized emails that look legitimate but contain malicious links or malware-infected attachments to be executed by the victim.

    b. **Zero-day exploits:** They take advantage of existing vulnerabilities in the specific versions of operating systems or applications that the target is using, previously unknown or with very little disclosure, to exploit them and enter undetected.

    c. **Social engineering:** They manipulate employees or suppliers to obtain access credentials or sensitive information.

3. **Establishing foothold:** Once attackers gain initial access, they install backdoor mechanisms or Trojan malware to maintain persistent access to the victim infrastructure and generate **command and control (C&C)**. These backdoors are designed to avoid detection and allow attackers to return at any time and provide instructions and orders to the victim system, even if the initial credentials are discovered and locked.

    Some examples of APT persistence techniques are shown in the following table, it includes:

Persistence technique	Description	Common Locations or usage	APT example
Registry Run Keys / Start-up Folder	Malicious executables added to automatically run at system boot	`HKCU\Software\Micro-soft\Windows\Current-Version\Run HKLM\Software\Microsoft\ Windows\CurrentVersion\ RunStartup folder`	APT28 (Fancy Bear)
Scheduled Tasks / Cron Jobs	Modified scheduled tasks to execute malicious scripts at intervals	Windows Task Scheduler (schtasks.exe)Linux crontab files	APT33

Persistence technique	Description	Common Locations or usage	APT example
WMI Event Subscription	Creates event subscriptions triggering malicious scripts	Windows Management Instrumentation events	APT32 (Ocean-Lotus)
Service Installation	Creates/modifies services to load malicious DLLs	`sc.exe` or PowerShell service manipulation	APT41
DLL Search Order Hijacking	Places malicious DLLs to be loaded by legitimate apps	Windows DLL search paths	APT29 (Cozy Bear)
Bootkits and Rootkits	Low-level malware hiding in boot sector or system	Boot sector, UEFI firmware	APT28 (LoJax)
Living off the Land	Abuses legitimate admin tools	PowerShell, WMIC, CertUtil	APT34 (OilRig)
COM/AppCert DLL Hijacking	Hijacks COM objects and application verification DLLs	Windows Registry COM entries	APT29
User Account Manipulation	Creates/modifies privileged accounts	Windows user management	APT32
Firmware/Hardware Implants	Modifies device firmware for persistence	UEFI BIOS, router firmware	APT28, APT41

Table 9.1: APT's persistence techniques

The following table shows examples of tools used to generate C&C for APTs, which include:

Tool / technique	Description	Example APT usage	Indicators of Compromise (IoCs)
CLNTEND	A remote access tool (RAT) supporting multiple network protocols, deployed via DLL sideloading through applications like Microsoft Word.	**Operation WordDrone** involved attackers deploying CLNTEND using remote desktop tools like UltraVNC, with the malware initiated by sideloading a rogue DLL via Microsoft Word.	• Presence of unexpected DLL files in application directories. • Anomalous process behaviors associated with Microsoft Word. • Network communications over unusual protocols or ports.

Tool / technique	Description	Example APT usage	Indicators of Compromise (IoCs)
Telemos Backdoor	A PowerShell-based script with backdoor functionality, delivered via spear-phishing emails containing malicious attachments.	In April 2024, an unidentified threat actor targeted Russian organizations, including the government sector, using the Telemos backdoor delivered through spear-phishing emails.	• Receipt of unsolicited emails with ZIP attachments containing. SCR or WSF files. • Execution of unexpected PowerShell scripts. • Unauthorized data collection from browsers and local drives.
SoftEther VPN	An open-source, cross-platform VPN solution used by attackers to maintain access to victim networks.	**China-aligned APT groups**, such as Flax Typhoon and Webworm, have increasingly relied on SoftEther VPN to maintain access to victims' networks, deploying it on compromised machines.	• Installation of SoftEther VPN on systems without prior authorization. • Unusual VPN connections originating from internal systems. • Presence of SoftEther-related files or services.
Tickler Backdoor	A multistage backdoor malware is developed to establish remote access to victim networks after initial compromise.	• **APT33 (Peach Sandstorm)** developed Tickler to gain persistent access and exfiltrate data from sectors like satellite, communications equipment, oil and gas, and government entities in the United States and the United Arab Emirates.	• Presence of Tickler-related files or processes. • Unusual outbound connections to attacker-controlled servers. • Modifications to system configurations facilitating persistence.

Tool / technique	Description	Example APT usage	Indicators of Compromise (IoCs)
Pipedream Toolkit	A modular malware framework designed to target **Industrial Control Systems (ICS)** and **Programmable Logic Controllers (PLCs).**	**State-level APT actors** developed Pipedream as a **Swiss Army knife** for hacking ICS, enabling them to scan for, compromise, and control devices like Schneider Electric and OMRON PLCs.	• Unauthorized scanning of ICS/SCADA devices. • Deployment of unexpected modules or code on PLCs. • Anomalous network traffic between control systems and external IPs.

Table 9.2: APT's C&C techniques and tools

4. **Privilege escalation**: To access sensitive information, attackers need to obtain elevated permissions and privileges. They use exploits and advanced tools to gain administrative privileges, allowing them to move freely within each of the compromised machines and, in some cases, the entire network if they achieve privileges within an Active Directory, for example.

The following table shows some examples of APT privilege escalation techniques, which include:

Tool / technique	Description	Example APT usage	Indicators of Compromise (IoCs)
Exploitation of CVE-2024-30088	A Windows Kernel Elevation of Privilege vulnerability allows attackers to execute arbitrary code with SYSTEM privileges.	**Earth Simnavaz (APT34)** exploited CVE-2024-30088 to escalate privileges and maintain persistence in targeted systems.	• Presence of exploit binaries related to CVE-2024-30088. • Unexpected processes running with SYSTEM privileges. • Modifications to critical system files or settings.

Tool / technique	Description	Example APT usage	Indicators of Compromise (IoCs)
Abuse of Password Filter DLLs	Installing malicious password filter DLLs to capture plaintext passwords during password change operations.	**Earth Simnavaz (APT34)** utilized this technique to extract plaintext passwords, compromising system integrity.	• Unauthorized password filter DLLs registered in the system. • Unusual access to LSASS process memory. • Unexpected network connections during password changes.
Exploitation of 'needrestart' Vulnerabilities	Leveraging vulnerabilities in the **needrestart** utility on Linux systems to gain root privileges.	Attackers exploit flaws in **needrestar** (for example, CVE-2024-48990) to execute arbitrary code as root during package installations or upgrades.	• Unexpected execution of **needrestart** by non-privileged users. • Anomalous changes to system files or configurations. • Logs indicating exploitation attempts of **needrestart**.
Process Injection via Metasploit's Win7Elevate Module	Injecting malicious code into legitimate processes to bypass **User Account Control (UAC)** and gain elevated privileges.	**Kimsuky APT Group** used the Win7Elevate exploit to inject code into **explorer.exe**, achieving stealthy privilege escalation.	• Unusual **explorer.exe** behavior or resource usage. • Presence of Metasploit-related files or modules. • Unauthorized modifications to UAC settings.
Exploitation of Microsoft Hyper-V Vulnerabilities (CVE-2025-21333, CVE-2025-21334, CVE-2025-21335)	Targeting zero-day flaws in Hyper-V's NT Kernel Integration VSP to gain SYSTEM-level privileges.	APT groups have exploited these vulnerabilities as part of post-compromise activities to escalate privileges within virtualized environments.	• Unexpected activities within Hyper-V environments. • Anomalous behavior of virtual machines or host systems. • Indicators of unauthorized access to virtualization services.

Table 9.3: APT's privilege escalation techniques

5. **Lateral movement**: Attackers scan machines connected to the internal network, identifying critical servers, storages, mail servers, Active Directory Servers, databases, and other sources of valuable information for their purposes. They use remote administration tools and stolen credentials to move from one system to another without being detected.

Some of the tools used for privilege escalation and lateral movement by APT can be found in this table with their IoC:

Tool / technique	Description	Example APT usage	Indicators of Compromise (IoCs)
SharpNBTScan	.NET-based tool used for network reconnaissance to identify open NetBIOS sessions, facilitating lateral movement.	**Stately Taurus** utilized SharpNBTScan to map network shares and identify potential targets for lateral movement.	• Execution of SharpNBTScan.exe in unusual directories. • Network scans targeting NetBIOS sessions. • Unexpected enumeration of network shares.
OpenSSH	A suite of secure networking utilities based on the SSH protocol, used for secure remote login and other secure network services.	**Void Manticore** employed OpenSSH clients to establish encrypted channels for lateral movement within compromised networks.	• Installation of OpenSSH clients on systems where it's not standard. • Unusual SSH connections between internal systems. • Presence of unauthorized SSH keys in `~/.ssh/authorized_keys`.
Living off the Land (LotL) Techniques	Utilizing legitimate system tools and built-in utilities to perform malicious activities, thereby evading detection.	**Volt Typhoon** leveraged built-in Windows tools like PowerShell and **Windows Management Instrumentation (WMI)** for reconnaissance and lateral movement without deploying traditional malware.	• Unusual execution patterns of legitimate system binaries. • Scripts or commands executed via PowerShell or WMI without proper authorization. • Anomalies in process creation logs involving system utilities.

Tool / technique	Description	Example APT usage	Indicators of Compromise (IoCs)
ScreenConnect (ConnectWise Control)	A legitimate remote desktop and meeting solution that can be repurposed by threat actors for unauthorized remote access and lateral movement.	**MuddyWater** APT group used ScreenConnect to remotely control compromised systems, facilitating lateral movement and further exploitation.	• Installation of ScreenConnect client on systems without prior authorization. • Unusual remote sessions initiated through ScreenConnect. • Network traffic to ScreenConnect servers not associated with legitimate use.
ShadowPad Backdoor	A modular backdoor platform that allows attackers to load various plugins for different functionalities, including lateral movement.	An unidentified threat actor deployed ShadowPad via DLL sideloading to maintain persistence and facilitate lateral movement within targeted networks.	• Presence of unexpected DLL files associated with legitimate applications. • Anomalous process behaviors indicative of DLL sideloading. • Network communications with known ShadowPad C&C servers.

Table 9.4: APT's tools for privilege escalation and lateral movement

6. **Data exfiltration:** Once the attacker(s) find valuable data, they use encrypted communication channels to extract the information without triggering security alerts. The data is sent to servers controlled by the attackers, often located in multiple geographic locations, to make it difficult to trace.

In this table, we present some of the most well-known methods used by APTs to extract information from their victims.

Tool / technique	Description	Example APT usage	Indicators of Compromise (IoCs)
Rclone	An open-source command-line program to manage files on cloud storage.	**LockBit**, **Black Basta**, and **Blacksuit** ransomware groups have utilized Rclone for data exfiltration due to its versatility and ability to blend into normal operations.	• Presence of `rclone.exe` in unusual directories. • Outbound connections to cloud storage services. • Unusual command-line executions involving Rclone.

Tool / technique	Description	Example APT usage	Indicators of Compromise (IoCs)
WinSCP	A popular free SFTP and FTP client for Windows, used to transfer files securely.	Threat actors have leveraged WinSCP for data exfiltration due to its trusted reputation and robust automation capabilities.	• Unexpected installations or executions of WinSCP. • Scripts automating file transfers to external servers. • Unusual outbound FTP/SFTP traffic.
cURL	A command-line tool and library for transferring data with URLs.	Attackers have employed cURL for data exfiltration because of its trusted reputation and robust automation capabilities.	• Execution of curl commands uploading data to external locations. • Presence of curl.exe in non-standard directories. • Unusual outbound HTTP/HTTPS requests.
PcExter 2.0	To. NET-based tool designed to collect and exfiltrate data, with an improved file search mechanism.	**ToddyCat** APT group developed PcExter 2.0 to enhance their data exfiltration capabilities.	• Detection of PcExter processes. • Anomalous .NET application executions. • Unusual file access patterns.
SQLULDR2	A high-performance Oracle database unloading tool used to extract data.	**APT41** utilized SQLULDR2 for copying data from databases during their operations.	• Execution of SQLULDR2 processes. • Large-scale data extraction from Oracle databases. • Unscheduled database export activities.
PINEGROVE	A tool used to exfiltrate data to Microsoft OneDrive, facilitating covert data transfers.	**APT41** employed PINEGROVE to exfiltrate data to Microsoft OneDrive, leveraging trusted cloud services to avoid detection.	• Unauthorized connections to OneDrive accounts. • Unexpected data uploads to external OneDrive repositories. • Presence of PINEGROVE-related scripts or executables.

Tool / technique	Description	Example APT usage	Indicators of Compromise (IoCs)
PuTTY	An open-source terminal emulator, serial console, and network file transfer application.	Threat actors have used PuTTY for data exfiltration by establishing secure remote connections.	• Presence of putty.exe in unusual locations. • Unexplained SSH/Telnet connections to external IPs. • Execution of PuTTY-related command-line activities.
Havoc Demon	An open-source post-exploitation tool designed for persistence, data exfiltration, and lateral movement.	**WIRTE** APT group used the Havoc Demon agent to establish persistence and exfiltrate data in targeted attacks.	• Detection of Havoc Demon agent processes. • Unusual network communications indicative of C2 activities. • Execution of unauthorized scripts or binaries.
Tickler Backdoor	A multistage backdoor malware that establishes remote access to victim networks.	**APT33 (Peach Sandstorm)** developed Tickler to gain persistent access and exfiltrate data from sectors like satellite and communications equipment.	• Presence of Tickler-related files or processes. • Unusual outbound connections to attacker-controlled servers. • Modifications to system configurations facilitating persistence.
Red Team Tools	Legitimate security tools repurposed by threat actors for malicious activities, including data exfiltration.	**Earth Koshchei** leveraged red team tools for espionage and data exfiltration in complex RDP attacks.	• Execution of known red team tools in unexpected contexts. • Network traffic patterns associated with data exfiltration. • Anomalous use of administrative utilities.

Table 9.5: APT's exfiltration methods

7. **Persistence and evasion:** To avoid detection, attackers employ advanced evasion techniques, such as rootkits, polymorphic malware (which constantly changes its signature), and code obfuscation. In addition, they delete activity logs to erase traces and use persistence techniques to maintain access even after system upgrades or

reboots. In the following table, you will preview persistent and evasion techniques that are currently in use by cybersecurity professionals and cybercriminals:

Tool / technique	Description	Example APT usage	Indicators of Compromise (IoCs)
HookChain Technique	A sophisticated evasion method combining IAT Hooking, dynamic SSN resolution, and indirect system calls to bypass **Endpoint Detection and Response (EDR)** systems.	Researchers introduced HookChain as a novel approach to evade traditional EDR solutions by redirecting execution flows within Windows subsystems, remaining undetected.	Absence of expected hooks in `Ntdll.dll`. Unusual execution flows in system processes. Discrepancies in API call monitoring logs.
Intra-Section Code Cave Injection	Injecting adversarial code within existing sections of Windows **Portable Executable (PE)** files to evade machine learning-based malware detectors.	Researchers demonstrated this technique by injecting code caves within the .text, .data, and `.rdata` sections of PE files, achieving high evasion rates against detectors like MalConv and MalConv2.	Presence of unexpected code within standard PE sections. Alterations in section sizes without corresponding functionality changes. Anomalies in file integrity checks.
CloudScout Toolset	To. NET-based post-compromise toolset designed for session hijacking and unauthorized access to cloud services.	**Evasive Panda**, a China-linked threat group, deployed CloudScout to hijack web session cookies, granting access to services like Google Drive, Gmail, and Outlook.	Unauthorized access to cloud service accounts. Presence of unfamiliar .NET assemblies related to CloudScout. Unusual activities in cloud service logs.

Tool / technique	Description	Example APT usage	Indicators of Compromise (IoCs)
Living off the Land (LotL) Techniques	Utilizing legitimate system tools and built-in utilities to perform malicious activities, thereby evading detection.	**Volt Typhoon**, a Chinese state-sponsored group, leveraged built-in Windows tools like PowerShell and **Windows Management Instrumentation (WMI)** for reconnaissance and lateral movement without deploying traditional malware.	Unusual execution patterns of legitimate system binaries. Scripts or commands executed via PowerShell or WMI without proper authorization. Anomalies in process creation logs involving system utilities.
Use of Open-Source Tools	Employing widely available open-source software for malicious purposes to blend in with legitimate activities and evade detection.	**Evasive Panda** relied on widely available tools rather than custom malware, forgoing advanced obfuscation techniques, to conduct cyber espionage campaigns.	Presence of open-source tool binaries in unexpected locations. Execution of open-source software without proper authorization. Network communications indicative of data exfiltration or C&C.

Table 9.6: APT's persistence techniques

Hunting for APTs and nation-state actors

Unfortunately, given all the TTPs we evaluated above, we understand that it is not easy to detect an APT that has managed to compromise our infrastructure and that is infiltrated by spying on us and exfiltrating data.

As there are so many variants within the APT attack, there are many places where we should look, but at the same time, this plays against us since we can overlook things or assume behaviors as normal, which belong to the actions of an APT. Within the *APT TTPs* section related to the TTPs of the APTs, we saw the details of some of the tools and procedures they currently use, but the recommendation here is really that we must have a global strategy that allows us to defend several fronts at the same time. This strategy involves the combination of four main factors:

- **Continuous monitoring**: Implementation of real-time monitoring solutions to detect unusual activities or events to detect potential intrusions.

- **Threat intelligence integration**: Utilizing the latest threat intelligence sources to identify Indicators of Compromiseassociated with known APT groups. There are many sources that we already covered in previous chapters that you can use. As an example, refer to the following table:

Source name	Description	Access Link
MISP Threat Sharing	An open-source platform for collecting, storing, and sharing cybersecurity indicators and threats.	**MISP Project**
Open Threat Exchange (OTX)	A crowd-sourced platform with over 180,000 participants sharing more than 19 million potential threats daily.	**OTX**
threatfeeds.io	Provides free and open-source threat intelligence feeds.	**threatfeeds.io**
Awesome Threat Intelligence	A curated list of threat intelligence resources, including APIs and feeds.	**GitHub Repository**
Open-Source Threat Intel Feeds	A repository containing freely usable threat intelligence feeds without additional requirements.	**GitHub Repository**

Table 9.7: Threat intelligence sources

- **Behavioral analysis:** The day-to-day behavior of users is one of the factors that APTs try to imitate to prevent their actions from being discovered. However, it is not entirely possible for an APT to disguise its malicious activities as regular user behavior. Therefore, it is vitally important to closely monitor for anomalies.

- **Incident response planning:** Being prepared for a crisis is part of the normal role of the blue team that monitors and controls the security of an entity, keeping the latest with both the response plans to the different potential incidents that could affect a company as well as knowing the latest developments and tactics used by criminals is an obligation for this staff.

Staying informed and adopting a proactive approach to cybersecurity is imperative in the face of these advanced threats.

AI and its repercussions on cyberattacks and APT

In line with the above, we must keep in mind that thanks to the advances in AI, the TTPs used by cybercriminals have changed, have been enhanced, and have advanced as a key informative document on how AI has improved cyberattacks, we can cite MITRE's ATLAS matrix as shown in the following figure:

ATLAS Matrix

The ATLAS Matrix below shows the progression of tactics used in attacks as columns from left to right, with ML techniques belonging to each tactic below. & indicates an adaption from ATT&CK. Click on the blue links to learn more about each item, or search and view ATLAS tactics and techniques using the links at the top navigation bar. View the ATLAS matrix highlighted alongside ATT&CK Enterprise techniques on the ATLAS Navigator.

Reconnaissance[&]	Resource Development[&]	Initial Access[&]	AI Model Access	Execution[&]	Persistence[&]	Privilege Escalation[&]	Defense Evasion[&]	Credential Access[&]	Discovery[&]	Collection[&]	AI Attack Staging	Command and Control[&]	Exfiltration[&]	Impact[&]
6 techniques	12 techniques	8 techniques	4 techniques	4 techniques	4 techniques	2 techniques	8 techniques	1 technique	7 techniques	3 techniques	4 techniques	1 technique	5 techniques	7 techniques
Search Open Technical Databases[&]	Acquire Public AI Artifacts	AI Supply Chain Compromise	AI Model Inference API Access	User Execution[&]	Poison Training Data	LLM Plugin Compromise	Evade AI Model	Unsecured Credentials[&]	Discover AI Model Ontology	AI Artifact Collection	Create Proxy AI Model	Reverse Shell	Exfiltration via AI Inference API	Evade AI Model
Search Open AI Vulnerability Analysis	Obtain Capabilities[&]	Valid Accounts[&]	AI-Enabled Product or Service	Command and Scripting Interpreter[&]	Manipulate AI Model	LLM Jailbreak	LLM Jailbreak		Discover AI Model Family	Data from Information Repositories[&]	Manipulate AI Model		Exfiltration via Cyber Means	Denial of AI Service
Search Victim-Owned Websites	Develop Capabilities[&]	Evade AI Model	Physical Environment Access	LLM Prompt Injection	LLM Prompt Self-Replication		LLM Trusted Output Components Manipulation		Discover AI Artifacts	Data from Local System[&]	Verify Attack		Extract LLM System Prompt	Spamming AI System with Chaff Data
Search Application Repositories	Acquire Infrastructure[&]	Exploit Public-Facing Application[&]	Full AI Model Access	LLM Plugin Compromise	RAG Poisoning		LLM Prompt Obfuscation		Discover LLM Hallucinations		Craft Adversarial Data		LLM Data Leakage	Erode AI Model Integrity
Active Scanning[&]	Publish Poisoned Datasets	Phishing[&]					False RAG Entry Injection		Discover AI Model Outputs				LLM Response Rendering	Cost Harvesting
Gather RAG-Indexed Targets	Poison Training Data	Drive-by Compromise[&]					Impersonation[&]		Discover LLM System Information					External Harms
	Establish Accounts[&]						Masquerading[&]		Cloud Service Discovery[&]					Erode Dataset Integrity
	Publish Poisoned Models						Corrupt AI Model							
	Publish Hallucinated Entities													
	LLM Prompt Crafting													
	Retrieval Content Crafting													
	Stage Capabilities[&]													

Figure 9.4: *MITRE's ATLAS Matrix*
(**Source:** *https://atlas.mitre.org/matrices/ATLAS*)

This tool will support us to be able to better profile the actions of cybercriminals that are supported by tools such as LLMs, Deepfakes, etc.

APT incident response and attribution

Throughout the chapter, we have talked about the actions that APT groups carry out step by step to compromise an infrastructure; being able to accurately attribute an attack to a point actor is a complex task that involves detailed analysis of technical indicators, behavioral patterns, and contextual evidence. Attributing an attack to a particular APT requires not only identifying the tools and tactics used, but also connecting these elements to known actors based on geopolitical motivations, goals, and contexts.

To get closer to accurate attribution, we can perform various types of analysis:

- **Analysis of Technical Indicators (IoCs): Indicators of Compromise (IoCs)** are pieces of information that suggest the presence of malicious activity. These include the following that are shown in the table:

Indicator	Description	Utility	Example
C2 IPs and Domains	Addresses and domains used for C&C	Identify shared infrastructure between campaigns	APT28 reused .net domains for multiple operations
Malware Hashes	Unique cryptographic signatures of malicious files	Correlate malware samples between attacks	APT29 reused MiniDuke malware variants

Network Patterns	Abnormal traffic behaviors and protocols	Detect hidden malicious communications	APT41 uses DNS tunneling for exfiltration
File Names	File and directory naming conventions	Identify related campaigns through nomenclature	APT32 uses legitimate Windows service names

Table 9.8: APT IoC's

Following are the tools used:

- o VirusTotal for malware analysis.

- o Shodan and Censys to track C2 infrastructure.

- o MISP and Threat Intelligence Platforms to correlate IoCs.

- **Analysis of Tactics, Techniques, and Procedures:** Each APT has a specific **modus operandi**, which means a unique set of TTPs that they use repeatedly. Following are suggestions for the analysis of TTPs:

  - o **MITRE ATT&CK framework:** Maps TTPs against a standardized framework included in their matrix.

  - o **Specific tools:** Some APTs prefer custom-made and tailored tools or adapt open-source tools for their purposes.

  - o **Scripts and code strings:** Coding and obfuscation conventions often reveal clues about authorship; some developers include some kind of "signatures" in their code.

Following are the example:

- o **APT28 (Fancy Bear)** uses **X-Agent** and **Sofacy**, while **APT29 (Cozy Bear)** prefers **Cobalt Strike** and advanced PowerShell techniques.

- o **APT33 (Elfin)** uses custom tools in conjunction with `Shamoon` for sabotage.

- **Infrastructure analysis:** Analysis of the network infrastructure used by the attacker can reveal links or connections to known APT groups or campaigns. Following are some suggestions for analyzing the infrastructure:

  - o **Domain and DNS records:** Investigating registration patterns, providers, and similar or reused domains.

  - o **Hosting services, Cloud providers, and proxies:** Some APTs use specific VPN and VPS infrastructures or proxies to anonymize their traffic.

  - o **Geolocation and activity times:** Matching time zones and activity hours can suggest the actor's geographic location.

Following are the examples:

- o **APT41 (Winnti)** uses infrastructure shared between espionage campaigns and financial activities.

- o **APT34 (OilRig)** reuses C2 servers and **Domain Name System (DNS)** tunnels in campaigns in the Middle East.

Following are the tools used:

- o **PassiveTotal** for domain analysis.

- o **Maltego** for infrastructure relationship analysis.

- o **ThreatCrowd** and **ThreatMiner** for C2 infrastructure correlation.

- **Malware analysis and tools used:** Thorough analysis of the malware and the tools used by the adversaries reveals critical information:

  - o **Code reuse:** APTs often reuse code snippets in different campaigns.

  - o **Encryption algorithms and obfuscation techniques:** These may be unique to certain groups.

  - o **Specific functionalities:** Such as backdoors, credential stealers, keyloggers or destructive capabilities.

Following are the examples:

- o Lazarus Group (APT38) uses malware with custom encryption algorithms to exfiltrate banking data.

- o Turla (Snake Group) employs modular backdoors for long-term espionage.

Following are the tools used:

- o IDA Pro and Ghidra for reverse malware engineering.

- o YARA Rules to identify codeshare patterns.

- o Sandboxing (Cuckoo Sandbox, Any.Run) for malware behavior analysis.

- **Analysis of motivations and geopolitical context:** The motivations and objectives behind the attack, help identify the actor:

  - o **Cyberespionage:** Aimed at collecting sensitive information (for example, APT29 and political espionage).

  - o **Sabotage and disruption:** Destructive attacks on critical infrastructures (for example, APT33 and Shamoon).

  - o **Financial theft:** Exfiltration of financial data or cryptocurrencies (for example, Lazarus Group).

o **Geopolitical influences:** Attack patterns aligned with national or political interests.

Following are the examples:

o APT28 (Fancy Bear) has attacked political institutions aligned with Russian interests.

o APT32 (OceanLotus) focuses on political dissidents and governments in Southeast Asia.

- **Comparison with profiles of known APTs:** By correlating the findings with the profiles of known APTs, authorship can be determined:

  o MITRE ATT&CK provides detailed profiles of known APTs.

  o Threat Intelligence Reports from companies such as TrendMicro, FireEye, CrowdStrike, and Kaspersky.

  o Intelligence sharing through platforms such as **Malware Information Sharing Platform and Threat Sharing (MISP), Open Threat Exchange (OTE)**, and VirusTotal Intelligence.

The following are the examples:

o Coincidences in TTPs and tools with those of APT28 point to operations linked to Russian military intelligence **Glavnoe Razvedyvatel'noe Upravlenie (GRU)**.

o Shared infrastructure and C2 reused with APT41 indicate a relationship with Chinese state-sponsored actors.

- **International collaboration and validation:** Effective attribution requires validation and collaboration:

  o Intelligence sharing with **Computer Emergency Response Team (CERTs)**, Interpol, and other international agencies.

  o Cross-validation of findings with other researchers and threat analysts.

  o Publication of technical reports to make the attribution process transparent and allow for peer review.

Conclusion

In this chapter, we have discussed APT. We analyze the different stages of the APT lifecycle and see similarities with the Kill Chain. We evaluated and defined which are the TTPs most used by them, and we discussed the changes generated by AI in the landscape of cyberattacks and their TTPs. We discussed the recommended strategy to be able to hunt APTs. Finally, we discussed how to achieve effective attribution in case of receiving an attack from an APT campaign. With all the above, we see that the world of APTs is complex and that meticulous work is required to detect them. However, it is a task that we can achieve with the right strategy and knowledge.

In the next chapter, readers will shift focus from analysis to action by exploring the *Incident Response lifecycle*. This includes understanding how incidents are detected and triaged, strategies for containment and mitigation, and the steps involved in investigating and analyzing an incident. The chapter will also cover post-incident activities such as recovery, reporting, and much more.

Points to remember

- The APT lifecycle has similarities to the kill chain cycle

- There are many TTPs that are often combined in different ways

- AI changed the Cyberattack Landscape

- Often, the different APT groups reuse code and tools.

- **Know your adversaries:** Align detections with specific APT behaviors, not just generic malware.

- **Focus on persistence**: Look for registry tampering, task scheduler abuse, and C2 implants.

- **Combine CTI and behavior**: Use ATT&CK mappings to overlay detection with threat actor profiles.

- **Attribution is hard**: It requires technical, geopolitical, and infrastructure correlation.

Multiple choice questions

1. **What is an advanced persistent threat (APT)?**

   a. A short-term, opportunistic attack aimed at financial gain.

   b. A sophisticated, targeted attack aimed at long-term espionage and data theft.

    c. A type of virus that replicates itself to infect multiple devices.

    d. A tool used for scanning networks for vulnerabilities.

2. **Which phase is typically the first step in the APT Lifecycle?**

    a. Lateral Movement

    b. Data Exfiltration

    c. Reconnaissance

    d. Privilege Escalation

3. **In the context of APT TTPs, which framework is commonly used to map them?**

    a. NIST Cybersecurity Framework

    b. MITRE ATT&CK

    c. ISO/IEC 27001

    d. COBIT 5

4. **Which of the following is NOT a method used for APT Attribution?**

    a. Analyzing Tactics, Techniques, and Procedures (TTPs)

    b. Tracking C&C infrastructure

    c. Analyzing Hashes of Malware Files

    d. Randomly guessing the origin based on geographical proximity

5. **When hunting for APTs, which approach is the most effective?**

    a. Waiting for alerts from antivirus software

    b. Using behavioral analysis and threat intelligence feeds

    c. Shutting down all systems until the threat is removed

    d. Deleting suspicious emails without investigation

Answers

1. b.

2. c.

3. b.

4. d.

5. b.

References

1. **MITRE ATT&CK Framework: https://attack.mitre.org/**

2. **Advanced Persistent Threat (APT)-CrowdStrike: https://www.crowdstrike.com/en-us/cybersecurity-101/threat-intelligence/advanced-persistent-threat-apt/**

3. **APT Groups-MITRE ATT&CK: https://attack.mitre.org/groups/**

4. **Tactics, Techniques, and Procedures-ANY.RUN: https://any.run/cybersecurity-blog/malware-ttps-explained/**

Join our Discord space

Join our Discord workspace for latest updates, offers, tech happenings around the world, new releases, and sessions with the authors:

https://discord.bpbonline.com

CHAPTER 10
Incident Response and Handling

Introduction

This chapter explores the best practices and strategies involved in effectively detecting, responding to, and recovering from cybersecurity incidents.

Readers will gain valuable insights into the incident response lifecycle, learning how to swiftly detect and triage incidents, contain and mitigate their impact, and conduct thorough investigations for analysis and future prevention, this chapter equips readers with the necessary resources and knowledge to understand the process with confidence.

Structure

In this chapter, we will discuss the following topics:

- Incident response lifecycle
- Incident detection and triage
- Incident containment and mitigation
- Incident investigation and analysis
- Post-incident activities and reporting
- Case study of ransomware attack response at CCSS

Objectives

In this book, we have seen many techniques that cybercriminals use to attack their potential targets, and we have discussed the IoC, the indications and clues that would allow us, at a certain time, to detect that we have been compromised and hunt the threats. Unfortunately, there is a high possibility that criminals will succeed precisely in these attempts to infiltrate different infrastructures because most factors play in their favor.

The objective of this chapter is precisely to give us a general outline about the proper handling of an incident and guidelines on how to respond in the best possible way.

Incident response lifecycle

The lifecycle of incident response has changed many times over time. On some occasions, stages have been added, and on others, they have been condensed or joined together. There are several reasons for these changes, for example, the new technologies that are developed and implemented day by day. Another is the increasingly high dynamism and sophistication in the attacks perpetrated by cybercriminals, including AI, for the purposes of the incident. In this section, we will present the latest special publication called *Incident Response Recommendations and Considerations for Cybersecurity Risk Management*.

NIST SP 800-61 Revision 3: (**https://nvlpubs.nist.gov/nistpubs/SpecialPublications/NIST.SP.800-61r3.ipd.pdf**)

This document was created on April 3, 2024, which changes the paradigm of incident management a bit and facilitates evolution. The following figure illustrates the incident response lifecycle:

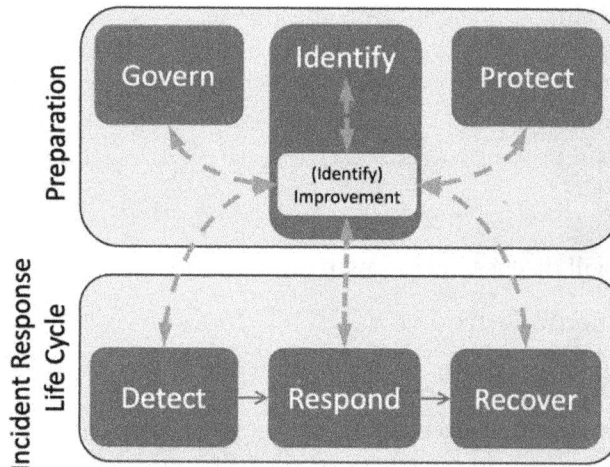

Figure 10.1: Incident response lifecycle
(Source: https://csrc.nist.gov/projects/incident-response)

We can see that the incident response lifecycle is made up of three steps: **Detect | Respond | Recovery**, but it becomes more interesting to see the dependencies connected with good preparation that involves the governance part, and connects with identification and protection. In fact, we know that a key element of the proper functioning and health of the IT areas of organizations is a robust connection with IT governance and connecting technological needs with business goals.

We recommend looking at the document, which is very interesting and presents a comparison between the previous and current lifecycle.

There are many aspects that we can evaluate of preparedness, such as that continuous improvement is specifically connected to the identify stage, but in this section of the book, we are concerned with the lifecycle of response to specific incidents, so we are going to limit ourselves to that area. The detailed information about the stages is mentioned in the following:

- **Detection:** This phase involves the identification of potential security incidents; this requires permanent monitoring infrastructure, capable of real-time analysis.

- **Response:** Upon confirming an incident, the response phase aims to contain and mitigate the threat; essential actions include containment, eradication, and communication.

  An appropriate and well-orchestrated response is vital to prevent further damage and to preserve evidence for forensic analysis. Remember, the digital evidence is very fragile.

- **Recovery:** Restoring normal operations and implementing measures to prevent recurrence, like lessons learned schemas, instructive and manuals update.

Incident detection and triage

The detection of an anomalous event that is later characterized as an incident is the origin of the entire incident response process from a practical point of view. This implies that we need to have the best conditions, policies, and mechanisms that allow us to make an early detection of any anomaly. To achieve this, there are several elements, which we can frame within our incident response strategy, in the following we can mention:

- **Continuous security monitoring and analytics:** We can use different technologies, but as we explained in previous chapters, you can use tools like **Security Information and Event Management (SIEM)**, **Extended Detection and Response (XDR)**, etc., to collect and analyze logs from across the network and from each host, to obtain a panoramic view of all activities, helping you detect anomalies early.

- **Behavioral analytics:** Modern attackers try to mimic the normal behavior of a user, and this does not always trigger traditional alarms. Behavioral analytics helps in detecting abnormal activities like unusual logins, abnormal web browsing, or data transfers, indicating potential breaches even if no malware is involved.

- **Threat intelligence integration:** The additional and the latest information obtained by integrating threat intelligence feeds allows you to learn from other attacks happening worldwide. This allows you to recognize attack patterns and stay ahead of emerging threats.

In the following figure, we can see different detection sources, which are processed and analyzed with the aim of debugging the events that really require a response:

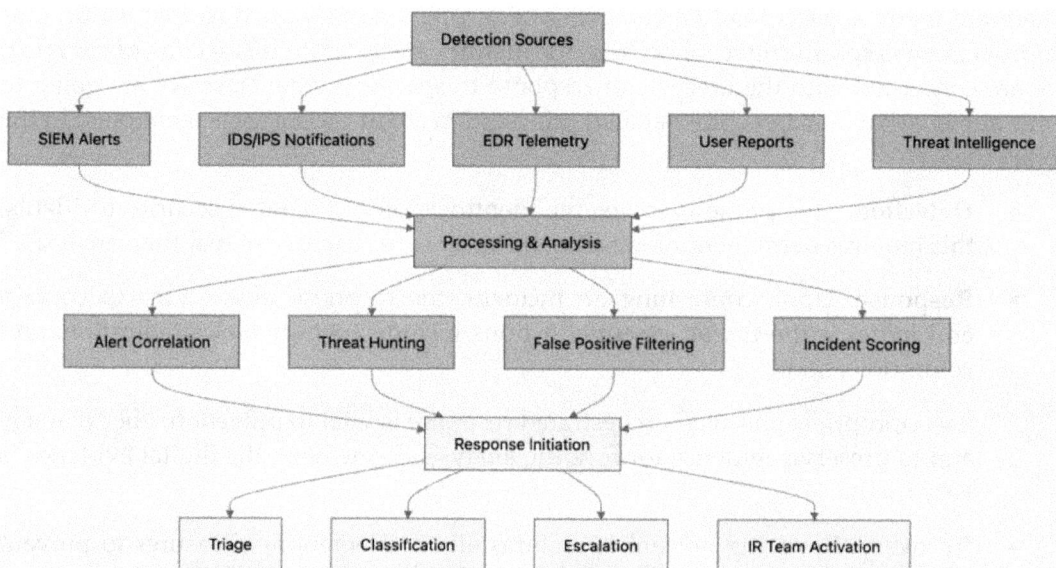

Figure 10.2: Detection sources

In the above figure, we see different possible sources of information, then that data could be processed in different ways and then analyzed to avoid false positives. For example, once it is confirmed that the incident is real, we go on to generate a response that could include some of the stages mentioned in the figure.

Incident triage

Once a potential incident is detected, the triage phase involves evaluating and prioritizing the incident based on its severity, impact, and urgency. This phase includes:

- **Classification:** Determining the nature of the incident (for example, active directory compromise, malware infection, unauthorized access, credentials leak, data exfiltration) to understand its potential consequences.

- **Prioritization:** Assessing the incident's impact on critical systems and business operations to allocate resources appropriately. Incidents threatening sensitive data or essential services are prioritized for immediate response.

- **Assignment:** Delegating the incident to the appropriate response team or individual with the expertise to handle the specific type of threat.

Effective triage ensures that incidents are addressed accordingly with their potential risk, optimizing the use of security resources and minimizing potential damage. Here is an example of a severity classification with details about the ranking:

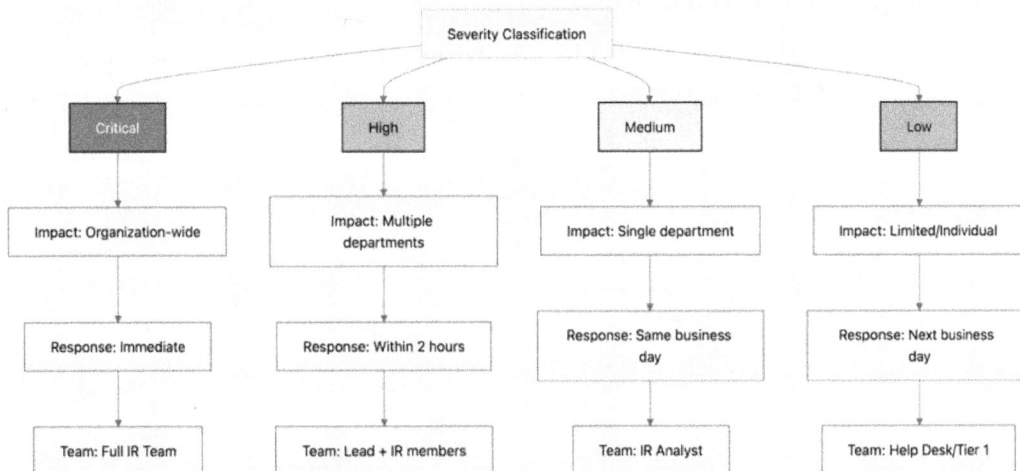

Figure 10.3: *Severity classification*

Figure 10.3 is an example of how triage can be applied to various types of incidents.

Incident containment and mitigation

Depending on the type of incident that an organization has suffered, we must initiate immediate actions to try to contain the extent of the compromise in the best possible way, or we must apply mitigation measures to reduce the impact. Let us explain it better with a couple of examples:

- **Incident A: Ransomware or worm-type malware attack**

    In this type of incident, there is always the risk that once patient zero has been contaminated, the malware will continue to spread throughout the network and therefore the entire infrastructure could be compromised. In this way, it is imperative to be able to contain the infection in the least amount of assets possible within the organization. This may require, for example, disconnecting network devices, isolating servers, shutting down storage devices, etc. Each case is different and it depends on the policies and **incident response plans** (**IRPs**) of each entity on how to proceed.

- **Incident B: Fall of the main communications operator**

  In this case we are not receiving an attack. We are only being affected by a problem that a supplier is suffering within our supply chain, given the nature of the problem here, containment does not apply but mitigation, since we need to resume communications as quickly as possible, so we could put in place contingency plans related to connectivity to another provider, or use a different channel from the same provider that is not affected.

The following figure illustrates the incident containment and mitigation diagrams, which will help us understand the process:

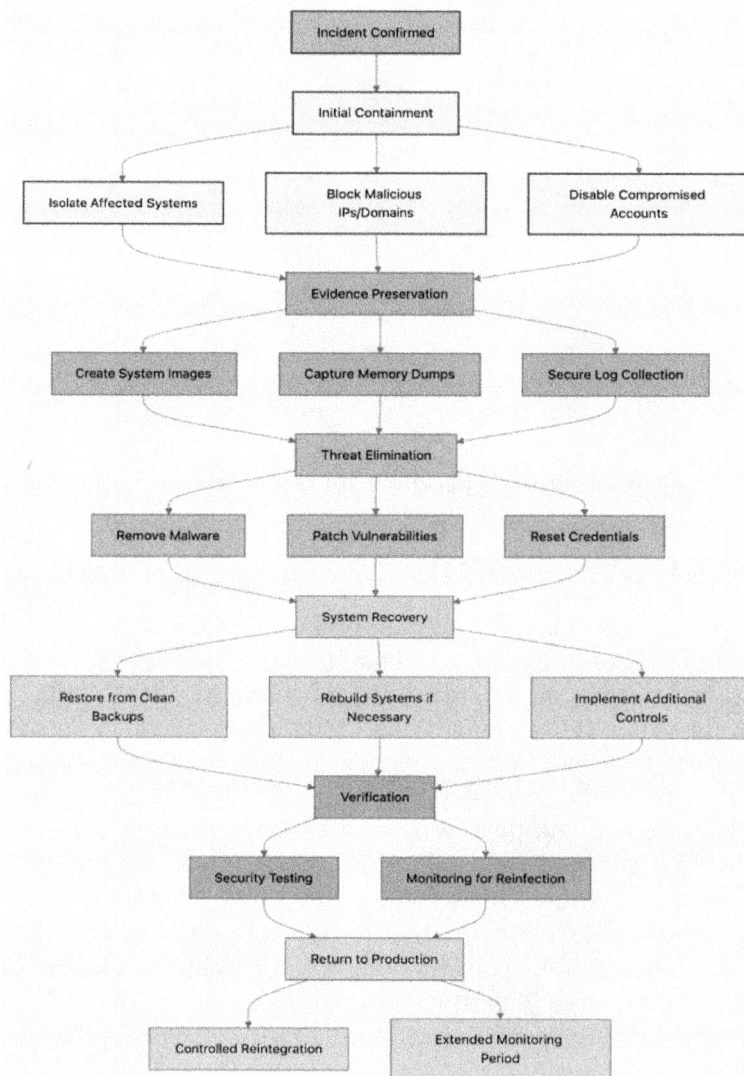

Figure 10.4: Incident containment and mitigation diagram

In the above figure, we can see some examples of potential incidents and steps that can be taken to mitigate or contain their actions. We see that the preservation of evidence is a very important step in the process.

Incident investigation and analysis

It is impossible to avoid being the target of the same attack on multiple occasions, if we do not learn from the first attack received. To this end, we must capture as much evidence as possible about the incident, so that we can analyze and understand it and thus learn the necessary lessons to avoid being caught in the same way in the future. To achieve this, we must carry out a detailed and careful procedure of investigation and analysis, starting with good data collection. The procedure of the investigation, starting with data collection, are mentioned in the following:

1. **Data collection:** The first step in any good investigation is gathering the evidence. This is about grabbing every digital crumb that the attacker has left behind. Here are some more details of places to collect data:

   a. **Log collection**: Centralize logs from all relevant sources: Firewalls, IDS, servers, endpoints and applications. These logs are very useful in tracking the movements of the attacker.

   b. **Network traffic analysis**: Use network traffic captures and network flow data to identify the path that the attacker took through the network. Tools like Wireshark, Zeek or TcpDump are very useful in this case.

   c. **Forensic imaging**: Make copies of the affected systems to analyze them in depth. This maintains the state of the system without altering the evidence thus preserving the integrity of the investigation process. (You can reference *Chapter 7, Computer Forensics*).

   d. **Memory dump analysis**: This involves capturing the RAM contents to see the running processes, network connections and any malware in the memory. This may detect fileless malware (LoLBas – LoLBin) or other complicated threats that do not write to the disk.

2. **Root cause analysis:** It is not just about what happened; it is about how and why it happened. Here are some more details of the root cause analysis:

   a. **Attack vector identification:** Determine the point of entry. Perhaps it was a phishing email or a misconfigured server or a zero-day exploit; Knowing the entry point is very valuable for remediation.

   b. **Lateral movement mapping:** See how the attacker moved around in the network. Maybe they executed privilege escalation or stolen credentials, they used secret keys, Used different devices and much more. This is useful in determining the full extent of the breach.

c. **Persistence mechanisms:** Determine how the attacker ensured that he or she retained access to the system. This could be through back doors, scheduled tasks, registry modifications, or compromised credentials. (You can reference *Chapter 9, Advanced Persistent Threats and Nation-State Actors*).

d. **Impact assessment:** Determine the extent of the damage. This includes data leakage, system integrity breach, financial loss, and reputational damage.

3. **Threat attribution:** This is the **identification of the author**. Although attribution is difficult, it is not impossible with the proper intelligence and tools (You can reference *Chapter 9, Advanced Persistent Threats and Nation-State Actors*). Here are some more details of threat attribution:

a. **Indicators of Compromise (IoCs)**: Gather and analyze IoCs like IPs, file hashes, domains, and URLs. These can be matched up against threat intelligence feeds with known enemies.

b. **Tactics, Techniques, and Procedures (TTPs)**: Compare the attack patterns against known TTPs in frameworks like MITRE ATT&CK. This allows the incident to be related to threat actors or APT groups. (You can reference *Chapter 9, Advanced Persistent Threats and Nation-State Actors*).

c. **Threat intelligence correlation**: Work with your threat intelligence partners or use commercial threat intel platforms to confirm the findings and add more context to the attack.

4. **Hypothesis testing and analysis:** An investigation is only as good as the questions it generates. This step includes developing hypotheses about the attack and testing them against the data. (You can reference *Chapters 3, Cyber Threat Intelligence and Indicators of Compromise*, and *Chapter 4, Tools and Techniques for Threat Hunting*). Here are some more details of hypothesis testing and analysis:

a. **Timeline reconstruction**: Construct the incident timeline by analyzing events against logs, alerts, and forensic artifacts. This shows the sequence and steps of the attacker's actions in detail.

b. **Attack path mapping:** Depict the attack's path from initial access through to movement within the network, privilege escalation, data exfiltration, and persistence.

c. **Scenario analysis**: Attack scenarios should be built and tested against hypotheses. This may include red teaming, or an adversary-simulated attack in a controlled environment.

d. **Continuous re-evaluation**: When new evidence is obtained, the hypotheses are updated and re-evaluated to ensure correct conclusions.

The following figure presents a diagram of the incident investigation and analysis process, highlighting the steps involved:

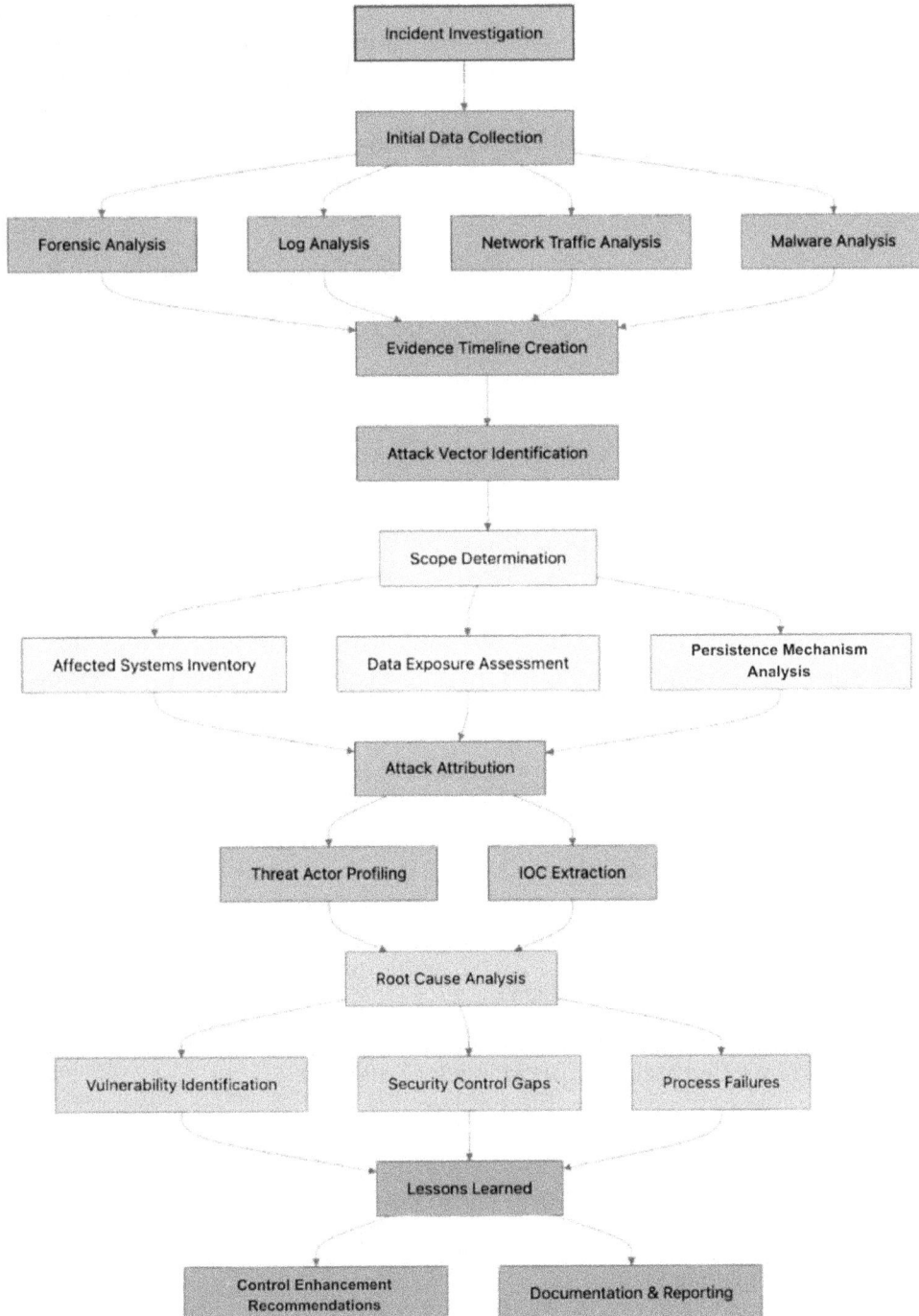

Figure 10.5: Incident investigation and analysis diagram

Post-incident activities and reporting

This is where the real learning happens after the incident. It is where you make sense of the chaos, turning a security incident into a learning experience that can be used to improve your defenses. This is where you **gain power from pain** by looking at what went wrong, what went right, and how to improve. The following figure presents a diagram of the post-incident activities and reporting, highlighting the process:

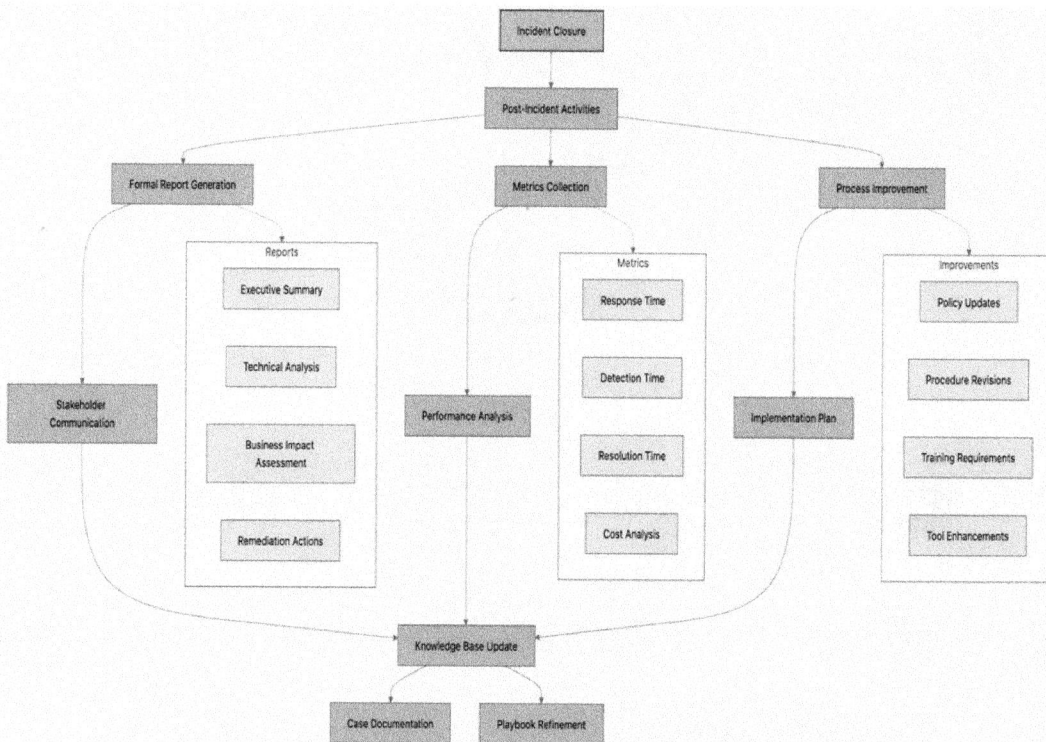

Figure 10.6: Post-incident activities and reporting

Incident documentation

This is important, not only for legal or compliance purposes, but also for creating the organization's knowledge base to support incident response.

Not all incidents are the same, but we suggest some of the sections that the reports could contain:

- **Incident report:** A comprehensive report detailing:
  - **Summary of the incident:** What happened, how it was detected, and the impact generated.
  - **Root cause and contributing factors:** Detailed analysis of how the incident occurred.

- o **Attack vector evaluation:** Review the incident timeline and identify the initial point of entry. This helps in understanding how the adversary gained access and what controls failed to stop them.

- o **Actions taken:** Every step of the response, from detection to recovery.

- o **Outcome:** Impact on systems, data, and business operations.

- o **Lessons learned and recommendations:** Insights gained and suggested improvements.

- **Technical analysis report:** For incidents involving complex technical details, a detailed discussion is often necessary. This includes:

  - o Forensic analysis results

  - o Indicators of Compromise

  - o Tactics, Techniques, and Procedures used by the attacker

- **Compliance and legal documentation:** Ensure reports meet regulatory requirements and preserve evidence for potential legal proceedings.

Metrics collection

Knowing how effective our actions were before, during and after the incident is very important, to generate that continuous improvement and readiness that we must always seek.

The metrics allow us to know these factors in detail; we can generate many metrics that will allow us to have a clear idea about whether we are failing in some aspect, what we need to improve, or what we need to change definitively. For example, assess how well your tools, teams, and processes worked. Did you detect the incident early enough? Was the containment swift? Where were the bottlenecks? In addition, you can evaluate how effectively the incident response team communicated, coordinated, and executed the response plan. Identify gaps in skills or knowledge that need to be addressed.

The following are some of the recommended metrics:

- Response time
- Detection time
- Resolution time
- Cost analysis

Process improvement

If your metrics detect some area to correct or improve, it is time to update your policies, procedures, and security controls to close the gaps. This is where continuous improvement happens. Here are some more details of the process improvement:

- **Incident Response Plan (IRP) review:** Update the IRP to reflect lessons learned, including modifications to escalation paths, communication protocols, and decision-making authority.

- **Security controls enhancement:** Implement or strengthen security controls identified as weak points during the incident. This may include:
  o Hardening configurations and baselines
  o Improving monitoring, detection and alerting systems
  o Deploying new security tools or technologies
  o Topology adjustment

- **Playbook refinement:** Adjust incident response playbooks for specific attack types (for example, ransomware, phishing, DDoS) to ensure a faster, more effective response in the future.

- **Communication and escalation protocols:** Optimize internal and external communication strategies to avoid confusion during future incidents and improve stakeholders' updates.

Case study of ransomware attack response at CCSS

On May 31, 2022, the **Costa Rican Social Security Fund (CCSS)**, which manages the country's public healthcare system, was targeted by the Hive ransomware group. This attack followed a wave of similar incidents by the Conti ransomware gang against other government institutions in the country:

- **Detection:** Unusual network activity was detected during the early hours of the attack. Hospital staff reported erratic printer behavior and the appearance of ransom notes. Systems critical to healthcare operations, including patient records and administrative services, became inaccessible.

- **Initial response:** The CCSS activated its IRP, which included:
  o Shutting down critical systems such as the Digital Health Record System (EDUS) and Centralized Collection System (SICERE).
  o Notifying national cybersecurity authorities and international partners.
  o Deploying contingency plans across 163 healthcare facilities to maintain service continuity.

- **Containment and eradication:** Forensic investigations revealed that over 800 servers and 9,000 endpoints had been compromised. A phased recovery was launched, involving:
  o Isolation of infected systems.

o Cleaning and validating backups.

o Preventing reinfection during system restoration.

- **Recovery:** Despite a $5 million ransom demand in Bitcoin, the CCSS chose not to pay. Instead, they restored services using verified offline backups and focused on long-term cybersecurity hardening.

- **Lessons learned:**

o Offline, up-to-date backups are essential for ransomware resilience.

o IRPs must be regularly tested and updated.

o End-user awareness and IT staff training are key to early detection and effective response.

Conclusion

In this chapter, we had a general and strategic view of incident response, which is linked to threat hunting in different ways. After reading the chapter, we see how our activities as threat hunters emerge once an incident is detected, and we see the connection points in each activity. In summary, our activity and the activities related to incident response must be adequately articulated with the aim of being more efficient, effective, and beneficial for the organization. The survival of a company after the materialization of a cyberattack can depend largely on this articulation.

In the next chapter, readers will be introduced to the fundamentals of threat hunting, including the essential skills and qualities needed to be effective in this proactive cybersecurity role.

Points to remember

- Incident response involves many activities
- The threat lifecycle changes in a dynamic form
- The incursion of AI forces us to improve detection and monitoring mechanisms
- Forensic computing should always be included within the incident handling process

Multiple choice questions

1. **Which of the following is the first step in the Incident Response lifecycle according to the new NIST framework?**

    a. Detection

    b. Containment, Eradication, and Recovery

    c. Preparation

    d. Post-Incident Activity

2. **What is the primary goal of the Incident Triage process?**

    a. To eradicate malware from affected systems.

    b. To monitor network traffic for anomalies.

    c. To generate forensic reports for compliance.

    d. To prioritize incidents based on their impact and urgency.

3. **Which of the following is NOT typically included in an Incident Response Plan (IRP)?**

    a. Detailed steps for implementing business continuity plans.

    b. Defined roles and responsibilities for the response team.

    c. Communication protocols during an incident.

    d. Escalation paths for unresolved incidents.

4. **What is the primary purpose of conducting a "lessons learned" session after an incident?**

    a. To blame those responsible for the incident.

    b. To improve incident response processes and prevent recurrence.

    c. To test backup and recovery procedures.

    d. To monitor systems for additional threats.

5. **Which of the following best describes the purpose of incident containment?**

    a. To identify the root cause of the incident.

    b. To notify stakeholders of the incident.

    c. To restore systems to normal operation.

    d. To prevent the attacker from gaining further access to systems.

Answers

1. a.
2. d.
3. a.
4. b.
5. d.

References

1. **NIST Incident Response Lifecycle: https://csrc.nist.gov/projects/incident-response**

CHAPTER 11
Threat Hunting Best Practices

Introduction

As we have gone through the chapters, we have covered many interesting topics such as malware, traffic analysis, operating systems, and many more; due to this, we can conclude that threat hunting is a long process that can take up a lot of time due to understanding of the problem, findings, analysis, normalization, and reporting. Given the sophistication of the threat hunting process, it is essential to implement best practices that enable us to detect and respond to threats before they can cause significant harm.

In this chapter, we will explore the fundamentals that a threat hunter must have as a skill set and the best practices for the threat hunting process, helping the readers save time in many aspects of threat hunting that can be extensive or avoiding running into many dead ends due to the cybercriminals being more proficient at hiding their actions.

The best recommendation we can give in this chapter is to practice each piece of advice and best practice presented in the chapter in order to refine their capacities and increase their knowledge. In this type of activity, practical experience makes all the difference at the level of capabilities. However, we must keep in mind that threat hunting is a very interesting activity that we can discuss in detail, but we will never feel that we have mastered it perfectly since its field of study is enormous, that feeling of appetite for unsatisfied knowledge, we must never lose it.

Structure

In this chapter, we will discuss the following topics:

- Essential skills and qualities of a threat hunter
- Planning and preparation for threat hunting
- Continuous monitoring and proactive hunting
- Measuring and improving effectiveness
- Best practices in cloud environments
- Threat hunting best practices in ICS
- Threat hunting best practices in IoT

Objectives

We already have a very well-equipped toolbox with concepts, knowledge, techniques, and tools, but now it is important to know how to proceed in the best way with the information we can gather about threats. So, this chapter is your guide for Industry threat hunting best practices.

Essential skills and qualities of a threat hunter

In the book, we have seen a large amount of material related to detection techniques both in networks and operating systems. We have discussed malware, how to analyze it, etc., making an X-ray of the knowledge required to be able to apply all these tools. We managed to understand that the threat hunter requires a complete group of skills and knowledge to execute their work, and that the field experience will increase the capacities and discernment of the researcher.

In detail, we have several indispensable capabilities for the threat hunter and several desirable abilities. Let us start by listing the essential ones related to personal soft skills:

- **Soft skills:** These personal attributes play a crucial role in a threat hunter's effectiveness. While technical skills are essential for uncovering threats, it is often soft skills that enable clear communication, critical thinking, and effective collaboration. The following soft skills are considered essential:

  o **Analytical thinking and problem solving:** The threat hunter needs the ability to think like an adversary to anticipate potential threats and identify unusual patterns; the hunter should be able to think about the step-by-step of an attack and be able to visualize the alternative paths that the adversary could take in case any point of his strategy fails.

Critical thinking is useful to connect disparate and separated indicators, in most cases extracted in a non-human readable form, and build a comprehensive attack timeline and narrative.

o **Communication and collaboration skills:** Ability to translate complex technical findings into clear and actionable reports for both technical and non-technical audiences.

Effective collaboration with the blue team, **Security Operations Center (SOC)** teams, incident responders, stakeholders, and management.

o **Attention to detail**: Precision in identifying subtle indicators in massive datasets and the ability to spot anomalies that others might overlook.

o **Patience and persistence**: Resilience to pursue long-term investigations that can take days, weeks, or even months and tenacity in following leads and hypotheses until they are proven or disproven.

o **Curiosity and a hacker mindset**: Natural drive to explore, dissect, and understand how attacks happen.

Passion for continuous learning about emerging threats and vulnerabilities.

o **Risk assessment and decision-making**: Capability to keep and maintain calm inside the chaos; ability to assess risk and prioritize threats based on business impact.

Confidence to make informed decisions swiftly during investigations.

o **Ethical integrity**: Adherence to the organization's policies and compliance requirements.

• **Technical skills:** A strong technical foundation is essential for any threat hunter. These skills enable the identification, analysis, and mitigation of threats across diverse systems and environments. The following technical capabilities are considered indispensable for effective threat hunting:

o **IT infrastructure knowledge**: The researcher requires knowledge about the operation and architecture of different services, such as cloud, databases, Microservices, APIs, etc., because, in most opportunities, he will carry out research in hybrid architectures.

o **Deep understanding of operating systems**: Mastery of Windows, Linux, and macOS internals, including kernel processes, registries, file systems, and knowledge of Active Directory structures and common attack vectors.

Network security knowledge: Proficiency in TCP/IP, DNS, HTTP/S, and SSL/TLS protocols.

Understanding of network-based attacks such as **Domain Name System (DNS)** tunneling, **Distributed Denial of Service (DDoS)**, and **man-in-the-middle (MitM)**.

- o **Malware analysis**: The hunter must have the capability to perform static and dynamic analysis of malware, understand how malware works, know the different types, what their **Indicators of Compromise (IoC)** potentials are, and how to proceed properly to prevent the spread of infection.

  Ability to detect fileless malware, **Living-off-the-Land (LotL)** techniques, and **Advanced Persistent Threats (APTs)**.

  A desirable capability will be an understanding of assembly language and binary analysis.

- o **Familiarity with attack tools and techniques**: Knowledge of penetration testing tools (for example, Rubeus, Nuclei, Metasploit, Nmap, Bloodhound).

  Understanding how adversaries use **command and control (C2)** techniques and how to detect them.

- **Threat hunting core competencies:** Beyond technical and soft skills, threat hunters must develop specific competencies that define the discipline itself. The following are considered essential:

  - o **Advanced threat detection and analysis**: Expertise in **identifying IoC** such as file hashes, IP addresses, domains, and registry changes.

    Proficiency in analyzing and interpreting **Security Information and Event Management (SIEM)** data.

  - o **Forensic computing**: It is not essential that the threat hunter be a forensic expert, but it is essential that he knows the proper handling of digital evidence and understands what the proper procedures are to avoid the alteration of evidence.

    Skills in **packet capture** (**PCAP**) analysis using tools like Wireshark and Zeek.

    Knowledge of **Endpoint Detection and Response (EDR)** solutions (for example, CrowdStrike, Carbon Black).

    Proficiency in forensic techniques like memory forensics and analysis of disk images.

  - o **Threat intelligence integration**: Ability to correlate external threat intelligence with internal telemetry for proactive defense.

  - o **Knowledge of security frameworks:** A detailed understanding of the MITRE ATT&CK framework for recognizing adversarial **Tactics, Techniques, and Procedures (TTPs)**.

    Familiarity with NIST SP 800-61 for incident handling and response.

- **Desirable skills:** While not strictly essential, these skills significantly enhance a threat hunter's effectiveness and versatility. Developing these skills can offer a strong competitive edge:

  o **Scripting and automation:** Proficiency in scripting languages such as Python, PowerShell, or Bash for automating threat-hunting tasks.

  Experience with **Security Orchestration, Automation, and Response (SOAR)** tools to streamline investigations.

Planning and preparation for threat hunting

Detailed planning and good preparation are the fundamental basis of an effective threat hunting process. It is ideal to have a proactive approach, which enables organizations to identify and mitigate potential threats that may bypass traditional security measures. Following are some recommendations to achieve effective planning and readiness of the threat hunting area in a company:

1. **Define objectives and scope:** Clearly identifying the objectives and scope provides direction and focus for the threat hunting activity. The following elements should be considered when defining this phase:

   a. **Establish clear goals:** Determine what you aim to achieve with threat hunting, such as detecting potential corporate espionage implants, identifying APTs, detecting insider threats, or uncovering unknown vulnerabilities.

   b. **Scope definition:** Decide which systems, networks, or applications will be included in the threat hunting activities to ensure focused and efficient operations.

2. **Assemble a skilled threat hunting team:** A capable and diverse team is critical to the success of any threat hunting initiative. The following skill sets should be considered when building the team:

   a. **Identify qualified personnel**: Select team members with expertise in cybersecurity, network analysis, and incident response. Experience in understanding attacker behavior and tactics is crucial.

   There are specific certifications on the market that are desirable in a threat hunter. Refer to the following table:

Certification	Provider	Focus Area	Website
GIAC Certified Forensic Analyst (GCFA)	SANS Institute	Advanced incident response and digital forensics for analyzing sophisticated threats	**https://www.giac.org/certifications/certified-forensic-analyst-gcfa**
eLearnSecurity Certified Threat Hunting Professional (eCTHP)	INE Security	Threat hunting and identification with emphasis on real-world scenarios	**security.ine.com**
CompTIA Cybersecurity Analyst (CySA+)	CompTIA	Behavioral analytics for threat detection and response	**https://www.comptia.org/certifications/cybersecurity-analyst**
Certified Threat Intelligence Analyst (CTIA)	EC-Council	Building effective threat intelligence including data collection and analysis	**eccouncil.org**
MTH - Certified Threat Hunter	Mosse Institute	Comprehensive threat hunting skills for security professionals	**mosse-institute.com**
TH-200: Foundational Threat Hunting Certification	OffSec	Threat hunting methodologies and practical skills	**offsec.com**
ISAC Certified Threat Hunter (ICTH)	ISAC	MITRE's ATT&CK framework, threat hunting approaches, and techniques	**https://isacfoundation.org/isac-certified-threat-hunter-icth**

Table 11.1: Threat hunting certifications

    b. **Continuous training**: Invest in ongoing education and certifications to keep the team updated on the latest threat landscapes and hunting techniques.

3. **Develop a threat hunting strategy**

A well-defined strategy guides the threat hunting process, aligning it with organizational goals and ensuring consistency across hunts. The following elements are key to building an effective strategy:

    a. **Hypothesis development:** You can formulate educated guesses about potential threats based on different informational sources, like threat intelligence, known vulnerabilities, or observed anomalies. This hypothesis-driven approach guides the hunting process and gives you a proper foundation.

b. **Methodology selection:** Choose appropriate threat hunting methodologies, such as:

    i. **Intelligence-driven:** Leveraging threat intelligence reports and feeds to identify IoC.

    ii. **Analytics-driven:** Utilizing machine learning and user behavior analytics to detect anomalies.

    iii. **Situational awareness-driven:** Focusing on critical assets and potential threats specific to the organization's environment.

4. **Collect and prepare data:** Threat hunting requires access to reliable and relevant data. This step involves collecting telemetry from key sources and applying validation measures to ensure the data is clean and usable:

a. **Data collection**: Aggregate relevant data sources, including:

    i. **Web access logs**: To detect abnormal navigation and user's internet access.

    ii. **DNS resolution logs**: To detect abnormal resolved hosts and behavior.

    iii. **Network traffic logs:** To monitor data flow and detect unusual patterns.

    iv. **Endpoint logs:** To observe activities on individual devices.

    v. **Authentication logs:** To track user access and identify unauthorized attempts.

    vi. **Active Directory logs:** To detect abnormal behavior from Users and Resources.

b. **Data validation and hygiene**: Ensure collected data is accurate, complete, and free from inconsistencies to facilitate effective analysis.

5. **Select appropriate tools and technologies:** Using the right tools is essential to support efficient and effective threat hunting. The following should be considered:

a. **Threat Intelligence Platforms (TIPs)**: Implement TIPs to aggregate and analyze threat data from multiple sources, enhancing situational awareness.

b. **Security Information and Event Management (SIEM) systems**: Deploy SIEM solutions to collect, correlate, and analyze security events in real-time.

c. **Endpoint Detection and Response (EDR) tools**: Install EDR solutions to monitor and analyze endpoint activities, facilitating rapid detection and response to threats.

6. **Establish procedures and playbooks:** Standardized procedures ensure consistency and repeatability in threat hunting activities. The following should be considered:

   a. **Develop Standard Operating Procedures (SOPs)**: Detailed guidelines for threat hunting activities, including data analysis techniques, escalation protocols, and documentation standards, are recommended, so you can replicate the activities and escalate them in a more effective way.

   b. **Incident response integration**: Threat hunting procedures should be aligned with the organization's incident response plan for seamless operation during threat detection and mitigation.

7. **Allocate time and resources:** Effective threat hunting requires dedicated time, personnel, and tools to deliver meaningful results. The following should be considered:

   a. **Define a timeline**: Set realistic timelines for each threat hunting activity based on the team's capacity and the complexity of the tasks. This is key to achieving good execution within the team and reducing frustration levels.

   b. **Resource allocation**: Threat hunting team should have access to necessary resources, including tools, data (present and historical), and support from other departments.

8. **Implement continuous improvement practices:** Threat hunting should evolve through ongoing learning and refinement of techniques. The following should be considered:

   a. **Post-hunt analysis**: Conduct reviews after each threat hunting mission to assess what was successful and identify areas for improvement.

   b. **Update threat models**: Regularly refine threat models and hypotheses based on new intelligence and findings from previous hunts. This keeps your models up to date.

   c. **Knowledge sharing**: Promote collaboration by sharing insights and lessons learned with relevant stakeholders and the broader security community.

Continuous monitoring and proactive hunting

Combining continuous monitoring with proactive threat hunting creates a robust cybersecurity framework. Continuous monitoring provides real-time visibility into the network, enabling immediate detection of known threats and anomalies. We must always remember that the time that a threat manages to go unnoticed, operating within our infrastructure, is irreparable and often impossible to measure in relation to its negative consequences. Proactive threat hunting complements this by actively seeking out unknown or sophisticated threats that may bypass automated monitoring systems. Together, they ensure a comprehensive approach to threat detection and response, enhancing an organization's ability to protect its assets and maintain trust.

Not all the tools available can connect continuous monitoring with threat hunting, but the following table is the list of some of the most relevant ones that have capabilities in this regard:

Tool Name	Type	Purpose	Key Features	URL
Grafana Cloud	Monitoring and Observability	Continuous Monitoring	Customizable dashboards, robust visualization	**https://grafana.com/products/cloud/**
Prometheus	Monitoring System	Continuous Monitoring	Time-series data collection, real-time alerting	**https://prometheus.io/**
Datadog	Monitoring and Analytics	Continuous Monitoring	Infrastructure monitoring, log management	**https://www.datadoghq.com/**
New Relic	Observability Platform	Continuous Monitoring	Full-stack monitoring, AI-driven insights	**https://newrelic.com/**
Zabbix	Network Monitoring	Continuous Monitoring	Performance monitoring, fault detection	**https://www.zabbix.com/**
Heimdal Threat-Hunting & Action Center	Threat Hunting Platform	Proactive Threat Hunting	Advanced threat detection, granular telemetry	**https://heimdalsecurity.com/**
Kaspersky **Anti-Targeted Attack Platform (ATAP)**	Threat Detection and Response	Proactive Threat Hunting	Advanced threat hunting capabilities	**https://www.kaspersky.com/enterprise-security/anti-targeted-attack-platform**
Trustwave **Managed Detection and Response (MDR)**	Managed Security Service	Proactive Threat Hunting	24/7 monitoring, incident response	**https://www.trustwave.com/**

Table 11.2: Threat hunting monitoring tools

Measuring and improving effectiveness

Organizations can significantly enhance the effectiveness of their threat hunting programs by systematically measuring performance through defined metrics and implementing continuous improvement strategies, leading to a more robust security posture.

Following is a comprehensive list of strategies for measuring and improving threat hunting effectiveness:

1. **Measuring threat hunting effectiveness:** Tracking performance helps validate the value of threat hunting and guides future improvements. The following should be considered:

    a. **Set clear objectives:** Define specific goals and milestones for the threat hunting program, such as reducing the MTTD threats or increasing the identification of previously unknown threats. Clear objectives provide a benchmark for measuring success.

    You can use historical data to start your charts and forecasts.

    b. **Key Performance Indicators (KPIs):** It is impossible to know if we are achieving the expected results if we do not have a clear measurement, So, it is advisable to implement KPIs to assess the efficiency and effectiveness of threat hunting activities:

        i. **Activity metrics:** Track the frequency and scope of threat hunting exercises to ensure consistent coverage across the organization's environment.

        ii. **Detection efficacy:** Evaluate the success rate of hunts in identifying genuine threats, indicating the precision of threat detection methods.

        iii. **Mean Time to Detect (MTTD):** Measure the average time taken to identify threats, aiming to minimize this duration to reduce potential damage.

        iv. **Mean Time to Respond (MTTR):** Assess the average time from threat detection to remediation, reflecting the responsiveness of the security team.

    c. **Threat hunting maturity models:** Use frameworks like the **hunting maturity model** (HMM) to evaluate the evolution and state of the threat hunting program in your organization. The HMM assesses factors such as data collection capabilities, data accessibility, and analysts' skill levels, assigning a maturity level from HMM0 (initial) to HMM4 (advanced). In the following figure, you will preview the maturity model:

Levels of the Threat Hunting Maturity Model

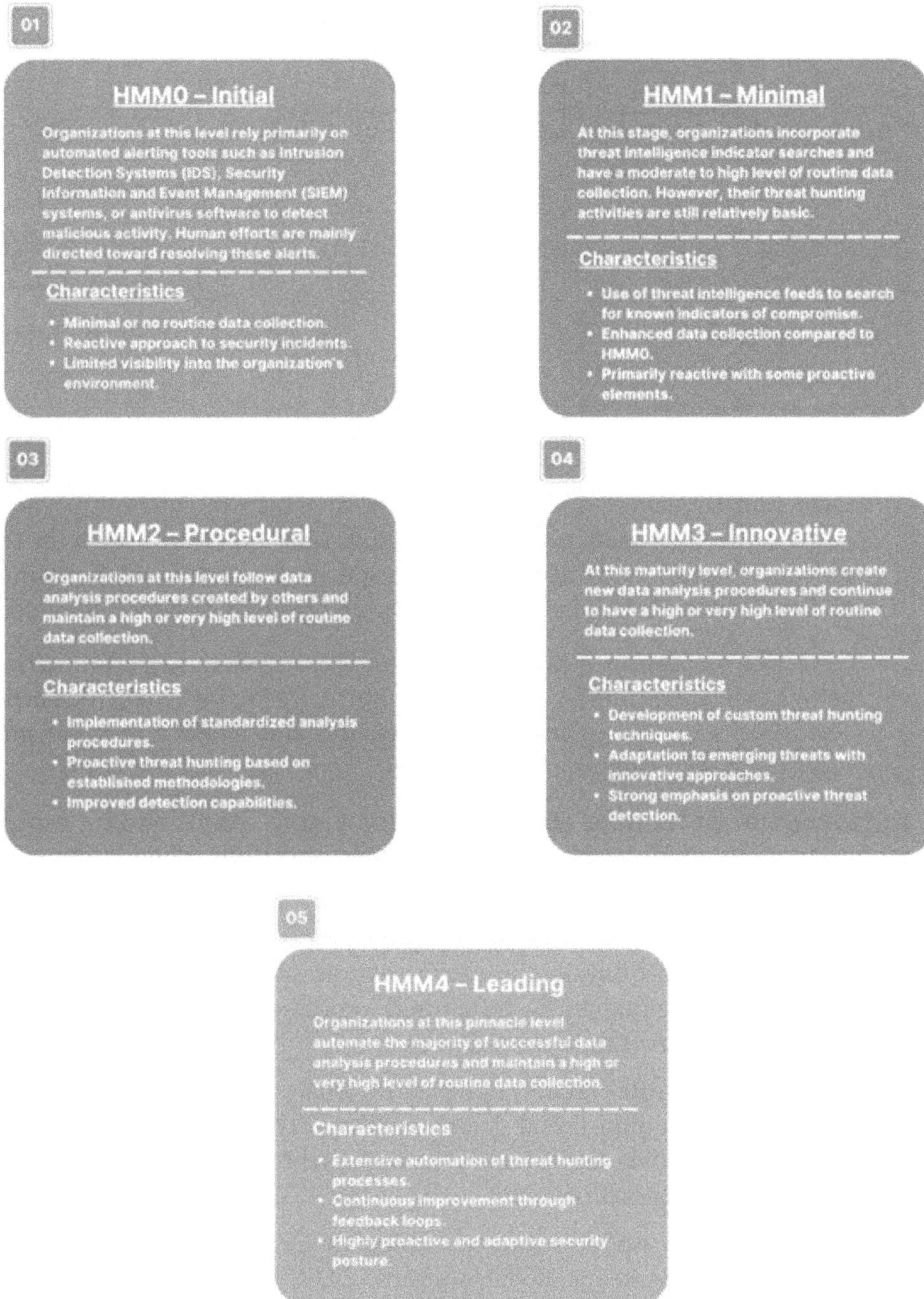

01

HMM0 – Initial

Organizations at this level rely primarily on automated alerting tools such as Intrusion Detection Systems (IDS), Security Information and Event Management (SIEM) systems, or antivirus software to detect malicious activity. Human efforts are mainly directed toward resolving these alerts.

Characteristics

- Minimal or no routine data collection.
- Reactive approach to security incidents.
- Limited visibility into the organization's environment.

02

HMM1 – Minimal

At this stage, organizations incorporate threat intelligence indicator searches and have a moderate to high level of routine data collection. However, their threat hunting activities are still relatively basic.

Characteristics

- Use of threat intelligence feeds to search for known indicators of compromise.
- Enhanced data collection compared to HMM0.
- Primarily reactive with some proactive elements.

03

HMM2 – Procedural

Organizations at this level follow data analysis procedures created by others and maintain a high or very high level of routine data collection.

Characteristics

- Implementation of standardized analysis procedures.
- Proactive threat hunting based on established methodologies.
- Improved detection capabilities.

04

HMM3 – Innovative

At this maturity level, organizations create new data analysis procedures and continue to have a high or very high level of routine data collection.

Characteristics

- Development of custom threat hunting techniques.
- Adaptation to emerging threats with innovative approaches.
- Strong emphasis on proactive threat detection.

05

HMM4 – Leading

Organizations at this pinnacle level automate the majority of successful data analysis procedures and maintain a high or very high level of routine data collection.

Characteristics

- Extensive automation of threat hunting processes.
- Continuous improvement through feedback loops.
- Highly proactive and adaptive security posture.

Figure 11.1: Threat hunting maturity model

Now that you have seen the descriptions and characteristics here is a more graphical way of the threat hunting maturity level:

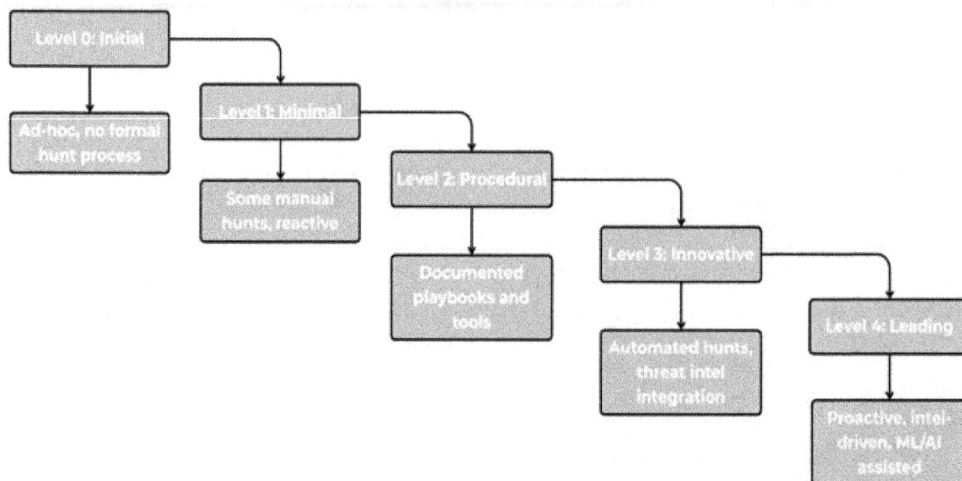

Figure 11.2: Threat hunting maturity model levels

    d. **Detection coverage**: Analyze the extent to which threat hunting activities address the organization's threat profile. Ensure that hunts are aligned with the most relevant and impactful threats specific to the organization's industry and environment. This helps to use existing resources in a more targeted way.

    e. **Detection validation**: Test and validate detection rules and alerts on a frequent basis; update the rules to ensure they effectively identify malicious activities. This process helps in fine-tuning detection and alerting mechanisms and reducing false positives.

2. **Improving threat hunting effectiveness:** Enhancing threat hunting capabilities requires ongoing refinement of tools, processes, and skills. The following should be considered:

    a. **Develop a structured threat hunting process**: Implement a formalized approach to threat hunting, involving hypothesis generation, data collection, analysis, and remediation. Structured processes enhance consistency and defectivity in threat hunting activities.

    b. **Leverage threat intelligence**: Integrate external and internal threat intelligence to inform and guide threat hunting efforts. This integration enhances the ability to anticipate and identify emerging threats, before they materialize inside your organization.

    c. **Invest in advanced tools and technologies**: Deploy the latest security tools such as SIEM systems, EDR solutions, XDR, behavioral monitoring, and advanced analytics platforms. These tools provide deeper visibility and facilitate efficient threat detection and analysis, reducing human effort and leaving the heavy lifting to the different integrated technologies.

d. **Continuous training and skill development**: Provide ongoing training for threat hunters to keep them updated on the latest attack techniques, tools, and methodologies. A well-trained team is more adept at identifying and responding to sophisticated threats.

e. **Conduct regular reviews and updates**: Periodically review threat hunting strategies, processes, and outcomes to identify areas for improvement. Updating threat models and methodologies ensures the program adapts to the evolving threat landscape.

f. **Foster collaboration and information sharing**: Encourage collaboration among security teams and participate in information-sharing communities. Sharing insights and experiences enhances collective knowledge and improves threat detection capabilities.

Now that we have seen some of the challenges and key aspects that we must have when we are threat hunting, the following figure shows a graphical way of the threat hunting process:

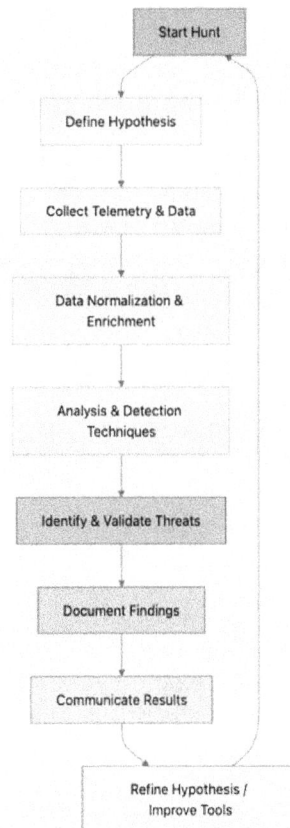

Figure 11.3: Threat hunting maturity model levels

Best practices in cloud environments

Cloud environments present unique challenges for threat hunting due to their dynamic nature, lack of visibility, and shared responsibility model.

Some of the most important challenges in cloud threat hunting are:

- **Visibility gaps:** Limited access to raw network data and infrastructure-level logs.

- **Shared responsibility:** Complexities in determining who manages what aspect of security.

- **Dynamic nature:** Ephemeral resources make tracking threats difficult.

- **Encrypted traffic:** Reduces visibility into potential threats.

- **Complex IAM configurations:** Expands the attack surface with misconfigurations.

- **Cloud-specific threats:** Requires new skills and tools to address unique TTP.

- **Cost of logging:** The high volume and cost of storing logs can limit effective hunting. In some cases, companies decide to forward all logs to on-premises infrastructure, which can grow with fewer limitations and costs.

Considering the challenges mentioned above, we provide some recommendations to make the threat hunting process in cloud computing environments more effective:

- **Implement comprehensive log management:** Effective threat hunting relies on thorough log management. Establishing a robust plan that includes centralized aggregation, appropriate filtering, and a suitable retention policy is crucial. Poorly managed logs can limit forensic and hunting operations. It is critical to know how each cloud provider handles logs and what logs can provide, since there is no global standard, and data may vary from one provider to another. In this way, a policy must be created in accordance with the capabilities of the service provider and our needs as a company.

- **Utilize advanced detection capabilities:** Investing in technologies such as machine learning-based anomaly detection, taking advantage of AI, and **cyber threat intelligence (CTI)** solutions can enhance the ability to detect subtle changes indicative of an attack. These advanced tools enable more proactive and effective threat hunting.

- **Conduct regular threat hunting sessions:** Proactive data collection and regular threat hunting sessions help organizations stay up to date on the latest infrastructural changes and avoid surprises. Collecting logs from across the infrastructure and storing them in a central repository, followed by using automated tools to examine them for suspicious activity, is recommended.

- **Align with established frameworks:** Aligning threat hunting activities with frameworks like the MITRE ATT&CK framework can provide a structured approach to identifying and mitigating threats. This alignment helps in understanding adversary TTPs, thereby enhancing threat detection capabilities.

Threat hunting best practices in ICS

Threat hunting in **Industrial Control Systems** (**ICS**) presents unique challenges due to the specialized and critical nature of these environments. Following are the key obstacles that include:

- **Legacy systems and obsolete technologies:** Many ICS environments operate with outdated hardware and software, such as Windows 98, 2000, and XP, which lack modern security features and are difficult to replace.

- **Limited logging and monitoring capabilities:** ICS devices often have restricted or limited logging functionalities, making it challenging to detect and analyze malicious activities.

- **Safety and availability prioritization:** The primary focus on operational safety and continuous availability can limit the implementation of security measures that might disrupt processes. In ICS, always apply: *if it is working, do not touch it!*

- **Convergence of IT and OT networks:** The blending of **Information Technology** (**IT**) and **Operational Technology** (**OT**) networks increases the attack surface, introducing vulnerabilities from IT systems into OT environments and vice versa.

- **Lack of specialized threat intelligence:** Traditional threat intelligence often overlooks the unique aspects of ICS, necessitating customized intelligence to effectively address OT-specific threats.

- **Shortage of skilled personnel:** There is a scarcity of professionals with expertise in both cybersecurity and ICS operations, making more difficult the threat hunting efforts.

- **Complex and proprietary protocols:** ICS environments utilize specialized communication protocols, which can be complex and proprietary, making it difficult for standard security tools to analyze traffic effectively.

- **Insufficient network segmentation:** Poorly segmented networks allow threats to move laterally across systems, increasing the potential impact of attacks.

- **Regulatory and compliance constraints:** Compliance requirements may limit the implementation of certain security measures, complicating threat hunting initiatives.

- **Evolving threat landscape:** Adversaries are continually developing sophisticated methods targeting ICS, requiring constant adaptation of threat hunting strategies.

We have already enunciated some of the main challenges to implementing an effective threat hunting strategy in ICS environments, here are some of the best practices to consider:

- **Understand the ICS environment:** Develop a comprehensive and thorough inventory of all ICS assets, including brand, hardware, software, protocols, OS, firmware, and communication channels. This foundational information is essential for effective threat detection. From our experience, most companies do not have an inventory of assets up to date; in this case, we are talking about both IT and OT, including other architectures such as Fog Computing.

- **Integrate threat intelligence:** Leverage CTI to stay informed about emerging threats and attack techniques targeting ICS. Sharing threat intelligence with relevant stakeholders enhances collective defense.

- **Implement continuous monitoring:** Continuous monitoring of network traffic and system logs to detect anomalies indicative of potential threats is mandatory. Given the unique nature of ICS environments, tailored monitoring strategies are essential.

- **Conduct regular threat hunting exercises:** Proactively search for IoC within the ICS network. Regular threat hunting allows to identify and mitigate threats that may bypass automated defenses.

- **Prioritize safety and reliability:** Ensure that threat hunting activities do not disrupt the operational safety and reliability of ICS. Collaborate with engineering teams to align security measures with operational requirements; remember that ICS normally controls critical mission operations inside the organizations.

- **Develop incident response plans:** Create and regularly update incident response plans tailored to the ICS environment. These plans should outline procedures for detecting, containing, and recovering from cyber threats.

- **Conduct regular assessments and training:** Perform regular security assessments, like Vulnerability Assessments or penetration testing exercises, to identify vulnerabilities within the ICS. Provide ongoing training for personnel to recognize and respond to potential threats effectively.

As we have previously seen the obstacles of threat hunting, here is the following figure showing the challenges of cloud and ICS:

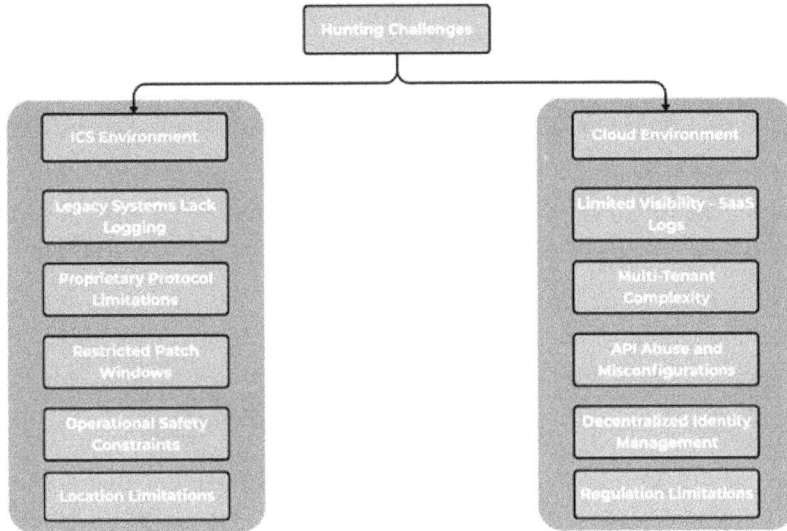

Figure 11.4: *Cloud/ICS Challenges.*

Threat hunting best practices in IoT

If carrying out effective threat hunting in OT environments is complex and full of challenges, being effective in IoT environments is even more difficult because there are additional limitations. Addressing these challenges requires a comprehensive approach, including implementing robust security protocols, ensuring regular firmware updates, enhancing device monitoring capabilities, and fostering industry-wide standardization to secure IoT environments effectively.

The following are some of the most important challenges:

- **Heterogeneity:** IoT ecosystems consist of a wide variety of devices with different hardware architectures, operating systems, and communication protocols, complicating the development of universal security solutions.

- **Limited resources:** Many IoT devices have constrained computational power, memory, and energy resources, limiting the implementation of robust security measures such as encryption and intrusion detection systems.

- **Inadequate security:** Weak authentication and lack of encryption; Many IoT devices utilize default or weak credentials, making them susceptible to unauthorized access and data transmitted by IoT devices is often unencrypted, exposing sensitive information to interception and tampering.

- **Outdated firmware and software:** IoT devices often run outdated firmware or software, leaving known vulnerabilities unpatched and exploitable by attackers.

- **Insufficient logging and monitoring:** Many IoT devices lack comprehensive logging and monitoring capabilities.

- **Scalability issues:** Massive device deployment, the large scale of IoT deployments makes it challenging to monitor and manage security across all devices effectively.

- **Physical security risks:** IoT devices are often deployed in unsecured or remote locations, making them vulnerable to physical attacks that can compromise device integrity.

- **Complex attack surfaces:** The integration of IoT devices into networks increases the attack surface for the adversaries.

- **Evolving threat landscape:** IoT environments are increasingly targeted by sophisticated APTs that are difficult to detect and mitigate.

- **Supply chain vulnerabilities:** The use of third-party hardware and software in IoT devices can introduce vulnerabilities, especially if components are sourced from untrusted suppliers.

Some of the best practices recommended for performing threat hunting in IoT environments are:

- **Develop a comprehensive asset inventory and categorization:** Understanding what needs to be protected is essential for focused and effective threat hunting. The following should be considered:

  o **Identify all IoT devices**: Maintain an up-to-date inventory of all IoT devices connected to the network, including device types, manufacturers, and firmware versions.

  o **Categorize devices**: Classify devices based on their functions and criticality to prioritize security measures effectively.

- **Implement strong authentication and access controls:** Controlling access to systems and data reduces the risk of unauthorized activity and lateral movement. The following points should be considered:

  o **Enforce unique credentials:** Replace default passwords with strong, unique credentials for each device.

  o **Utilize Multi-Factor Authentication (MFA):** Implement MFA to add an extra layer of security for accessing IoT devices and management interfaces.

- **Ensure regular firmware and software updates:** Keeping systems updated helps close known vulnerabilities and reduce exploitable attack surfaces. The following details should be considered:

  o **Patch management:** Establish a process for timely updates of device firmware and software to address known vulnerabilities.

    o **Automated updates:** Where possible, enable automated updates to ensure devices receive critical patches promptly.

- **Segment networks appropriately:** Network segmentation limits the spread of threats and improves visibility and control over traffic flows. The following network details should be considered:

    o **Isolate IoT devices:** Place IoT devices on separate network segments or VLANs to make it easier to traffic monitoring and detection and reduce attack surface.

    o **Implement firewalls:** Use firewalls to control and monitor traffic between IoT devices and other network segments.

- **Continuous monitoring and anomaly detection:** Implement advanced monitoring solutions to track device behavior and network traffic, enabling the early detection of anomalies and threats.

- **Implement AI and machine learning for threat detection:** Take advantage of artificial intelligence and machine learning technologies to analyze patterns, detect anomalies, and predict potential vulnerabilities in real-time.

- **Regular security audits and risk assessments:** Conduct periodic security audits and risk assessments to identify vulnerabilities and implement necessary mitigations.

Conclusion

Reaching the point of being an effective threat hunter requires effort, study, and practice, since it requires a large number and types of skills, both soft and hard. On the other hand we see that planning and preparation are key in the hunt for threats. If we do not have them, the process can become very difficult and partial, generating a kind of blindness to certain indicators. On the other hand, in this chapter we have explored an extensive group of best practices recommended to create effective threat hunting strategies in cloud environments, which are complex and in many cases far from our control and we end up with best practices in more complex environments and less taken into account for some tools such as OT and IoT.

In the next chapter, readers will explore the importance of threat intelligence sharing to enhance detection and response capabilities across organizations. Topics will include an overview of both the benefits and challenges involved in sharing threat information in a connected and evolving threat landscape, and much more.

Points to remember

- Planning and preparation are key to developing an effective threat hunting strategy.

- There are some specific tools that facilitate the continuous monitoring and proactive hunting, some of them are open source.

- You need metrics to validate the effectiveness of your threat hunting policies and strategies.

- Cloud, OT, and IoT environments are commonly used by adversaries as an attack surface; so, they need to be included in any threat hunting strategy.

Multiple choice questions

1. **When conducting threat hunting in IoT environments, which practice is considered most effective for reducing attack surfaces?**

    a. Enabling default credentials for easy management

    b. Implementing network segmentation and isolating IoT devices

    c. Using outdated encryption protocols

    d. Disabling all security logging to reduce data volume

2. **Which of the following techniques is best for detecting APTs during threat hunting?**

    a. Signature-based detection

    b. Log analysis and anomaly detection

    c. Manual packet inspection only

    d. Static IP blocking

3. **What is the primary benefit of using threat intelligence feeds in threat hunting?**

    a. To limit data collection requirements

    b. To replace the need for human analysts

    c. To provide context and IoCs for detecting threats

    d. To increase network latency for attackers

4. **Which of the following is NOT considered a best practice in threat hunting?**

    a. Establishing a hypothesis before starting a hunt

    b. Conducting threat hunts on a regular schedule

    c. Ignoring user behavior analytics to focus only on network traffic

    d. Using threat hunting frameworks like MITRE ATT&CK

5. **In the context of threat hunting, what is the main purpose of hypothesis-driven investigations?**

   a. To test specific assumptions about potential threats based on known tactics and observed data.

   b. To confirm alerts generated by SIEM systems without further analysis.

   c. To automate all security responses.

   d. To prioritize compliance over security.

Answers

1. b.

2. b.

3. c.

4. c.

5. a.

References

1. **Technical Approaches to Uncovering and Remediating Malicious Activity**

   https://www.cisa.gov/news-events/cybersecurity-advisories/aa20-245a

2. **Enhanced Visibility and Hardening Guidance for Communications Infrastructure**

   https://www.cisa.gov/resources-tools/resources/enhanced-visibility-and-hardening-guidance-communications-infrastructure

3. **Identifying and Mitigating Living Off the Land Techniques**

   https://www.cisa.gov/sites/default/files/2024-02/Joint-Guidance-Identifying-and-Mitigating-LOTL_V3508c.pdf

Join our Discord space

Join our Discord workspace for latest updates, offers, tech happenings around the world, new releases, and sessions with the authors:

https://discord.bpbonline.com

CHAPTER 12
Threat Intelligence Sharing and Collaboration

Introduction

Criminals day by day try to innovate their TTPs, changing their infection method due to a new technology vulnerability or a new Living off the Land malware that is embedded in a file undetectable by anti-malware systems, and being in vanguard of the new fingerprints and IoCs of a zero-day vulnerability or malware is almost impossible. For this reason, the cybersecurity and threat intelligence community developed a series of networks to be connected and share their findings for the **Indicators of Compromise (IoC)** or to help each other analyze new threats.

In this chapter, we will explore the importance of sharing new findings in the threat intelligence community, where we can find new IoCs, what information we can share with the community, and the legal implications we need to be aware of when sharing this type of information.

Structure

In this chapter, we will discuss the following topics:

- Importance of threat intelligence sharing
- Threat intelligence sharing
- Legal and ethical considerations

- Collaborative threat hunting
- Benefits and challenges
- Use cases

Objectives

Knowing where we can share and find out information about new threats, techniques, and vulnerabilities is fundamental for a threat hunter. The objective of this chapter is to explore the benefits and challenges of intelligence sharing, explore key platforms and communities dedicated to this purpose, and examine the legal and ethical considerations that threat hunters must have in sight.

Importance of threat intelligence sharing

In the world of threat hunting, knowing a way to find a possible compromise is key, and having this information available on how to identify the newest threat would bring a potential compromise to a stop. However, threat intelligence is not only about how accurate and how fast organizations can share what they know, whether it will be a success or failure. Threat intelligence sharing is about defending systems from cybercriminals that have its members in underground forums sharing tips on how to use and improve their attacks.

Adversaries already exchange tools, tactics, and new (zero-day) vulnerabilities in the dark web markets. When organizations and people exchange information about threats, it takes away the attacker's advantage. It is no longer a lone threat hunt but a coordinated effort. The following are some of the advantages of threat intelligence sharing:

- Disrupts adversary advantage
- Accelerates detection and response
- Optimizes resources
- Enables continuous learning
- Promotes trust and collaboration
- Improves visibility of threats
- Provides strategic insights
- Enhances resilience

To expand more on the subject, the following figure will show a collaboration flow:

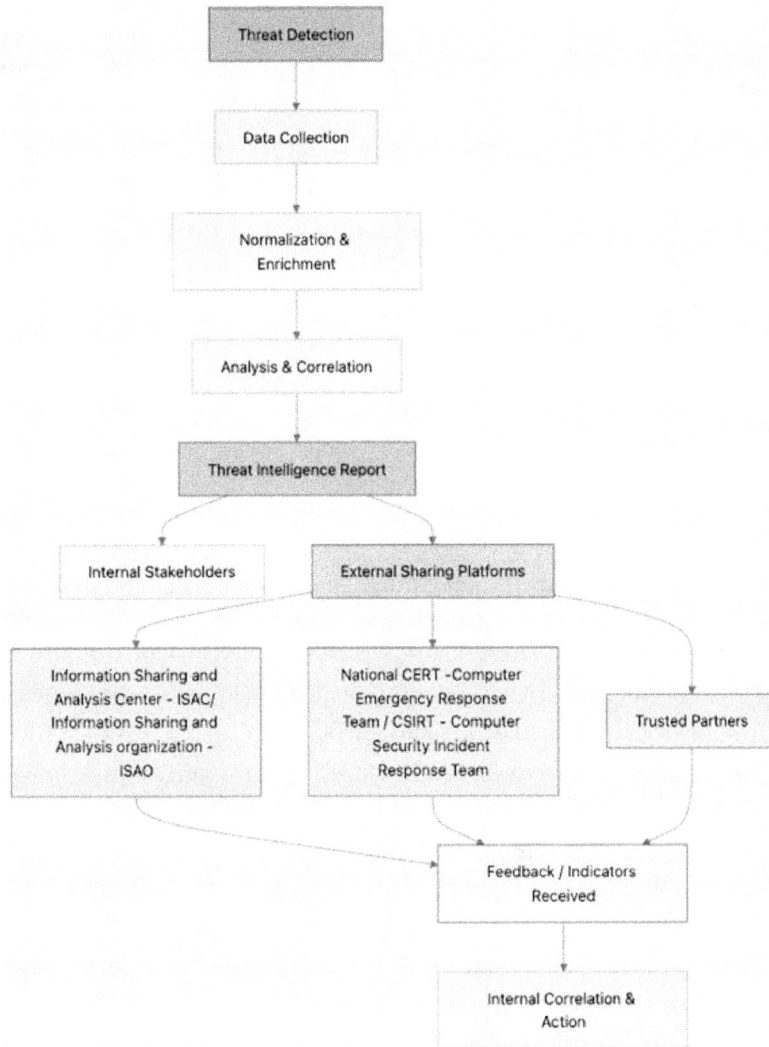

Figure 12.1: Threat intelligence sharing collaboration flow

Threat intelligence sharing

Threat intelligence sharing platforms and communities play a crucial role in bridging information gaps by providing trusted environments for exchanging insights, IoCs, and tactical information about adversaries. The following table shows some threat intelligence-sharing platforms:

Platform	Description	Type	Link
Malware Information Sharing Platform (MISP)	Open-source platform for sharing IoC and threat data.	Free	https://www.misp-project.org/
ThreatConnect	The platform for aggregating, analyzing, and sharing threat intelligence.	Paid	https://threatconnect.com/
Open Threat Exchange (OTX)	Free, open threat intelligence community by AlienVault.	Free	https://otx.alienvault.com/
Recorded Future	Intelligence-driven security platform with real-time threat insights.	Paid	https://www.recorded-future.com/
Palo Alto Networks AutoFocus	Threat intelligence service focusing on malware and threat actors.	Paid	https://www.paloalto-networks.com/cyber-security/threat-intelligence/autofocus
IBM X-Force Exchange	Cloud-based threat intelligence platform for sharing and analyzing threat data.	Free and Paid	https://exchange.xforce.ibmcloud.com/
FireEye Threat Intelligence	Intelligence platform with insights on nation-state actors and APTs.	Paid	https://www.fireeye.com/services.html
Kaspersky Threat Intelligence Portal	Offers threat data feeds, APT reports, and malware analysis.	Free and Paid	https://opentip.kaspersky.com/
LookingGlass Cyber Solutions	Threat intelligence platform focusing on internet and dark web threats.	Paid	https://www.looking-glasscyber.com/
EclecticIQ	Threat intelligence management and sharing platform for large organizations.	Paid	https://www.eclecticiq.com/
Flashpoint	Intelligence platform focused on deep and dark web monitoring.	Paid	https://flashpoint.io/
DomainTools	Focuses on domain-based threat intelligence for proactive defense.	Paid	https://www.domain-tools.com/

Table 12.1: Threat intelligence sharing platforms

The following table shows some communities:

Community	Description	Type	Link
Cyber Threat Alliance (CTA)	A non-profit organization that enables intelligence sharing among cybersecurity vendors.	Paid	**https://www.cyberthreatalliance.org/**
Forum of Incident Response and Security Teams (FIRST)	Global organization for incident response and threat intelligence sharing.	Paid	**https://www.first.org/**
NH-ISAC (Health-ISAC)	ISAC focused on healthcare industry threats and best practices.	Paid	**https://h-isac.org/**
Financial Services ISAC (FS-ISAC)	Community focused on sharing threat intelligence for the financial sector.	Paid	**https://www.fsisac.com/**
Automated Indicator Sharing (AIS)	DHS initiative for automated threat intelligence sharing in the U.S.	Free	**https://www.cisa.gov/topics/cyber-threats-and-advisories/information-sharing/automated-indicator-sharing-ais**
Research and Education Networks ISAC (REN-ISAC)	Intelligence sharing for higher education and research institutions.	Paid	**https://www.ren-isac.net/**
Shadowserver Foundation	Non-profit organization providing free threat intelligence feeds globally.	Free	**https://www.shadowserver.org/**
Cybersecurity and Infrastructure Security Agency (CISA)	U.S. government agency facilitating threat intelligence sharing.	Free	**https://www.cisa.gov/**
No More Ransom Project	Initiative for sharing intelligence and tools to combat ransomware.	Free	**https://www.nomoreransom.org/**
Anti-Phishing Working Group (APWG)	Community focused on sharing threat intelligence related to phishing.	Free and Paid	**https://apwg.org/**

Table 12.2: Threat intelligence communities

Legal and ethical considerations

Threat intelligence sharing offers significant benefits, but it also involves legal and ethical challenges that organizations must carefully address to avoid negative consequences. The following table explores the key legal and ethical considerations:

Consideration	Description	Example
Privacy Compliance	Ensuring compliance with regulations like GDPR when sharing threat intelligence.	Ensuring that shared threat data does not contain user information in violation of GDPR.
Anonymization of Data	Removing **Personally Identifiable Information (PII)** to protect privacy during data sharing.	Removing IP addresses and user IDs from logs before sharing them with external partners.
Consent and Notification	Obtaining consent from affected parties before sharing information and notifying them appropriately.	Notifying customers if their data is included in a threat intelligence report shared externally.
Intellectual Property Protection	Safeguarding intellectual property rights when sharing threat intelligence.	Sharing threat intelligence without exposing proprietary algorithms or software code.
Liability and Legal Risks	Understanding legal risks associated with sharing intelligence, including the possibility of sharing inaccurate information.	Validating threat data to prevent false positives that could harm third parties.
Safe Harbor Provisions	Leveraging legal frameworks that protect organizations sharing intelligence in good faith.	Using **Cybersecurity and Infrastructure Security Agency (CISA's) AIS Automated Indicator Sharing (AIS)** program to share threat intelligence with liability protection.
Attribution and Accuracy	Ensuring the accuracy of shared intelligence to avoid wrongful attributions.	Sharing only verified IoC to prevent misattribution of attacks.
Code of Conduct and Ethics	Establishing clear guidelines on what information can be shared and under what circumstances, respecting ethical principles.	Defining what types of threat data can be shared under an organization's ethics policy.
Cross-Border Data Sharing	Navigating regulations that affect cross-border intelligence sharing.	Complying with both U.S. and EU regulations when sharing threat intelligence internationally.

Table 12.3: Ethical and legal considerations

Collaborative threat hunting

Due to privacy, competitive, or legal concerns, many organizations are reluctant to share their threat intelligence data. To address these barriers, it is necessary to establish trust, to ensure that data is anonymized before sharing, and to define clear legal foundations. Threat hunting in a collaborative manner is not only a strategic position, but also the future of cybersecurity. In this way, organizations can greatly improve their detection and response capabilities by removing barriers and creating a community of trust and knowledge.

In today's world, defending against adversaries is complex, and with the continual emergence of new and updated cyber threats, collaborative threat hunting will be the answer to staying ahead or being a victim.

Benefits and challenges

Despite its significant advantages, threat intelligence sharing is not without its challenges, such as legal complexities, trust issues, standardization problems, and the risk of information overload present substantial complications. However, it brings us many benefits that we are currently not exploiting the way we should, and that is one of the reasons why criminals are always ahead. The following is a table of the benefits vs challenges:

Benefits	Challenges
Improved threat detection: Enables early detection of threats by sharing IoCs and TTPs.	**Legal and compliance risks:** Difficulty in complying with regulations like GDPR and CCPA.
Cost efficiency: Reduces costs by leveraging shared resources instead of in-house builds.	**Trust and reluctance to share:** Concerns about exposing sensitive information.
Enhanced situational awareness: Provides a comprehensive view of the threat landscape.	**Standardization challenges:** Lack of common formats for sharing intelligence complicates integration.
Strengthening collective defense: Facilitates a unified defense against large-scale attacks.	**Information overload:** Risk of overwhelming security teams with excessive intelligence data.
Continuous learning: Promotes skill development through shared intelligence and practices.	**False positives risk:** Potential for sharing inaccurate intelligence leading to resource wastage.
Proactive defense: Enables organizations to implement preventive measures based on shared intelligence.	**Attribution challenges:** Difficulty in verifying the source and credibility of shared intelligence.

Access to advanced threat intelligence: Smaller organizations gain access to high-quality intelligence they could not afford.	**Technical integration issues:** Challenges in integrating shared intelligence into existing security systems.
Faster response times: Shared intelligence enables quicker implementation of countermeasures.	**Competitive concerns:** Fear of losing competitive advantage by revealing information about attacks.
Building trust and alliances: Encourages partnerships and collaboration among organizations.	**Operational security risks:** Sharing intelligence can inadvertently reveal vulnerabilities to adversaries.
Compliance with industry standards: Demonstrates proactive risk management to regulators and stakeholders.	**Resource constraints:** Processing and analyzing shared intelligence can strain limited security resources.

Table 12.4: Benefits versus challenges of threat intelligence sharing

Use cases

Case 1: Operation Tovar, Coordinated Disruption of Gameover Zeus and CryptoLocker. In 2014, an international task force composed of private cybersecurity companies (CrowdStrike, Dell SecureWorks, Symantec), academic researchers, and law enforcement agencies (FBI, Europol) executed **Operation Tovar**, aimed at dismantling the **Gameover Zeus** botnet and the associated **CryptoLocker** ransomware campaign.

The following are examples of threat intelligence sharing in action:

- Multiple actors contributed malware reverse engineering, botnet tracking, and infrastructure mapping.
- IoCs, DNS data, encryption key analytics, and command-and-control infrastructure details were shared across jurisdictions in near real-time.
- A coordinated DNS sinkholing operation was launched to sever the botnet's communication with its controllers, effectively neutralizing it.
- TI exchange enabled rapid development of decryption tools for victims.

The following is the impact:

- Operation Tovar not only disrupted a botnet responsible for over $100 million in financial theft but also prevented further ransomware propagation. This operation remains one of the clearest demonstrations of how tactical and strategic threat intelligence sharing, when tightly orchestrated, can dismantle complex transnational cybercriminal infrastructures.

Case 2: APT29 and COVID-19 vaccine espionage, joint attribution, and alerting. In July 2020, a joint security advisory from the UK's NCSC, the US CISA, and Canada's CCCS publicly attributed cyber-espionage activities to **APT29** (aka Cozy Bear), an advanced persistent threat group linked to Russian intelligence. The group targeted COVID-19 vaccine research institutions across North America and Europe.

The following are examples of threat intelligence sharing in action

- The three agencies jointly published detailed threat reports including TTPs, IoCs, and YARA rules.
- **Shared telemetry from multiple sectors:** Healthcare, pharma, government, enabled detection of intrusion attempts leveraging custom malware (e.g., WellMess and WellMail).
- The collective dissemination of actionable threat intelligence to both public and private entities enabled real-time hardening of systems.

The following is the impact:

- This case set a precedent for proactive multinational threat attribution and real-time defense. It showcased the critical role of structured collaboration in disrupting state-sponsored operations before data exfiltration or sabotage could occur.

Conclusion

As we come towards the end of this book, in a world where cyber threats are only going to become more sophisticated, collaborative defense strategies are now essential because of the existence of the cybercriminal community. Sharing threat intelligence helps organizations reduce their time to detect, improve their time to respond, have more attack surfaces covered, and build a collective defense. This is because the sharing of information on IoCs, TTPs, and other valuable information makes the organizations and people not only improve their own security posture but also help to enhance the overall security of the cyber ecosystem.

As this chapter and book end, it is an appropriate moment to thank the reader for taking the time to explore the *Threat Hunter's Handbook*. The interest and effort to gain knowledge and confront cyber threats highlight the importance of developing and maintaining capable and knowledgeable individuals in the cybersecurity field. It is hoped that this book has been helpful and has provided techniques that can be applied in day-to-day activities, and a clear understanding of the threat hunting process.

Points to remember

- Sharing threat intelligence strengthens collective defense by enabling organizations to respond to threats more effectively.
- Access to shared IoCs allows for earlier detection of emerging threats.
- Collaborating on threat intelligence reduces costs by allowing organizations to share resources and expertise.

- This is a unified effort to make the cybersecurity world a more proactive and defensive shield.

Multiple choice questions

1. **What is the primary benefit of threat intelligence sharing for organizations?**
   a. Reducing the need for compliance with regulations
   b. Limiting access to external threat data
   c. Increasing the cost of cybersecurity operations
   d. Enhancing collective defense against cyber threats

2. **Which of the following is a key challenge associated with threat intelligence sharing?**
   a. Ensuring compliance with GDPR and CCPA
   b. Simplifying integration with all security systems
   c. Reducing information overload for security teams
   d. Eliminating the need for internal threat detection

3. **How does sharing IoCs benefit organizations?**
   a. By delaying the detection of threats
   b. By reducing the number of alerts generated
   c. By enabling earlier detection of emerging threats
   d. By limiting the scope of threat analysis

4. **What is a common reason for organizations to hesitate to share threat intelligence?**
   a. Lack of useful intelligence to share
   b. Concerns about exposing sensitive information
   c. The high cost of intelligence-sharing platforms
   d. Difficulty in detecting advanced threats

5. **Which factor is most important for ensuring the success of threat intelligence sharing?**
   a. Implementing automated tools without human oversight
   b. Focusing only on historical data instead of real-time threats
   c. Limiting the sharing of threat data to internal teams
   d. Ensuring the accuracy and reliability of shared information

Answers

1. d.

2. a.

3. c.

4. b.

5. d.

References

1. NIST Computer resource center vulnerability and threat information: https://csrc.nist.gov/projects/incident-response/life-cycle-resources

2. Guide to Cyber Threat Information Sharing: https://csrc.nist.gov/pubs/sp/800/150/final

3. The importance of collaborative defense: https://keepnetlabs.com/blog/the-importance-of-collaborative-defense

Join our Discord space

Join our Discord workspace for latest updates, offers, tech happenings around the world, new releases, and sessions with the authors:

https://discord.bpbonline.com

Index

C

www.ingramcontent.com/pod-product-compliance
Lightning Source LLC
Chambersburg PA
CBHW061801210326

41599CB00034B/6837